BODIES IN CONTACT

Bodies in Contact

Rethinking Colonial Encounters in World History

Edited by Tony Ballantyne and Antoinette Burton

DUKE UNIVERSITY PRESS   Durham and London 2005

© 2005 DUKE UNIVERSITY PRESS. All rights reserved.
Printed in the United States of America on acid-free paper. ∞
Designed by Rebecca M. Giménez. Typeset in Carter & Cone
Galliard by Keystone Typesetting. Complete republication
acknowledgments appear on pages 443–44. Library of
Congress Cataloging-in-Publication Data appear on
the last printed page of this book.

This book is dedicated to EVIE AND OLIVIA:

women of the future, women of the world

CONTENTS

ACKNOWLEDGMENTS

Many people have helped us realize this collection and we are grateful to all of them. First, we want to thank the contributors, most of whom we have been in direct communication with, for their exhilarating and innovative scholarship. It goes without saying that their work is the sine qua non of our project to reimagine both colonial and world histories. We have also been aided along the way by invaluable critical feedback from Amanda Brian, Barbara Brookes, Clare Crowston, Ian Fletcher, Yael Simpson Fletcher, Durba Ghosh, Brian Moloughney, Fiona Paisley, Adele Perry, Mrinalini Sinha, Heather Streets, and Margaret Strobel. Anu Rao's counsel has been especially invaluable. Joan Catapano offered some crucial bibliographical information as well as her ongoing support for the project of women's and gender history. Students in Jean Allman and Antoinette Burton's graduate seminar, "Gender and Colonialism," in spring 2003 at the University of Illinois helped to test the efficacy of our arguments by discussing a number of the essays that have made their way into the collection. We are especially grateful to Erica Fraser, Keguro Macharia, and James Warren for their astute readings.

Our engagements with world history in recent years have, for better or worse, been shaped by discourses of globalization. One formative experience we shared was in a 2001–2002 NEH-funded seminar in the History Department at Illinois, entitled "Transforming the Undergraduate History Core in a Global Age" and co-organized with Peter Fritzsche. Much of what this book is about stems from conversations with our colleagues here and elsewhere, and we appreciate their role in shaping what it has become. Miriam Angress at Duke University Press has been a constant source of good advice, goodwill, and good humor, for which we are grateful. Not least, we have relied on the labor of James Beattie, Ciara Breathnach, Jason Hansen, and Deborah Hughes for the photocopying and scanning of the essays, and we thank them. Without Paul Arroyo's technical assistance (and so much more), this book would not have been possible. In addition to preparing the index, Sally Henderson provided great advice and support (as ever!).

Bodies in Contact is dedicated to the youngest among us. May they grow up to encounter each other and change the world.

Tony Ballantyne and Antoinette Burton

Introduction: Bodies, Empires,

and World Histories

We live in a world profoundly shaped by cross-cultural encounters, slavery, colonization, and migration. These forces
have not only been central in determining the distribution
of wealth and power at a global level, but they have also molded the
world's demographic profile, dictated where national boundaries have
been inscribed, influenced the legal regimes that govern people's lives,
and shaped the ways different ethnic, religious, racial, and national communities relate to each other. The impact of colonialism and the results of
empire building are not restricted to "high politics" and state practices,
but also shape everyday life at a global level, influencing the languages we
speak, the clothes we wear, the food we eat, the music we listen to, and the
arts and culture we are inspired by. The legacies of slavery, empires, and
mobility are frequently painful, but they are inescapable: in many ways,
these legacies are at the heart of what it is to be modern, what it is to be
human, at the start of the twenty-first century.

As a distinctive approach to the past, one that focuses on cross-cultural
encounters, institutions, and ideologies and the integrative power of various types of networks, world history allows us to scrutinize the diverse
forces that have brought various communities into contact, concert, and
conflict. World history has enjoyed renewed popularity in recent years, in
part because economists, sociologists, anthropologists, and other students of the present moment are increasingly interested in how areas of
the globe that were once thought to be distinct have actually been interconnected for a very long time. It is no longer possible, or even desirable,

to uncritically think in terms of "the West," "Asia," "Europe," or "the Third World"—not only because each of those categories tends to homogenize the geographical region it evokes, but equally because all of those places have been interdependent from the fourteenth century onward, if not before. Scholars have been at work investigating what many of us in the first decades of the twenty-first century take for granted in the present: that because of trade, migration, revolution, war, religion, and travel, goods, people, ideas, and civilizations themselves are all the result of transnational processes. In other words—and to use a common buzzword of the moment—they are the result of "globalization." Here we agree with Laura Briggs that the term *globalization* is often "a placeholder, a word with no exact meaning that we use in our contested efforts to describe the successors to development and colonialism."[1] Current debates on globalization emphasize some of the same processes of interconnection and mutual dependence that practitioners of world history have examined in the past twenty years. Their teaching and research have suggested that far from being fixed within borders or limited to local communities and national states, many of the world's most important commodities, political systems, and spiritual practices are the consequence of diverse cultural encounters over time and space—so much so that we now have to rethink terms like "European progress," "Chinese trade," and "Western Christianity." Coming to these subjects from the perspective of world history allows us to appreciate how they came to be identified with such geographical precision. It also underscores the limits of understanding them merely as insular national or territorially based phenomena. World history, in short, enables us to take a global view of ostensibly local events, systems, and cultures and to reevaluate the histories of connection and rupture that have left their mark, in turn, on our contemporary condition.

The influence of societies on each other across regions and, in some cases, across the globe does not mean, of course, that they have been uniform or anything like united, even at the same moments in history. This is in large part because empires and imperial ambitions have been among the most powerful sponsors of "cultural contact"—and of the processes of intermixture, borrowing, fusion, and appropriation that such contact has given rise to over the course of centuries. So, for example, European cultures have been immeasurably shaped by their encounters with African, Indian, and Mesoamerican peoples in ways that make

Europe itself one of the greatest examples of transnationality in the world. But the often violent imposition of European modernity on "subject peoples" in the form of technology, capitalist labor practices, and the Christian civilizing mission has meant that cultures on the receiving end of such contact have been in a reactive and at times defensive posture with respect to dominant forms of "global" influence. Nor are such imperial strategies unique to the "West." Both the Han and the Mughal empires produced similar forms of colonial encounter with the indigenous communities they came into contact with, models of which later, Western imperial advocates (notably the British) were acutely aware. The impact of empires on global processes and transformations has thus been considerable, as well as historically significant. That is why this collection focuses on the role of imperial ideologies — their agents and their enemies, their collaborators and their resisters — in helping to shape world history.

A few caveats are in order. We use the term "empire" quite loosely here, intending it to mean webs of trade, knowledge, migration, military power, and political intervention that allowed certain communities to assert their influence and sovereignty over other groups.[2] In other words, these "imperial webs" functioned as systems of exchange, mobility, appropriation, and extraction, fashioned to enable the empire-building power to exploit the natural resources, manufactured goods, or valued skills of the subordinated group. In offering the image of the web, we want to emphasize interconnected networks of contact and exchange without downplaying the very real systems of power and domination such networks had the power to transport. The web's intricate strands carried with them and helped to create hierarchies of race, class, religion, and gender, among others, thereby casting the conquerors as superior and the conquered as subordinate, with important and lingering consequences for the communities they touched. We do not wish to suggest that empires functioned as colossal juggernauts, razing everything in their paths and putting into place systems of domination that were unaffected by "native" agency or uncontested by indigenous interests. Indeed, the image of the web also conveys something of the double nature of the imperial system. Empires, like webs, were fragile and prone to crises where important threads were broken or structural nodes destroyed, yet also dynamic, being constantly remade and reconfigured through concerted thought and effort.

As the essays that follow amply demonstrate, empires have not simply been carriers or enablers of global processes, they have in turn spawned new hybrid forms of economic activity, political practice, and cultural performance that take on lives of their own — in part because of the ways colonized peoples and cultures have acted on or resisted imperial political and social forms. Nor do we want to imply that all world history can be reduced simply to the fact of empires. Not only does such a claim stake too much ground for imperial histories, but it is in danger of blinding us to stories large and small which cannot always be glimpsed through the archives that empires leave behind. But we do believe that targeting empires is *one* way of making sense of world history because it requires us to pay attention to big structural events and changes as well as to ask what impact they had on microprocesses and the historical subjects who lived with and through them. Tracking empires in a global context is, in other words, one way of reimagining the world's history so that both its monumental quality and its ultimately fragmented character can be captured simultaneously.

Why the focus on bodies as a means of accessing the colonial encounters in world history? Quite simply, we are seeking a way to dramatize how, why, and under what conditions women and gender can be made visible in world history — a challenge on many levels. Women do not tend to enter the primary source materials that remain from imperial and colonial archives because, for the most part, they did not hold positions of official power. This absence has meant that it is difficult to see them, and to understand their historical roles, in world civilizations. There are exceptions, of course. Queens and elite women can be recaptured from obscurity through texts and visual images; they dot the landscape of world history textbooks and even some books devoted to women of the past across the globe. But this leaves us with a less than satisfying view of how women experienced the movement of history, how dominant and indigenous regimes saw them, and what role gender has played in helping to shape civilizational attitudes as well as transnational movements and processes.

What is striking, however, is the extent to which women's bodies (and, to a lesser degree, men's) have been a subject of concern, scrutiny, anxiety, and surveillance in a variety of times and places across the world. Whether it was native Indian women's sexuality that caused concern for a colonizing Catholic Church in colonial Mexico or that of Japanese women under postwar U.S. military occupation, the female body has gotten—and kept—the attention of imperial officials in ways that demonstrate how crucial its management was believed to be for social order and political stability. The stakes of this stability were perhaps especially high for imperial powers, which were de facto trying to impose specific political forms and cultural practices on often unwilling populations. What this means is that the body can be read by us as evidence of how women were viewed by, and how gender assumptions undergirded, empires in all their complexity. Some of the essays in this collection focus on the body very explicitly, as in Patrick McDevitt's essay on contact sport as a national pastime in colonial Ireland and Hyun Sook Kim's on the fate of "comfort women" in the context of World War II. Other essays use the body as a metaphor for citizenship and the nation, as in Elisa Camiscioli's work on interwar French immigration controls as expressions of concern about the racial purity of the "national body." Others focus on examples of cultural contact through bodies literally in motion, like Siobhan Lambert Hurley's essay on the begam of Bhopal and Carter Vaughn Findley's research on the Ottoman traveler and writer Ahmed Midhat. Still others, like Melani McAlister's essay that begins with Muhammad Ali, show how famous bodies can be used as a jumping-off point for seeing connections between local communities (African Americans during the cold war) and transnational events with global significance (the Arab-Israeli War and the international Islamicist movement).

The volume is divided into three sections. The first section, "Thresholds of Modernity: Mapping Genders," focuses on the place of race, gender, and sexuality in empire building during the early modern period. Although the essays range over disparate geographic and social contexts, they underscore the centrality of the body in the articulation of imperial ideologies and in the often fraught dynamics of cross-cultural contact. More generally still, the contributions in this first section reveal how the operation of early modern empires began to reconfigure understandings of the body at a global level, as the languages of gender and race grew in authority and imperial systems began to "globalize" and universalize legal regimes, religious beliefs, and understandings of sickness and death. The essays that make up the second section of the volume, "Global Empires, Local Encounters," examine a wide array of very specific local colonial encounters from the close of the eighteenth century to the middle decades of the twentieth century. These essays chart the diverse locations where understandings of the body were defined and contested: from the sports fields of Ireland to Australian courtrooms, from the prairies of the American Midwest to the clubs of colonial India, from swimming holes in Mozambique to the British Columbia frontier. The contributions to this section foreground the ways the boundaries of race and gender were negotiated, policed, and reinforced in an age of colonial modernity and demonstrate the processes that increasingly undermined the flexibility and fluidity that characterized many earlier social formations.

The third section of the volume, "The Mobility of Politics and the Politics of Mobility," focuses on the battles over empire from the final decade of the nineteenth century to the late twentieth century. While many of the essays examine the politics of anticolonialism and nationalism, they all reflect on the ways our modern world was shaped by greater mobility, whether in travel, migration, the flow of ideas and information, war, or imperial expansion itself. The fierce debates over imperialism reconstructed in this section turn on the body, how it was managed, how it could be represented, and how the brutalities visited on particular types of bodies should be remembered or understood. The collection closes with a final essay that reflects on the volume as a whole and that uses the notion of "bodies in contact" to map some future directions for both world history research and teaching.

THE ESSAYS COLLECTED here have, then, a dual purpose. First, they emphasize the centrality of bodies — raced, sexed, classed, and ethnicized bodies — as sites through which imperial and colonial power was imagined and exercised. By thus foregrounding the body, this volume marks a fundamental reconception of the nature and workings of empires: we focus on the material effects of geopolitical systems in everyday spaces, family life, and on-the-ground cultural encounters. Rather than privileging the operations of the Foreign Office or gentlemanly capitalists, for example, this attention to bodies means that the plantation, the theater, the home, the street, the school, the club, and the marketplace are now visible as spaces where people can be seen to have experienced modes of imperial and colonial power. Although the past two decades have witnessed a tremendous boom in scholarly production on colonialism and empire, with feminist historians taking the lead in the project of recovering the experiences of women and other "others," this research has not received the attention it should in world history textbooks and hence in world history courses. There, high politics and commerce still dominate accounts of empire in ways that certainly remain useful. Women and gender are now scrupulously attended to but most often not in ways that underscore their constitutive role in the shaping of global power or cross-cultural social organization.[3] Long after women's history has moved beyond the "add women and stir" formula, world history surveys still tend to take an additive approach, so that each unit "covers" women, but discretely; rare enough is the approach taken by Peter Stearns, which emphasizes "particular historical episodes" in tension with "higher-level analysis of patterns over time."[4] And, as shall be discussed in more detail below, scarcely any attention is paid to masculinity as a cultural (let alone a political) category.[5] This is especially regrettable because colonial projects and their processes were frequently believed to throw white male bodies into crisis (making them vulnerable to disease, insanity, and hybridization), and the supposed "femininity" of colonized men was frequently used as a political tool to justify their exclusion from positions of power and as a means of justifying their colonization in the first place.[6] The abstractions, omissions, and facile categorizations that tend to follow from a historiographical literature that overlooks gendered subjectivities and experiences need qualification and elaboration. This is all the more important because the quest for generalization can take people — especially women, children, and "natives" — out of the story, thereby often relegating human agency in its particulars to the margins of historical understanding.

This is not to say, of course, that women, gender, and sexuality represent the full extent of what bodies in history can and do signify. Bodies evoke birth and death, work and play, disease and fitness; they carry germs and fluids as well as a variety of political, social, and cultural meanings; they are the grounds of political economies and the pretext for intrusion, discipline, and punishment at both the individual and the collective levels. Although the essays that make up this collection treat subjects as diverse as slavery and travel, ecclesiastical colonialism and military occupation, marriage and property, nationalism and football, immigration and temperance, we do not propose to offer anything like a global history of the body.[7] For our purposes, the gendered bodies invoked by the authors collected here serve as entrées into larger discussions of how the body can give shape to themes of relevance to world history, as well as how they can reorient that project so that it encompasses different bodies of evidence.[8] Of equal importance is the opportunity to bring into view research published in venues that may be ignored or underutilized by European or American audiences, such as the *Indian Journal of Gender Studies*, the *Journal of African History*, and *Australian Feminist Studies*. In doing so we can better appreciate both the applicability of Euro-American theoretical models of gender and the body to diverse geographical sites and the very real limits of those frameworks for historicizing "global" realities. *Bodies in Contact*, in short, enables readers to access some of the most recent and significant scholarship on women, gender, and the colonial encounter so that students with a variety of disciplinary interests can appreciate the tensions between macro and micro perspectives on the globe — and so that the constitutive impact of gender and sexuality in all their historical complexity can be more fully appreciated.

Second, the volume insists on the centrality of imperial and colonial bodies in the circuits of global politics, capital, and culture. This commitment stems from our conviction that historically, empires have been constitutive of global systems, but that in contemporary debates about how to think and teach world history and globalization the centrality of imperial power and knowledge is often excised or downplayed or occluded, a situation that may or may not change with the arrival of new forms of U.S. imperialism at work in the global arena. Collectively these essays map the transformative power of imperial systems and the ways in which the development of global empires have been entwined historically with bodies in contact: that is, bodies not just involved in intimate personal, sexual, or social relations but bodies in motion, bodies in subjection, bodies in struggle, bodies in action. This move effectively recasts readers' understanding of the contemporary world, where empires are clearly not over, even and especially in this particular global moment. Each of the essays we have chosen makes visible the ideological work of imperial or colonial mentalities in a specific moment and a specific set of locations, demonstrating both the need for historical contingency when creating global narratives and the fundamentally transnational operation of colonial power. Once again, feminist scholarship has been crucial to recent developments in comparative, imperial, and world histories, but in ways that have not been easily accessible to students in the classroom.[9] *Bodies in Contact* thereby offers students of globalization an opportunity to appreciate the role of empires in shaping world systems by tracking embodied experiences across historical time and cultural space. It also makes recent scholarship available to instructors, who can then test it against the over-arching claims and theories made in the textbooks that are inevitably used in large courses. This, we hope, creates a series of heretofore unavailable pedagogical opportunities by setting up supposedly "small" histories that may ratify some established syntheses, question others, and perhaps even chip away at the long-standing distinction between big and small processes of historical continuity and change.[10] In the process, *Bodies in Contact* also enables students to interrogate the totalizing narratives that can arise under the rubric of "world history" and to ask when, why, and under what conditions the global is a desirable category of historical analysis.[11]

If this collection brings together a series of essays that foreground race, gender, and sexuality in ways that challenge the traditional foci of global narratives, many of the essays reflect perhaps the most important contribution of recent world history research: the critique of long-established narratives of "the rise of the West." The emergence of world history as a distinctive approach to the past in the early twentieth century coincided with a moment of European paramountcy and a widespread faith in the West's civilizing mission. Within such a context, it was hardly surprising that early world histories, written by H. G. Wells, Oswald Spengler, and Arnold Toynbee, played a central role in consolidating Europe and North America at the heart of understandings of global history and articulating a powerful narrative that molded the complex, fragmentary, and hetero-geneous nature of the human past into a striking account of the creation, consolidation, and extension of the power of the "West."[12] Even as world history slowly became professionalized after World War II, this narrative continued to provide a key framework for understandings of the global past in undergraduate lecture halls, graduate seminar rooms, and faculty lounges. In turn, this model was fortified by sociologists and area studies specialists who promulgated world system and dependency theories that firmly located Europe and North America as the "core" of the modern world.[13] In 1963 W. H. McNeill published his paradigmatic *The Rise of the West*, a work that had sold over 75,000 copies by 1990 and that continues to be widely used in college classrooms and to attract a wide public audience. The subtitle of McNeill's work (*A History of the Human Community*) reduces human history to a narrative of the "rise of the West" and underscores the profoundly teleological assumptions that shaped world history in the 1960s and 1970s.[14]

Such assumptions do linger today, but research undertaken by world historians since the early 1980s has explicitly challenged the primacy attached to Europe or the West as the prime historical agent of cross-cultural integration. The work of Janet Abu-Lughod, for example, called into question the belief that Europeans were central in driving cross-cultural exchanges, by drawing attention to the complex circuits of long-distance trade that integrated Eurasia in the thirteenth and fourteenth centuries.[15] This emphasis on the importance of changes taking place in central Asia has been extended by other scholars who have identified the "Mongol explosion" in this period as marking the emergence of the first truly "world empire."[16] Most important, however, it has been the historians who work on China and its connections with inner Asia, Southeast Asia, the rest of East Asia, and Europe who have transformed our understandings of the basic pattern of world history. At the same time, research on the economic history of South Asia has both revised an image of a corrupt and weakening Mughal empire inherited from British colonial discourse and has emphasized that the Indian Ocean was the center of a series of interlocking commercial networks that reached out as far as East Africa and Indonesia. Europeans were latecomers to this cosmopolitan commercial world and their arrival caused little concern to the Jewish, Arab, Gujarati, Tamil, Malay, and Chinese traders who dominated the bazaars and shipping routes of the region. It was only as a result of the militarization of trade during the eighteenth century and the growing colonial aspirations of European East India Companies that Europeans gradually came to dominate the long-established markets and commercial hubs around the Indian Ocean.

In effect, this work on Asian economic history and Asia's trade with Europe has both called into question the exceptional status so frequently accorded to Europe and recast our understandings of the chronology of world history.[17] One of the crucial debates that continues to exercise world historians is the relationship between Europe's rise, imperialism, and the emergence of global capitalism. While some historians, such as David Landes, continue to attribute Europe's rise to power to supposedly intrinsically European cultural qualities ("work, thrift, honesty, patience, tenacity"), recent research has tended to underscore the centrality of imperialism in the New World in both allowing Europe to escape from its ecological constraints (by making a host of new natural resources and valuable commodities available to Europe) and constituting the very nature of European culture itself.[18] Moreover, where McNeill might have given shape to history by discerning the rising dominance of the West, what has emerged out of recent world historical research is an image of a multicentered world during the period between 1250 and 1800, when China was perhaps the single most powerful region. In the 1800s, it seems that Europe did exercise increasing power at a global level as a result of the military-fiscal revolution that consolidated its military advantage over non-European nations, its harnessing of its natural resources, especially coal, to its industrial revolution, and a sustained period of imperial expansion beginning from the 1760s.[19]

Of course, the spectacular rise of European empires from the middle of the eighteenth century was also intimately connected with the "hollowing out" of the Safavid and Mughal empires and the ability of European agents to turn these older imperial structures to their own advantage.[20] At the same time, the consolidation of imperial authority at the margins of Europe (especially in Ireland and the Mediterranean) and the thrust of European powers in South Asia, Southeast Asia, and the Pacific incorporated vast territories into the political, commercial, and religious ambit of European colonial systems. There is no doubt that this new age of global imperialism marks a profound disjuncture in world history, as the pull of European markets, the practices of imperial/colonial states, the "universal" languages of science and statistics, and the international reach of missionary organizations fashioned new and profoundly uneven forms of interconnection and interdependence.[21] Many of the essays in this collection trace these transformations, reconstructing how specific colonial encounters produced understandings of gender, race, and sexuality and revealing the ways these local exchanges were increasingly assimilated into broader imperial debates over cultural difference. The tremendous variety of human social arrangements remained a key concern of the scientists, historians, and theorists of empire in the mid-nineteenth century. And although a great range of cultural variation remained, the reach of European empires rendered much of this complexity legible through the (distorting) languages of race and gender.

But the thrust of much recent work is that European ascendancy was never uncontested and Europe's position as the global center of imperial power was relatively short-lived. The United States, the Soviet Union, and Japan emerged as both industrial forces and imperial powers around the turn of the twentieth century, and Tokyo, Hong Kong, Singapore, and Bombay emerged as new commercial, cultural, technological, and migratory centers. World history research on migration, economics, empires, and ideologies suggests that history cannot be imagined as an inexorable march to Western dominance and global homogeneity, but is a more complex and ambiguous set of interwoven and overlapping processes driven by a diverse array of groups from a variety of different locations.[22]

These arguments frame this volume, and in various ways, the essays in this collection reinforce this emergent image of a multicentered, even a de-centered, world, evoking a fluidity that gender and the body, especially when read as performative categories, contingent for its manifestations as much on space as on time, can help us immeasurably to appreciate. While many of the authors pay close attention to the uneven power relations of colonialism and the profound inequalities created by European imperial systems, they explore the imperial projects carried out by non-European powers, reconstruct the ability of subaltern groups to challenge colonial authority and puncture colonial ideologies, and map the sophisticated cultural complexes created by peoples at the supposed "periphery" of empires.

Equally important, however, this collection foregrounds the body in a way that world history scholarship to date has resisted. World history, at least in its dominant institutional form, has not only clung to an "additive" view of women's history but has also generally remained insulated from (if not resistant to) new directions in cultural history, especially gender history. As a result, "masculinity" is an analytical category that remains, for all intents and purposes, unheard of in the field. Reconstructing the variable and culturally contingent historical forms of masculinity, and their relationship to economics, politics, culture, religion, class, and sexuality, is a project that has only just begun. Rosalind O'Hanlon's essay on imperial masculinities in Mughal north India, Patrick McDevitt's examination of the place of sports in Catholic masculinity in Ireland, and Joseph Alter's examination of celibacy and the place of masculine constraint in Indian nationalist thought suggest the important insights into the place of gendered bodies and embodied subjectivities in empire building, anticolonial resistance and nationalist ideologies that critical histories of masculinity offer. Much of the pioneering work in the field, especially with regard to modern imperial masculinities, has suggested that the male-dominated archives that are the stock in trade of the world historian can be read in new and interesting ways. Rather than searching only for notable women or seeking to access an unmediated female subjectivity, we can assemble a richer understanding of the operation of gender in world history by examining the ways these archives articulate competing visions of and anxieties about masculinity, while attending equally to the pressures that class, racial, ethnic, and religious affiliations have historically exerted on it as both an embodied and a performative articulation of identity.

Whether interpreted broadly or narrowly, then, the category "bodies in contact" can enable us to appreciate histories we might not otherwise have seen and to make visible connections between the colonial and the global that scholars are, in some instances, just beginning to make into "history." As important, recovering women and gender in world history not only permits us to see them as historical subjects, it also means that we have to understand empires as gendered projects — endeavors in which, it turns out, women and gender mattered tremendously. Our focus on bodies, then, reorients both imperial history and world history by rooting the phenomenon of "encounter" in a gendered, sexualized context, and often throws light on practices of daily life and experience that are otherwise obscured. As important, it allows us to reimagine the global past as a space of contact between women and men, between "woman" and colonizer, between colonizing men and cultures that were often considered "effeminate" by imperial observers. The fact that these gendered relationships recur fairly consistently across empires, across the world — as exhibited from the early modern period down to the late twentieth century, from China to the Americas and in a variety of locations in between — suggests that it is a subject that undergraduates need to learn about if they are to have as full an understanding of world history as possible. This collection represents a beginning in that direction; we hope it will stimulate debate, discussion, and even perhaps a new generation of historians interested in further exploring the relations between bodies, empires, and the worlds of the past.

Notes

1. Laura Briggs, *Reproducing Empire: Race, Sex, Science and U.S. Imperialism in Puerto Rico* (Berkeley: University of California Press, 2002), 1.
2. This vision of empires and imperial history is developed in Tony Ballantyne, *Orientalism and Race: Aryanism in the British Empire* (Basingstoke, England: Palgrave-

Macmillan, 2001). More recently, a slightly different vision of the "web" has been harnessed to world history in J. R. McNeill and William H. McNeill, *The Human Web: A Bird's-eye View of World History* (New York: Norton, 2003).

3. One recent exception is Robert Tignor et al., *Worlds Together, Worlds Apart* (New York: Norton 2002).

4. Peter N. Stearns, *Gender in World History* (London: Routledge, 2000), 4.

5. For a discussion of this problem, see Margaret Strobel, "Women's History, Gender History, and European Colonialism," in *Colonialism and the Modern World: Selected Studies*, ed. Gregory Blue, Martin Bunton, and Ralph Crozier (New York: M.E. Sharpe, 2002), 51–68.

6. Many thanks to Adele Perry for this point.

7. For an extremely compelling version of this project, see Valerie Traub, "The Global Body," in *Early Modern Visual Culture: Representation, Race and Empire in Renaissance England*, ed. Peter Erickson and Clark Hulse (Philadelphia: University of Pennsylvania Press, 2000), 44–97.

8. We are grateful to Clare Crowston for urging this point.

9. For one exception, see Sarah Shaver Hughes and Brady Hughes, eds., *Women in World History*, 2 vols. (New York: M.E. Sharpe, 1997).

10. See, for example, Charles Tilly, *Big Structures, Large Processes, Huge Comparisons* (New York: Russell Sage Foundation, 1984).

11. For more on teleologies of globalization from a feminist perspective, see Jean Allman and Antoinette Burton, eds., "Destination Globalization? Women, Gender and Comparative Colonial Histories in the New Millennium," *Journal of Colonialism and Colonial History* 4, 1 (2003) http://muse.jhu.edu/journals/cch/.

12. Oswald Spengler, *The Decline of the West* (London: Allen and Unwin, 1922); Arnold J. Toynbee, *A Study of History*, 10 vols. (Oxford: Oxford University Press, 1934–1954); H. G. Wells, *Outline of History* (London: Cassell, 1920). Spengler certainly recognized the significance of non-Western civilizations, but for him only "Western Civilization" had fulfilled its potential, and the crisis that he diagnosed in the early twentieth century reflected a crisis born out of the decline of "Western Civilization."

13. For a bracing account of the stakes of American civilization for 1990s politics, see Thomas C. Patterson, *Inventing Western Civilization* (New York: Monthly Review Press, 1997), 9–15. For an equally compelling analysis of Western Civ textbooks, see Daniel A. Segal, "Western Civ and the Staging of History in American Higher Education," *American Historical Review* 105, 3 (2000); also available at http://www.historycooperative.org/journals/ahr/105.3/ah000770.html.

14. McNeill reflects critically on the "Rise of the West" model in his essays: "The *Rise of the West* after Twenty-five Years," *Journal of World History* 1, 1 (1990): 1–21 and "World History and the Rise and Fall of the West," *Journal of World History* 9, 2 (1998): 215–236. In J. R. McNeill and William H. McNeill, *The Human Web*, his work is fashioning a new understanding of the multiple forms of contact and interdependence that have shaped human history.

15. Janet L. Abu-Lughod, *Before European Hegemony: The World System A.D. 1250–1350* (New York: Oxford University Press, 1989).

16. See S. A. M. Adshead, *China in World History* (Macmillan, 1987) and *Central Asia in World History* (New York: Macmillan, 1993); David Christian, *A History of Russia, Central Asia, and Mongolia* (Oxford: Blackwell, 1998).

17. Much of this work is synthesized in the *Cambridge History of China*. For a collection of work that explores the connections between the development of the Chinese economy and global trade, see Dennis O. Flynn and Arturo Giráldez, eds., *Metals and Monies in an Emerging Global Economy* (Brookfield, Vt.: Variorum, 1997). Also see the provocative arguments forwarded in Dennis O. Flynn and Arturo Giráldez, "Born with a 'Silver Spoon': The Origin of World Trade in 1571," *Journal of World History* 6, 2 (1995): 201–221. On South Asia and the Indian Ocean, see Satish Chandra, *The Indian Ocean: Explorations in History, Commerce and Politics* (New Delhi: Sage, 1987); K. N. Chaudhuri, *Trade and Civilisation in the Indian Ocean: An Economic History from the Rise of Islam to 1750* (Cambridge, England: Cambridge University Press, 1985); Kenneth McPherson, *The Indian Ocean: A History of People and the Sea* (Delhi: Oxford University Press, 1993).

18. David Landes, *The Wealth and Poverty of Nations: Why Some Are So Rich and Some So Poor* (New York: Norton, 1998), 523; compare the works listed in the next two notes.

19. Kenneth Pomeranz, *The Great Divergence: China, Europe, and the Making of the Modern World Economy* (Princeton, N.J.: Princeton University Press, 2000); Kenneth Pomeranz and Steven Topik, *The World That Trade Created: Culture, Society, and the World Economy, 1400–the Present* (Armonk, N.Y.: M.E. Sharpe, 1999); and the essays in the forum on the "great divergence" in *Itinerario* 24, 3/4 (2000).

20. See C. A. Bayly, *Imperial Meridian: The British Empire and the World 1780–1830* (White Plains, N.Y.: Longman, 1989) and *Empire and Information: Intelligence Gathering and Social Communication in India, 1780–1870* (Cambridge, England: Cambridge University Press, 1996).

21. C. A. Bayly, "The First Age of Global Imperialism, c. 1760–1830," *Journal of Imperial and Commonwealth History* 26, 2 (1998): 28–47; Tony Ballantyne, "Empire, Knowledge and Culture: From Proto-globalization to Modern Globalization," in *Globalization in World History*, ed. A. G. Hopkins (London: Pimlico, 2001), 115–140.

22. See, for example, Arjun Appadurai, *Modernity at Large: Cultural Dimensions of Globalization* (Minneapolis: University of Minnesota Press, 1990); Michael Geyer and Charles Bright, "World History in a Global Age," *American Historical Review* 100, 4 (October 1995): 1034–1060; Akira Iriye, "The Internationalization of History," *American Historical Review* 94, 1 (February 1989): 1–10; Adam McKeown, *Chinese Migrant Networks and Cultural Change: Peru, Chicago, Hawaii, 1900–1936* (Chicago: University of Chicago Press, 2001).

I

THRESHOLDS OF MODERNITY:

MAPPING GENDERS

Rosalind O'Hanlon

Masculinity and the Bangash
Nawabs of Farrukhabad

Understandings of gender were as fundamental to the culture of early modern Islamic empires as they were to the maritime empires constructed by European powers. Mughal authority in India rested on the creation of alliances with rival warrior kingdoms, and codes of masculine sociability were prominent in courtly culture. During the eighteenth century, these imperial traditions were increasingly challenged by a range of insurgent groups (Sikhs, Marathas, and Pathans) that fostered distinctive military traditions and visions of manhood. Through its examination of the Pathan soldier and courtier Muhammad Khan Bangash's manipulation of these competing codes of masculinity, this essay underscores that the performance of gender identities was a crucial cross-cultural means of establishing hierarchies and affirming common identities within the cosmopolitan world of Mughal imperial politics.

This paper focuses on rulership, warfare, and masculinity in eighteenth-century north India, and for three reasons. First, it is very difficult to specify how the coming of colonial society changed gender roles and identities without knowing very much about the eighteenth century, although this has not deterred many historians from trying.[1] Second, and following on from this, one of the wider questions for any historian of gender in South Asia arises out of suggestions by Ashis Nandy and others that precolonial Indian societies worked with rather fluid and permeable gender identities, in which ideas about bisexuality and androgyny featured strongly and in which "softer" forms of creativity and intuition were not strongly identified with femininity, nor values of violence and power with masculinity. It was on these malleable and multiplex identities, Nandy argues, that Victorian colonial culture imposed its much more rigid and dichotomous ideologies of gender, setting masculine against and above feminine and establishing a homology between political and sexual dominance that juxtaposed the manliness, rationality, courage, and control of British rulers — essentially British middle-class sexual stereotypes — against degenerated, effete, and superstitious colonial subjects. In this way, Nandy argues, the rather small sectors of Indian society in which the martial values of the Kshatriya order predominated came during the colonial period to threaten and partially to displace those more fluid and diffuse identities of Indian tradition.[2] This reconstitution of Indian gender values and identities under colonialism is an important one, and a starting point for me is the late precolonial period.

Third, the recent work of Mrinalini Sinha on "colonial masculinity" in late-nineteenth-century Bengal has raised some extremely important questions about the significance of masculine identities as a cross-cultural means of establishing hierarchies and affirming common identities. Sinha examines the ideological constructs of the "manly Englishman" and "effeminate Bengali" in a range of different political contexts. She shows how colonial rulers and Indian elites alike employed them in complex ideological maneuvers, sometimes to institute a hierarchy, sometimes to suggest commonalities.[3] This is a very interesting approach, in that it extends into the field of masculine identities questions about the links between gender, race, and imperialism which are already the subject of intense scrutiny and debate from the perspective of women's histories.[4] These latter have illustrated how colonial officials, missionaries, Indian reformers, and nationalists came to agree that the domains of women and family, "custom" and community lay properly outside the normal realm of politics and the state. This emerging consensus about the domains of the public and private, politics and the "domestic" helped establish a significant framework for cooperation between Indian politicians and the colonial state.[5] Sinha adds greatly to this discussion by showing how conceptions of masculine identity could also in some contexts help cement this consensus. However, these insights again raise the question of colonial change, and of how far there may be elements of an older north Indian practice in these interplays between masculine identity and political power.

HOW, THEN, MIGHT these concerns contribute to our understanding of political culture in eighteenth-century north India? This was, of course, an extraordinarily fluid world, as the political reach of Mughal power shrank and was superseded in many parts of the subcontinent by a wide array of large and small regional power holders. Some of these, such as Bengal, Awadh, and Hyderabad, had once been Mughal provincial governorships; some, such as the Jats of the Punjab and the Marathas of western India, represented elements of popular peasant insurgency against Mughal power; and some were "Rajput" kingdoms, representing the martial values and kingly aspirations of the dominant Hindu landholding communities of Rajasthan. Some again were established by successful warrior mercenaries, such as the Afghan Rohilla kingdoms around Delhi, or by skilled revenue farmers who, with the support of Hindu bankers and local clansmen, were able to assume the powers and appurtenances of Hindu kings. In this wider north Indian context, the archetypal Hindu warrior order of the Rajputs provided the most obvious example of high-profile martial values, and their elaborate codes of honor have consistently attracted the attention of colonial chroniclers and modern historians alike. However, this essay examines masculinity in some rather different contexts, because my aim is to suggest some general arguments rather than to explore in detail the history of a particular group. I wish to examine the gendered culture surrounding those alliances — between kings and their lesser political clients, between rulers and their military servants, between mercenary leaders and their warbands — that was the stuff of eighteenth-century politics and warfare. Here, I want to argue that codes about martial bravery and correct manly behavior formed part of a wider common language and set of assumptions that have remained largely unexamined in the historiography of precolonial north India.

John Richards has extensively studied the codes of martial honor in the Mughal empire at its height from the later sixteenth through to the early eighteenth centuries.[6] The Mughal state needed to bring about key changes in the martial cultures of its most important military servants. In particular, the "free" warrior aristocrats of local north Indian society and the self-sacrificing individual *ghazis* or warriors of the Indo-Muslim tradition had to be persuaded that the primacy of individual or group honor in battle should be second to the needs and disciplines of imperial service. Richards and others have mapped the novel ideological, institutional, and ceremonial devices through which the Mughal state worked to achieve these aims, often with extraordinary success. Stuart Gordon has also broadened our understanding of the way martial codes worked in pre-colonial India. He has drawn our attention to what he sees as three distinct "zones of military entrepreneurship," marked primarily by cultural rather than military differences. The Rajput/Mughal zones emphasized heavy cavalry mounted on costly imported horses; an ethic of personal devotion and self-sacrifice; service based on the *mansabdari* system of graded ranks, which was difficult to enter, costly to maintain, and operated over very large distances; and the special patronage of a small number of prominent Rajput families who were able to consolidate their "kingly" powers through Mughal service.[7] The Maratha zone of western India, based on pioneer peasant settler communities who returned home from campaigning to their fields in the monsoon season, included light cavalry mounted on local horse, tactics of guerrilla warfare specifically designed to frustrate heavy cavalry, plain, low-capital, and informally run military service, and the patronage of locally dominant landholding communities deeply attached to their land rights in western Maharashtra. The *nayaka* warrior ethos of south India emphasized infantry-based armies, the devolution of many state functions in service grants that helped establish local power holders, and the close involvement of nayaka warriors with Hindu temples and sects. Gordon argues that the persistence of these very different military cultures provides fresh insights into Mughal failures in central and southern India. The Mughals possessed only one model for the integration of local military talent, which was a successful blending of Mughal and Rajput. Holding blindly to this single norm for a correct cavalryman, warrior tactics, and terms of service, the Mughals failed to assimilate and deploy the cultural symbols and assumptions that might have enabled them to find solid bodies of imperial servants among the Maratha communities of the Deccan.[8]

Although these accounts have been illuminating, they overlook the important ways in which these were masculine as well as simply martial identities. Gender actually stood at the heart of Mughal attempts to recruit an elite of committed supporters. The Mughals, under the emperor Akbar in particular, sought to make imperial service not just one path to successful manhood in the field of worldly action, but the only path. Only in the emperor's service, which blended together Persian courtly skills with the warrior traditions of the central Asian steppe, could a man realize his highest inner qualities: of purposeful action and heroic striving for the highest ideals, of resolute personal courage tempered by discretion and self-control, of personal honor expressed and safeguarded through dignified personal submission to the legitimate authority of the emperor, who was himself presented as the "perfect man."[9] These codes were explicitly contrasted with the qualities of women on the one hand, and on the other, with the crude, uncultivated, and inferior forms of masculinity that lay outside Mughal service: intemperate warriors, petty rulers little better than robbers and thieves, unwashed rusticity. While at first remarkably effective in creating a distinctive ethos for an "elite" imperial service, this effort to project a single ideal of cultivated manliness faltered as its monopoly gradually weakened over the course of the seventeenth century as divergent norms and models emerged. This was in part a result of the increased brilliance and luxury of the Mughal court under the emperors Jahangir and Shah Jahan and the elaboration of much more complex codes for courtly and cultivated forms of masculinity, increasingly divorced from the ethos of warriorship: man as refined gentleman connoisseur, patron of fine arts, judge of the exquisite in fabrics and gems, a gourmet of fine foods, elegant in person and fastidious in dress.

Challenges to Mughal models also emerged in the encounter with other forms of normative military masculinity that were current among the Marathas, Sikhs, and Afghans who were drawn into the north Indian military labor market and sometimes into service with Mughal armies. Often peasant brotherhoods in arms, these emphasized a soldierly plainness and informality, as Gordon had described, but also carried important codes for martial masculinity. Set against the simplicity and straight comradeship of the warband were not only the feminine worlds of women and home, but also the dandified luxury of the court, where men were adorned with jewels instead of arms, and gold was the coin of devotion to the empire rather than the lives of loyal soldiers. From this perspective, the "feminized" worlds of the court and the harem were drawn into a kind of homology, to suggest a model of simple and soldierly masculinity ultimately superior to Mughal norms.

Thus, the "zones of military entrepreneurship" that Gordon discusses do not actually contain within them a single homogeneous military culture, but rather rival attempts to establish hierarchies of masculinity in the manner described above.[10] These distinct, competing, and publicly displayed norms powerfully shaped what it meant to be a man in eighteenth-century north India at the level of individual identity and experience.

Rival masculinities also offered a means of defining and assigning value to different realms of activity. They were powerful foci in the struggles to create and sustain new group loyalties that were so central to state formation from the late seventeenth century. They could make the difference between success and failure in military and diplomatic negotiations of many different kinds, in which a military commander's personal reputation and frequent pubic display of the right qualities of martial masculinity could play a crucial role. As we shall see, however, there also continued to exist shared basic norms of martial masculinity, about what constituted bravery and correct manly behavior in warfare, set against the values of women and the domestic. If men were different from one another in the manner of their military service, these differences receded before the larger divide between men and women.

I look at these processes through the early-eighteenth-century example of the Mughal military servant and founder of the city of Farrukhabad, Muhammad Khan Bangash (ca. 1665–1743). As a Pathan, a soldier with enormous personal battle experience and a Mughal military servant, Muhammad Khan was adept at manipulating these competing codes of masculinity and gaining advantage at strategic public moments through his assertion of his own plain soldierly Pathan style. Yet he was able to selectively draw on other codes, to show his competence in the knowledge and skills of the court and also command its material luxuries.

THE BANGASH NAWABS of Farrukhabad were Pathan mercenaries and service people who came to Hindustan in the late seventeenth century and settled in Mau-Rashidabad in the Doab region of north India.[11] After two decades of service among the warring rajas of Bundelkhand, Muhammad Khan himself entered the imperial service in 1712 in support of Farrukhsiyar, one of the princely contenders for the Mughal throne who led the coup that displaced the emperor Jahandar Shah. With Farrukhsiyar's victory, Muhammad Khan was raised to the rank of a commander of four thousand, given assignments on revenue in Bundelkhand to support his troops, and styled Nawab. Like other emergent state builders, he proceeded rapidly to found his new city, Farrukhabad, as the center for his household and those of his twenty-two sons. Here also he settled his *chelas* (followers), the "sons of the state" whom he recruited in great numbers from almost every social source: fellow Pathans, local rajas and Rajputs, Brahmans, Bamtela Thakurs, some four thousand by the end of his life. These favored young men whose loyalty seemed more predictable than that of troublesome and ambitious brother Pathans, were entrusted with great responsibilities: in the military as soldiers, bodyguards, and paymasters; in the household; and even as revenue collectors and deputy governors of provinces.

With this formidable apparatus, Muhammad Khan entered on his career as a powerful player in the political upheavals in Delhi following Farrukhsiyar's deposition in 1719. Petitioned by the rival successors Abdullah Khan and Muhammad Shah in 1720, he threw in his lot with the latter and fought in the main body of the battle which brought Muhammad Shah to victory. Raised in rank and granted the title of *ghazanfar jang*, Lion in War, he spent the 1720s engaged with his sons and chelas in subduing the mutinous Hindu rajas of Bundelkhand, and much of the 1730s trying to put together alliances to contain the Marathas in their northward expansion. This demanded those classic skills of negotiation and alliance building that historians have identified as so central to eighteenth-century politics and warfare. Muhammad Khan needed to maintain his credit and continue to press his claims at court. He had to win allies among the Bundela rajas and lesser chiefs, such as the powerful Chattersaul raja, whom he persuaded to submit to imperial authority in 1729, only to learn that powerful factions in Delhi were trying to undermine him by inciting Chattersaul to further hostilities. He had to build friendships with powerful players in the wider political system, such as Sa'adat Khan of Awadh, then himself receiving overtures from the Bundelas and to whom Muhammad Khan appealed for aid as the Marathas pushed northward later that year; and with Nizam-ul Mulk, with whom he concerted in 1731 against the Marathas in Malwa. He needed at the same time to maintain control over his threatened estates in Bundelkhand and later in Malwa. Most of all, Muhammad needed to be able to attract good troops and keep them loyal, even when he had little to pay them and it was clear that his star in the imperial court was waning.

In many ways, then, Muhammad Khan's path to power was a common one, and the political and military relationships he needed to sustain are now familiar to historians. Central to these relationships were the codes for martial masculinity discussed above. At one level, these codes were shared ones. A man was most a man as a soldier, in the company of other men. What distinguished a man was his prestige as a skillful and fearless fighter, his ability to draw other battle-hardened warriors to his standard, his aura of success as a commander, his soldierly dignity in the conduct of diplomacy, and his fierce regard for the honor of his household and his women. These qualities were displayed in very direct and physical ways: in the splendor of men's physiques, the dazzle of equipage, the grim efficiency of their weapons, and the magnificence of their fighting animals. Here, allies, troops, patrons, and rivals continually weighed and judged, challenged and affirmed each other's possession of the manly qualities and competence deemed essential in the successful ruler, ally, military commander, and warrior. Ridicule and failure always loomed as possibilities, as the qualities of the inner man revealed themselves to this audience of his fellows and were appraised by practiced eyes. Here, as suggested in the foregoing, men constructed and sustained masculine identity very much in relation to their peers.

Juxtaposed against these codes, and running through William Irvine's 1878 account of the Bangash Nawabs, is the contrast with the realms of women, the household and harem. Of course, the brilliance of a man's household demonstrated his control over women, and their display for the enjoyment of honored allies formed an essential tool of diplomacy. But too much association with women made a man womanly; his real place lay with his fellow men and soldiers. As we shall see, a defining moment in the gathering of an army lay in a commander's appeal to his men that those who preferred to be at home with their women and children should leave and only those prepared for danger and death set out together on campaign, pledged to mutual loyalty. Running alongside this theme in the life of Muhammad Khan is the parallel contrast between his own soldierly plainness and the luxurious, effete, and money-oriented world of foppish amirs and urbane courtiers in Delhi. Here, we see him making the worlds of the court and the harem homologous, juxtaposed to his own superior martial simplicity. Moreover, this was not only a tactic in Muhammad Khan's negotiation with Muhammad Shah. It was also used against him by his own chelas, and formed an important theme in the way he received and entertained other rulers and military men in the search for prospective allies.

Let us look at the four contexts in which these themes worked themselves out in Muhammad Khan's career: juxtapositions between household, court, and harem; the staged fighting contests between picked warriors that were such an important part of court entertainment; the hunting and animal fights that figured equally importantly as court recreation; and the battlefield.

Muhammad Khan played very interestingly with themes of luxury and plainness, masculinity and effeminacy, and the world of the warrior and of the harem. He had an enormous female establishment: twenty-two sons and twenty-two daughters who reached adulthood, 1,700 concubines in the private apartments of his palaces, and nine further establishments, each containing women drawn from all classes: Kachi, Chamar, Koli, Rajput, Banya, Brahman, Sayyad, Mughal, Pathan, and Shekh. Irvine describes his principal pleasure-house in the Paen Bagh as magnificent.[12] Yet Muhammad Khan made a very deliberate point of keeping his own public style austerely plain. According to Irvine: "He always wore clothes of the commonest stuff. In his audience hall and in his house the only carpet consisted of rows of common mats, and on these the Pathans and *chelas* and all persons, high or low, had to be content to sit." The point, however, was not just to display a soldierly plainness, for this might be taken as poverty. Muhammad Khan intended rather that his visitors should see this as a deliberate preference over luxury and pomp. Irvine describes how: "When any noble from Delhi visited the Nawab, no change was made, the same mats were spread to sit on, and the same food presented. The visitors were astonished at the contrast between his great wealth and power, and the simplicity of his personal habits. Then, for each day after their arrival, the Nawab would name a *chela* to entertain the visitor sumptuously."[13] The implication here was that Muhammad Khan understood his visitor's weakness for luxury and feasting, and so indulged it through one of his chelas, but was himself above it.

This comes out very clearly in Irvine's account of the visit of Nawab Umdat-ul-Mulk Amir Khan to Farrukhabad. Umdat-ul-Mulk and his followers seem to have affected the mannered style of fashionable dandies, with lamp black on their eyelids, their teeth blackened, their hands and feet reddened with henna, rings on their fingers and ears, and bracelets on their wrists. Muhammad Khan and his son Kaim Khan evidently decided to have some fun with them. The nawab was invited over for an audience, and Muhammad Khan received him in the most austere style: the reception room set out with common white cloths and pillows, the utensils for distribution of *pan* (betel) leaves of wood and base metal, and Muhammad Khan himself very simply dressed. "Nawab Amir Khan was much amused at this poor display. On the road back he said to Kaim Khan, 'Though your father is a Bawan Hazari [a holder of very high military rank], he looks like a villager, why do you not teach him better?'" Meanwhile, Muhammad Khan ordered his chela Ja'far Khan to prepare the most stunning reception for the nawab. "Ja'far Khan got out some thousands of silver vessels, he cut up many thousand rupees' worth of gold brocade, and spread scarlet broadcloth all over his *bagh* [garden]. He sent for all the favourite singers, and made ready the most exquisite meats." After the dinner, many of the most valuable items, the silver dishes and gold brocade, were casually given away to the servants and the singing women. Muhammad Khan completed this elaborate piece of public one-upmanship on Amir Khan's next visit. He gave him a handsome present and made apologies for his own humble style of entertainment. For, as he said, "he was only a soldier."[14]

These publicly made juxtapositions between the worlds of the soldier on the one hand, and on the other of the womanly realm of the harem and the luxurious world of the court, emerge again and again. During the battle of Karnal in 1739 against the invading Persian forces of Nadir Shah, Muhammad Shah put Muhammad Khan in charge of his women. After the defeat of the Mughal forces, Muhammad Shah enraged Muhammad Khan by reproaching him bitterly for his absence from the battlefield. The latter kept to his house and evaded all efforts to make him come to the court until Nadir Shah's own men were sent to bring him. Muhammad Khan told his men that his last hour had come and went to the court evidently prepared to recover his reputation or die in the attempt. He went arrayed in full battle armor, with mail shirt, breastplate and backpiece, helmet and gauntlets, with his shield, sword, and dagger at his wrist. Nadir Shah and Muhammad Shah were seated together in the hall, along with two hundred men with naked swords on either side. "The master of ceremonies announced Muhammad Khan, stating that he was armed and refused to leave his sword at the door, on the grounds that he was a soldier, not a noble, and that a soldier's jewels were his arms." This gambit worked, for Nadir Shah ordered him to be admitted armed and then congratulated Muhammad Shah on the loyalty of his servant Muhammad Khan. The latter followed up his advantage, remarking to Nadir Shah that actually "none was so faithless as he; for had he been staunch His Majesty would not have easily come so far; and he regretted that he had not been posted to the van of the army." Muhammad Khan's credit continued to rise, and Nadir Shah invited him forward to receive the costliest of robes. Muhammad Khan then delivered his final salvo: "Putting on the robes, he made his obeisance, but gave no money offering. Nadir Shah's wazir, thinking this was wrong, asked the reason. Muhammad Khan answered that it was not a soldier's business to give tribute of gold and silver: that he left to amirs and wazirs. He was only a soldier, and his head was his offering."[15]

Evidently, the defense of the harem was a persistent source of difficulty, for at the battle of Panipat twenty-two years later, we find Muhammad Khan's son Ahmad Khan in much the same situation, "directed to guard the women, his force being so small. The Nawab refused indignantly, saying that such work was fit for eunuchs, he would fight in the front."[16]

These themes of martial values over those of harem or court could be played with in interesting ways and used in a variety of situations to enhance a man's reputation and strengthen his bargaining position. Muhammad Khan found himself at the other end of these tactics in dealings with his chela Daler Khan. By birth a Bundela Thakur, Daler Khan was a warrior of legendary daring and courage. He also delighted in the splendor of his troops, and spent a year's income from the province he governed in equipping a magnificent body of 1,700 horse. Pressed urgently by Muhammad Khan for remittance of revenue, Daler Khan marched his men in state to the fort and presented them in all their splendor to Muhammad Khan as he sat in court. Protesting his humility as a mere soldier, "Daler Khan took up the Nawab's shoes and stood behind his seat, saying, 'I am only fit to carry your shoes, you may give the Subah to whom you like, one who will bring you heaps of money; these seventeen hundred men are all the revenue you will get from me.' Again this worked: it made Muhammad Khan smile, he embraced Daler Khan and sent him back to his district."[17]

Public contests between picked warriors offered opportunities for the display of qualities of martial masculinity that were more generally shared. Here, of course, there were very long-established Mughal precedents. For Mughal elites, sports and games of many kinds were a source of court recreation, an arena in which aspirants for promotion could catch the emperor's eye and, of course, a means of training and character building. The emperor Akbar's close advisor Abu'l Fazl described these aims quite explicitly in his justification for the game of *chaughan*, the Indian form of polo that served so importantly as a means of training Mughal heavy cavalry. Some, he said, viewed chaughan just as a game, "but men of more exalted views see in it a means of learning promptitude and decision. It tests the value of a man, and strengthens the bonds of friendship. Strong men learn in playing this game the art of riding and the animals learn to perform feats of agility and to obey the reins. Hence his majesty is very fond of this game. Externally, the game adds to the splendour of the court, but viewed from a higher viewpoint, it reveals concealed talents."[18]

For eighteenth-century courts, too, public contests of picked warriors had important practical benefits, keeping men fit outside the campaigning season, honing battle skills, and building an esprit de corps. But such occasions also served a number of vital political purposes, combining display with sociability, prestige with the consolidation of loyalties and friendships. Allies could be entertained with feasting and women, joint projects for military expansion discussed, and the disposition of enemies surmised. Equally important, these occasions were nodal points for generating information about the relative dynamism of different military and political players in the field, information that was both fed into wider military labor markets in north India and disseminated through the courts and armies of other potential opponents or friends. On such occasions, allies, rivals, and subordinates could scrutinize one another's troops, appraise their bodies, skills, and equipage, and gauge their military élan.

Muhammad Khan had to survive this kind of public testing shortly after his reputation was redeemed with Nadir Shah and Muhammad Shah. He attended another public audience with the two kings, taking with him a renowned Indian Muslim archer, wonderfully expert but slight of stature. Nadir Shah called out a champion, a great big man, from among his own troops, and asked Muhammad Shah to match him. The little archer offered to go, but Muhammad Khan refused: "He did not want to be turned into the laughing stock of the army." But the archer insisted on putting himself forward. With his man in the ring, the spotlight was firmly on Muhammad Khan, and his mettle now publicly to be tested, "the perspiration poured down Muhammad Khan's body from anxiety, and he muttered a prayer to God." Seeing his opponent, the Persian said he would lift him and carry him off on his lance point. The two galloped at one another inconclusively, until the Persian's lance struck home, lifting the archer's body from his horse like a tumbler. It looked as though Muhammad Khan was to be humbled: "Nadir Shah began to laugh, and the countenances fell of those on the other side." But then, wounded as he was, the Indian turned and let fly an arrow with such violence that it penetrated the Persian's headpiece, so that the man sat dead on his horse. Full of praise, Nadir Shah bestowed a dress of honor on him, no doubt much to Muhammad Khan's relief.[19]

Often, these public contests could involve players from far afield. Muhammad Khan's son Kaim Khan was himself a renowned lancer, so much so that a Maratha warrior came all the way from Poona to try him. Kaim Khan put him up and entertained him while he checked his credentials. Having done so, he fixed a day for the tournament, which was to be held in an open space in the Ganges riverbed where the troops usually exercised. His soldiers all assembled to watch, and the two warriors rode out into the plain: "There they contended till full noon, but neither had been touched. Now, the Mahratta had a handkerchief round his arm, such as they usually tie above their other clothes. The Nawab decided to try and loose this handkerchief with the point of his spear. He touched it repeatedly, but being wet with perspiration the knot had become extremely tight. After some hours, however, the Nawab succeeded in untying it with his lance and carried it off on his point."[20]

A further context in which these shared qualities of martial masculinity could be demonstrated lay in dealings with animals. Eighteenth-century India was a context in which humans and animals lived in close proximity and came into contact in many daily situations. Animals thus offered a vivid and immediate means of symbolizing a whole range of human relations and qualities. At a simple level, celebrating a man's war animals offered another means of talking about his own qualities. Thus the bards celebrated Daler Khan's horses, the sheer physicality of their descriptions almost as an extension of himself as a warrior: "Their hoofs stamp the ground as soon as the foot touches the stirrup; they go like the wind, these milk-white steeds . . . by strong chains two grooms lead them; they pull at the chains and plunge and prance. They have arched backs, are white, youthful, strong and young. They are as if formed in moulds out of gold, they are of beautiful shape and form. They have cloths of gold stuff and brocade of every colour green, yellow, black, white, purple . . . they leap and bound, in strength they are like elephants. Sahib Asgar, these are the steeds of a great lord."[21]

In rather more complex ways, courtly hunting provided a multiplex arena for the display of manly and martial qualities. Many historians have described the multiplicity of purposes served in the royal progress of the court through the countryside: the display of kingly wealth and the ability to offer protection; maneuvers for the army, by which potential rebels could be overawed; an opportunity to inquire into local affairs and offer access to humble subjects.[22] For armies on the move, hunting and war were very closely related, providing not only fighting practice and a test of the troops' resolve under stress, but an arena for individuals to display their courage and a means of scouting for information about enemy positions. Thus, in the days before his final battle with the Bundela rajas, Daler Khan slowly advanced through the Bundela countryside toward Maudha to meet them, hunting in the forests as he went within a few miles of the Bundela armies and testing the courage of his troops so close to the enemy. Muhammad Khan, too, used hunting in this way. Having persuaded the Chattersaul raja to offer his submission to the emperor, Muhammad Khan spent much of his time with the raja's eldest son, Harde Sah, and they "frequently made excursions and hunting expeditions together, and talked of setting out together on a *mulkgiri* [expedition of conquest]."[23]

What is not clear is how far the killing of animals offered a means for the expression of individual masculinity homologous to the excitement and release of sexual conquest, as John MacKenzie has described for a later generation of colonial British hunters.[24] Of course, the courtly hunt in India used hunting animals, such as the cheetah and falcon, on a much larger scale than did colonial hunters, with their greater enthusiasm for combat between the individual hunter and his quarry. It may be that themes of dominance and conquest in the Indian context were enacted more in the formalized contests between fighting animals of all kinds, which featured as a large part of both courtly and popular recreation. Certainly, the staging of fights of large animals formed a centerpiece in every ruler's demonstration of his power and majesty, and the size and rich variety of their animal parks were always an important index of prestige.[25] Many contemporary descriptions of warriors in battle liken them to fighting animals. Thus the bardic tradition celebrating Daler Khan describes how his men "leapt into the midst of the foe, like the chitah seizes and shakes a deer . . . like elephants black as lamp-black, maddened, lifting up their tusks, they drove all before them."[26] Elephant fights carried particular meaning. They could be used as symbolic struggles for the throne, as when Akbar staged a fight between elephants belonging to his rival sons to get an omen as to his successor.[27] The staging of elephant fights also expressed royal status and had been a jealously guarded prerogative of the Mughal throne until the eighteenth-century emergence of regional powers beyond Mughal control, anxious to exercise their own kingly powers. Ahmad Khan employed them in 1761, to the evident fury of Shuja-ud-Daulah: "The newswriters sent letters to Shuja-ud-daulah, informing him of Ahmad Khan's daily life and stating that he rode in a *palkhi* (a litter, as in a form of conveyance), that he caused elephants to fight, that he had established a Gulalbari or royal pavilion, and had assumed other privileges of royalty. Shuja-ud-daulah writhed like a snake when he read this, and at once he made a minute report to the Emperor, adding that to mount the throne was the only step, which now remained for Ahmad Khan to take."[28]

Just as important a public arena for the display of these qualities was, of course, the battlefield itself. It is no accident that contemporary accounts abound with detailed descriptions of the ebb and flow of battles, for these were the dramatic theaters where a man's mettle could be displayed to most brilliant advantage and put most violently to the test. The chela and matchless warrior Daler Khan generated, as Irvine describes, a very rich folk tradition in celebration of his martial qualities. In these Hindi folk songs, we can see many of the themes illustrated above. As he carried his hunting party closer and closer to the enemy, local Muslims reproached Daler Khan for his rashness and urged him to turn back, but that way, he said, lay disgrace. There followed the familiar moment of combat between men and military commanders, the appeal to choose war and honor over home, wives, and children: "Turning to his troops he harangued them, and offered to pay up and discharge all those who held their wives and children dearer than honour." Some of his men left him, and with the others he went forward to the violent three-day battle in which he lost his life. Many Hindi bards and contemporaries celebrated his qualities. In body, he was a perfect specimen of manhood, "his chest a yard wide," and the Pathans and Bundelas named him *surman*, brave, bold, "the mark of which is that a man's arms are so long that his hands touch his knees when standing up. Daler Khan had this peculiarity."[29] The descriptions of Daler Khan's last battle interweave themes of hunting, the dust and roar of combat, and the bloody grappling of warriors: "They gathered in Sihunda-garh, when came word of the war; they took up bow and arrow and repaired to the hunting ground of Mungas." The tradition graphically describes the fight, "like that of practised wrestlers; the blood flowed and turned the earth into mire," and the flash and roar of the guns as Daler rode in to attack: "In many ways did he thrust with his spear, did brave Daler, the mighty. The cannon roared, the swords clashed, the rockets flashed like lightning clouds. They drew their chapual, look at them once! On every side the Mughal and the Bundelas are mingled in one wave."[30]

MOST OF MY examples in the foregoing are from Farrukhabad. However, I hope that I have illustrated something of the way Farrukhabad diplomacy may have been part of a wider martial culture of "imperial masculinity" that was a very important part of the north Indian political system. This was a complex rather than a monolithic culture, incorporating both competing efforts to establish a hierarchy of higher and inferior forms of masculinity and shared codes that juxtaposed men as soldiers generally against the social world of women. Peter Hardy and others have suggested that outdoor activities in Mughal India provided an arena for Hindu-Muslim contact, and that shared ideals about bravery and correct manly behavior in warfare, games, and hunting helped promote intercommunal fellow feeling.[31] This is an important point to appreciate about these shared codes of martial masculinity. Much of the social world in which they were expressed was essentially an outdoor world, consciously and deliberately juxtaposed to the indoor realms of court household and harem. Men lived as particular social beings — as Hindu or Muslim, Rajput, Maratta, or Pathan, as commander or common trooper, noble or servant — mostly within the indoor realm of the household. In the outdoor world of the contest, the game, the hunt, and the battlefield, the sectional values and identities of the household receded and the common pursuits and codes of martial masculinity could find freer play.

It is also clear from the foregoing that the British were not the first to use masculinity in the way that Mrinalini Sinha has described, as a cross-cultural means of establishing hierarchies and affirming common identities. The strength of what she identifies as "colonial masculinity" may well owe something to longer-established north Indian practice. Furthermore, these martial codes were above all syncretic and inclusive in character. This seems difficult to reconcile with Ashis Nandy's depiction of India's martial traditions as mainly Kshatriya or Rajput in character. In particular, Nandy seems to me mistaken in seeing Kshatriya tradition as a minor part of Indian culture that became inflated and generalized under the influence of British "hypermasculinity," so as to efface a precolonial world of fluid and multiple gender identities. Precolonial martial values and practices were neither simply Kshatriya in origin, nor were they only a minor part of north Indian culture. Although they have been largely invisible to historians, they stood as an essential integrative aspect of more formal political and military institutions. These codes drew men together both in contests about and in recognition of commonalities of gender that often transcended other forms of cultural difference.

Last, it is worth asking what the longer-term implications of these codes and identities may have been for gender relations in India, particularly in view of the colonial drive to pacification and demilitarization. Of course, this drive was never fully successful, and the colonial state was only gradually more effective than its predecessors in disarming rural populations. Nevertheless, we do know that the British East India Company's destruction of the military labor market and disbanding of armies through the first half of the nineteenth century denied military careers, whether seasonal or full time, to a very significant proportion of the rural population. Many historians have recognized that one of the consequences of colonial peace was to stifle opportunity for many sectors of the rural population, and so to lead to a hardening of caste boundaries. As suggested in the foregoing, there may have been implications here too for communal boundaries. These processes also had important implications for women. As other opportunities for mobility declined and social distinction came increasingly to rest on the niceties of social propriety, women's conduct became an increasingly sensitive index of status. Declining opportunities for the expression of martial masculinity may have been important here, too, as the outdoor world in which they were affirmed contracted, thus focusing attention more closely on the indoor realm of household and family.

Notes

1. *Editors' note*: In 1765 the British East India Company became *diwan* of Bengal, Bihar, and Orissa and as such assumed responsibility for revenue collection and the administration of the law over some 20 million South Asians. This is traditionally seen as marking the beginning of formal British colonialism in South Asia.

2. Ashis Nandy, "The Psychology of Colonialism: Sex, Age and Ideology in British

India," in Ashis Nandy, *The Intimate Enemy: Loss and Recovery of Self under Colonialism* (Delhi: Oxford University Press, 1983), 1–63. *Editors' note*: Kshatriya refers to caste groups who traditionally functioned as warriors and military leaders. They were the second-highest grouping in the classical fourfold *varna* model of caste hierarchy.

3. Mrinalini Sinha, *Colonial Masculinity: The "Manly" Englishman and the "Effeminate" Bengali in the Late Nineteenth Century* (Manchester, England: Manchester University Press, 1995).

4. Partha Chatterjee, *The Nation and Its Fragments: Colonial and Postcolonial Histories* (Delhi: Oxford University Press, 1995); Partha Kumari Jayawardena, *The White Woman's Other Burden: Western Women and South Asia During British Rule*. (New York: Routledge, 1995); Kumkum Sangari and Vaid Suresh, eds., *Recasting Women: Essays in Colonial History* (New Delhi: Kali for Women, 1989).

5. Rosalind O'Hanlon, *A Comparison between Women and Men Tarabai Shinde and the Critique of Gender Relations in Colonial India* (Madras: Oxford University Press, 1994).

6. J. F. Richards, "The Formulation of Imperial Authority under Akbar and Jahangir," in *Kingship and Authority in South Asia*, ed. J. F. Richards (Madison: University of Wisconsin, 1981), 255–289; J. F. Richards, "Norms of Comportment among Imperial Mughal Officers," in *Moral Conduct and Authority: The Place of Adab in South Asian Islam*, ed. Barbara Daly Metcalf (Berkeley: University of California Press, 1984); J. F. Richards, *The Mughal Empire* (Cambridge, England: Cambridge University Press, 1993).

7. *Editors' note*: a *mansabdar* was a "holder of rank" in the Mughal state. In return for their powerful official position, mansabdars supplied a specified number of soldiers for the Mughal army. This system was inaugurated by the emperor Akbar in 1577 and it formed the foundation of both the Mughal military and administrative systems.

8. Stuart Gordon, "Zones of Military Entrepreneurship in India," in Stuart Gordon, *Marathas, Marauders and State Formation* (Delhi: Oxford University Press, 1994), 182–208.

9. S. A. A. Rizvi, *Religious and Intellectual History of the Muslims in Akbar's Reign* (Delhi: Munshiram Manoharlai, 1975).

10. R. W. Connell, *Masculinities* (Oxford: Polity Press, 1995). See also Stuart Gordon, "Zones of Military Entrepreneurship in India," in *Marathas, Marauders and State Formation*, 182–208.

11. William Irvine, "The Bangash Nawabs of Farrukhabad—A Chronicle (1713–1857), Part 1," *Journal of the Asiatic Society of Bengal* 47 (1878): 277–358. See also William Irvine, "The Bangash Nawabs of Farrukhabad—A Chronicle (1713–1857), Part 2," *Journal of the Asiatic Society of Bengal* 48 (1879): 41–174. As will be seen, Irvine forms my major source for this essay, which is closely based on contemporary Persian and Urdu sources, including a large collection of Muhammad Khan's own letters. For an excellent discussion of the political context, see Seema Alavi, *The Sepoys and the Company: Tradition and Transition in Northern India* (Delhi: Oxford University Press, 1995), 195–202.

12. Irvine, "The Bangash Nawabs Part 1," 277.

13. Ibid., 277–358.

14. Ibid., pp. 338–339.

15. Ibid., 331–332.

16. Irvine, "The Bangash Nawabs Part 2," 127.

17. Irvine, "The Bangash Nawabs Part 1," 286.

18. Fazl Abu'l [1873]. *Ain-i Akbari*, vol. 1, translated by H. Blochmann (New Delhi: Asiatic Society of Bengal, 1977).

19. Irvine, "The Bangash Nawabs Part 1," 333.

20. Ibid., 372.

21. Ibid., 370.

22. Stephen P. Blake, *Shahjahanabad: The Sovereign City in Mughal India, 1639–1739* (Cambridge, England: Cambridge University Press, 1991); John MacKenzie, *The Empire of Nature: Hunting, Conservation and British Imperialism* (Manchester, England: Manchester University Press, 1988); M. N. Pearson, "Recreation in Mughal India," *British Journal of Sports History* 1, 3 (1984): 335–350.

23. Irvine, "The Bangash Nawabs Part 1," 297.

24. MacKenzie, *The Empire of Nature*, 42–43.

25. See, for example, descriptions of the impressive animal parks in the north Indian state of Awadh, in Abdul Halim Sharar, *Lucknow: The Last Phase of an Oriental Culture*, translated by E. S. Harcourt and Fakhir Hussain (Delhi: Oxford University Press, 1984), 116–122.

26. Irvine, "The Bangash Nawabs Part 1," 369.

27. Fazl, *Ain-i Akbari*, 467.

28. Irvine, "The Bangash Nawabs of Farrukhabad," 136.

29. Ibid., 368–369.

30. Irvine, "The Bangash Nawabs of Farrukhabad," 368–369.

31. Peter Hardy, "The Growth of Authority over a Conquered Political Elite: The Early Delhi Sultanate as a Possible Case Study," in *Kingship and Authority in South Asia*, ed. J. F. Richards (Madison: University of Wisconsin Press, 1981), 112–121.

Emma Jinhua Teng

An Island of Women:

Gender in Qing Travel

Writing about Taiwan

Unlike early modern Europeans, who viewed the continent of Africa as a "virginal" space, Chinese writers of the same period did not see Taiwan as a sexualized terrain. As the Europeans did with Africa, however, they pathologized indigenous Taiwanese and Vietnamese women as hypersexualized "others," highlighting their reproductive, marital, and sexual habits. Tales of female dominance, or "gender inversion," were rife in premodern Chinese ethnic discourses about foreign lands. Nor were these stereotypes limited to China's external others: writers approached China's southern tribal peoples with the same gendered visions, effectively equating them with the "savages" beyond their borders. Of particular note is the legend of Baozhu, a Han courtesan who became the female chieftain of an indigenous tribe, thus both fulfilling and challenging dominant Chinese notions about the relationship between women, sexuality, and power.

Seventeenth- and eighteenth-century Chinese travelers to the island colony of Taiwan perhaps imagined that they had stumbled upon the mythical Kingdom of Women, the Chinese equivalent of the land of the Amazons. Encountering a land with female tribal heads, uxorilocal marriage, and matrilineal inheritance, travel writers noted with astonishment that native custom gave precedence to the female sex.[1] "The savages value woman and undervalue man" became a commonplace of Qing ethnographic writing on the Taiwan indigenes. As a direct inversion of the Confucian patriarchal maxim "Value man and undervalue woman" (*zhongnan qingnü*), this expression indexed the utter alterity of Taiwan in Chinese eyes. The anomalous gender roles of the indigenous peoples became one of the most popular topics in Qing travel writing on Taiwan. Female sex roles, in particular, attracted intense interest not only because they appeared strange in and of themselves, but also because they served as a marker of the strangeness of Taiwan as a whole. The discourse of gender was thus central to Qing colonial representations of Taiwan's "savagery."

Gender and ethnicity are closely intertwined in premodern Chinese ethnographic discourse, where the trope of gender inversion (the reversal of normative sex roles) was commonly used to represent foreignness, especially in accounts of Southeast Asia and the West. The rigidity of sex roles in Confucian ideology meant that deviations from normative definitions of femininity and masculinity were readily interpreted as signs of barbarism. Hence, the discourse of gender became a means of demarcating the "civilized" from the "uncivilized." Other gendered tropes, such as hypermasculinization and hyperfeminization, were also employed to establish the alterity of non-Chinese groups.

In Qing colonial discourse, gendered or sexualized tropes are employed not only as a means of signifying the "otherness" of the colonial subject, but also quite often as a form of denigration. Thus, gender functions much as it does in the European discourses of discovery and colonialism: as a metaphor for conceptualizing inequality or for signifying power relations. A critical point of difference, however, is that Qing colonial discourse does not represent the colonized land itself as metaphorically feminine or as virgin. Exploration and conquest, in turn, are not figured as sexualized acts of penetration and possession. Qing travel writers did, however, represent colonial expansion as a masculine quest for sexual experience, a trope that postcolonial scholars have identified as a major theme of Western imperialist writings. Colonial relations, too, are sexualized in their textual representations, colonial power and ethnic prestige being symbolized by Chinese sexual license with the native women. The Qing colonial discourse of gender therefore overlaps with European colonial discourses, although it is not identical. The gender dynamics found in travel literature about Taiwan reveal that insights from Western colonial theory can provide useful tools of analysis, but also that the gendered tropes of this particular literature are derived from within the Chinese literary tradition.

This essay examines the representation of the "savage woman" in Qing travel accounts of Taiwan and the linkages between gender and ethnicity in Qing colonial discourse. I argue that gender inversion is fundamental to the construction of the ethnic difference of the Taiwan indigenes. One aspect of this inversion, the feminization of the indigenous men, may be regarded as a means of expressing the subordinate status of the colonized subject. However, it is less the feminization of the men than the anomalous roles of women that preoccupy the Chinese travel writers. This fascination stems in large part, I argue, from their desire to imagine "another world." Taiwan frequently served as a projection of this desire in travel literature, whether as a world of the past, a world of marvels, or a "Kingdom of Women."

The savage woman not only symbolized difference to Chinese observers, she was also a pivotal figure in the representation of colonial relations: colonial dominance was frequently represented in terms of Han Chinese access to indigenous women. Qing writings thus typically hypersexualized the savage woman, depicting her as more erotic, more promiscuous than the Chinese woman. Intermarriage between Han Chinese settlers and indigenous Taiwanese women became a source of contention, with women serving as a kind of contested terrain for colonizers and colonized. At the same time, this intermarriage was an important vehicle for transcultural exchange in colonial Taiwan: a two-way process of acculturation. At other times, the discourse of gender was less about Taiwan itself than about the internal concerns of Qing society, in particular the changing roles of women. The idealization of the non-Chinese woman became a common trope for self-reflexive critiques of Chinese society: the foreign woman serves as a projection for Confucian ideals perceived to be losing their hold in China. The figure of the savage woman, then, could serve a variety of rhetorical purposes, often opposing, to suit the needs of the travel writer.

FEW CHINESE EYEWITNESS accounts of Taiwan exist from the period prior to the Qing, when the island was a Dutch colony and later an outpost of Ming loyalist rebels. The only firsthand account of Taiwan from the Ming is Chen Di's *Record of the Eastern Savages* (*Dongfan ji*, 1603), which was regarded as highly authoritative by Qing readers. After the Qing colonization of Taiwan in 1683, the number of accounts written by Chinese, mainly colonial officials, military men, and others who traveled on behalf of the Qing colonial enterprise, increased dramatically. The best-known Qing accounts include Lin Qianguang's *Brief Record of Tai-*

wan (*Taiwan jilue*, ca. 1685), the first eyewitness account of Taiwan writ-ten after the Qing conquest; Yu Yonghe's *Small Sea Travelogue* (*Pihai jiyou*, 1697), a diary of a sulphur expedition; and Wu Ziguang's *Taiwan Memoranda* (*Taiwan jishi*, ca. 1875), a series of essays written by a Chi-nese settler. These accounts, among others, are emphasized here because of their representative status and their use by later writers. Owing to the high degree of intertextuality in accounts of Taiwan, the conclusions drawn here may be used to generalize about Qing representations of the island.

Chinese travel writers may have been predisposed to view Taiwan as a gynocentric society in part owing to their familiarity with tales of King-doms of Women (much as Sir Walter Ralegh was predisposed to find the Amazons in South America). Their representations of the Taiwanese in-digenes were also influenced by a tradition of regional stereotyping in both literary and historical materials. By the Tang dynasty, a tradition of feminizing the southern borderlands and masculinizing the northern frontiers had been firmly established in the Chinese literary tradition. The south was associated with sensuality, languor, literary refinement, femi-ninity, and female promiscuity; the north with barrenness, ruggedness, martial valor, and machismo. This divide between hyperfeminized south-erners (peoples such as the Miao and the Dai) on the one hand and hypermasculinized northerners (peoples such as the Mongols and Jur-chens) on the other means that the simple structural equation male/fe-male paralleling major/minor is untenable. Rather, the Han Chinese configured the other in terms of polarized opposites of sexual excess, centering the Han self as the norm.

Newly incorporated into the Chinese empire in the seventeenth cen-tury, Taiwan seemed to fit neatly into existing images of matriarchal and hypersexualized "southern barbarians"; in fact, writers often borrowed tropes from earlier accounts of the Miao, the Lao, and even the people of Thailand to describe the indigenous peoples of Taiwan. The gendering of the south as feminine thus provides an important context within which to read Qing representations of the "savage woman" of Taiwan.

CERTAIN PRACTICES EMERGED as indices of gender inversion in the travel literature: uxorilocal marriage, matrilineal inheritance, the "prefer-ence" for female children, sexual assertiveness of women, sexual division of labor, absence of postpartum seclusion, and the fact that women were not sequestered. Although the existence of female tribal heads among certain groups represented an obvious inversion of the Chinese norm of male rulership, it was the domestic roles of native women that became the focus of attention in the travel accounts. Chinese writers theorized that it was the savage woman's position in the family that accounted for her social dominance.

Descriptions of uxorilocal marriage and matrilineal descent among the Taiwan indigenes commonly invoked the notion of inversion. As Chen Di wrote in his *Record of the Eastern Savages*:

> The girl hears [the suitor's music] and admits him to stay the night. Before daylight he straightaway departs, without seeing the girl's parents. From this time on he must come in the dark and leave with the dawn when the stars are out, for years and months without any change. When a child is born, she for the first time goes to the man's home and [brings him back to her home] to be welcomed as the son-in-law, as [the Chinese] welcome a new bride, and the son-in-law for the first time sees the girl's parents. He then lives in her home and supports her parents for the rest of their lives, while his own parents can no longer regard him as their son. Therefore they are much happier at the birth of a girl than of a boy, in view of the fact that a girl will continue the family line, while a boy is not sufficient to establish the family succession.[2]

This passage clearly represents an interpretation of native customs through the lens of Chinese gender ideology. Chen Di employs the discourse of inversion in likening the savage bridegroom to the Chinese bride. The phrase "to be welcomed as the son-in-law, as [the Chinese] welcome a new bride" sets up the equation savage man = Chinese woman. At the end of Chen's description, he delivers what would become a quintessential formulation of gender inversion: "they are much happier at the birth of a girl than of a boy." This inversion of normative Chinese values serves as a basic index of the difference between Chinese and savage. Rather than simply marveling at the strange nature of this inversion, however, Chen provides a rationale for this reversal of values. As it is the savage women who assume the function of continuing the family succession (an all-important role in Chinese culture), an inversion of value results: daughters, not sons, become the privileged progeny. In identifying the inheritance system as the root of the strange gender hierarchy,

Chen represents gender inversion as a product of social convention and economic relations. Such an explanation serves at once to distance the savages (they are matrilineal and we are patrilineal) and to normalize them (they, like us, value the sex that assures the succession of the family line).

Following Chen Di, discussions of marital customs and their effects on the gender hierarchy became a standard element of descriptions of indigenous customs. Yu Yonghe provides this account of native courtship:

> In marriage they have no go-betweens; when the girls are grown, their parents have them live separately in a hut. The youths who wish to find a mate all come along, playing their nose-flutes and mouth-organs. When a youth gets the girl to harmonize with him, he goes in and fornicates with her. After they fornicate, he goes home of his own accord. After a long time, the girl picks the one she loves and "holds hands" with him. The "hand-holding" is to make public the private commitment. The next day, the girl tells her family, and invites the "hand-holding" youth to come to her home. He knocks out the two top bicuspids to give to the girl and she also knocks out two teeth to give to the boy. They set a date to go to the wife's house to marry, and for the rest of his life he lives at the wife's residence. . . . The parents are not able to keep their son. Therefore, after one or two generations the grandchild does not know his ancestors; the savages have no family names.[3]

Highlighting female agency in mate selection, Yu paints a vivid picture here of the "sexual assertiveness" of the savage woman, an image that would have been most shocking to Chinese audiences, for whom arranged marriage was the norm. For Yu, gender inversion signaled the disruption of the entire kinship system, leading the savages to forget their own ancestors. The notion that the indigenes did not recognize their ancestors was another indication of their savagery. For Chinese, ancestor worship was one of the cornerstones of civilization.

Other writers decried the "subordination" of the savage male by uxorilocal marriage practices, viewing him as debased and emasculated.[4] To these authors, uxorilocal marriage was not simply different and strange, but contemptible. The equivalence drawn in Chinese eyes between the savage groom and the Chinese bride provided an impetus for this interpretation of gender relations. That is, the notion of inversion, of a "mirror world," conditioned Chinese understandings of gender relations that differed from the Confucian norm.

THE INVERSION OF gender was also represented in the travel literature by descriptions of the sexual division of labor. Numerous Chinese observers expressed surprise at the fact that it was the indigenous women, and not the men, who were engaged in agricultural production. This perceived reversal of sex roles was interpreted by the Chinese as female "industriousness" and male "idleness," as Chinese literati did not recognize the male occupation of hunting as "productive" activity. As Lin Qianguang declared: "All of the tilling is done by the wife; the husband on the other hand stays at home waiting to be fed."[5] This image of the man's childlike dependence on his wife's labor recurred frequently in the literature, providing yet another rationale in Chinese eyes for female dominance.

THE DEPICTION OF Taiwan as a matriarchal land can be regarded as part of a long tradition of southern exoticism in classical Chinese literature and historiography. A popular theme of this literature was the native woman bather. The Dai became particularly famous for the custom of bathing openly in streams, an image that remains popular among PRC tourists today.[6] Indeed, the hypersexualization of non-Han in southern China has maintained a certain consistency over the centuries.

Female dominance, or gender inversion, was another favorite motif of accounts about "southern barbarians." An entry on "The Lao Women" from the *Accounts Widely Gathered in the Taiping Era* (*Taiping guangji*), for example, focuses on gender inversion as its central point of interest:

> In the south there are Lao women. They give birth to children and then get up. Their husbands lie in bed. Their diets are exactly the same as a nursing mother. They do not protect their pregnant women in the least. When the women go into labor, they give birth on the spot. They do not suffer in the least. They prepare food and gather firewood as usual. It is also said that according to Yue custom, if a wife gives birth to a child, after three days, she bathes in the stream. When she returns, she prepares gruel to feed her husband. The husband bundles the infant in the bedclothes and sits up in bed. They call him the "parturient husband." Their inversion is to such a degree.[7]

This feminization of the south was contrasted against the masculinization of the northern frontiers in both literary and historical sources. These gendered stereotypes were influenced by several factors: the existence of matrilineal customs among southern "barbarians"; the association of northern "barbarians" with warfare; theories of environmental determinism of human character (the environment of the north being rugged and that of the south being wet and fertile); and the relative strength of the expansionist northern dynasties vis-à-vis the overrefined and declining southern dynasties during the Six Dynasties era. These stereotypes were further developed in Tang literary treatments of the northern frontiers and the southern borderlands. The southern male was in effect emasculated not only by contrast to the empowerment of the southern female, but also as part of a general feminization of the region. The feminization of southern peoples and the masculinization of northern peoples served to center the ideal Han Chinese self of the "central plains" as a privileged norm. The feminization of the Taiwan indigenes should thus be understood not simply as part of a general case of "feminizing the other," but also as part of this particular economy of regional stereotypes within the Chinese literary tradition.

The image of Taiwan as part of the exotic/erotic southland was promoted by descriptions of female bathers, native sexual habits, and remarks on female beauty. Yu Yonghe, for example, frequently includes notes in his travelogue about the physical appearance (and, indeed, sexual attractiveness) of the women whom he encounters. His diary entry for one day includes the note, "Of the savage women that we saw, many were fair-skinned and beautiful." On another day he observes: "There were also three young girls working with mortar and pestle. One of them was rather attractive. They appeared in front of outsiders naked, but their composure was dignified."[8] Although there is frequent reference in the literature to both male and female nudity (nakedness in general being a sign of impropriety and thus cultural inferiority), it is only the savage woman's lack of shame concerning nudity that receives comment from the travel writers. One of the chief markers of proper femininity in Chinese culture being the shrouding of the body, the savage woman's lack of shame regarding her body must have appeared to Chinese observers as particularly strange and offensive (and titillating).

Travel writers expressed great interest in the bathing habits of indigene women, noting in particular the frequency and openness of this practice. Liu-shi-qi, a Manchu official who traveled to Taiwan in the mid-eighteenth century, devoted an entire entry of his account to "Bathing in the Stream." His description eroticizes the act of bathing by linking it with play, flirtation, and voyeurism. This objectification of women is also particularly apparent in Qing ethnographic illustrations, where women are often depicted in festival dress or bare-breasted.

The image of Taiwan as a land of exotic sensuality was perhaps most promoted by descriptions of native courtship and marriage practices. A standard favorite in the Taiwan literature was the anecdote about youths sealing partnerships with young girls based on their ability to harmonize with them on the mouth organ, "to harmonize" being a pun on "to couple." For a Chinese audience, such anecdotes were reminiscent of poetic motifs in the ancient *Classic of Poetry* and thus conjured up images of a primitive past. At the same time, the notion that the savages lacked an understanding of sexual propriety signaled their uncivilized status.

Chinese observers also took the lack of both segregation of the sexes and proscriptions against physical contact as marks of sexual impropriety among the savages. However, travel writers who disparaged the savage practice of men and women sitting together "mixed" or "without order" often themselves indulged in voyeurism and other behavior taboo in their own society. Liu-shi-qi, for example, made this note under the heading of "Suckling the Child": "The savages have no taboos against contact between male and female. When the savage woman nurses her child, those who see will play and tease from the side. She will be very pleased, thinking that people adore her child. Even if one touches her breast she will not prevent it."[9] Contrasting the savage woman's body with the Chinese female body, which ideally remained out of sight and beyond touch, added titillation to ethnographic description. It bolstered the image of Taiwan as a fantasy island where Chinese men had free license with the indigenous women.

The image of Chinese men in unrestricted sexual intercourse with savage women was used in travel writing to buttress the self-image of the colonizer. Interethnic marriage or sexual relationships served in numerous narratives as a means of representing the ethnic hierarchy of the colonial society, the unequal status of Chinese and indigene. Yu, for example, observes of the Chinese men on the island, "They take the barbarian women as their wives and concubines. Whatever is demanded of them they must comply with; if they make a mistake they must take a flogging.

And yet the barbarians do not hate them greatly." Yu attributes the availability of indigenous women to ethnic privilege: "Should the [Chinese] guests take liberties with them [the women], they do not get angry. A husband, seeing a guest becoming intimate with his wife, is very pleased, saying that his wife is really charming, and that therefore Chinese like her. . . . However, should one of their own people fornicate with [a savage's wife], then he will take his bow and arrows, search out the adulterer, and shoot him dead. But he will not hold it against his wife."[10] For a Qing audience, such stories portray the indigenes as subordinate to the Chinese, supplying women and labor without animosity, and confirm its own superior status. In such narratives, the savage woman is reduced to an object in a contest for power.

Other travel writers contradicted Yu's claim regarding the liberties allowed Chinese men, recording conflicts between Han settlers and indigenes over such relations. Indeed, as rates of intermarriage increased during the Qing, owing to an unfavorable sex ratio among the settlers, colonial officials came to view the Chinese demand for indigenous women as a source of ethnic conflict.[11] After a local revolt, the Qing administration prohibited intermarriage between Han Chinese men and indigenous women in 1737.

Yet, there were no social prohibitions against such couplings. John Shepherd found that "the Chinese perceived no racial divide between Han and aborigines that would impede the ability of aborigines to acquire Chinese status characteristics or deny legitimacy to mixed marriages and their offspring." In fact, intermarriage between Han Chinese and indigene was even perceived by some officials as an expedient means of assimilating the indigenes.[12] As one local official argued: "With marriage and social intercourse, there will be no separation between the savages and the people. If the officials do not segregate them as a different race [*zhong*], then after some time they will naturally assimilate [*hua*]."[13] As wives, then, indigenous women could be regarded as key vehicles for transculturation.[14] Indeed, anthropologist Melissa Brown has argued that during the Qing, "intermarriage was the primary mechanism for introducing and spreading Chinese values and practices into Aborigine communities."[15]

AS HAN WOMEN rarely married indigenous men until the late Qing, few such marriages are mentioned in the Qing literature other than the fascinating legend of Baozhu, a Han Chinese courtesan who became the female chieftain of an indigenous tribe. One nineteenth-century traveler, Ding Shaoyi, reconstructs the identity of this mysterious figure by entwining two items of local lore, one about a female chieftain and the other about the Chinese consort of an indigenous ruler:

> Prefect Deng Chuan'an of Fuliang says in his *Measuring the Sea with a Calabash*: "During the Jiaqing period (1796–1821), the female chieftain Baozhu made herself up like an aristocratic lady of China. In her administration, she followed the law. Someone sent the officials a memorial [stating that her tribe] followed the law obediently and respectfully, not killing people, not rebelling. Even though this place is beyond the pale, how is it different from China proper?" Legend has it that during the Zhu Yigui rebellion, the chief of the Beinanmi, Wenji, decided to get a beauty for his consort. There was a courtesan in Taiwan city who heard of this with delight and volunteered to go. The savages value women to begin with, and since the chieftain got a courtesan, he doted on her to the extreme, doing whatever she commanded. Then they got rid of their old customs, and were civilized with the rites and laws of China. Therefore the seventy odd villages of the Beinanmi are the most orderly, and their customs were long different from those of the other savages. "Baozhu" is not like a savage woman's name. Perhaps this so-called female chieftain is after all a prostitute?[16]

The equivalence between these two figures, Baozhu and the Han courtesan, is based on one central point of coincidence: the woman's role in initiating the assimilation of her tribe to Chinese culture. It is an equivalence that is also allowed for by the liminality of both women, one a savage who resembles a Chinese, one a Chinese who resembles a savage. Ding thus speculates that they must be one and the same.

By crossing ethnic boundaries to live among the savages, this figure Baozhu was able to take advantage of both the gender inversion in savage society and the superior status of her ethnicity to elevate her standing; in other words, she placed herself in a position in which both her femininity and her Chineseness were valued. The story thus nicely demonstrates how, in certain cases, it is ethnicity that brings privilege, while in other cases, it is gender that brings privilege. In dramatically rising from the station of a prostitute to that of a chieftain, Baozhu crossed not only ethnic boundaries but also status lines, "dressing herself up like an aristocratic lady of China." Baozhu's identity thus remained in a liminal state, between the savage and the civilized, between the lowly and the noble, between the matriarchal and the patriarchal. It is from this liminality, this ambiguous status, that Baozhu derived her power. The figure of Baozhu serves as a metaphor for the unique culture produced in the "contact zone" of the frontier; it is in "giving up" her Chineseness that Baozhu induces the savages to "give up" their savagery.[17] By straddling the insider/outsider opposition, by becoming a "hybrid," Baozhu in effect obliterates this opposition. As Deng Chuan'an phrased it: "Even though this place is beyond the pale, how is it different from China proper?" In being placed at this point of cultural transference, on the cusp between different ethnicities and different gender ideologies, the figure of Baozhu illustrates how ethnicity and gender combine variously in the constitution of power.

GENDER INVERSION WAS also employed as a rhetorical device, often in a self-reflexive critique of Chinese mores. The device is generally linked to the mode of primitivism, in which the "less civilized" other is seen as a repository of values associated with a more virtuous, simple past. The status of the foreign woman as other made her a figure on which not only undesirable, but also idealized traits could be projected, making her a foil against which to contrast the flaws of Chinese womanhood.

This technique is employed in a Qing story about a merchant's travels to Vietnam. Entitled, "On a Journey to Vietnam a Jade Horse Miniature Is Exchanged for Crimson Velvet" (*Zou Annan yuma huan xingrong*, ca. 1661), the story uses the exotic setting of Vietnam to demonstrate a moral lesson about the laxity of contemporary Chinese women. Two of the central devices employed to establish the foreignness of Vietnam are the familiar tropes of gender inversion and hypersexualization. In particular, it is the violation of Chinese norms of gender segregation that captures the attention of the narrator. However, a satirical twist in the story's rhetoric shifts the story into the mode of self-reflexive critique. While proclaiming Vietnamese women to be inferior in their customs and lax in their sense of public propriety, the narrator reveals his true object of criticism to be Chinese womanhood. A description of the public bathing habits of Vietnamese women becomes an opportunity to satirically deride Chinese women for their hypocrisy. He declares:

[The Vietnamese women] cannot measure up to our Chinese women, who close the door so tightly when they take a bath that no breeze gets through and furthermore insist that the maid stand outside the window for fear that someone will peep on them. But these women's false pretenses are really just a big show. Just look at our women of the south, all day they go touring in the mountains or by the waters, visiting temples, leaning on gates and standing in doorways, going to plays or societies; they let the public see their powdered faces. And yet they want to criticize the shortcomings of men! Commenting and laughing at the looks of passersby, they do not know how to cherish the "face" of the family. But if the breeze so much as lifts up their skirts to reveal a bit of leg, or if they are feeding a baby and their breast is exposed, or if they are going to the toilet and their "thing" is exposed, they make a hundred gestures to cover this and conceal that, and put on airs of distress. They do not know that "face" and the body are one: if they want to cherish the body they should cherish "face"; if they want to conceal the body, they should cover the "face." The ancients said it well: "if the fence is secure, the dogs will not get in." If you had not let outsiders see your face, how would they think of violating your body?[18]

Although the author portrays the Vietnamese as less civilized on account of their failure to segregate the sexes, his criticism is aimed at the moral degeneracy of Chinese women, as manifest in their transgressions of gender norms. The structure of the story allows the author simultaneously to indulge in exotic fantasy and to advocate greater conservatism in gender roles.

The nineteenth-century writer Wu Ziguang engaged in a similar self-reflexive critique, idealizing the indigenous women of Taiwan as paragons of ancient simplicity and virtue: "Their clothing is all frugal and plain . . . and they have a profound understanding of the proprieties of antiquity. Moreover, they do not use cosmetics, just like the lady of Guo who feared being stained with color. They do not paint their eyebrows: even if they had the brush of Zhang Chang they would not use it. Their manners are far superior in virtue to those of Chinese women."[19]

Wu makes the claim here that it is the savages rather than the women of China who maintain the proprieties of Chinese antiquity. The women of China, he implies, have conversely become degenerate and frivolous.

Rather than seeing an inversion of gender in the foreign culture, Wu projects a hyperrealization of Chinese gender ideals. The idealization of the foreign woman as a foil to contemporary Chinese womanhood may have expressed an anxiety concerning the new social roles for women emerging during the late Ming and Qing.[20] Confucian ideals that were no longer upheld by Chinese women were thus projected onto foreign women.

The most famous Qing example of this type of gender play is Li Ruzhen's celebrated novel, *Flowers in the Mirror.* In this work, Li creates a number of fantastically learned foreign female characters whose understanding of the Confucian classics far surpasses that of the average Chinese male. Throughout the novel, female literary talent is given an aura of glamour, and it is implied that China would be well served by the development of such talents among the female population. Li furthermore employs gender inversion in the Kingdom of Women episode of this novel, to satirize, and thereby denaturalize, Chinese sex roles. In particular, he calls into question the humanity of practices such as footbinding. Through both satire and utopian vision, Li Ruzhen presents an idealized model of accomplished (albeit still Confucian) femininity, embodied in the women of fabulous countries.

Whether through the idealization of the foreign woman or through gender inversion, gender serves as a ready vehicle for the expression of ethnic otherness in Qing travel accounts. The linkage between gender and ethnicity is particularly strong because the difference that is built into gender can be readily converted into the difference of the foreign, and vice versa. In Qing ethnographic writing, Woman became a stand-in for the Other; the strangeness of the "savage" woman of Taiwan represents the strangeness of her culture. The figure of the indigenous woman also mediates between colonizer and colonized, expressing relations of desire, domination, and exchange. The multiplicity of gendered images, moreover, demonstrates that the linkages between gender and ethnicity are not simply based on a direct metaphoric equivalence, the analogy Chinese : savage :: male : female. This is particularly true in the colonial or cross-cultural context, where gender itself is already racialized, or ethnicized, creating an instability around the terms of gender. Therefore, although feminization may be a form of denigration, not all women are denigrated. What it meant to be a Han Chinese woman in colonial Taiwan was vastly different from what it meant to be an indigene woman, as the legend of Baozhu so nicely illustrates.

THE CONTINUITIES BETWEEN Qing and modern discourse are aptly demonstrated in a media article from the 1960s entitled "Aborigine Women of Taiwan March toward the Realm of Civilization," which touts the achievements of the KMT in modernizing indigenous lifestyles.[21] The author, Yang Baiyuan, not only employs many of the old tropes of gender inversion but also argues that owing to the vital role played by women in the matrilineal indigenous societies, governmental efforts at "civilizing" the indigenes must be directed primarily at the women. Once again, indigenous women are expected to serve as vehicles for the transmission of Chinese culture. The discourse of hypersexualization has also continued to be employed, with some very real consequences for indigenous women, namely, their commodification in the tourism and sex industries.

Poverty is a driving force behind this phenomenon. Also at play, however, are stereotypes about the indigenes' propensity for heavy drinking, which are used to justify the "natural" suitability of indigenous women as bar hostesses and night club entertainers. Beginning in the 1980s, the feminist and indigenous rights movements in Taiwan generated greater social awareness of discriminatory attitudes toward indigenous women, and we have seen a rejection of some of the older colonialist discourse. It remains to be seen what new images will emerge.

Notes

1. *Editors' note*: In uxorilocal marriages the husband lives with the wife's family or at her place of residence.
2. Translated in Laurence Thompson, "The Earliest Chinese Eyewitness Accounts of the Formosan Aborigines," *Monumenta Serica*, xxiii (1964), 173–174.
3. Yu Yonghe, *Pihai jiyou* (Small Sea Travelogue), 35. Unless otherwise noted, all translations from Chinese are Emma Teng's.
4. Nineteenth-century writer Deng Chuan'an, for example, writes: "According to savage custom, the men who marry uxorilocally are just like women who marry virilocally [in China]. Obedient and dutiful, they do not dare to take their own initiative; they are debased to such a degree." Deng, *Lice huichao* (Measuring the Sea with a Calabash), 10.
5. Translated in Thompson, "The Earliest Chinese Eyewitness Accounts of the Formosan Aborigines," 181.
6. Charles McKann, "The Naxi and the Nationalities Question," in *Cultural Encounters on China's Ethnic Frontiers*, ed. S. Harrell (Seattle, 1995), 45.

7. *Taiping guangji*, 3629.

8. Yu, *Pihai jiyou* (Small Sea Travelogue), 18–19.

9. Liu-shi-qi, *Fanshe caifeng tukao* (Taipei, 1961), 7.

10. Thompson, "Earliest Accounts," 196, 192–193.

11. Melissa Brown notes that specific rates of intermarriage cannot be estimated. Brown, "On Becoming Chinese," 52.

12. John Shepherd, *Statecraft and Political Economy on the Taiwan Frontier, 1600–1800*, 379, 462 n. 85. Shepherd notes that the Dutch regarded intermarriage as a vehicle for Christianizing the Taiwan indigenes.

13. Jiang, *Taiyou riji* (Travelogue of Taiwan), 46.

14. The term "transculturation" was coined by Fernando Oritz in the 1940s. Mary Louise Pratt defines it thus: "Ethnographers have used this term to describe how subordinated or marginal groups select and invent from materials transmitted to them by a dominant or metropolitan culture." Pratt, *Imperial Eyes: Travel Writing and Transculturation*, 6.

15. Brown, "On Becoming Chinese," 45.

16. Ding Shaoyi, *Dongying zhilue* (Brief Record of the Eastern Ocean), 78.

17. Pratt, *Imperial Eyes: Travel Writing and Transculturation*, 6.

18. Zhuoyuantingzhuren, "Zou Annan yuma huan xingrong" (On a journey to Vietnam a jade horse miniature is exchanged for crimson velvet), 61–62.

19. Wu Ziguans, *Taiwan jishi* (Taiwan Memoranda), 31. Zhang Chang was a native of Pingyang during the Han dynasty who became governor of Chang'an under Xuandi. He was famous for having painted his wife's eyebrows.

20. See Ko, *Teachers of the Inner Chambers: Women and Culture in Seventeenth-Century China*.

21. Yang Baiyuan, "Jinru wenming lingyu de bensheng shandi funü," 163–169.

Jennifer L. Morgan

Male Travelers, Female Bodies, and the

Gendering of Racial Ideology, 1500–1770

Drawing on the writings of the seventeenth-century English explorer Richard Ligon, this essay examines the preoccupation of early travel writers with the African female bodies they encountered when they ventured beyond the confines of the so-called civilized world. Although images of black women had a history in Western writing from the Greeks onward, early modern writers focused on their breasts and their reproductive capacities more generally as sites of fascination and markers of primitiveness. Together with Amerindian women whom writers observed in the "new world," African women emerged in the sixteenth- and seventeenth-century imagination as monstrous and inhuman, thereby helping to justify the many faces of European colonialism (economic, political, cultural). Equally important, writers like Ligon were instrumental in carrying such images back to metropolitan centers like London, where readers who would never travel beyond their own shores could learn about the linkages being made between nonwhite sexuality and savagery and could participate in the colonial experience, however geographically distant.

In June 1647, the Englishman Richard Ligon left London on the ship *Achilles* to establish himself as a planter in the newly settled colony of Barbados. En route, Ligon's ship stopped in the Cape Verde Islands for provisions and trade. There Ligon saw a black woman for the first time; as he recorded the encounter in his *True and Exact History of . . . Barbadoes*, she was a "Negro of the greatest beauty and majesty together . . . that ever I saw in one woman. Her stature large, and excellently shap'd, well favour'd, full eye'd, and admirably grac'd. . . . [I] awaited her comming out, which was with far greater Majesty and gracefulness . . . than I have seen Queen Anne . . . descend from the Chaire of State."[1] Ligon's rhetoric may have surprised his English readers, for seventeenth-century images of black women did not usually evoke the ultimate marker of civility — the monarchy — as the referent.

Early modern English writers conventionally set the black female figure against one that was white — and thus beautiful. In *Pseudodoxia Epidemica* (1646), Sir Thomas Browne argued that blackness and beauty were mutually dependent, each relying on the other as antithetical proof of each one's existence.[2] As recent scholars have shown, male travelers to Africa and the Americas contributed to a European discourse on black womanhood. Femaleness evoked a certain element of desire, but travelers depicted black women as simultaneously unwomanly and marked by a reproductive value dependent on their sex. Writers' recognition of black femaleness and their inability to allow black women to embody "proper" female space served as a focus for representations of racial difference. During the course of his journey, Ligon came to another view of black women. As he saw it, their breasts "hang down below their Navels, so that when they stoop at their common work of weeding, they hang almost to the ground, that at a distance you would think they had six legs." For Ligon, their monstrous bodies symbolized their sole utility: their ability to produce both crops and other laborers.[3]

Ligon's narrative is a microcosm of a much larger ideological maneuver that juxtaposed the familiar with the unfamiliar, the beautiful woman who is also the monstrous laboring beast. As the tenacious and historically deep roots of racialist ideology become more evident, it becomes clear also that, through the rubric of monstrously "raced" Amerindian and African women, Europeans found a means to articulate shifting perceptions of themselves as religiously, culturally, and phenotypically superior to those black or brown persons they sought to define. In the discourse used to justify the slave trade, Ligon's beautiful Negro woman was as important as her six-legged counterpart. Both imaginary women marked a gendered whiteness that accompanied European expansionism. Well before the publication of Ligon's work, New World and African narratives that relied on gender to convey an emergent notion of racialized difference had been published in England and Europe. Although this essay is primarily concerned with England and its imperial expansion, by the time English colonists arrived in the Americas they already possessed the trans-European ethnohistoriographical tradition of depicting the imagined native in which Ligon's account is firmly situated.[4]

Ligon's text indicates the kind of negative symbolic work required of black women in early modern English discourse. As Ligon penned his manuscript while in debtors' prison in 1653, he constructed a layered narrative in which the discovery of African women's monstrosity helped to assure the work's success. Taking the female body as a symbol of the deceptive beauty and ultimate savagery of blackness, Ligon allowed his readers to dally with him among beautiful black women, only seductively to disclose their monstrosity over the course of the narrative. Travel accounts, which had proved their popularity by the time Ligon's *History . . . of Barbadoes* appeared, relied on gendered notions of European social order to project African cultural disorder. I do not argue here that gender operated as a more profound category of difference than race. Rather, this essay focuses on the way racialist discourse was deeply imbued with ideas about gender and sexual difference that, indeed, became manifest only in contact with each other. White men who laid the discursive groundwork on which the "theft of bodies" could be justified relied on mutually constitutive ideologies of race and gender to affirm Europe's legitimate access to African labor.

Travel accounts produced in Europe and available in England provided a corpus from which subsequent writers borrowed freely, reproducing images of Native American and African women that resonated with readers. These travelers learned to dismiss the idea that women in the Americas and Africa might be innocuous, unremarkable, or even beautiful. Rather, indigenous women bore an enormous symbolic burden as writers from Walter Ralegh to Edward Long employed them to mark metaphorically the symbiotic boundaries of European national identities and white supremacy. The struggle with perceptions of beauty and assertions of monstrosity such as Ligon's exemplified a much larger process through which the familiar became unfamiliar as beauty became beastliness and mothers became monstrous, all ultimately in the service of racial distinctions. Writers who articulated religious and moral justifications for the slave trade simultaneously grappled with the character of the female African body—a body both desirable and repulsive, available and untouchable, productive and reproductive, beautiful and black. I argue that these meanings were inscribed well before the establishment of England's colonial American plantations and that the intellectual work necessary to naturalize African enslavement, that is, the development of racialist discourse, was deeply implicated by gendered notions of difference and human hierarchy.

EUROPE HAD A long tradition of identifying Others through the monstrous physiognomy or sexual behavior of women. Pliny the Elder's ancient collection of monstrous races, *Historia Naturalis*, catalogued the long-breasted wild woman alongside the oddity of Indian and Ethiopian tribal women who bore only one child in their lifetime.[5] Medieval images of female devils included sagging breasts as part of the iconography of danger and monstrosity. The medieval wild woman, whose breasts dragged on the ground when she walked and could be thrown over her shoulder, was believed to disguise herself with youth and beauty in order to enact seductions that would satisfy her "obsessed . . . craving for the love of mortal men."[6] The shape of her body marked her deviant sexuality; both shape and sexuality evidenced her savagery.

Thus, writers commonly looked to sociosexual deviance to indicate savagery in Africa and the Americas and to mark difference from Europe. According to *The Travels of Sir John Mandeville*, "In Ethiopia and in many other countries [in Africa] the folk lie all naked . . . and the women have no shame of the men." Further, "they wed there no wives, for all the women there be common . . . and when [women] have children they may give them to what man they will that hath companied with them."[7] Deviant sexual behavior reflected the breakdown of natural laws: the absence of shame, the inability to identify lines of heredity and descent. This concern with deviant sexuality, articulated almost always through descriptions of women, is a constant theme in the travel writings of early modern Europe. Explorers and travelers to the New World and Africa brought expectations of distended breasts and dangerous sexuality with them. Indeed, Columbus exemplified his reliance on the female body to articulate the colonial venture at the very outset of his voyage when he wrote that the earth was shaped like a breast, with the Indies composing the nipple.

Richard Eden's 1553 English translation of Sebastian Munster's *A Treatyse of the Newe India* presented Amerigo Vespucci's voyage to English readers for the first time. Vespucci did not mobilize color to mark the difference of the people he encountered; rather, he described them in terms of their lack of social institutions ("they fight not for the enlargeing of theyr dominion for as much as they have no Magistrates") and social niceties ("at theyr meate they use rude and barberous fashions, lying on the ground without any table clothe or coverlet"). Nonetheless, his descriptions are not without positive attributes, and when he turned his attention to women, his language bristles with illuminating contradiction: "Theyr bodies are verye smothe and clene by reason of theyr often washinge. They are in other thinges fylthy and withoute shame. Thei use no lawful coniunccion of mariage, and but every one hath as many women as him liketh, and leaveth them agayn at his pleasure. The women are very fruiteful, and refuse no laboure al the whyle they are with childe. They travayle in maner withoute payne, so that the nexte day they are cherefull and able to walke. Neyther have they theyr bellies wimpeled or loose, and hanginge pappes, by reason of bearinge manye chyldren."[8]

The passage conveys admiration for indigenous women's strength in pregnancy and their ability to maintain aesthetically pleasing bodies, and it also represents the conflict at the heart of European discourse on gender and difference. Vespucci's familiarity with icons of difference led him to expect American women with hanging breasts; thus, he registers surprise that women's breasts and bodies were neither "wimpeled"[9] nor "hanginge." That surprise is inextricable from his description of childbearing. His admiration hinges on both a veiled critique of European female weakness and a dismissal of Amerindian women's pain. The question of pain in childbirth became a central component of descriptions of Africa and Africans. Vespucci presented a preliminary, still ambiguously laudatory account of Amerindian women. Nonetheless, he mobilized the place of women in society as a cultural referent that evoked the "fylth" and shamelessness of all indigenous people. Thus, the passage exposes early modern English readers' sometimes ambivalent encounters with narratives that utilized women's behavior and physiognomy to mark European national identities and inscribe racial hierarchy.

Contrary to what one might expect, the label "savage" was not uniformly applied to Amerindian people. Indeed, in the context of European national rivalries, the indigenous woman became somewhat less savage. In the mid- to late sixteenth century, the bodies of women figured at the borders of national identities more often than at the edges of a larger European identity. The Italian traveler Girolamo Benzoni, in his *History of the New World*, utilized sexualized indigenous women as both markers of difference and indicators of Spanish immorality. His first description of a person in the Americas (in Venezuela in 1541) occurs at the very beginning of his story: "Then came an Indian woman . . . such a woman as I have never before nor since seen the like of, so that my eyes could not be satisfied with looking at her for wonder. . . . She was quite naked, except where modisty forbids, such being the custom throughout all this country; she was old, and painted black, with long hair down to her waist, and her ear-rings had so weighed her ears down, as to make them reach her shoulders, a thing wonderful to see. . . . her teeth were black, her mouth large, and she had a ring in her nostrils . . . so that she appeared like a monster to us, rather than a human being."[10]

Benzoni's description invokes a sizable catalogue of cultural distance packed with meaning made visible by early modern conventions of gendered difference. *His* "wonder" situates *her* distance. In the context of a society concerned with the dissemblance of cosmetics, her black-faced body was both cause for alarm and evidence of a dangerous inversion of norms. Her nakedness, her ears, and her nose, all oddities accentuated by willful adornment, irrevocably placed her outside the realm of the familiar. Her blackened teeth and large mouth evoked a sexualized danger that, as Benzoni himself explicitly states, linked her and, by implication, her people to an inhuman monstrosity.

Benzoni utilized the pathetic figure of the fecund mother and the sexually violated young girl against the Spaniards. Such a move was common in the aftermath of Las Casas's *In Defense of the Indians* (ca. 1550) and amid the intensified resentment over access to the Americas directed toward Spain by other European nations. In "Discoverie of the . . . Empire of Guiana" (1598), Ralegh stated that he "suffered not any man to . . . touch any of [the natives'] wives or daughters: which course so contrary to the Spaniards (who tyrannize over them in all things) drewe them to admire her [English] majestie."[11] While permitting himself and his men to gaze upon naked Indian women, Ralegh accentuated their restraint. In doing so, he used the untouched bodies of Native American women to mark national boundaries and signal the civility and superiority of English colonizers—in contrast to the sexually violent Spaniards. Moreover, in linking the eroticism of indigenous women to the sexual attention of Spanish men, Ralegh signaled the Spaniards' "lapse into savagery." Benzoni, too, inscribed the negative consequences of too-close associations with indigenous women. For him, sexual proximity to local women depleted Spanish strength. As he prepared to abandon the topic of Indian slavery for a lengthy discussion of Columbus's travels, he again invoked motherhood to prove Spanish depravity: "All the slaves that the Spaniards catch in these provinces are sent [to the Caribbean] . . . and even when some of the Indian women are pregnant by these same Spaniards, they sell them without any consciences."[12]

AMERICAN NARRATIVES CONTRIBUTED to a triangulation among Europe, America, and Africa. English travelers to West Africa drew on American narrative traditions. Richard Hakluyt's collection of travel narratives, *Principall Navigations* (1589), brought Africa into the purview of English readers. *Principall Navigations* portrayed Africa and Africans in positive and negative terms. The authors' shifting assessments of Africa and Africans "produc[ed] an Africa which is familiar and unfamiliar, civil and savage, full of promise and full of threat." Sixteenth-century ambivalence concerning England's role in overseas expansion required a forceful antidote. In response, Hakluyt presented texts that, through an often conflicted depiction of African peoples, ultimately differentiated Africa and England and erected a boundary that made English expansion in the face of confused and uncivilized people reasonable, profitable, and moral.

On the West African coast, women's bodies, like those of their New World counterparts, symbolized the shifting parameters of the colonizing venture. English writers regularly directed readers' attention to the sexually titillating topic of African women's physiognomy and reproductive experience. In doing so, they drew attention to the complex interstices of desire and repulsion that marked European men's gaze on Amerindian and African women. Sixteenth- and seventeenth-century writers conveyed a sexual grotesquerie that ultimately made African women indispensable, in that it showed the gendered ways of putting African savagery to productive use. Although titillation was certainly a component of these accounts, to write of sex was also to define and expand the boundaries of profit through productive and reproductive labor.

Some thirty years after the original Hakluyt collections were published, other writers continued to mobilize African women to do complex symbolic work. In 1622, Richard Jobson's *The Golden Trade* appeared in London, chronicling his 1620–1621 trading ventures up the Gambia River. Jobson described strong and noble people on the one hand and barbarous and bestial people on the other, and African women personified his nation's struggle with the familiar and unfamiliar African, a struggle that can also be located along the axis of desire and repulsion. Jobson's association with the "Fulbie" and "Maudingo" people furnishes evidence of this struggle. He described Fulbie men as beastlike, "seemingly more senselesse, then our Country beasts," a state he attributed to their close association with the livestock they raised. Unlike many of his contemporaries, Jobson regarded African women with admiration. In contrast to Fulbie men, the women were "excellently well bodied, having very good features, with a long blacke haire." He maintained that the discovery of a "mote or haire" in milk would cause these dairywomen to "blush, in defence of her cleanely meaning." This experience of shame encapsulated a morality and civility to which only women had access. Among the Maudingos of Cassan, newly married women "observ[e] herein a shame-fast modestie, not to be looked for, among such a *kinde of blacke or barbarous* people." Despite his well-meaning description of African women, Jobson recorded those behaviors associated with English civility only inasmuch as they deviated from that which he, and his readers, expected. His appreciation of Fulbie women and Maudingo people was predicated on their ability to exceed his expectations. To Jobson, African women proved the precarious nature of African civility. His narrative, even at its most laudatory, always returned to inferiority. While describing the history of kingship and the great importance of ancestral honor among the Maudingos, Jobson still contended that "from the King to the slave, they are all perpetuall beggers from us." His "wonder" at women's modesty alerted his readers to the culture's abnormality and, implicitly, to its larger absence of civility. Even as he depicted them positively, women became part of the demonstration that, despite kings and history, these Africans were barbarous and ripe for exploitation.[13]

African women's Africanness seemed contingent on the linkages between sexuality and a savagery that fitted them for both productive and reproductive labor. Women enslaved in the seventeenth and early eighteenth centuries did not give birth to many children, but descriptions of African women in the Americas almost always highlighted their fecundity along with their capacity for manual labor.[14] Seventeenth-century English medical writers, both men and women, equated breastfeeding and tending to children with work. Erroneous observations about African women's propensity for easy birth and breastfeeding reassured colonizers that these women could easily perform hard labor in the Americas while simultaneously erecting a barrier of difference between Africa and England. Sixteenth- and seventeenth-century English women and men anticipated pregnancy and childbirth with extreme uneasiness and fear of death, but at least they knew that the experience of pain in childbirth marked women as members of a Christian community. African women entered the developing discourse of national resources via an emphasis on their mechanical and meaningless childbearing. Early on, metaphors of domestic livestock and sexually located cannibalism relied on notions of reproduction for consumption. By about the turn of the seventeenth century, as England joined in the transatlantic slave trade, assertions of African savagery began to be predicated less on consumption via cannibalism and more on production via reproduction. African women were materialized in the context of England's need for productivity. The image of utilitarian feeding implied a mechanistic approach to both childbirth and reproduction that ultimately became located within the national economy. Whereas English women's reproductive work took place solely in the domestic economy, African women's reproductive work could embody the developing discourses of extraction and forced labor at the heart of England's national design for the colonies.

By the eighteenth century, English writers rarely employed black women's breasts or behavior for anything but concrete evidence of barbarism in Africa. In *A Description of the Coasts of North and South-Guinea*, begun in the 1680s and completed and published almost forty years later, John Barbot "admired the quietness of the poor babes, so carr'd about at their mothers' backs . . . and how freely they suck the breasts, which are always full of milk, over their mothers' shoulders, and sleep soundly in that odd posture."[15] William Snelgrave introduced his *New Account of Some Parts of Guinea and the Slave-trade* with an anecdote designed to illustrate the benevolence of the trade. He described himself rescuing an infant from human sacrifice and reuniting the child with its mother, who "had much Milk in her Breasts." He accented the barbarism of those who attempted to sacrifice the child and claimed that the reunion cemented his goodwill in the eyes of the enslaved, who, convinced of the "good notion of White Men," caused no problems during the voyage to Antigua. Having utilized the figure of the breastfeeding woman to legitimize his slaving endeavor, Snelgrave went on to describe the roots of Whydah involvement in the slave trade and its defeat in war at the hands of the Kingdom of Dahomey (both coastal cities in present-day Ghana). "Custom of the Country allows Polygamy to an excessive degree . . . whereby the land was become so stocked with people" that the slave trade flourished. Moreover, the wealth generated by the trade made the beneficiaries so "proud, effeminate and luxurious" that they were easily conquered by the more disciplined (read: masculine) nation of Dahomey.[16] Thus, women's fecundity undermined African society from without and within as they provided a constant stream of potential slaves.

Abolitionist John Atkins similarly adopted the icon of black female bodies in his writings on Guinea. "Childing, and their Breasts always pendulous, stretches them to so unseemly a length and Bigness that some . . . could suckle over their shoulder." Atkins then considered the idea of African women copulating with apes. He noted that "at some places the Negroes have been suspected of Bestiality" and, while maintaining the ruse of scholarly distance, suggested that evidence "would tempt one to suspect the Fact." The evidence lay mostly in apes' resemblance to humans but was bolstered by "the Ignorance and Stupidity [of black women unable] to guide or controll lust."[17] Abolitionists and antiabolitionists alike accepted the connections between race, animality, the legitimacy of slavery, and black women's monstrous and fecund bodies. By the 1770s, Edward Long's *History of Jamaica* presented readers with African women whose savagery was total, for whom enslavement was the only means of civility. Long maintained that "an oran-outang husband would [not] be any dishonour to an Hottentot female; for what are these Hottentots?" He asserted as fact that sexual liaisons occurred between African women and apes. Nowhere did he make reference to any sort of African female shame or beauty. Rather, Long used women's bodies and behavior to justify and promote the mass enslavement of Africans. By the time he wrote, the association of black people with beasts — via African women — had been cemented: "Their women are delivered with little or no labour; they have therefore no more occasion for midwifes than the female oran-outang, or any other wild animall. . . . Thus they seem exempted from the course inflicted upon Eve and *her daughters*."[18]

If African women gave birth without pain, they somehow sidestepped God's curse upon Eve. If they were not her descendants, they were not related to Europeans and could therefore be forced to labor on England's overseas plantations with impunity. Early modern European women were so defined by their experience of pain in childbirth that an inability to feel pain was evidence of witchcraft. In the case of England's contact with Africa and the Americas, the crisis in European identity was mediated by constructing an image of pain-free reproduction that diminished Africa's access to certainty and civilization, thus allowing for the mass appropriation that was the transatlantic slave trade.

AFTER RICHARD LIGON saw the black woman at Cape Verde, he pursued her around a dance hall, anxious to hear her voice, though she ultimately put him off with only "the loveliest smile that I have ever seen." The following morning he came upon two "prettie young Negro Virgins." Their clothing was arranged such that Ligon viewed "their breasts round, firm, and beautifully shaped." He demurred that he was unable "to expresse all the perfections of Nature, and Parts, these Virgins were owners of." Aware of the image of African womanhood already circulating in England, he assured his readers that these women should not be confused with the women of "high Africa . . . that dwell nere the River of Gambia, who are thick lipt, short nos'd, and commonly [have] low forheads."[19] As though their breasts did not adequately set these women apart, Ligon used these qualifiers to highlight the exception of their beauty. As were many of his contemporaries, Ligon was quite willing to find beauty and allure in women who were exceptional — not "of high Africa," but whose physiognomy and "education" marked them as improved by contact with Europe.[20]

In the face of Ligon's pursuit, these women, like the beautiful woman he met the evening before, remained silent. Ligon tried, unsuccessfully, to test the truth of their beauty through the sound of their speech. Language had been a mark of monstrosity for centuries; Pliny identified five of his monstrous races as such simply because they lacked human speech. It appears that decent language, like shame, denoted civility for Ligon in the face of this inexplicable specter of female African beauty. Finally, Ligon begged pardon for his dalliances and remarked that he "had little else to say" about the otherwise desolate island.[21] To speak of African beauty in this context, then, was justified.

By the time the English made their way to the West Indies, decades of ideas and information about brown and black women predated the actual encounter. In many ways, the encounter had already taken place in parlors and reading rooms on English soil, assuring that colonists would arrive with a battery of assumptions and predispositions about race, femininity, sexuality, and civilization. Confronted with an Africa they needed to exploit, European writers turned to black women as evidence of a cultural inferiority that ultimately became encoded as racial difference. Monstrous bodies became enmeshed with savage behavior as the icon of women's breasts became evidence of tangible barbarism. African women's "unwomanly" behavior evoked an immutable distance between Europe and Africa on which the development of racial slavery depended. By the mid-seventeenth century, that which had initially marked African women as unfamiliar — their sexually and reproductively bound savagery — had become familiar. To invoke it was to conjure up a gendered and racialized figure who marked the boundaries of English civility even as she naturalized the subjugation of Africans and their descendants in the Americas.

Notes

1. Richard Ligon, *A True and Exact History of the Island of Barbadoes* (London, 1657), 12–13.

2. Thomas Browne, *Pseudodoxia Epidemica: or Enquiries into very many received tenents and commonly presumed truths* (1646), cited in Kim F. Hall, *Things of Darkness: Economies of Race and Gender in Early Modern England* (Ithaca, 1995), 12.

3. Ligon, *True and Exact History . . . of Barbadoes*, 51.

4. Peter Hulme, *Colonial Encounters: Europe and the Native Caribbean, 1492–1797* (London, 1986), 18.

5. Pliny, *Natural History in Ten Volumes*, trans. H. Rockham (Cambridge, Mass., 1969), 2: 509–527; Herodotus, *The History*, trans. David Grene (Chicago, 1987) 4, 180, 191.

6. Richard Bernheimer, *Wild Men in the Middle Ages: A Study in Art, Sentiment, and Demonology* (Cambridge, Mass., 1952), 33–41, quotation on 34. See also Peter Mason, *Deconstructing America: Representations of the Other* (New York, 1990), 47–56.

7. *The Travels of Sir John Mandeville: The Version of the Cotton Manuscript in Modern Spelling*, ed. A. W. Pollard (London, 1915), 109, 119.

8. *A Treatyse of the Newe India by Sebastian Munster* (1553), trans. Richard Eden (microprint), (Ann Arbor, Mich., 1966), [57].

9. *Editors' note*: rippled.

10. Girolamo Benzoni, *History of the New World* (1572), trans. W. H. Smyth (London, 1857), 3–4.

11. Sir Walter Ralegh, "The discoverie of the large, rich, and beautifull Empire of Guiana," in Richard Hakluyt, *The Principal Navigations Voyages Traffiques & Discoveries of the English Nation* (1598–1600), 12 vols. (Glasgow, 1903–1905), 10: 391.

12. Benzoni, *History of the New World* (emphasis added).

13. Richard Jobson, *The Golden Trade or a Discovery of the River Gambra . . . by Richard Jobson* (1628), (Amsterdam, 1968), 35, 33, 36, 56, 58, 52, 54.

14. Jordan, *White over Black*, 39.

15. John Barbot, *A Description of the Coasts of North and South-Guinea*, in *A Collection of*

Voyages, ed. A. Churchill (London, 1732), 36.

16. William Snelgrave, introduction to *A New Account of Some Parts of Guinea and the Slave-trade* (1734), (London, 1971), 3–4.

17. John Atkins, *A Voyage to Guinea, Brazil, and the West-Indies* (1735), (London, 1970), 50, 108.

18. Edward Long, "History of Jamaica, 2, with notes and corrections by the Author" (1774), British Library, London, Add. Ms. 12405, P364/f295, P380/f304 (emphasis added).

19. Ligon, *True and Exact History*, 13, 15–16.

20. Another example can be found in John Gabriel Stedman's relationship to the mulatto woman Johanna in his *Narrative of a Five Years Expedition Against the Revolted Negroes of Surinam: Transcribed . . . from the Original 1790 Manuscript*, ed. Richard Price and Sally Price (Baltimore, 1988).

21. Ligon, *True and Exact History . . . of Barbadoes*, 17.

Rebecca Overmyer-Velázquez

Christian Morality in New Spain: The Nahua
Woman in the Franciscan Imaginary

Rarely is the impact of conquest on the colonizers so clear as in this essay about the
Florentine Codex, *a compilation of historical and ethnographic information
about the Aztecs assembled by the Franciscan Bernadino de Sahagún. Produced
at the behest of the officials of his order, the* Codex *reflects the attempts of the
colonizing Catholic Church to gather knowledge about the peoples whom it
hoped to convert. Book 10, which is the focus of this essay, illustrates how crucial
gender ideologies — and especially the control of female sexual behavior — were to
the colonizing project in New Spain. It also demonstrates in rich detail the
collision of two cosmologies: that of the Nahua, which privileged "gender parallelism," or complementarity between the sexes, and that of the ruling Spanish
church, which emphasized the morally transgressive nature of women. The
Franciscans actively targeted Nahua women's bodies as sites of behavioral reform, which they saw as the pathway not just to conversion, but to redemption as
well. In addition to illustrating how the sexual ideologies of ecclesiastical colonialism were conceptualized, this analysis of Book 10 reveals the very real struggles and disillusionment that Sahagún was subject to as he repeatedly overlooked
the complexities of indigenous society in his attempts to impose his evangelical
project on the Nahua.*

The *Florentine Codex* (also known as the *Historia General de las
Cosas de la Nueva Espana* or *A General History of the Things of New
Spain*) is an encyclopedia of Aztec beliefs and practices compiled
in colonial Mexico during the second half of the sixteenth century.[1] In
twelve books this work details the spiritual and secular lives of the people

commonly known as the Aztecs, increasingly referred to as the Nahua, the dominant cultural/linguistic group in the Central Valley of Mexico. Book 10, entitled "The People," describes such categories of society as nobility, commoners, and ethnic groups, as well as the kin relationships, occupations, and daily social life of women and men. Like the other books of the *Historia*, Book 10 is the result of work initiated by Fray Bernardino de Sahagún in 1558 at the request of the provincial of the Franciscan order in New Spain.

Sahagún arrived in New Spain in 1529 and began training young Nahua noblemen to collaborate with him in his efforts to convert the indigenous population to Christianity. The friar became a master of the Nahuatl language spoken by the majority of peoples in central Mexico, while his young collaborators became fluent in Spanish and Latin and proficient at writing Nahuatl in Latin script. The purpose of the work was to provide priests and other Spaniards with a detailed description of Nahua culture, especially its religious practices and beliefs, in order better to recognize "idolatry" in everyday colonial life and attempt to stamp it out forever. Toward that end, Sahagún prepared an outline of topics to examine, created a questionnaire, and, with the help of the young Christianized Nahua noblemen in his employ, asked the elder noble leaders of the communities of Tepepulco and Tlatelolco how they lived before the Spaniards arrived in 1519. The text of each book was arranged in two columns: Nahuatl on the right and Spanish translations and illustrations on the left. Throughout this process, Sahagún worked closely with the Nahua men he had trained and, because the friar wrote only in Spanish, the younger men played a crucial role in creating the codex.[2]

Book 10 is explicitly informed by a Christian emphasis on a good/evil dualism; thus, for every category of person (niece, nobleman, sorcerer, weaver, etc.), she or he is described first in terms of "good" qualities and then in terms of "bad" qualities. The "inimical [hostile; malevolent] woman" was the nemesis of Sahagún and helped to represent, for him, the reason behind the failure of the Christian mission in New Spain. Her construction in Book 10 reveals the severe dualism of a late medieval Catholicism careful to clarify the distinction between good and evil. In their zeal to make this distinction, the friars in New Spain continued at a metaphysical level what they had already partly accomplished at a material level: the destruction of Nahua religious life. The Catholic worldview manifested in Book 10 serves this destruction by eliminating complicated

Nahua conceptions of the human relationship with the cosmos as one that is interdependent, ambiguous, and precarious, yet in balance. It replaces, or at least attempts to replace, these conceptions with exclusive, hierarchical categories of good and evil, God and devil, male and female. As a result, these "new" Christian categories served to deny the power and authority traditionally held by Nahua women, whose status in Nahua society was not understood or valued by the Spaniards. (It is nevertheless true, of course, that Nahua women were excluded from most positions of overt religious and political power, both before and after the conquest, much like their Spanish counterparts.) This text, then, is one of the first articulations in Spanish America of the contact and conflict of two very different worldviews, a conflict whose outcome—in religion, the triumph at least of an external Spanish form—left Nahua women the obvious losers.

Nahua women in this period were able to make independent decisions about their lives, most of which unfolded in rural areas far from Spaniards and direct Spanish influence. But over time, the introduction of Catholic ideology (as well as related theories of law and politics) facilitated the erosion of the practices and memories of a time when the role of women was conceived in very different terms.[3] This process of erosion, I contend, began in the sixteenth century with such colonial religious literature as the *Historia*, among other media, in which Nahua moral tropes were used to explain and translate Christian concepts in Nahuatl. Thus, the women in Book 10 are overwhelmingly portrayed as excessive in terms of sexuality, appearance, and intoxication and related to decenteredness and deception, all of which, in the Nahua worldview, refer to chaos and immorality. Although these are tropes of a distinctly Nahua morality, the emphasis in Book 10 on excessive female sexuality distorts their original significance and points to a Christian preoccupation with virginity and chastity. While women are also described as "good" and men as "bad" in this text, the qualitative differences between women and men are significant, and the consistent negative association of women with a dangerous and disruptive sexuality is strikingly Christian.

THROUGHOUT HIS COMMENTS on Book 10, Sahagún repeatedly refers to two Nahua "traits" that serve as explanations for the failure of the missionary project. The one for which he condemned the Indians, both female and male, most strongly was excessive sexuality; the second was deception. For Sahagún, the climate of New Spain exacerbated the inherent lustfulness of the people; their deceit in keeping their "former" ways was proof of how little they were to be trusted. But the friar did not simply mistrust the Nahua. The familial relationship developed by Sahagún and other friars with their converts encouraged strong feelings of personal betrayal among the former when they witnessed their Indian charges "relapse . . . into idolatry."[4] These relations also permitted mendicant violence. Sahagún's explicit association of the Nahua with licentiousness served to reinforce the preoccupation in Book 10 with dangerous sexuality. To put it another way, the contrasting representations of women and men in Book 10 underscore the Franciscan's disillusion and increasing sense of his betrayal by the Indian people.

For the Nahua, however, sexuality and the role of women before the Spanish invasion were conceived in different terms from those brought by Spanish missionaries. Nahua morality emphasized moderation in all things, from personal appearance to drug use and expressions of sexuality. For a woman to be made up and dressed well, for example, so long as she was not done up excessively, was not immoral for the Nahua; it was, in fact, a sign of self-respect. Immorality was defined as *tlatlacolli*, a word that refers to something damaged and is characterized by the disruption of order and the promotion of decay and randomness. Entropy — cosmic, social, and individual — was the essence of immorality.[5] Similarly connected to immorality was the distinction between the center and the liminal and dangerous periphery. The earth was slippery because life was inherently precarious and close to chaos and the abyss. To preserve itself, human life had to stay within the ordered center. Movement into and out of ordered space was, therefore, morally fraught, and the act of movement was equated with the immoral deed. Both women and men were told to behave well to avoid being cast out to wander among strangers. In sum, Nahua immorality was equated with stupidity or madness; to be moral was to act with common sense and do what was obviously desirable.[6]

The basic dilemma of human existence in Nahua culture was the need to live in balance between order and chaos. The goal was to establish and sustain the order, continuity, and stability required for social and cultural survival while taking just enough fertilizing energy to ensure biological survival.[7] "Negative" forces were essential parts of the cosmos, and chaos was as necessary as order. In fact, order was always believed to be temporary, with chaos lurking on the periphery. The stress was on the movement of the cosmos, not on a permanent structure or static hierarchy of being, which preoccupied Neoplatonist Scholastics like Sahagún. Among the Nahua, then, opposites complemented each other; out of disorder came order and out of death came life. This dialectical dualism, typical of Mesoamerican thought, is irreducible to discrete polar opposites. In contrast, Christianity most often asserted unity by denying, not incorporating, the second element of a pair (usually characterized as the evil of sin or, in medieval Christianity, the devil).[8] Thus, Christianity's dualities were always in conflict, refusing resolution into a whole.

The complex nature of femaleness and maleness was not abandoned in daily social life, even though women's and men's roles were strictly defined. Susan Kellogg uses the phrase "gender parallelism" to describe the structure of the relationship between women and men in Nahua society, in which each gender occupies separate but parallel social structures. Although this parallelism does not ensure gender equality, it expresses the high value placed on women's roles and the belief that the genders complemented each other.[9] After an infant's birth, a midwife bathed the child and buried the girl's umbilical cord near the hearth, while the boy's was to be buried on the battlefield. This ritual reflects each gender's primary activities. In contrast, both girls and boys were sent to schools, and women and men could be administrative authorities in local, neighborhood, and religious associations. Women did all the household work, including spinning, weaving (a sacred Nahua art), cooking, performing daily religious rituals, and caring for children, but they also worked in temples, markets, schools, and craftworkers' organizations. They were considered autonomous beings, not the dependents of men.[10] Nahua women, then, had at least limited access to power and authority in all spheres of life, a fact that tended to outweigh the importance of gender hierarchy because women's roles were equally necessary. The importance of women in society paralleled the cognatic system of descent, in which an individual traced her or his descent equally from female and male antecedents and in which women and men inherited property. (The right of inheritance was shared by Spanish women as well.) The basis for this parallelism was the Nahua emphasis on complementary duality, which stressed both the contrasts and merging of differences into a larger unity.[11]

This idea of gender parallelism also affected expressions of Nahua women's sexuality. The friars, following logically from a belief in a rigid good/evil dichotomy, preached moderation but with an emphasis on *avoiding* pleasure.[12] Like Christ and the devil, the soul and the body fought each other, with the result that the self was always divided and never in balance, as the Nahua conceived it. The friars were more interested in sexual abstinence than in maintaining equilibrium, and this had an impact on women in particular. An example of the Christian disregard for Nahua complementarity and balance is Sahagún's characterization of the complicated Tlazolteotl as "another Venus," explicitly associated with the morally transgressive Eve. Fray Juan de Torquemada was blunt in his similar identification of Tlazolteotl with Venus: "For a goddess of loves and sensualities, what can she be but a dirty, filthy, and stained goddess?"[13]

Consequently, Franciscans like Sahagún favored a constricted life for women. They urged parents to tell their daughters not to go out in public, not to laugh, and not to enjoy themselves. Girls, furthermore, were not to look or smile at men, and were to rush when out of the house. Franciscans exhorted Nahua women to model their lives after saints' lives and criticized noblewomen for their love of fine clothes, telling them to live as Saint Clare did, who shaved her head and wore only a hair shirt.[14] Virtuous Christian women, according to the friars, had no hair, never looked at anyone, and never went outside. This was hardly a Nahua ethic of moderation. Kellogg claims, "One of the most potent forces for change in indigenous women's lives during the sixteenth and seventeenth centuries was a religious ideology that laid a new stress on female honor and purity."[15]

Christian virginity was explicitly associated with women, and priests encouraged women to stay in the house while men provided for the family, even though this was not feasible for the vast majority of the Indian population. There was no word for "virgin" in Nahuatl, however. The closest terms were *ichpochtli* and *telpochtli*, which applied respectively to young women and men past adolescence but not yet of adult status, the age at which one married and established a family. This adult status had nothing specifically to do with a person's sexual status. But Sahagún repeatedly praised Mary's virginity in his sermons, and told the young woman who was no longer a virgin, "'Already the tlacotecolotl [the Devil] carries you about . . . now you already pertain to the promiscuous women. . . . Now you are just equal to filth."[16] Men were to be responsible for observing religious rites in the household and at church. This ideology of purity and enclosure subverted the possibility of women's holding formal authority. Instead, young Spanish women, "enclosed . . . behind twenty walls" (according to Fray Geronimo de Mendieta), were held up as examples for Indian women who supported their families with work outside the home.[17] Clearly, while the ideal of female enclosure was applied to all women, it was practical only for noble daughters, the specific targets of this rhetoric, not nonelite women who had to work to survive. Nevertheless, even the status of nonelite women was affected after the invasion. Many of the institutions in which women had participated with some authority disappeared and parallel institutional structures for both genders began to weaken as traditional religious, political, and economic structures collapsed.[18]

IN 1576, A year the plague ran rampant in Mexico City, Sahagún was hurrying to finish the Spanish translation of his monumental *Historia* before the Crown officials he was expecting soon would come to seize it from him once and for all. Royal *cedulas* had been issued which demanded the confiscation of all manuscripts and their delivery to royal officials. This was a complete reversal of former Crown policy that had encouraged the production of an *historia moral*, a project strongly supported by Juan de Ovando, president of the Council of the Indies. When Ovando died and the Tridentine decisions were implemented in New Spain, few writings concerning "the superstitions and way of life these Indians had" were safe.[19] This time, Sahagún was a palsied old man who relied entirely on the younger Nahua men he had trained in Spanish and Latin to act as translators and copyists. He was able to pay them for their work after five years, between 1570 and 1575, during which all his funds had been cut off, thanks to Fray Rodrigo de Sequera, a fellow Franciscan well placed in the Inquisition who had appreciated the potential value of the *Historia* in the work of Christian conversion. After a year spent collecting his writings that were scattered throughout central Mexico in 1570, Sahagún took two years to compile and translate the *Historia*'s twelve books. Ironically, after Father Sequera took the *Historia* to Spain with him, saving it from royal censors, Sahagún never saw the manuscript again. He continued to wonder about its existence until he died.

Something had gone terribly wrong for mendicants like Sahagún who had spent half a century preaching Christianity among the Indian peoples in New Spain. The millennial promise signaled by the arrival of the first mendicants to arrive after the Spanish invasion in 1524, the Franciscan

Twelve, was now, more than fifty years later, totally unfulfilled. War, slavery, overwork, and disease had wiped out huge numbers of indigenous people, the very people Sahagún had hoped would carry on the work of Christianization far into the future. Worse still, the linguistic and ethnographic work of Spanish Christians such as Sahagún revealed that Indians who had managed to survive Spanish domination had also retained their spiritual beliefs despite the presence of the friars among them. The earlier Franciscan belief that the Indians of New Spain were innocent children simply in need of Christian instruction had evaporated and been replaced by the dour conviction that these children, if they were still children, were willfully disobedient and completely in thrall to the devil. The *Historia* was written in response to this perceived crisis.

Sahagún's comments in the *Historia* reveal his deep disappointment with the turn of events. He writes: "We can take it for granted that, though preached to more than fifty years, if [the Indians] were now left alone, if the Spanish nation were unable to intercede, in less than fifty years there would be no trace of the preaching which had been given them."[20] It was in his interest to paint as bleak a picture as possible, for he was appealing to the Spanish king to intercede in favor of the mendicant project of conversion. This was a particularly turbulent period for the Franciscans. Between the 1560s and the 1580s, the order was rent by feuds between creoles and peninsular Spaniards and the increasing tensions between anti-Indian and pro-Indian factions. Attacks on the order by the Crown and episcopate, combined with an increasing worldliness that openly exploited the Indians, reduced morale among the friars.[21] After 1550, the monarchy favored the secular over the regular clergy, a favoritism clearly expressed in 1574 with the *Ordenanza del Patronazgo*, which formally initiated the replacement of regulars by secular priests. (Earlier, the Council of Trent had decreed that all clerics with parochial powers were to be under episcopal control.) "From the royal point of view the regulars had accomplished their purpose and the time had come to establish the orderly, traditional episcopal hierarchy everywhere."[22]

In the midst of this changing political situation, Sahagún blamed the Nahua. He was unequivocal that the friars had been deceived and that the indigenous were incorrigible sensualists. In other words, there was no possibility, in Sahagún's thinking, that the Indians could be complex human beings as the Nahua understood human nature, human beings, that is, as always at the mercy of a capricious world. Instead, the Franciscans had placed all their millennial hopes on a people they initially believed were entirely without guile and entirely "good" despite the Indians' having been misled by the devil and his minions. The only other possibility for Sahagún, convinced as he was that the world was structured in terms of good and evil, was that the Indians lacked goodness and were therefore evil and could not be trusted.

His comments on Book 10, however, are a fascinating example of a dualistic logic unable to reconcile apparent oppositions. Sahagún idealized preconquest Nahua society for its ability to regulate behavior and prevent excessive sexuality, yet he bemoaned the inherent licentiousness of the Nahua that went unchecked in the colony. He criticized colonial Spanish secular society for its depredations but nevertheless blamed native drunkenness for pervasive social decay. He praised the native ability to replicate European arts and crafts but felt betrayed by the deception they practiced behind their mimetic religious mask. Thus, Sahagún was unable to articulate what he knew was the uncertain relationship between mimicry and deceit. He scorned Nahua religion but had high praise for the Franciscans' attempt to imitate the Nahua tradition of raising children in temples under religious supervision.[23] For Sahagún, the destruction of the Nahua religious/social system could not be a cause of the social decay in colonial Indian society because this religion was thoroughly demonic. While he connected Christianity with the state and moral society (he understood, in other words, that religion and the state worked together), in his discussion of Nahua religion he made no such connection.[24]

Sahagún believed that the inculcation of Christian belief and behavior was the only way effectively to combat the excesses of sexuality and idolatry. Early in the colonial period, the Franciscans built colleges and strictly raised Nahua boys who had been taken from their families. They sent Nahua girls to convents, where some learned to read and write.[25] Looking back in 1576 on these moribund institutions, Sahagún waxed nostalgic for the days when indigenous children were roused to prayers and self-flagellation. The Franciscans taught the sons of Nahua nobility to read, write, and sin, while they taught the sons of commoners only Christian doctrine. Within a short time, the friars were able to assemble both groups of boys, and together they demolished Nahua temples "so that no vestige of them remained."[26] According to Sahagún, boys were especially useful in this task. They acted as spies on village preparations for Nahua religious festivals, and often as many as one hundred boys would lead the friars to these festivals, where they attacked, bound, and dragged the participants to the college to be punished until they repented. "And so they came forth therefrom [*sic*] instructed in Christian doctrine and punished, and the others learned a lesson from them and dared not do anything similar."[27] This process was repeated frequently, and it is clear from the text that Sahagún was impressed with how the people feared these children, even when the boys were few in number.

Decades later, Sahagún regretted that the boys no longer lived among the friars, who were no longer able to sequester and discipline idolaters. Indeed, Sahagún believed feasts, orgies, and native singing were performed openly because Christian priests did not understand their demonic meaning. Family members persecuted and killed his boy spies when they discovered that the young men had informed on them.[28] The awful power of Spanish Christianity in the New World that Sahagún celebrated turned parents against children and children against their own parents and traditions, and reflected an ambivalence between power and tenderness that was "mirrored in the ambiguity of power and love in God and Jesus Christ."[29] Sahagún did not understand these boys, however; he wrote that it was not many years after the college started that the friars realized they had been deceived. He stressed that with plentiful food and tenderness the boys "began to feel a strong sensuality and to practice lascivious things."[30] This immense doubt Sahagún feels about the success of the Christian project reappears. On the one hand, he longed for the time when the Franciscans were apparently in control (though he was all too aware that they were not), but, on the other hand, he gravely mistrusted the very people on which he would have to rely to reconstruct those heady days ("[they] were not capable of such perfection").[31] He was caught in a web of deceit and betrayal he had woven for himself.

IN BOOK 10 Nahua men and women are defined through their relationship to the Spanish world, which is positively valued by the friar: Nahua men are almost exclusively and positively marked with "Spanishness," while women are almost never represented wearing Spanish dress or participating in Spanish occupations. Images of "good" noblewomen invariably show them seated on mats (not Spanish stools), wearing the traditional *huipil* (women's traditional loose-fitting blouse) and skirt. By contrast, men are sometimes shown sitting on stools. Women, even if they are "good," have considerably less association with Spanish markers and with the positive valuation these markers signify. The "bad noble," on the other hand, is ostensibly a preconquest Nahua man who is depicted as a bearded Spaniard wearing a tailored shirt with a collar and pants. In the image of the "youth," the pants are distinctively Spanish and he wears a European-style hat. Pants replaced the traditional Nahua *maxtlatl* (loin-cloth), which revealed too much of the body for the friars. Patricia Ana-walt observes that the maxtlatl was used as a male given name and was always found worn on top of a *tlahuitztli* (warrior costume). She suggests that the loincloth was "probably synonymous with virility."[32] If this is so, then the "de-sexing" of men, compared to the "oversexing" of women in Book 10 is quite emphatic. Yet these men retain their *tilmatli* (capes) and they go barefoot. By 1550, the European fitted and buttoned shirt (*camixatli*) was very popular, even among the poorest Indian men, who would wear a loincloth underneath. (Pants, however, were slower to come into general acceptance.)

In addition to wearing Spanish clothing, carpenters are shown using European tools to construct a Spanish building (a chapel?), and the "wise man" gives his advice in one of the best examples in the book of a Spanish interior in realistic perspective. The image of the "wheat sellers," in which Nahua men are represented as Spaniards, epitomizes the association of maleness with Spanishness. The Spanish visual markers in Book 10 render Nahua males more familiar to European readers even as they remain definitively marked "Indian."

In each of these images, the clothing the men wear (or do not wear, as no one wears shoes and one of the carpenters is without pants) at times reminds us of their "Indianness," while the distinctly Spanish settings reflect the fact that, during the colonial period, Nahua men, particularly elite men, had the most consistent contact with Spanish power.[33] Nahua women did not hold public office, and, although women were numerous in religious *cofradias* (sodalities), elite men always held the high-ranking positions that would have brought them into contact with Spanish secular officials and priests. Women continued to wear the huipil and skirt until the eighteenth century, even as they made Spanish clothes for the males in the family. Women also continued to sell traditional medicinal plants until the end of the colonial period, a practice that persists today.[34] At the same time, the sacred art of weaving by noble and commoner women alike, from which women also could obtain an income, was gradually taken over by male-owned mechanical looms. Furthermore, later in the colonial period, witnesses to wills and other documents were almost always men, most likely due to Spanish influence. During the early colonial period, Nahua women had served as witnesses in almost equal numbers as men, which was a striking contrast to Spanish wills, for which women rarely served as witnesses. Lockhart speculates that due to the large female membership in cofradias it is likely that Nahua women exerted a de facto predominant influence in these organizations. This "hidden power" of women (not apparent in the sources) may have been true in local secular organizations as well, but it is difficult to verify.[35] Still, the sources show us that in material culture, as in Christian religious ideology, Nahua women were relegated to the margins of Spanish colonial power structures. Thus, the images of Nahua men and women in Book 10 tell a colonial story about the lower-status position of Indian women relative to Indian men within the dominant Spanish social system.

The "prostitute" is the only woman in this work associated with Spanish markers, though these markers are associated with transgressive sexuality. Her representation is especially odd because not only does she wear a Spanish man's collared shirt under her huipil, but it appears a Nahua woman's hairstyle was added as an afterthought. (We know that Nahua women did not wear Spanish shirts.) Without this addition her hair is short, curly, and light in color, which makes it look more like a Spanish man's. The prostitute offers alcohol to a patron, who presents her with a Spanish coin, images that mark the transaction as immoral to a European reader, who would most likely associate this woman with the "mother of harlots" in the book of Revelations.[36] The images of the crossroads and the footprints, however, are Nahua symbols and reflect concerns that this woman is "restless on the water, living on the water, she is flighty . . . she nowhere finds lodging . . . she [wakes at] dawn anywhere."[37] The road itself connoted danger and immorality, and the crossroads even more so, as it was called the "crotch of the road," signifying its connection with excessive female sexuality. And yet, for the Nahua, the crossroads was simultaneously a place where illness could be cured by leaving one's tlatlacolli at a shrine to women who died in first childbirth. Such liminal places were rich in creative/destructive power. Coincidentally, for medieval Europeans, the crossroads had a diabolical association, as it was where witches and sorcerers were said to hold their meetings with the devil. In addition, Peterson suggests that the prostitute's red feet (striking in the original) are a European allusion to lascivious women.[38]

Contrary to positive associations of men with "Spanishness," the prostitute's association with European / Spanish markers, including male hair and clothing, is an entirely negative one. Her image bristles with a potent mix of Christian and Nahua moral symbols that in combination signify to European and Nahua readers, in different ways (and in spite of the more complex and balanced Nahua conception of the crossroads), the immorality of wayward women.

It is important to note that the ambiguous gender manifest in the prostitute is strongly proscribed in Book 10, though the "badness" of this appears to derive from the dangerous perversion of maleness with femaleness, not ambiguousness as such. The hermaphrodite, for example, is described as having a man's body, build, and speech ("good" qualities) but is nevertheless "a woman with a penis." Similarly, the sodomite, like the male pervert, is effeminate and plays "the part of a woman." The "chicle chewer" is dressed as a Nahua woman, but is made to look ugly; it is as if the image corresponds to the text, which asserts that "men who publicly chew chicle achieve the status of sodomites; they equal the effeminates." This may in fact be an "effeminate" as his / her hair is loose and the text tells us that only married women cannot chew chicle in public. On the other hand, the text also asserts that "bad women, those called harlots," chew in public and along the roads.[39] It is unclear exactly where a woman crosses the boundary to become "bad." In either case, however, it is the association with female sexuality that signifies immorality.

By now it should be apparent that the central descriptive difference between women and men that reveals a distinctly Christian morality is the consistent association of "bad" women with excessive sexuality and deception, along with the characteristics of "bad" men, including laziness, inebriation, and general disobedience. Similarly, it is sexuality that distinguishes the daughter from the son. When a daughter is good she is chaste and a virgin, but gone bad she is a whore, showy, and a drunken pleasure seeker. The good son is obedient and humble; the bad son is a disobedient dunce. The bad woman physician is distinguished from the bad male physician by her uncontrolled sexuality. Not only is she a sorceress and seducer like her bad male colleague, but she also has "a vulva, a crushed vulva, a friction-loving vulva."[40] Furthermore, the female pervert is distinguished from the hermaphrodite and the sodomite by her excessive sexuality. Both the bad mother and bad grandmother are deceivers who lead others into evil / immorality / chaos (the forest, cliff, desert, water's current, or crag). Falling and tripping into caves or torrents are Nahua metaphors for moral aberration and the literal departure from social norms. A bad father is lazy and unreliable, whereas a bad grandfather is simply senile; he, like the father, has no active desire to disrupt. A woman, however, is actively disruptive and dangerous. One bad noblewoman, for example, "goes about besotted; she goes about demented," and the corresponding image shows her holding a stick as a symbol of her reckless violence. In the background are two figures in a scene resembling a pieta, suggesting perhaps that the demented woman is the cause of this misfortune (the text is not specific).

In sum, the bad woman is like a prostitute: she is not careful with her sexuality, which "wanders." Moreover, through deception she leads others astray, evidence that immorality is contagious. For the friars, sin acted like a disease, infecting others and making them participate in the sin. Thus, Fray Andres de Olmos wrote that the "'secret prostitute'" endangered good women, "like a rotten fruit by which good fruit goes bad."[41] That a human being could induce immoral behavior in others was absurd to the Nahua, for whom life without tlatlacolli was impossible; and truly absurd was the notion that humans could cause "sin." Humans could not cause nor choose sin, for sin was considered a part of life on earth, independent of human actions or intent. The implication is that passages in Book 10 that speak of "leading others astray" are products of Christian theology. The procuress, "the messenger of the devil," is an obvious example of this Christian interpretation of infectious sin.[42] In this case, the scribes (and/or Sahagún) abandoned Nahua symbols in favor of an unequivocal statement about the diabolical nature of female sexuality.

BOOK 10 OF the *Historia* tells us about the changing status of Nahua women in Spanish colonial religious ideology and how this change was perhaps connected to changes in daily social life. By the seventeenth century, for example, Nahua women in Mexico City participated in far fewer property transactions than they had in the previous century, and they no longer served as legal guardians of minor children in lawsuits.[43] By this time, an Indian woman's legal identity was connected to her husband's, and even when women inherited property in dispute, the husband had initiated the lawsuit. Husbands typically spoke for their wives, and brothers represented sisters in litigation. This was in contrast to the early colonial period, when Spanish officials were astonished to witness Nahua women speaking for their male relatives in court, even answering for these men when they were asked to give their names. One reason for the decline in women's legal status was the decline of the social institutions in which women had had some authority before the Spanish invasion. Connected to the disappearance of these social institutions was the gradual replacement of traditional Nahua gender ideology by a Christian ideology that had no notions of gender parallelism or life in balance.

Book 10 reveals the flattening effects Spanish intolerance had on the definition of what constituted a virtuous woman. Despite the vitality of the Nahua worldview and its attendant symbols, a Christian gender ideology predominated, radically disrupting traditional Nahua conceptions of how women could live in the world. But therein lies the rub: a study such as this one must confront the limits of cultural continuity and change. While a Nahua (or Mesoamerican) worldview certainly survived the imposition of Spanish religious forms, it could not help but be transformed by a conversion to Catholicism.[44] The point is not to determine which ideology won out in the end but to suggest that profound change occurred in Nahua religious and social ideology at the expense of women, whereas certain cultural values and forms nevertheless endured Hispanic oppression. This process took place over centuries, giving rise to forms that were neither completely Spanish nor completely Nahua. Over the years, the Nahua claimed outwardly Hispanic concepts, patterns, and institutions, as if they had always been theirs.[45] In this way, Christian gender ideology became Nahuatized as former Nahua gender roles and relations were gradually forgotten.

It is important to remember, however, that this process never added up to a final syncretic union of the Nahua and the Christian. As we have seen, elements of these two worldviews might be placed in an uneasy juxtaposition, but neither could easily assimilate the other. On the contrary, in Book 10 it is clear that Christian disparagement of sexuality, especially female sexuality, necessarily distorted the Nahua celebration of sexual expression as essential to a happy life. The book's one-sided accusation that women are dangerously sexual and deceptive was also a violation of the ideal of balance in life and in relations between the sexes. The Franciscan understanding of the complex and powerful Nahua goddess Tlazolteotl as Eve-like and evil underscores the total misunderstanding that accompanied this cultural encounter. For Nahua women, the demonization of their power as women could not bode well for the future.

Notes

1. Bernardino de Sahagún, *Florentine Codex: General History of the Things of New Spain*, 11 vols., trans. and ed. Arthur J. O. Anderson and Charles E. Dibble (Salt Lake City: School of American Research, 1950–1982). Note that Book 10 is actually volume 11 of this work.

2. Jorge Klor de Alva, H. B. Nicholson, and Eloise Quinones Keber, introduction to *The Work of Bernardino de Sahagún: Pioneer Ethnographer of Sixteenth-Century Aztec Mexico*, ed. J. Jorge Klor de Alva, H. B. Nicholson, and Eloise Quinones Keber (Albany, N.Y.: Institute for Mesoamerican Studies, SUNY, 1988), 9.

3. Some evidence of this erosion has been noted by anthropologist James Taggart, *Nahuat Myth and Social Structure* (Austin: University of Texas Press, 1983). See also Alan R. Sandstrom, *Corti Is Our Blood: Culture and Ethnic Identity in a Contemporary Aztec Indian Village* (Norman, Okla.: University of Oklahoma Press, 1992).

4. John Keber, "Sahagún's Psalmodia: Christian Love and Domination in Sixteenth-Century Mexico," in *Chipping Away on Earth: Studies in Prehispanic and Colonial Mexico in Honor of Arthur O. Anderson and Charles E. Dibble*, ed. Eloise Quinones Keber (Lancaster, Calif.: Labyrinthos, 1994), 52.

5. Louise Burkhart, *The Slippery Earth: Nahua-Christian Moral Dialogue in Sixteenth-Century Mexico* (Tucson: University of Arizona Press, 1989), 29.

6. Ibid., 71.

7. Ibid., 38.

8. See Jeffrey Burton Russell, *Lucifer: The Devil in the Middle Ages* (Ithaca, N.Y.: Cornell University Press, 1984) for a detailed discussion of the medieval personification of evil.

9. Susan Kellogg, *Law and the Transformation of Aztec Culture, 1500–1700* (Norman, Okla.: University of Oklahoma Press, 1995), 88.

10. Ibid., 95.

11. Ibid., 92.

12. Burkhart, *Slippery Earth*, 134.

13. Ibid., 93.

14. Ibid., 139.

15. Kellogg, *Aztecs*, 114.

16. Burkhart, *Slippery Earth*, 156.

17. Kellogg, *Aztecs*, 115, quotation on 116.

18. Ibid., 107.

19. Sahagún, *Florentine Codex*, 1:37.

20. Ibid., 1:38.

21. John Leddy Phelan, *The Millennial Kingdom of the Franciscans in the New World*, 2d ed. (Berkeley: University of California Press, 1970), 57. *Editors' note*: the episcopate was the ruling body of bishops.

22. Charles Gibson, *Spain in America* (New York: Harper and Row, 1966), 78.

23. Sahagún, *Florentine Codex*, 1:77.

24. Ibid., 1:75.

25. Ibid., 1:9.

26. Ibid., 1:79.

27. Ibid., 1:80.

28. Ibid.

29. Keber, "Sahagún's *Psalmodia*," 52.

30. "Pero como no se exercitauan en Jos trabajos corporales, Como solian, y *como demanda la condicion de su briosa sensualidad*, tambien comjan mejor, de lo que acostu-brauan en su republica antigua" (emphasis added). Sahagún, *Florentine Codex*, 1:78.

31. Ibid.

32. Patricia Anawalt, *Indian Clothing before Cortes: Mesoamerican Costumes from the Codices* (Norman, Okla.: University of Oklahoma Press, 1981), 209.

33. See Charles Gibson, *The Aztecs under Spanish Rule: A History of the Indians of the Valley of Mexico, 1519–1810* (Stanford: Stanford University Press, 1964), 218, 243–244.

34. Ibid., 353.

35. James Lockhart, *The Nahuas after the Conquest* (Stanford: Stanford University Press, 1992), 228.

36. Jeannette Favrot Peterson, "The *Florentine Codex* Imagery and the Colonial *Tlacuilo*," in *The Work of Bernardino de Sahagún*, 284.

37. Sahagún, *Florentine Codex*, 11:94.

38. Peterson, "The *Florentine Codex* Imagery," 285.

39. Sahagún, *Florentine Codex*, 11:38, 11:90, 11:89.

40. Ibid., 11:53.

41. Burkhart, *Slippery Earth*, 180.

42. Sahagún, *Florentine Codex*, 11:57.

43. Kellogg, *Aztecs*, 111.

44. See, for example, Guillermo Bonfil Batalla, *Mexico Profundo: Reclaiming a Civilization*, trans. Philip A. Dennis (Austin: University of Texas Press, 1996); David Carrasco, *Religions of Mesoamerica* (San Francisco: Harper and Row, 1990); Lockhart, *The Nahuas after the Conquest*; Brenda Rosenbaum, *With Our Heads Bowed: The Dynamics of Gender in a Maya Community* (Albany, N.Y.: Institute for Mesoamerican Studies, SUNY, 1993); Sandstrom, *Corti Is Our Blood*; Taggart, *Nahua Myth*.

45. Lockhart, *The Nahuas after the Conquest*, 446.

Julia C. Wells

Eva's Men: Gender and Power at
the Cape of Good Hope

*In many cross-cultural contact situations, women played key roles as transla-
tors, go-betweens, and mediators. This essay explores the key role played by one
Khoena woman, Krotoa (known to the Dutch colonists as Eva), who acted as an
intermediary between the agents of the Dutch East India Company and various
kin and tribal groups on the Cape Colony's frontiers. Eva's crucial role in
translating, guiding the Dutch in their diplomacy with African leaders, and
enabling the creation of new economic relationships placed her in a powerful but
precarious position between cultures and reveals the heavy reliance that colonial
powers placed on local knowledge in the early stages of colonization. Eva's ambiguous relationship with Dutch commander Jan Van Riebeeck and subsequent
marriage to Pieter Van Meerhoff, a Danish surgeon, suggests that racial
boundaries were not initially strictly policed on the South African frontier and
also raises important questions about the place of intimacy and sexuality in the
construction of colonial authority.*

Q uite possibly, Eva, born Krotoa, is the most written about
African woman in South African historiography. Her name
fills the journals of the Dutch East India Company almost
from the very start of their little feeding station at the Cape of Good Hope
in 1652. She is known as a Khoena girl taken into Dutch commander Jan
Van Riebeeck's household from the age of about twelve, who later became a key interpreter for the Dutch, was baptised, married Danish surgeon Pieter Van Meerhoff, but then died as a drunken prostitute after his
death.[1] Yet her persona remains an enigma.

Virtually all of the representations of Eva construct her as a helpless victim of vicious culture clashes. Today's racial consciousness, laced with assumptions of inevitable African-European hostility, is often read back into the historical record. Frustratingly large gaps in that record leave room for a wide range of interpretations, depending heavily on the subjectivities of the historian. Virtually all previous writers, however, have judged Eva primarily by the tragic circumstances of her death, while minimizing the considerable achievements of her earlier years.

None of the existing images does justice to the complexities of her life and times. Yet, another story can be told, that of a woman who exercised an extraordinary level of control and influence over the key men in her life. Her story dramatizes the initial dependency of the Dutch newcomers on anyone who provided reasonably reliable information about the local inhabitants. In Eva's case, this usefulness was compounded by her sexuality in an environment where women were scarce. She also exploited gender stereotypes which cast her as a "safe" person to be entrusted with full access to the Van Riebeeck household. Her life reflects both high levels of acceptance within Dutch society, as well as the frustrations and limitations a transcultural person faced.

Her life also exposes the range of ambivalent Khoena feelings about the Dutch presence in their first decade at the Cape. During this period, the Khoena did not unilaterally view the Dutch as enemies or invaders. Some saw in them an opportunity for unparalleled personal gain as middlemen in the livestock trade; others saw them as potential allies against old enemies; still others used them to secure valued trade commodities. Eva herself evolved considerably over time. At the peak of her career, she subscribed to the belief that the Dutch presence could be mutually beneficial to both sides. In many ways, Eva's story exposes that brief historical moment when Dutch and Khoena peacefully coexisted and strove to live in harmony.

THE REASONS FOR Eva's presence with the Dutch from the earliest days of their settlement have a direct bearing on the nature of her subsequent status in both Dutch and Khoena societies. Circumstantial evidence supports the possibility that Krotoa lived with her "uncle" Autshumato (called Harry by the Dutch) at the time of the Dutch landing. The records confirm that she was separated from her sister in infancy and the fact that Eva showed consistent hostility to the Goringhaiqua clan and to her own mother, who lived with them. In contrast, her fate and fortunes were closely tied with those of Autshumato, for whom she clearly expressed deep concern and compassion on several occasions.

The implications are quite important, as Autshumato's Goringhaicona people were sedentary, nonpastoral hunter-gatherers who collected shell-fish in the vicinity of Table Bay. For years before the Dutch came to settle, Autshumato served as a postal agent for passing ships from a number of countries, having been taken to Java by the English in 1631. He and his followers camped at Table Bay and greeted Van Riebeeck when he landed. They then lived adjacent to the Dutch tents during the construction of the first fort and became the first Africans proletarianized by the Dutch colonial presence. Thus, if Krotoa lived with Autshumato when the Dutch first arrived, her going into service with them might have been a relatively smooth transition, as many Goringhaicona readily did odd jobs for the Dutch in return for food, tobacco, or drink. Her mother's people, the Goringhaiqua, by contrast, were pastoralists only rarely seen by the Dutch during their first year.

Possibly, the Dutch needed more than casual help when, only a few months after arriving, the first baby was born to the chaplain / sick-healer, Willem Barentssen Wijlant, and his wife.[2] Two days after the birth, both the new father and Mrs. Van Riebeeck came down with a virulent disease that had been spreading rapidly through the settlement, leaving a few casualties. Extra assistance with the new baby could thus have become particularly urgent.[3] The sick-comforter, Wijlant, routinely led short excursions out of the fort to try to barter with Khoena. Like Van Riebeeck, he was an evangelical Calvinist, eager to find converts among the local people. In view of his religious zeal, and possibly the need of his wife for assistance with the new baby, he might have initiated negotiations to obtain the services of a young Khoena girl. They probably turned to Autshumato first, as he already had a long history of working for Europeans. Perhaps he selected Krotoa because of her status as ward, separated from her biological parents.

Although Krotoa was certainly too young to have exercised much free will about where she lived and worked, her service in the commander's household could have been viewed as an honor and a form of apprenticeship by the Khoena. Contemporary evidence from the journal kept by Van Riebeeck describes a young African girl raised in the home of a nonrelated but prestigious chief and hence honored as highly as if she were his daughter. A German officer, Ludwig Alberti, described similar customs among the amaXhosa nearly a century and a half later. Clearly, the people among whom Krotoa lived differentiated between low- and high-ranking Dutch, greeting ships' captains or the commander as long-lost friends, throwing their arms around their necks in warm embrace.[4] From the Khoena point of view, the presence of a young girl in the home of a neighboring "chief" might be seen not only as an honor, but as a token of friendship and a useful way to gather intelligence.

The flimsiness of the initial Dutch encampment and their high dependency on good relations with their Khoena neighbors suggests a tenuous situation, unlikely to serve as a "prison" in which a captive girl could have been kept against her will and the will of her kin, as Abrahams alleges.[5] In fact, Krotoa entered Dutch service twice in the first few years after their arrival. The first time, as suggested, probably arose from her easy availability and Dutch need. The second entry more clearly signified a gesture of friendliness and goodwill on the part of the Khoena, smoothing over a serious rift with the Dutch. It appears that Autshumato removed Eva from the Dutch in October 1653, when he stole all of the Company cattle, killing a Dutch herd-boy in the process. A few months later, Wijlant spotted Eva, Autshumato's wife and children, and all the missing cattle among the followers of Gogosoa, chief of the nearby Goringhaiqua.[6] Van Riebeeck reported that he restrained himself from using force to recover the stolen livestock, instead entering into negotiations. During this crisis, Gogosoa and his wife made repeated visits to the fort in the interests of restoring peace. Possibly at this time they also made a more formal arrangement for Krotoa to return to the fort, as a gesture of good intentions; the record does not say. But soon after, Krotoa did reenter service to the Dutch, and relations between the Dutch and the Goringhaiqua improved considerably.

OVER THE NEXT few years, Eva developed a persona in the records, not simply as "Van Riebeeck's favourite maid," but as a highly valued interpreter.[7] For her, it was a period of relative isolation from her people and of significant acculturation among the Dutch. Living with the Van Riebeeck family, she took advantage of her position to learn Dutch fluently, "almost as well as a Dutch girl."[8] Her induction into the Dutch language and way of life may also have been facilitated by Van Riebeeck's two nieces, of relatively comparable ages to Eva. One of these, Elizabeth Van Opdorp, years later took in Eva's children while she was incarcerated on Robben Island.

Eva's standing with the Dutch, however, went beyond her enthusiastic embrace of the Dutch language and culture. Despite clear efforts to present a picture of respectability and decorum regarding Eva, Van Riebeeck reveals a high level of personal concern for her. His journal conveys a muted sense of a father-daughter relationship, stresses Eva's closeness to Van Riebeeck's wife, Maria, and highlights efforts to convert Eva to Christianity. All these themes appear to justify the vast amounts of attention lavished on her. Van Riebeeck represented himself as cautious and critical of her motives at all times. However, her greatest offense was flattering the Dutch too much. This comes across as rather trivial compared to the behavior of her fellow male interpreters, who stole the Company livestock and led rebellions.

Although the evidence is entirely circumstantial, a case can be made that Van Riebeeck had an intimate relationship with Eva at some point. The most compelling evidence comes from the larger picture, taken as a totality. The trust and reliance that Van Riebeeck invested in Eva clearly transcended the boundaries of a conventional master-servant relationship. He invited her to important meetings, explained important decisions to her, consulted her privately about vital issues, gave her freedom to come and go, and made her an active sales agent. Perhaps most revealing is the sharp contrast between Van Riebeeck's attitude toward Eva and that of his successor, Zacharius Wagenaar. The new commander treated Eva with outright churlishness and hostility, hardly appropriate behavior toward one who had proved herself so invaluable. By comparison, Van Riebeeck had been gentle, considerate, tolerant, indulgent, and trusting of Eva in a highly subjective way.

If Van Riebeeck was intimate with Eva, it is not surprising that it was carefully concealed in the Company journals. He clearly tried hard to represent her in a detached, professional manner. She appeared simply as being the right person conveniently on the spot whenever needed. But her words and views commanded extraordinary respect and authority, as revealed in comments such as "this was also observed by Eva," "Eva said the same," "we must attend Eva's last parting advice," and "this Eva had often told us."[9] Despite all efforts to sustain propriety, Van Riebeeck also comes across in the journal as a man who took great interest in indigenous women. As an employee of the Dutch East India Company, his first major Company assignment was to secure peace and congenial trade cooperation with the powerful Queen of Achin in Sumatra.[10] After arriving at the Cape, he showed a keen fascination with the story of a chief's wife, bedecked with gold and jewels, insisting that she be brought into the fort. He even offered to go out to meet her himself. Though the tale eventually collapsed as largely fictitious, what is significant is the commander's near-obsessive absorption in the story, giving it great prominence in the journal. It is also interesting to note Eva's role in spinning the yarn while acting as interpreter, suggesting that she might have been deliberately playing on his weaknesses, which she knew firsthand.[11]

Not surprisingly, no hint of Dutch suspicion about their relationship comes through the journal. Van Riebeeck represented himself as a model husband, father, and family man, who led an exemplary life. But from the Khoena, a somewhat different picture emerged. The journal noted that the Khoena predicated their treatment of Eva on their perception of her extraordinary relationship to Van Riebeeck. Indeed, their closeness ensured both her safety when she traveled outside the fort, and his, as long as she was at hand. At one point, Van Riebeeck reported Eva as claiming that her enemies would have killed her had it not been for their fear of Van Riebeeck's wrath. At times when she left the fort, he expressed fear for his own safety.[12] This confirms the idea that the Khoena viewed her presence with the Dutch as a token of peace and goodwill. Conversely, her absence removed a special safeguard, leaving Van Riebeeck feeling particularly vulnerable.

Although the journal fails to confirm details of an intimate relationship between Eva and Van Riebeeck, it constructs a picture of complex dynamics which she exploited for her own interests. During the second half of the 1650s, Eva, though still only in her teens, actively and steadily placed herself in a central position within the Dutch establishment. She quickly learned just how much the Dutch valued "insider" information about Khoena thinking, plans, and movements. As newly arriving colonizers, they were vulnerable, not only because of their numerical weakness, but because of their ignorance of the local people and customs. Invariably, they placed a high premium on acquiring information on which their very survival hinged. Because of its character as a refreshment station for passing ships, the settlement depended heavily on cross-cultural understanding and cooperation. Food supplies came almost entirely from livestock traded with the indigenous people for tobacco, copper, beads, and drink. The more familiar colonial strategy of conquest and plunder always loomed in the background as perhaps an easier option. However, as Jay Naidoo has shown, despite Van Riebeeck's persistent eagerness to use force, directives from Amsterdam ultimately restrained him.[13] The ruling Chamber of Seventeen thoroughly committed itself to getting as much as it needed out of the Cape at the lowest expense. This depended entirely on good relations with the Khoena.

EVA'S SUCCESSFUL CAREER as an interpreter rested not only on her good language skills and her closeness to the commander, but also on her unique ability to acquire information about the Khoena of interest to the Dutch. Previous studies have tended to assume that she simply "knew" about political developments in the hinterland because she was Khoena herself. But much of what she shared with the Dutch went beyond what could have been known or understood by the twelve-year-old girl who first entered their service.

It is far more likely that she sought out information networks, constantly acquiring fresh input. This flow of information no doubt went both ways, although only the Dutch record of what they received from her is evident. On numerous occasions, however, various Khoena leaders used her to convey their wishes and interests to the Dutch. In fact, the first mention of Eva's involvement in the political affairs of the Dutch appears in January 1656, when she informed Van Riebeeck of her uncle Autshumato's intentions to move in closer to the fort.[14] A negative reply must have been communicated, as Autshumato, still only suspected of stealing Dutch livestock in 1654, kept his distance for some time.

After another year and a half, Eva clearly favored Dutch interests when she took advantage of her role as interpreter for Chainhantima, a chief of the Chainouqua people, who lived to the east of the Cape and had never before encountered the Dutch. The information she provided confirmed for Van Riebeeck what he had always suspected: that Autshumato had been obstructing the Dutch from learning much about the interior for fear they would seize land and wealth by force and threaten his vital position as a middleman in the livestock trade. Eva's translations drove Autshumato (by now back in service as an interpreter) into such a rage that he spat on the floor and stomped in the spittle.[15]

Two important points surface at this time. One is Eva's willingness to please the Dutch with fresh information at the expense of breaking rank with her own kinsman and other Khoena interpreters. The other is the beginning of her involvement in the Dutch quest for expanded contacts in the interior, a sphere of influence she later embraced wholeheartedly. Further, Van Riebeeck suspected that her interpretations went beyond simply conveying what informants said, extending to significant amounts of embellishment on her part.[16] Her role as an interpreter was scarcely passive or simply functional. She projected herself in a highly interventionist way, whetting the Dutch appetite to expand.

Eva's reputation as a Dutch collaborator is even more unmistakable during the course of a serious hostage crisis the following year. By mid-1658, the Dutch had started importing slaves, only to find that they quickly absconded into the interior. Van Riebeeck clearly found Eva far more sympathetic to his wish to have local Khoena participate in returning the runaways than his chief male interpreter, a Goringhaiqua named Doman. After spending a year in Java, Doman returned, highly suspicious of colonial intentions. The journal records how, in a private conversation between Van Riebeeck and Eva, she poured out her heart about the intense rivalry between herself and Doman. She accused him of telling the Khoena too much about the Dutch, to which he replied: "I am Hottentoosman, and not Dutchman, but you, Eva, *soubat* [curry favor with] the Commander."[17] She further alleged that it was Doman's people, the Goringhaiqua, who had the slaves and were likely to sell them into the interior in exchange for *dagga* (cannabis).

The Dutch then gave Eva all the credit (or blame) for proposing they take two sons of the Goringhaiqua chief, Gogosoa, as hostages, until all the slaves were returned. Considering the level of restraint the Dutch had exercised to date against using force with their Khoena adversaries, this implied a significant revision of policy. Malherbe suspects that the Dutch set up Eva as a scapegoat, as the tactic of hostage taking was in no way unfamiliar to them. In fact, the free burger (and husband of Elizabeth Van Opdorp) Jan Reijnertz had held Gogosoa hostage just a month previously to secure the return of some stolen cattle.[18] If hostage taking was already a common strategy, it is more likely that Eva only suggested names of effective candidates. Whatever her level of complicity, Doman and his people presumed her guilty of openly assisting the Dutch. Fearing for her life, Van Riebeeck ordered her not to leave the fort.[19]

However, tensions soon spiraled out of control. The hostages languished in the fort for over a week, and only a few missing slaves reappeared. The hostages themselves argued that they should be joined by other hostages from all the local Khoena chiefdoms. So the Dutch took more, including Eva's uncle, Autshumato, and seized all of his cattle. In the process, the Dutch killed one of his followers, the first Khoena death at their hands. Within two days, all parties concluded a peace treaty which freed the hostages and secured the return of the slaves. Significantly, it also contained clauses stating that the Goringhaiqua now gave up all claims to the Cape peninsula. So what had started out as a tussle over runaway slaves ended up with a Khoena cession of land to the Dutch, the imprisonment of Autshumato, the confiscation of his cattle, and a Khoena death — and both sides blamed Eva!

It was a messy affair, which reportedly left Eva "depressed" and no doubt urgently raised the issue of where her loyalties lay. She promptly visited Autshumato, who had been sent to Robben Island as a prisoner for his role in stealing company livestock five years earlier. But nothing she said or did could undo his sorry fate. Van Riebeeck compared her to Esther, pleading for her uncle Mordecai. Doman's accusations of her traitorous behavior escalated, with the journal reporting him as saying: "'See! There comes the Hollander's advocate again, she is coming to deceive her own countrymen with a parcel of lies, and to betray to the last,' and other expressions to make her odious."[20] If ever Eva needed friends and allies it was now, for her thorough identification with Dutch interests at this stage could have sealed her off from Khoena confidence altogether. Instead, the reverse happened, as Eva embarked on a bold new strategy to shore up her position.

IRONICALLY, THE DEPRESSION in the livestock trade during the crisis created an opportunity for Eva to redeem herself. Few Khoena came near the fort for fear of being taken hostage. Within a few days of the treaty, Eva and Doman, now acting in concert, requested permission "to pay a visit to their friends" in order "to make them known to us." It was the first time that Eva acted as a trade agent in her own right, although the male interpreters frequently did so. Because one of the hostages had been a Cochoqua, named Boubou, it is possible that Eva surmised that she could expect a warm reception from his people.[21] After all, the great Cochoqua cochief, Oedasoa, had gone to the trouble of taking Eva's sister as a wife after kidnapping her from another chief.

Armed with brass, iron, beads, tobacco, bread, and brandy for "her mother and friends," Eva set out. Her immediate change of apparel from Dutch clothes into Khoena skins shocked the Dutch, who liked to view her as having become one of them. No doubt it signified her strong wish to identify more fully with her own people and to seek their acceptance. She received a mixed reception. The Goringhaiqua apparently perceived her as an irredeemable sell-out. Even her own mother refused to have anything to do with her. In contrast, Chief Oedasoa and her sister, "who had not seen her since infancy," warmly welcomed her. This contact not only launched Eva on the most active stage of her career, but also turned the tide in northern trade for the Dutch. Her activities as intermediary between the Dutch and the Cochoqua proved pivotal. First, she dispelled myths and rumors that had kept them apart. She adamantly insisted that Doman was a liar when he claimed that the Cochoqua wanted to kill all the Dutch. Her descriptions of Cochoqua wealth in livestock actively whetted the Dutch appetite for new trading partners free from trouble-some middlemen. To Oedasoa, she painted a glowing picture of the Dutch as fair and reasonable people. She reportedly had "taken every opportunity of informing Oedasoa minutely of the customs of our na-tion, in particular of our inclination for a friendly intercourse and trade with them. She had also told how she was brought up in the house of the Commander's wife, that she had learnt our language and in some mea-sure, our religion."[22] Further, she convinced Oedasoa that trade with the Dutch could yield special benefits for him and his people. In other words, she convinced both sides to trust each other sufficiently to open direct negotiations.

Once the door opened, Eva remained involved, making suggestions to the Dutch of new trade goods which they had not previously offered, including cinnamon, cloves, nutmeg, mace, pepper, and sugar. She also successfully persuaded them to send along a few good violinists and a Dutch clown to entertain the chief! When the Dutch soldiers and traders returned to the fort after their first visit, they conveyed wondrous stories of a chief who could muster a thousand armed men, who had armories full of weapons and livestock as far as the eye could see. As they left the Cochoqua, the Dutch noted Eva's place of prestige among them: "She was, like her sister and brother-in-law, according to their national custom, mounted upon an ox, like a great lady, instead of travelling on foot with the rest."[23]

At this stage, Eva gave the Khoena a serious try. Her sister had promised to find her a husband, a chief rich in cattle and sheep.[24] So, after the initial Dutch trade expedition, Eva remained behind while the Dutch returned to the fort. However, her reculturation was extremely short-lived. Exactly why she returned to the fort within six weeks is not very clear. She claimed she came back because Oedasoa had been seriously mauled by a lion. According to the journal, she blamed herself for having made "repeated requests" to him to go on a hunting expedition to secure a wild horse and ivory for the Dutch.[25] Did other Khoena blame her and make her feel unwelcome? This hardly fits into the larger context of increasingly friendly relations between the Cochoqua and the Dutch.

Perhaps more to the point, the journal also alleged that Oedasoa and Eva's sister asked her to return to the fort to prepare for extensive further contacts. They anticipated an official visit in which Eva's sister would call on Mrs. Van Riebeeck and Oedasoa on Van Riebeeck, "for the sake of society, like sisters and brothers." Also, they planned to leave behind at the fort some young children "that they might be taught from their youth upwards" about Dutch ways.[26] This suggestion tends to confirm the possibility that something similar had been arranged in Eva's youth. It also gives a more plausible reason for her return to the fort: Oedasoa wanted to use her as his own agent within the heart of the Dutch establishment.

Whether Eva herself felt reluctant to remain within the pastoralist lifestyle or was not keen on marrying the chosen chief, the records do not tell us at this stage. Clearly, her ambassadorial role took precedence over other considerations. Malherbe interprets Eva's return as "an expedient retreat" from Khoena life. However, far more was at stake than Eva's personal wishes and feelings. From this stage on, her career not just as interpreter but as a key trading agent and intelligence-gathering functionary for Oedasoa took off.

However, Eva also continued to serve Dutch trading interests somewhat independently of the Cochoqua. Early in 1659 she provided the Dutch with elaborate descriptions of the Namaqua, an even more powerful chiefdom to the north of the Cochoqua and, it would emerge later, their sworn enemies. On the basis of her accounts, Van Riebeeck authorized a northward expedition of exploration by free burger volunteers in early February. Eva suggested which inland people would provide the best guides for the journey and insisted that the Namaqua could link the Dutch with the powerful inland Chobona, and eventually the Monomotapa and Vigiti Magna River. This intelligence from Eva demonstrates her immersion in the Dutch beliefs and aspirations of the day. They trusted heavily in a map, now known to be largely mythical, drawn up by Huygens Van Linschoten and published in Amsterdam in 1623, which portrayed a northward-flowing river named Vigiti Magna, on the banks of which sat the kingdom of the Monomotapa, believed to be rich in gold, ivory, and pearls. Although historians blame Eva for feeding the Dutch false information that whetted their appetite for inland exploration, it is more likely that she wove together a little fact and a little fiction to create a plausible story. However, the first northern expedition traveled scarcely thirty miles from the fort before returning, frustrated by barren, arid conditions.[27] The enthusiasm to explore the north then had to be postponed due to the outbreak of hostilities.

When the interpreter Doman led his Goringhaiqua people in open rebellion against the Dutch presence in May 1659, the Dutch viewed it as their "first war" against Khoena. For Eva, it proved to be the conflict that put her intermediary position to its severest test to date. In the ensuing power struggle, she capitulated to Oedasoa's wishes and, for the first time, clearly misled the Dutch.

During the early stages of the conflict, Eva maintained her familiar stance of marked hostility to the Goringhaiqua. She warned the Dutch of the Goringhaiqua strategy of attacking during the rain, when Dutch guns would not fire properly. Eva alone, of all the Khoena in service to the Dutch, remained inside the fort as the conflict escalated. With the eruption of open hostilities, her relationship to the Dutch was very much in question. From her position inside the fort, Eva raised Dutch expectations that Oedasoa might ally with them and join in the attack on the Goringhaiqua. However, Oedasoa consistently dodged this approach, projecting a position of studied neutrality. In an attempt to demonstrate his continuing trust and cooperation with the Dutch, he again offered a state visit from his wife, Eva's sister. Another proposal suggested that Oedasoa should come to the fort himself so that he and Van Riebeeck could cooperate "like two brothers with one heart and soul."[28] Neither plan quite materialized. Throughout June and July 1659, Eva traveled back and forth between the fort and the Cochoqua, camped in the vicinity of Saldhana Bay, at times by boat to avoid hostilities and dangers on the overland journey. While tensions bristled between the Dutch and their Goringhaiqua adversaries, the prospects of trade with Oedasoa and his Cochoqua people blossomed.

By the time the rebellion ended, however, Oedasoa had proved to be far from neutral. Not only did he decline to attack the Goringhaiqua and refuse to give the Dutch any intelligence about enemy whereabouts, but he gave shelter to the rebels and eventually negotiated a peace settlement on their behalf. The evidence suggests that Oedasoa had to neutralize Eva's independent actions. She spent much of the second half of 1659 at Saldhana Bay, where she could not influence the Dutch prosecution of the war.

Clear differences between Eva and Oedasoa surfaced when she urged the Dutch to send a wagon to fetch him to come into the fort. He refused to come, claiming the wagon ride would be too uncomfortable and that he wanted to attend to a sick child. Although a relatively trivial event, it exposed open conflict and disagreement between Eva and Oedasoa. His unwillingness to take up arms against fellow Khoena became more and more apparent to Van Riebeeck, who also began to lose trust in Eva, expressing many doubts and misgivings.[29] He was bitterly disappointed that Oedasoa's Cochoqua would not help the Dutch in their war against the Goringhaiqua.

When Eva left the fort in July 1659, she hinted that she might not return. However, after spending three months with the Cochoqua, she resurfaced as Oedasoa's chief negotiator in peace talks. By this stage, she conformed completely to the Cochoqua position and tried to soothe the tensions by stressing the importance of achieving peace rather than point fingers at one another for past transgressions. In other words, she completely dropped her vituperations against the Goringhaiqua. From the tone and the style of the journal, it is clear that the Dutch saw Eva, by early 1660, as having swung over to serve Cochoqua interests more than their own. Some free burgers who had visited Saldhana Bay warned Van Riebeeck that Oedasoa was using Eva as a spy, taking advantage of Van Riebeeck's having "such faith in Eva."[30]

Although Eva came out of the conflict decidedly more committed to the Khoena than ever before, she resumed her life as interpreter at the fort. She continued to help the Dutch find new trading allies; in 1660 she described in great detail the potential wealth of the Hessequa and even set up an uncle from among the Chainouqua as a specially trained and coached trading agent. However, the journal no longer portrays her as the insider whose advice on everything was so eagerly sought. In addition to her growing Khoena loyalties, Van Riebeeck might well have been shaken in his relationship with her by the active entry into her life of Pieter Van Meerhoff, who arrived in the Cape in March 1659.

SURPRISINGLY LITTLE SERIOUS attention has been given by scholars to the nature of the relationship between Pieter and Eva. The relationship was a durable one, lasting seven years and producing three children. The couple remained unmarried for four years, then married in 1664 and remained together until Pieter's death in 1666. Eva's subsequent inability to cope with life surfaced following his death, suggesting that his loss had a devastating impact on her, perhaps triggering a full mental breakdown. Further circumstantial evidence, however, suggests that the pair also shared considerably in advancing the trading interests of the Dutch and Khoena, an enterprise for which they were, together, ideally suited. Given the broad outlines of their relationship, one can just as easily project theirs as a romantic liaison of choice.

Hailing from Copenhagen, Pieter first enlisted in the Dutch East India Company as a soldier and was subsequently appointed undersurgeon, the rank he held upon his arrival in the Cape in 1659. The chances are that Pieter and Eva struck up an intimate relationship soon after his arrival in 1659, since by 1663 they had two children. This implies that the relationship started just prior to or during the period of Doman's rebellion, at a time when Eva was at the peak of her intermediary role. If Pieter acted opportunistically, it was to share in Eva's power and prestige, not her weakness. An unconfirmed report from an employee of the Dutch East India Company who passed through the Cape in 1660 mentioned that Eva had a child by a European man.[31] The author claims the father was a Frenchman who was heavily fined for making her pregnant, none of which is recorded elsewhere. Unfortunately, this memoir is rife with inaccuracies and repetitions from earlier accounts, casting doubt on its full reliability. If Van Riebeeck had indeed imposed a heavy fine on his rival — a thoroughly unprecedented measure — it is not surprising that he kept it out of the official record. However, a birth in 1660 fits into known chronologies.

Once the rebellion ended, Pieter flung himself wholeheartedly into the pursuit of the Namaqua and greater riches, a quest initiated by Eva even before his arrival. He alone volunteered to travel on all six northern exploration expeditions over the next four years. In any case, Pieter's enthusiasm for expeditions closely echoes Eva's eagerness to provide the Dutch with fresh information about outlying chiefdoms. Their dedication to expanding trade, perhaps for personal gain, became a common thread in their relationship.

Because Pieter kept the official company journal for the second and third northern expeditions, it is possible to see how, in his own words, he understood himself. He frequently wrote in great detail about his acts of bravery and drew on experience gained during his first expedition to portray himself as an expert on local conditions. He rescued servants from an attacking lion simply by shouting at it; leapt onto the back of a charging quagga, suffering a kick to the face when it bolted into a river; stuck to elephant or rhinoceros paths to get the oxen through difficult passages; and knew how to get around treacherous mountains. He reveled in the magnificence of a mountain named after him.[32] But perhaps most notable is the way Pieter represents himself as particularly skilled and sensitive in his dealings with Africans. For one thing, he did not let his men fall prey to the incessant rumors of hostility between one chiefdom and another, nor to the frequent threats to kill off the Dutch. In every case, his skepticism eventually proved to be correct, suggesting that he had acquired an insider's knowledge of Khoena political rivalries from Eva.

He also comes across as especially congenial in his personal dealings with wary chiefs and warriors. In his initial encounters with both Souqua hunter-gatherers and eventually the Namaqua, he first took time to teach them how to smoke tobacco, then plied them with drink and other gifts. He boldly strode into the Namaqua king's kraal and secured an invitation into his house to open up business negotiations. When befriending the elusive Namaqua, he stitched up the ear of the chief's son and created a rage for red caps by giving the king his own nightcap. Pieter portrayed various Khoena leaders as happy to see him personally, paving the way to further contacts and negotiations.[33]

This friendly approach paid great dividends. Not only had Pieter found the Namaqua, but he gained their promise to negotiate further about opening up trade. Hostilities between the Namaqua and the Cochoqua appeared to be the only obstacle. Accordingly, four days after his return from the exciting first encounter with the Namaquas, the Dutch governing council sent Pieter to bring Oedasoa into the fort. Oedasoa had previously claimed he did not need their help to deal with the Namaqua, whom he could easily defeat on his own.[34]

At this point it becomes evident that Pieter already had a strongly established personal relationship with Oedasoa, Eva's primary contact and kinsman. He successfully convinced Oedasoa to come in to negotiate. Once in the fort, Oedasoa initially refused to cooperate, but then changed his mind overnight. The next morning he agreed to send three ambassadors northward with Pieter to discuss a peace settlement. The scenario suggests close collaboration between Pieter and Eva. Eva's effective and sympathetic interpretation services would have been vital. As the two were already lovers, with one child, their cooperation with one another is highly probable. Even before securing Oedasoa's cooperation, the Council had resolved to send Pieter off immediately as leader of another expedition to induce the Namaqua to come into the fort for trade. The Company also hastily arranged to send a generous supply of red caps and sixteen varieties of beads, tactfully chosen to please the Namaqua chiefs.[35] At this point, Pieter is clearly pivotal, with all decisions revolving around him and his capacity to deliver.

He did not let the Company down. Pieter's expedition returned within a month's time, reporting complete success in its objectives. Although the Namaqua had moved off further into the interior seeking pastures, they had delegated ambassadors to remain behind with their friends, the Chariguriqua, for the express purpose of meeting Pieter and working out a peace settlement with the Cochoqua. Pieter triumphantly reported that not only had he brokered peace between the Namaqua and Cochoqua, but he had also brought into the agreement the Souqua hunter-gatherer raiders, who had been pestering both.

The success of this mission nearly drove the Dutch into a frenzy of speculation about their imminent access to great wealth from the interior. The Namaqua had agreed to send people to the fort at the end of the rainy season (October) with all sorts of trade goods obtained in the interim from their trading partners further north.[36] Two of Oedasoa's ambassadors who had been on the journey convinced Van Riebeeck of the nearness of the Monomotapa cities, rich in gold and ruled by a powerful leader called Chobona.[37] Responding to Van Riebeeck's reports, the Chamber of Seventeen exulted from Amsterdam, "You have found the thread of the clue."[38] Hopes soared of a new southern African El Dorado that might offset all the costs incurred in setting up the station at the Cape.

This journey, Pieter's third expedition to the north, marks the high point of his career as an explorer. In a way, his transcultural skills brought too much success too soon for a Company employee of such junior rank. When in October the Namaqua failed to appear at the fort with trade goods, the Council resolved to send out another expedition to find them. With the hopes of striking it rich still running high, the Council appointed as leader Sgt. P. Evrard, a man with sterling Company credentials, a commander of the military, who had served long in India and was a member of the local Council. He could better represent the "maxims and honour of the Company than one of inferior rank."[39] Pieter went as second-in-command, relieved of the duty of keeping the journal.

Neither this nor the subsequent two expeditions in which Pieter participated produced the results anticipated. One problem was that the Namaqua resided on the far side of a barren stretch of desert that the Dutch could not cross. But the finesse and sensitivity of Pieter's leadership style were also clearly missing. The Dutch fell victim to rumors circulated by Cochoqua and Souqua about Dutch aggressive intentions. Opportunities to dispel or discount the ever-present rumors of intergroup hostility and to negotiate peace painstakingly proved evasive.

At least one reported incident reveals tensions, if not mutiny, within the Dutch ranks over leadership style. During the fifth expedition, when the Dutch came across a Souqua kraal consisting only of women and children, Commander Cruythoff ordered their execution and the destruction of their huts. His subordinates, no doubt including Pieter, "would not agree to the proposal on any account, stating that they were not willing to take revenge on these poor creatures."[40]

THE DETERIORATION AND eventual abandonment of the Namaqua quest in many ways embodies the shifting climate that also marginalized the unique chemistry of Pieter and Eva working together as a team. As it became clearer that the Monomotapa empire was not at hand and that the great river to the north could not provide access to wealthy trading partners, the enthusiasm for sensitive and friendly contacts with the indigenous people faded. The whole spirit of Dutch-Khoena contact shifted to cruder pragmatism, laced increasingly with racism and militarism. Eva's relationships with the key men in her life changed dramatically, one by one.

By 1666, she had clearly fallen out with Oedasoa. The Company commander Zacharias Wagenaar speculated that Oedasoa began avoiding contact with Eva because she had married a European, but this seems implausible because Pieter had been well-known to Oedasoa and apparently trusted by him for several years and the couple already had two children together. In fact, in 1664 Oedasoa had made an unusually generous offer to Eva of one hundred cattle and five hundred sheep.[41] As this was also the year that Pieter and Eva formally married, it is possible that the offer was intended as a wedding gift, sometimes given to orphans without other forms of support. Two months after the wedding, Pieter and Eva traveled together to visit Oedasoa, at his invitation, perhaps in an effort to collect, but Oedasoa never paid up and stopped coming into the fort. Perhaps Oedasoa expected Pieter and Eva to leave Dutch employment as his gift to them would have made them wealthy enough to live independently. It appears more likely that Oedasoa became disaffected with the Dutch in general and the church wedding signified the young couple's commitment to live in conformity with the dictates of Dutch society.

In the journal Wagenaar probably obscured the more deep-rooted reasons for the falling out between Oedasoa and the Dutch. During early 1664, the chief had become a regular visitor to the fort, bringing in large contingents of Cochoqua to be regaled and entertained by the Dutch. He often arrived with fifty people just as the Dutch were sitting down to church or dinner, much to the chagrin of Wagenaar, who resented his presence as an intrusion. Oedasoa undoubtedly detected Wagenaar's blatant racism. To the journal, Wagenaar confided that he saw Oedasoa and his followers as "these incomparably greedy and beggarly men" — a sharp contrast to Van Riebeeck's perception of Oedasoa as "stately and dignified."[42]

Perhaps Oedasoa's biggest disappointment with the Dutch in this period came in the early months of 1664, when he actively sought their military assistance in a war against his Hessequa enemies. He offered to pay the Dutch generously in cattle if they agreed. The Dutch, however, declined on the grounds that they wanted to remain friendly with all Khoena chiefs and not show favoritism. Oedasoa soon stopped coming into the fort, although the Cochoqua trade in livestock continued.

Wagenaar's clearly racist attitude toward Eva probably triggered the couple's decision to have a church wedding after so many years together. Initially, it appears that Wagenaar saw Eva as an ordinary concubine, whom he also treated as a company servant. His first mention of her, a year and a half after his arrival in 1662, was scathing. At the time, Pieter was away on his last northern expedition. Wagenaar accused Eva of running away with the children without his permission, saying, "The thoughtless wench has played us the same trick before, throwing aside her clean, neat clothing and resuming old stinking skins of animals, like all the other filthy Hottentoo women." When she was apprehended (at a house that fits the description of the location of Elizabeth van Opdorp-Reinertz's home) and returned, he briskly dismissed her explanation that she had gone to visit her niece who had just given birth.[43] In sharp contrast to Eva's freedom of movement in the Van Riebeeck era, Wagenaar did not grant her the right to maintain free relationships with her Khoena kin. He considered leaving the fort without consulting him or getting his permission as intolerable behavior.

The timing of Pieter and Eva's formal engagement a few months after this event no doubt reflects the changing dynamics of their worlds. Eva was treated like a slut in Pieter's absence, the Namaqua quest had fizzled out, and Oedasoa was disaffected. Pieter and Eva, the preeminent contact people to new interior populations, had outlived their usefulness. Though the Company occasionally sent Pieter on short bartering expeditions and Eva still interpreted frequently for Wagenaar, basic trade contacts were now well-established.

In this context, the formality of marriage made sense. It certainly gave Eva greater status in Wagenaar's eyes and removed any possibility of his treating her as an ordinary servant. It also signaled the couple's capitulation to living as socially acceptable members of Dutch society and an end to their in-betweenness. Their bid for conformity worked well. Along with a proper Christian marriage, the couple received a wedding banquet, a promotion for Pieter, and a special marriage gift for Eva, the same as for all Company employees. About one year later, Pieter was again promoted, this time to the position of superintendent of Robben Island, moving there with a pregnant Eva and their two children. This appointment lasted two years before Pieter was given command of a prestigious expedition to Madagascar and Mauritius, key new spheres of influence for the Dutch. Clearly, his superiors still appreciated his intercultural skills, as his instructions admonished him to treat the natives there well, not like the other Dutch. However, without the invaluable coaching from Eva and her kin, he misjudged his new native contacts, who killed him while trying to negotiate on the beach of Antongil Bay in Mauritius in 1666.[44]

By the beginning of 1667, Eva had effectively lost all the influential men in her life. The loss of Pieter triggered a dramatic downhill slide that ended only with her dishonorable death on 29 July 1674. During those years the Dutch commanders accused her of abandoning her children, of rowdy drunken behavior, of promiscuity and producing several more children. They incarcerated her on Robben Island several times, allowing her back on promises of improved behavior, but claimed she never reformed. Despite her disgraceful demise, the Dutch community gave her a Christian burial and a few years later laid down strict terms for the adoption of her two surviving children, fathered by Pieter.[45]

What killed Eva was not simply her inability to adapt to Dutch society, as some believe, but rather the dynamic within colonialism that so soon made bridging, transcultural people like her and Pieter redundant. This became all the more painful to her after she had tasted the extraordinary power and influence that she could exercise as a woman trusted by both sides in the initial colonial encounter. Eva died her slow and miserable death in a world in which the illusion of harmony had already evaporated. The cause into which she had thrown her life no longer existed. Van Riebeeck's restraint in dealing with the Khoena and his personal indulgence toward her left when he did; Oedasoa decided to tolerate the Dutch at arm's length, disgruntled that they could not be made to bend to his will; and Pieter died seeking a new frontier. When the dream shattered, so did Eva.

While Eva's story appears to rest on a unique intersection of personalities and context, it no doubt also contains within it elements common to many intercultural relationships. Surely, themes such as the non-threatening indigenous woman pressed into service and learning European languages and ways, powerful chiefs using such women as their eyes and ears in the strange new settlement, the ambitious and brave young explorer also seeking romance, and the heavy dependency of the tiny numbers of intruders on friendly relations with the locals could easily appear on virtually every colonial frontier. Similarly, on all such frontiers, the interlude in which interracial couples capitalized on having the best of both worlds was destined to be brief. As colonial hegemony took hold, reliance on good quality relationships gave way to less kind forms of coercion, dominance, and dispossession. Other Evas and Pieters appear quietly and marginally scattered throughout the history of not only South Africa, but probably wherever two cultures have met.

Notes

1. I choose to use the term "Khoena" over the more familiar "Khoikhoi" or "Khoisan" as it is grammatically gender-inclusive, simply denoting "people," whereas Khoikhoi translates as "men of men." I also choose to use the name Eva over Krotoa because the only information available about her comes through the Dutch who used this name. It is an indication of the bias in the accounts in which she is always perceived in terms of her relationship to them and never simply as a Khoena woman. As such, it signifies the unfortunate loss of her Khoena identity in the historical accounts.

2. H. B. Thom, *Journal of Jan Van Riebeeck* (Cape Town, 1952), i, 43 (6 June 1652); Donald Moodie, *The Record or a Series of Official Papers relative to the Condition and Treatment of the Native Tribes of South Africa*, 3 vols. (Amsterdam, 1960), i, 110 (31 Oct. 1657), Van Riebeeck's journal.

3. Thom, *Van Riebeeck*, i, 44 (8 June 1652).

4. L. Alberti, *Ludwig Alberti's Account of the Tribal Life and Customs of the Xhosa in 1807* (Cape Town, 1968; first published 1815 in German), 83; Thom, *Van Riebeeck*, i, 30 (10 Apr. 1652).

5. Yvette Abraham, "Was Eva Raped? An Exercise in Speculative History," *Kronos: Journal of Cape History* 22 (Nov. 1996): 3–21.

6. V. C. Malherbe, *Krotoa, called Eva: A Woman Between* (University of Cape Town, Centre for African Studies, Communication no. 19, 1990), 8; Thom, *Van Riebeeck*, i, 208 (28 Jan. 1654).

7. David Gordon, "From Rituals of Rapture to Dependence: The Political Economy of Khoikhoi Narcotic Consumption *c.* 1487–1870," *South African Historical Journal* 35 (Nov. 1996): 66.

8. Moodie, *The Record*, i, 247.

9. Ibid., i, 148, 149, 184, 172.

10. Thom, *Van Riebeeck*, i, xxi.

11. Moodie, *The Record*, i, 110.

12. Ibid., i, 146 (29 Oct. 1658), i, 210 (30 June 1660).

13. Jay Naidoo, "Was the 'Van Riebeeck Principle' a Plea for Peace or a Plea for Plunder?" in Jay Naidoo, *Tracking Down Historical Myths* (Johannesburg, 1989), 18–34.

14. Moodie, *The Record*, i, 82.

15. Ibid., i, 114–115.

16. Ibid., i, 135, 203–204, 247.

17. Ibid., i, 128.

18. *Editors' note*: "Free burger" is the term used for servants of the Dutch East India Company who had been freed to farm their own land.

19. Malherbe, *Krotoa*, 16.

20. Moodie, *The Record*, i, 138, 141, 139.

21. Ibid., i, 141, 142.

22. Ibid., i, 145.

23. Ibid., i, 145–149.

24. Ibid., i, 150.

25. Ibid., i, 151.

26. Ibid., i, 152.

27. Thom, *Van Riebeeck*, iii, 9 (1 Feb. 1659).

28. Moodie, *The Record*, i, 174.

29. Ibid., i, 179, 180.

30. Ibid., i, 198.

31. R. Raven-Hart, *Cape of Good Hope 1652–1702: The First 50 Years of Dutch Colonisation as Seen by Callers*, 2 vols. (Cape Town, 1971), i, 68.

32. Moodie, *The Record*, i, 224, 230, 232.

33. Ibid., i, 231–233.

34. Thom, *Van Riebeeck*, iii, 359, 360.

35. Ibid., iii, 361.

36. Moodie, *The Record*, i, 235.

37. Thom, *Van Riebeeck*, iii, 374.

38. Moodie, *The Record*, i, 240.

39. Ibid., i, 241.

40. Ibid., i, 263.

41. Ibid., i, 289.

42. Ibid., i, 148, 275.

43. Ibid., i, 271.

44. Ibid., i, 180, 279.

45. Ibid., i, 354.

Sean Quinlan

Colonial Bodies, Hygiene, and Abolitionist
Politics in Eighteenth-Century France

*Both slavery and colonialism raised fundamental questions about the human
body and its ability to adapt to new physical environments, climates, and labor
regimes. This essay examines the ways in which understandings of racial difference were produced, and in turn conditioned, by medical practice in the French
empire during the eighteenth century. The very different impacts of migration to
the Antilles on enslaved Africans and free Europeans opened up a series of
debates over the ways in which the nature of the human body varied between
racial groups and how the bodies of both slaves and free settlers should be regulated in order to minimize morbidity and mortality in the Caribbean. These
exchanges had broad political significance in French colonies and in the metropole itself, as doctors, reformers, and intellectuals debated the morality of slavery
and the place of people of African descent in the French nation and empire and
explored the limits of the "liberty, equality, and fraternity" that the French
Revolution promised.*

In the Western imagination, contact and conquest in the "torrid climates" of Africa and the New World have long been associated with
disease and death. Moreover, the expansion of European empires
has also been linked to the growth and dissemination of medical knowledge and power. This essay explores the reactions of French physicians
and social commentators in the eighteenth century to the health experiences of the European and African slave populations in the French West
Indies. Specifically, my main intent is to delineate the extent to which
physicians utilized categories of race and class and concepts of pollution

and purity to explain the incidence of disease among Europeans and Africans in the Caribbean tropics. The unique conditions in the Antilles colonies significantly challenged physicians' assumptions about metropolitan health and hygiene and opened new discussions on race and the politics of public health during the French Revolution.

The colonial experience presented eighteenth-century medical personnel with a bewildering array of lethal pathogens. French physicians and surgeons observed that two outsider population groups, Africans and Europeans, responded quite differently to the exigencies of the Caribbean tropics, and they sought to explain these variations through contemporary theories of disease causation and avoidance. In contrast to physicians in Europe (who emphasized differences of class), colonial doctors frequently laid stress on biological differences of a racial type. Yet, in their desire to regulate and "police" African health, doctors invited investigation of and debate on the somatic effects of slavery, as commentators speculated that oppressive social and political institutions engendered the high rates of disease, degeneration, and depopulation within the slave community. These controversies carried explicit resonance in the broader sphere of French political culture. On the eve of the French Revolution, abolitionist writers such as Abbé Gregoire, Daniel Lescallier, and Lecointe-Marsillac widely denounced as excessive the morbidity and mortality of Africans subject to the slave traffic and seized on health and hygiene as means of rehabilitating the potentially liberated African body. In this manner, French abolitionists appropriated earlier medical preoccupations with the "physical and moral" constitution of the African body to advocate a specific program of "regeneration" and assimilation.

UNLIKE EARLIER COLONIAL physicians, who viewed the process of tropical "seasoning" (acclimatization) in the English Americas and West Indies in more favorable light, French doctors in the eighteenth century overwhelmingly accentuated the pathological and destabilizing nature of the Caribbean environment. The air, the most fickle and lethal of all external influences, continued to be seen as the principal cause of disease. Yet while their European counterparts carried out various "medical police" measures to alleviate the miasmic origins of sickness, colonial physicians adopted a preventive framework based on the other regularity of eighteenth-century hygienic thought: the growing trade in health catechisms instructing readers on preventive strategies and the perils of ill health. In this literature physicians addressed what they viewed as a strikingly middle-class clientele. They urged that the preservation and extension of life was contingent on the organism's ability to discipline its functions within the animal economy. In the struggle to achieve sanguinary equilibrium, as George Cheyne, Achille Le Begue de Presle, and others argued, it was easier to "preserve health than to recover it, and to prevent disease than to cure them [*sic*]."[1] What made this doctrine so novel was that physicians encouraged the middle classes to actively control their own bodies. Health became the self-disciplinary mark of the middle classes. Moreover, this self-regulating control demarcated not only social class; in the colonies it also distinguished race.

Physicians recognized that the process of physical degeneration followed the Europeans' arrival in the Antilles. Many Europeans quickly succumbed to the ravages of tropical illness, and the established settler and slave populations often spoke of yellow fever as a lethal "stranger's disease." Jean Damien Chevalier (1682–1755), in his 1752 work on disease and botanical variations in Saint-Domingue, carefully enunciated the pathological nature of the milieu:

> When the heat of the climate, through considerably increasing perspiration and exciting even continual sweating, leaves nothing more in the vessels than thickened liqueurs, while it simultaneously diminishes the ability of the solid parts; the equilibrium so necessary for health and life is soon shattered. The thickened liqueurs offer more resistance to the moving parts. . . . The solids require more effort to push [the thickened liqueurs], and they advance less: they swell the vessels, force their diameters, enter the canals, which in the state of health must not admit them; they dilate the sanguinary and lymphatic capillary arteries; there, they form varices, opening the ways to haemorrhages; in a word, they totally reverse the oeconomy of the human body, and become a source of deadly illness, and principally, malignant fevers.[2]

Antoine Bertin (1752–1790) proposed a similar explanation in his *Des moyens de conserver la santé des blancs et des nègres* (1768). He observed that the recently disembarked male European suffered immediately from "depleted" blood, maintaining that the circulatory system was highly susceptible to inflammation or other feverish distemper. The "unexpected heat" of the colonial milieu excited the vital properties of the organism and hastened decay and putrefaction of the organs and humors. Worse yet, the body produced an overabundance of bile. Not only did this predispose the body to weaknesses, degeneration, and stagnation, but additionally, the constitution of the blood could not defend the body against the "generation" of parasitic worms so common in the colonial environment.

Physicians recognized that disease did not merely signify an individual pathology; sicknesses occurred in specific social groups or races, as well. Bertin claimed that although the acclimatized populations of the Antilles suffered heavily from bodily degeneration, the hostile environment was host to the most severe illnesses for European settlers: "The Europeans who arrive come mostly with rich blood and strong, taut fibres that the heat soon slackens, which do not suddenly lose their initial strength and initial vigour. It is only with time . . . that the solids and fluids, by the constant action of the hot and more often humid atmosphere, by the change of nutrition, or by the effects of illness, absolutely lose their initial constitution, they *creolize* [*se creolisent*], as we say, and the temperament begins to unify with the climate."[3]

The process of "creolization" was intimately linked to eighteenth-century theories of degeneration and death. Philosophes, such as Buffon and d'Holbach, claimed that living and dying were reciprocal processes in the life cycle. Death slowly rotted the human frame from within: the fibrous muscles, bones and blood slowly congealed and lost their earlier sensibility. This, in turn, prevented the organism from resisting the anarchic properties of sickness and disease; the life course was nothing but a history of degeneration. For physicians such as Bertin and Antoine Poissonnier-Desperrières, the pathological milieu of the Antilles only hastened the physical destruction of the body.

The question thus arose: If the diseased body was only an indicator of an inherently diseased environment, how could one avoid or prevent sickness in tropical climates? What physicians in the mid-eighteenth century emphasized, above all, was direct control of the body and its natural functions. In an environment that seemingly bred the most pathological of all nonnatural causes, perhaps there was little more that the physician could offer. In a bizarre contradiction, doctors suggested that the male European body, because of its superior solids, fibers, and intellect, seemed more predisposed to disease. It was as though illnesses selected the best-adapted bodies. No small wonder that women, whom physicians claimed to have weaker fibers and liquid substances, seemed less inclined to colonial pathogens. Against such odds, it became the responsibility of the male individual—and more so in the colony than in the metropole itself—to diligently regulate the exogenous causes of disease through personal hygiene and bodily regimen.

While physicians extolled the unique character of each European body, they based their health care proscriptions on their idea of normal behavior. Chevalier claimed that individuals should carefully monitor food intake; gluttonous behavior, for example, would only swell the humors and encourage "regrettable" diseases. If necessary, the body should be bled and purged, and the traveler ought to "live soberly" at all times.[4] Bertin was more explicit. He cautioned against overexposure to the sun and encouraged moderate eating habits, consumption of citrus drinks, strict control of the passions, carrying a parasol when out in the sun, wearing sensible clothing, and engaging in sensible exercise. Dancing was discouraged. Individuals should place themselves under a hygienic regimen, no matter what the inconvenience might be. He grimly pronounced, "Within the islands, most of the sick die by a lack of care that did not depend on the physician."[5]

As might be expected, the consumption of alcohol and sexual activity were seen to contribute to the degeneration of the body. Intemperance shattered the fragile interactions between the solids and the fluids, facilitating the onslaught of disease. Most important, however, was careful control of one's sexuality. One should eschew the "commerce of women, and above all, that of Negresses," as Poissonnier-Desperrières cautioned. Significantly, eighteenth-century physicians were obsessed by the threat of "spermatic loss." Of all the excretions, the seminal fluid was the most precious, and its undue expense could entirely wreck the impressionable passions of the mind. Poissonnier-Desperrières stated: "Now, according to this disposition in the humors, they are only waiting for the favourable opportunity to enter by their acrimony the entire excited nervous and vascular systems, and this opportunity presents itself after large evacuations of seminal liqueur, which . . . had it re-entered the humors in a sufficient quantity, would have tempered their acrimony in such a way to render it impotent and kept the vessels in a state of suppleness far removed from excitability."[6] Ordinarily, such "large evacuations" of seminal fluid resulted only in madness or complete physical debilitation. In an environment that had thoroughly destabilized the animal economy, however, such negligence could cause malaria, yellow fever, or even death.

Physicians therefore stressed that colonists must adopt self-regulating mechanisms to avoid disease and preserve personal health. Their discussion reflected the highly stratified class barriers within the colonial white population: Chevalier, Poissonnier-Desperrières, and Bertin clearly maintained that a long life, healthy body, and productivity were all contingent on the maintenance and inculcation of modified bourgeois norms. Wealth and upper-class social standing would do little to divert sickness, as Bertin stated; what mattered was sobriety, temperance, and diligent sense.[7] Moreover, good health depended on disciplining the unpredictable passions and strict control of sexuality.

If Europeans could avoid disease through regulating their bodies, then the morbidity of the African slaves posed new problems for the physician. Numbering some 500,000 in St. Domingue alone on the eve of the French Revolution, here were people who clearly had no control over their own bodies. The question of whether the black slave could internalize the necessary hygienic regimen complicated this issue. As early as 1684, an anonymous author in the *Journal des Sçavans* had pronounced blacks a race separate from Europeans and implied that they carried innate physiological and intellectual inadequacies.[8] Following the Enlightenment's stress on the physical environment, natural historians, notably Buffon and J. F. Blumenbach, speculated that blacks had "degenerated" because of the African climate, geographic dispersal, and insufficient nutrition. In light of the pattern of disease in the French West Indies, however, this paradigm became problematic. Why did some sicknesses devastate European colonists, while the black population remained intact? By contrast, why did some diseases, such as dirt eating (*mal d'estomac*), tetanus, and yaws, decimate the African slave population? Physicians claimed that the physiological inferiority of women prevented the onslaught of some tropical pathogens; unfortunately, this failed to explain why the African body languished under such unique pathogenic entities. The selective nature of disease defied consistent explanation.

Pierre Barrère, in his *Dissertation sur la cause physique de la couleur des Nègres* (1741), was one of the first physicians to suggest an inherent morbid otherness to the African body. He concerned himself foremost with the causes of pigmentation. During many dissections, Barrère claimed that he discovered large quantities of black bile within the layers of the skin, and he posited that Africans were black for no less reason than an overabundance of the morbid substance. He also inferred an intimate link between pigmentation and sexuality: "One judges that the bile is naturally abundant in the blood of the Negroes by the strength and the rapidity of their pulse, by their extreme lustfulness and the other impetuous passions, and especially by the considerable heat of the skin that one notices in them. Experience shows, moreover, that the heat of the blood is proper to forming much bile, since one sees milk turn yellow among whites, when a nursing woman has a fever."[9]

Barrère's scalpel cut far deeper: the dissected cadaver revealed that the liver, blood, and vascular systems were awash with bilious matter. Even the epidermal pores released a "disagreeable odour." His work reflects the morbid anatomy practiced in colonial hospitals: physicians who opened up colonial corpses claimed they found bile interspersed in the anatomical recesses of Africans, mulattoes, and European alike. The implication was that bodies displaying such humoral imbalances were either predisposed to ill health or were themselves sources of disease.

Barrère's dissertation provoked unfavorable responses. An anonymous reviewer claimed that the Cayenne physician was grossly incorrect and virtually incompetent: blacks vomited yellow bile, suffered from jaundice, and even excreted the same infectious materials as whites. The author did note however, that under some forms of disease Africans suffered from a visible overabundance of black bile.[10] Dr. C.-N. Le Cat, in a largely ignored tract on African skin coloration, dismissed Barrère's efforts and insisted that anatomists did not consider his research seriously. In his view, it was the nervous system that decided pigmentation, and he compiled case studies of female hysteria, apoplexy, and syncope to prove that nervous disorders could create "blackened" skin color.[11] Yet, despite their different emphases on the hereditary or environmental factors that determined skin coloration, it should be emphasized that both Barrère and Le Cat are emblematic of the broader European racial discourse that sought to abjectify and feminize the African body. Their discussion of bilious organisms and fragile nervous systems suggests that some physicians believed that Africans possessed inherently pathological characteristics.

To preserve European health and prevent the degenerative process of "creolization," physicians posited that colonists should disassociate themselves from another source of pollution: the African slave. As we have seen, Poissonnier-Desperrières had warned that settlers should avoid sexual contact with black females. Accordingly, he documented a case study of a subject seized with a malignant fever. After diligent care and thorough purging, the patient seemed well on his way to recovery. On the last day of his treatment, however, the patient suffered a severe relapse, and before succumbing, he confessed to Poissonnier-Desperrières that he had "caressed a Negress" the night before.[12]

Two diseases fascinated European doctors: yaws (pians or framboesia) and tetanus. Yaws is a nonvenereal form of syphilis; the organism (*Treponeona pertenue*) usually penetrates the body through cuts and abrasions on the legs, below the genitalia. Massive tissual damage can occur in extended cases, and eighteenth-century physicians often confused the advanced stages of yaws with leprosy. Colonial doctors recognized the disease's selective nature and the sickening decimation and high rates of infection that it wrought upon the slave population:

> There are perhaps no other countries where venereal disease is as common as it is in these islands. All the male and female slaves carry it from Guinea; the children who are born there are consequently infected, engendering others even more corrupted than themselves.
>
> There are very few Whites who would not have had commerce with these Negresses, and it would be a great miracle that they would not communicate their disease to them.[13]

There remained some hesitation concerning the actual cause of the illness. On the one hand, physicians such as Chevalier suggested that environmental considerations encouraged the distribution of the disease. He believed that the "tough" constitution of the skin and the constant exposure to the sun or elements caused the "eruption" of pustules that covered the skin. The disease, transmitted by heredity, eventually degenerated into leprosy. J.-B. Dazille, in his *Observations sur les maladies des nègres* (1776), further insisted that slavery itself contributed to the incidence of disease and "dépopulation" among Africans. As he noted, "It is to be presumed that the venereal virus does exercise its activity principally on poorly-nourished, tired and nervous bodies, since then it produces accidents more serious, more murderous, and less susceptible to curation."[14] On the other hand, others saw the disease as an inherent pathological stigmata of the black: "There must be . . . in Negroes, a particular, predisposing cause, one that is not found in Whites, or that is not found in the same proportion, since if pians is not an illness from which Whites are excluded, it is always very rare among them, while it is very common with the former. It is necessary, by consequence, that a humor exists which has an analogy more particular with the nature of this virus."[15]

This internal debate aside, physicians increasingly suggested that the brutal demands of slavery directly contributed to the degeneration and mortality within the black Caribbean population. Of course, this suspicion had a substantial pedigree in Western medicine. Originally, the Hippocratic *Corpus* claimed that oppressive government and climate had molded the "mental flabbiness," "cowardice," and poor constitution of Asian peoples, and eighteenth-century philosophes had discerned a similar interrelationship between tyrannical institutions and a subject's somatic condition. However, medical writers who did post a direct correlation between structural or conjunctural deprivation and the incidence of disease still intimated that black diseases resulted from an a priori degenerate constitution — only now this "degraded" state stemmed from the harsh exigencies of slavery.

These themes were particularly accentuated in the colonial medical literature concerning the transmission and infection of tetanus. Although tetanus appeared to afflict both European and black populations alike, physicians remained highly concerned with the occurrence of lockjaw in the slave communities and the frequency of this disease in the black infant population. Eighteenth-century doctors were aware of the correlation between "cuts and abrasions" and the advent of tetanus. Medical personnel usually attributed the disease to a bodily exposure (for example, an open wound) to the "bad airs" from without. Observers noted that the black population remained highly subject to such occurrences and that the conditions of slavery perpetuated the sources of infection.

In 1786, Felix Vicq d'Azyr approved a volume addressed to the Société Royale de Médecine de Paris that detailed the grisly occurrence of tetanus and neonatal tetanus in the Antilles colonies. The reporting physicians opined that although both colonists and slaves were affected by the dreaded illness, blacks appeared to suffer to a far greater degree. According to these doctors, such illnesses were caused by nothing less than the lifestyle to which the slaves were exposed:

> In truth, the whites are infinitely less subject to this disease [tetanus] than are the blacks, although both are equally exposed to the impressions of the same air; but the particular reasons that could determine or encourage the invasion of these sicknesses are multiplied in the blacks; their particular cares, their precautions are much less; their lifestyle [*manière de vivre*], exercises, and the means of both are much

different: the blacks are much more exposed to the intemperance and vicissitudes of the air; they are exposed to it always without precaution, whether for themselves or for the affairs of their masters; they are less covered, engaged in the longest, roughest and most exhausting labour; blacks go about with their legs and feet naked; though heated or in a sweat, they walk on cold objects, go into the water, cross through marshes, streams, and rivers; they are exposed to the rain, evening dew, and wind: finally, they are more subject to wounds than are the whites; they go about with naked feet; they walk on hard, often sharp ground that injures them; they often make use of their feet in their work, and are more exposed to wounding them.[16]

In this discussion, the physician focused his gaze more on the exogenous causes of disease; not only did the environment create variable disease patterns, but perhaps the norms and forms of the "peculiar" institution were to blame. Everywhere, the black was subject to the direct causes of illness: immense physical labor in the hot and humid climate, poorly ventilated living quarters, newborn children exposed to foul airs and the burning rays of the sun, acute malnutrition, and overcrowding on the slave galleys all contributed to the incidence of disease. Whereas physicians such as Bertin estimated that humoral peculiarities predisposed the Caribbean slave to sickness, other observers, such as Dazille, could not help noticing that the brutalities of slavery and the slave trade begot conditions that were detrimental to the black population. Slavery, perhaps, was hazardous to African health.

While physicians may have expressed paternalistic concern over the health of the slave population, they certainly did not suggest that blacks could exert the necessary hygienic control over their bodies. Quite the contrary, it was the plantation slave owners who should maintain the slaves' physical well-being, and for no less reason than promoting their economic interests. The doctors reporting to the Société Royale de Médecine in 1786 warned, "It is yet easier to prevent than to stop its progress [tetanus]; the precautions that will appear minute, subjugative and unpleasant, could be very important, and one could do irreparable harm in wanting to avoid them: the Owners of Negroes, interested in their conservation, ought to be the first to take the precautions that could be beneficial to them." These physicians, including Antoine Poissonnier-Desperrières, encouraged slaveholders to exercise diligent medical care over their human property: owners should "entrust" their slaves to the "methodical treatment" of *gens de l'art* to conserve "a mass of individuals who are still more useful to them than to the State."[17]

"Policing" African health raised many political concerns. In one sense, physicians such as Poissonnier-Desperrières, Pierre Poissonnier Barrère, and J.-B. Dazille hoped that the centralization of colonial medical care would increase the naval health services' authority over the established (and fiercely independent) local medical communities. It was certainly no accident that Dazille dedicated his *Maladies des nègres* to the state minister of the navy, Sartine. Yet there were more subtle prerogatives at stake, as well. Populationist thought during the Enlightenment, in the form of mercantilist or physiocratic doctrine, strongly associated the health of the population with the physical well-being of the state: both organisms depended on self-regulating and disciplinary apparatuses to further productivity, power, and prestige. In the old regime and Revolutionary society that increasingly eschewed the corporate notion of the social body, however, the personal health of each citizen assumed highly politicized dimensions. The dual conceptions of political and animal economy collapsed upon one another and appear almost indistinguishable in the complex Revolutionary discursive plays on notions of regeneration and therapeutics for the truncated body politic. Considering the debates over the right to public health and medical reform throughout the Revolutionary period, it is not surprising that abolitionist writings on the so-called colonial question voiced concerns over the hygienic and reproductive capabilities of the slave population. If the state decided to assimilate the Caribbean slave into the restructured social body, it followed that the black would be subject to the same disciplinary mechanisms.

During the French Revolution, the subject of slave morbidity and mortality became a particular theme in abolitionist writings. As historian David Geggus has argued, the "colonial question" effectively "tested the universalistic claims of the French revolutionaries," raising powerful concerns over autonomy, racial equality, and the incongruence of slavery with bourgeois liberal society.[18] Although antislavery advocates found an organizational base with the founding of the Société des Amis des Noirs by Jacques-Pierre Brissot in February 1788, it remained primarily an elite movement that, unlike its British counterpart, failed to garner popular support. Abolitionists further encountered fierce opposition from powerful colonial lobbyists — notably, the notorious Club Massiac — and the full-scale revolt in St. Domingue in 1791 intensified existing political divisions within the Constituent Assembly. Revolutionaries achieved only a hesitant consensus on legislation related to ethnicity and slavery: the piecemeal Jewish emancipation of 1791, decrees on colonial racial equality in 1792, and the full abolition of slavery in 1794 (reinstated by Napoleon in 1802) each encountered determined opposition and qualifications.

Perhaps more significant, even ardent abolitionists, such as Grégoire, Brissot, and Condorcet, believed that the immediate abolition of slavery was an unfavorable and preemptive event. According to them, any actual change in the plantation system and slave society was dependent on cooperation between the various states engaged in slave trafficking and the gradual assimilation of the black population. Although Grégoire claimed that blacks possessed the "capacity for improvement," his endeavors to have blacks "become our equals" called for the imposition of European values such as Christianity, monogamous unions, proper work ethic, and hygienic care.[19] "If their physical and moral degradation is our work," the Abbé Sibire noted, "the less they reflect on it, the more it must interest us."[20] The problem was not only the destruction of the vices created by the slave culture, but encouraging blacks' innate ability to become virtuous citizens in the regenerated French nation.

Much of this discussion centered on economic prosperity and depopulation in the Antilles colonies or the African coasts. Although antislavery writers expressed reserved outrage over the problem of slavery, the damage inflicted on the African population aroused their productive-minded sympathies. Pruneau de Pommegorge, a former slave trader, argued in his *Description de la nigritie* (1789) that the trade directly contributed to the significant depletion of the African coasts, marking the African population with a brutal and "ferocious" character. The demographic estimates of this devastation varied widely: Brissot, Jérôme Pétion, and Benjamin-Sigismond Frossard estimated the population loss anywhere between 4, 60, and 300 million.[21] According to one anonymous writer, attempts to supplement the slaughtered indigenous populations of the Antilles were carried out under the mistaken assumption that blacks were best adapted to the exigencies of "torrid" climates: "The suffering of the Negroes during the [Atlantic] crossing weakens their strengths and chafes their temperament; the serious illnesses that they sustain in America and, usually, their short life-span, only demonstrate that they are imperfectly accustomed to this temperature." Thus, the plantation owners' desire to fill the colonies with "a generation of robust Blacks" capable of "sustaining the hardest labours" proved an illusory hope. Quite simply, "Without liberty, man is a degraded being in his moral and physical faculties."[22] Antoine Bonnemain's later volume, *Régénération des colonies* (1792), claimed that only the abolition of the slave trade and tempered care of the Caribbean slaves could encourage a burgeoning, healthy black population and facilitate full-scale abolition and assimilation.[23]

One of the first abolitionist writers to articulate the myriad black health problems was Daniel Lescallier. His primary focus remained the relationship between slavery and France's economic productivity, noting that the Caribbean sugar and coffee trade remained one of France's greatest political interests. He nevertheless connected the trade to the morbidity and mortality in the slave population, insisting that the state take active interest in promoting the physical well-being of the African slaves. For Lescallier the first step toward emancipating the Caribbean slaves remained their indoctrination into the norms and values necessary for a stable civil society. According to him, the conditions wrought by the slave trade engendered the poor quality of the black slaves. Like Grégoire, he seemed reluctant to take immediate measures for emancipation; the process was contingent on gradual assimilation. Lescallier argued that through abolition of the slave trade and careful attention to the conditions and lifestyle of the Caribbean slaves, the subsequent release of human and economic activities would prove far more profitable than the current situation.[24]

Lecointe-Marsillac provided the most powerful denunciation of the slave trade and its physical effects on blacks. He divided his impassioned 1789 volume into two specific parts: the first detailed the actual conditions inherent in slave transportation (which he claimed was based on the memoirs of a former slave), and the second analyzed the political and social ramifications of abolition. Images of morbidity and mortality permeated Lecointe-Marsillac's writing, as evinced by the provocative chapter titles in his work, such as "Treatment of sea-sick Negroes," "Mortality of slaves at sea," and "Causes of the depopulation and the mortality of Negroes." In his twelve-point outline for the abolition of slavery, moreover, Lecointe-Marsillac placed nourishment and untainted food supplies as the third step toward eventual emancipation.

According to Lecointe-Marsillac, the slave trade and social stratification within the plantations bred the pathologies that occurred in the black population. Conditions in the galley ships were so unsanitary that surgeons dreaded to treat the diseased blacks, for "they themselves fear breathing the pestilential air." As a result, he estimated that almost a quarter of the slaves died before reaching their Caribbean destination. The situation deteriorated after arrival, as "a quarter more slaves" succumbed to tuberculosis, phthisis, "putrid" fevers, or "a sharp species of fever that indistinctly attacks all strangers."[25] Unfortunately, those attending physicians only contributed to the pathetic condition of the subjugated slave: "[The surgeons] remain with us for only a few instants, and prescribe to us haphazardly those remedies that, always poorly indicated and poorly administered, do us more harm than good. . . . At the crack of a whip, they force us to swallow those poorly-made remedies that increase our grievous distress, and we are thus made to die. Finally, it is in these sepulchres of pestilential corruptions that all the horrors of convulsions, putrefaction, despair and the most painful miseries of the end of man seem to unite to offer sensible souls the most revolting spectacle of human sufferings; no, not even Hell would be so cruel."[26] The surgeons who treated blacks served another agenda, for they assured that the slaves were healthy enough to fetch a good price on the open market. Lecointe-Marsillac further denounced the lodgings, working conditions, and the nourishment provided for the slaves.

Yet, despite his outrage and powerful prose, Lecointe-Marsillac did not favor the immediate abolition of the slave trade. For him, the gradual assimilation of the Caribbean slave into the general population remained of the utmost importance. Throughout, he never placed this prerogative with the Caribbean slave; rather, the tempered treatment, dissemination of proper state values, and even dietary controls were to be imposed from above. This suggests that abolitionist writers who addressed the pressing issues of sickness and death in the slave population frequently adopted a program that mirrored earlier physicians' health care proscriptions for blacks: the Caribbean slaves did not know what was best for themselves or their bodies. And while abolitionists vehemently opposed conceptions of race that emphasized the innate, physiological inferiority of the African, they nevertheless suggested that, given the social and cultural exigencies of the period, the black was incapable of achieving "physical and moral" regeneration without explicit support of European philanthropists and institutions.

TOWARD THE CLOSE of the eighteenth century, therefore, physicians and school commentators drew on health and hygiene to reinforce specific social agendas. Originally, hygienic thought emphasized the critical interaction between the endogenous and exogenous causes of disease. Through diligent control of lifestyle and self-regulation of bodily functions, the European individual could avoid disease and prolong life. Within its continental eighteenth-century context, health and hygiene encouraged the active separation and segregation between social classes. In the colonies, by contrast, this discourse reflected both the powerful class and racial boundaries in the Antilles colonies. What distinguished the male European was his ability to mediate, regulate, or transform organismal functions in accordance with powerful exogenous forces. In a sense, the diseased body became the ultimate signifier of not just the pathological milieu, but the total lack of physical self-control exercised by the European individual.

With regard to the Caribbean slave population, physicians speculated that their predisposition toward a plethora of pathogenic entities indicated that either the African body was innately predisposed to sickness or that institutions and the tropical milieu facilitated the occurrence of disease. On the eve of the French Revolution, however, abolitionist writers insisted that the slave trade itself was the source of black health problems and claimed that the eventual dissolution of slavery would restore the African's political, moral, and physical well-being. These writers believed that the disciplinary functions of a dietary and hygienic regimen — along with the more obviously enunciated contingencies of Christianity, education, family life, and respect for property — remained the major tenets for assimilating the potentially liberated African slave. For them, this physical transformation would precede the very inclusion of the African slave into the body politic of the revolutionary French Republic.

Notes

1. George Cheyne, *An Essay of Health and Long Life* (London, 1724), xiii–xiv, 1–2; Achille Le Bègue de Presle, *La conservateur de la santé, ou avis sur les dangers qu'il importe à chacun d'éviter pour se conserver en bon santé et prolonger sa vie* (Paris, 1763), ii. All translations from the French are Sean Quinlan's.
2. Jean Damien Chevalier, *Lettres à M. le Jean, docteur-regent de la Faculté de Medicine en université de Paris. 1. Sur les maladies de St.-Domingue* (Paris, 1752), 27–28.

3. Antoine Bertin, *Des moyens de conserver la santé des blancs et des nègres aux Antilles ou climats chauds et humides d e l'Amerique* (Paris, 1768), 15–16.

4. Chevalier, *Lettres*, 27.

5. Bertin, *La Santé*, 33, 36–42; Antoine Poissonnier-Desperrières, *Traité desfièvres de l'isle de St. Domingue*, 2nd ed. (Paris, 1766), 95–97, 118.

6. Poissonnier-Desperrières, *Traité*, 106, 114–115.

7. Bertin, *La Santé*, 18–21.

8. "Nouvelle division de la Terre, par les differentes Espèces ou Races qui l'habitent, envoyée par un fameux Voyageur," *Journal dès Scavans* 12 (1684): 148–153.

9. Pierre Barrère, *Dissertation sur la cause physique de la couleur des nègres, de la qualité de leurs cheveux, et de la degeneration de l'un et l'autre* (Paris, 1741), 5–6.

10. Review of Barrère's *Dissertation sur la cause physique de la couleur des nègres, Journal dès Scavans* 127 (1742): 23, 45.

11. C.-N. Le Cat, *Traité de la couleur de la peau humaine en générale, de celle des negrès en particulier et de la métamorphose d'une de ces couleurs en l'autre, soit de naissance, soi acciden-telletnent* (Amsterdam, 1765), 1–4, 73–76, 173–174; Le Cat, *A Physical Essay on Senses* (London, 1750), 4–7, 149.

12. Poissonnier-Desperrières, *Traité*, 190–191, 204–206.

13. Chevalier, *Lettres*, 84.

14. J.-B. Dazille, *Observations sur les maladies des nègres, leurs causes, leur traitements, et moyens de les prevenir* (Paris, 1776), 255–256.

15. Bertin, *La Santé*, 90.

16. *Projet d'instruction sur une maladie convulsive, fréquent dans les colonies d'Amerique, connue sous le nom de Tétanos* (Paris, 1786), 29–30.

17. Ibid., 44, 95–96.

18. David Geggus, "Racial Equality, Slavery and Colonial Secession during the Constituent Assembly," *American Historical Review* 94 (1989): 1291.

19. Abbé Grégoire, *An Enquiry concerning the intellectual and moral facilities, and the literature of Negroes*, trans. D. Warden (Brooklyn, 1810), 158. He later insisted that blacks were incapable of great improvement (160).

20. Abbé S.-A. Sibire, *L'Aristocracie négrière, ou refléxions philosophiques et historiques sur l'esclavage et l'affranchissement des Noirs* (Paris, 1789), 122.

21. Jérôme Pétion, *Discourse sur la traite des noirs* (April 1790), 8–9; B.-J. Frossard, *Observations sur l'abolition de la traite des nègres présentées à la Convention rationale* (Paris, 1793), 20; Sibire, *L'Aristocracie*, 4.

22. *Réflexions sur l'abolition de la Traite et la liberté des Noirs* (Orleans, 1789), 6–7.

23. A. J. T. Bonnemain, *Régénération des colonies* (Paris 1792), 30–57.

24. Lescallier, *Réflexions sur le sort des Noirs dans nos colonies* (Paris, 1789), 6, 10, 57.

25. *Editors' note*: during the eighteenth century "phthisis" was applied to a wide range of wasting diseases, particularly diseases that afflicted the lungs and respiratory system.

26. Lecointe-Marsillac, *Le More-Lack* (Paris 1789), 45–46, 61, 63.

II

GLOBAL EMPIRES, LOCAL ENCOUNTERS

Mary Ann Fay

Women, Property, and Power
in Eighteenth-Century Cairo

This essay explores the complex sexual, familial, and economic relationships that shaped the social position of women in eighteenth-century Egypt, presenting a nuanced counterimage of gender relations in the Islamic world that undercuts both the figure of the subjugated Muslim woman and the grossly sexualized images of the harem that have been the stock in trade of Orientalism. Careful examination of sources such as waqfiyyat *(deeds of religious endowments) not only enables the reconstruction of the marital history and social position of individual women, but also provides important insights into the substantial property rights and very real economic power that Muslim women exercised. Against the backdrop of political turbulence, freed slave-concubines, such as Shawikar Qadin, constructed important gendered and ethnic networks that provided social cohesion and enabled the demographic renewal that was fundamental to the Mamluk (slave) revival that increasingly undercut Ottoman authority prior to Napoleon's incursion into Egypt in 1798.*

From what is left by parents
And those nearest related
There is a share for men
And a share for women
— Qur'an, s.IV:7

In 1762, a former slave-concubine, Shawikar Qadin, registered her *waqf* (religious endowment) in the main Cairo court of al-Bate al-'Ali. The property she was alienating and from which she would derive an income included two houses, agricultural land, a number of shops and rental units, an apartment building, and shares in one of the most lucrative investments of eighteenth-century Cairo, a *wakala*. This was a complex of storerooms, shops, workshops, and living units that was the foundation of the transit trade and the commercial economy of Ottoman Egypt.[1]

More than twenty-five years earlier, Shawikar arrived in Cairo, probably from Circassia, a penniless slave. We know that she was born a European Christian from her full name as recorded in her waqf deed, but the details of her life before she reached Egypt are largely unknown. However, if Shawikar's experiences were similar to those of other young women and men from the Caucasus, her impoverished family sold her to a slave dealer who brought her to Egypt and resold her to an elite Cairene household. The eighteenth-century chronicler 'Abd al-Rahman al-Jabarti as well as Shawikar's waqf reveal that while in Cairo, Shawikar became the favorite concubine of one of the most powerful amirs, 'Uthman Katkhuda al-Qazdughli. After he was killed in 1737 in one of the internecine struggles that characterized this period, his freed slave, Sulayman Jawish, seized his estate and Shawikar, whom he subsequently manumitted and made his legal wife. By the time she registered her waqf twenty-five years later, Sulayman was dead and Shawikar had remarried for the third time and was again the widow of an important military and political figure.

Shawikar's rise from slave-concubine to wealthy widow is attributable to a number of factors: her family sold her to a prominent household in which she became the concubine of a wealthy and powerful man; she possessed certain characteristics—such as political skills and shrewdness necessary for survival and success in a milieu noted for its bloody rivalries and ferocious in-fighting—that abetted her ascendance in status and wealth; and she was a woman living in a society in which women of all classes had the legal right to own property.[2]

Women's right to property is derived from the verse in the Qur'an quoted at the beginning of this essay. Muslims believe the Qur'an is the word of God as revealed to the prophet Muhammad and is one of the sources of Islamic law (*shari'a*). The revelation relating to women's property ownership is found in *sura* (chapter) IV, *aya* (verse) 7. Under the law, a woman has the right to own and manage her own property, to will it to her heirs after her death, and to endow it as waqf. The only legal restriction on women's property ownership is the same as that on men's:

the property of the deceased is subject to division according to the law. Females are entitled to half the share of males. Additionally, the law stipulates that a woman, not her family or husband, directly receives the *mahr* (dowry) and maintains control of it. After her marriage, a woman retains possession of her property, and neither spouse has a legal claim to or interest in the property of the other. A woman is not legally responsible or obligated to use her personal wealth or property to support her husband or family. Maintenance — providing food, clothing, and lodging — is the primary responsibility of the husband.

Shawikar's story, as sketchy and incomplete as it is, demonstrates vividly the ways in which property ownership empowered women. It also shows the advantages that women in early modern Islamic societies had when compared to most European and North American women during the eighteenth century. The property rights that women living under Islamic law exercised since the seventh century A.D. (first century A.H.) were not granted to women in Great Britain, the United States, or Canada until the passage of married women's property acts in the mid-nineteenth century. The property rights that Islamic law grants to women, the way women (such as Shawikar) exercised these rights to amass estates of considerable size, and the relationship between women's property ownership and their position in the household are the subject of this essay.

Fortunately for the field of women's history in Islamic societies, an abundance of primary documents is available to researchers searching for evidence of women's ownership, administration, and inheritance of property. Because women in Islamic societies have property rights and the shari'a recognizes women as legal persons, court records, especially the *waqfiyyat* (religious endowment deeds), form a particularly rich archival source for the study of Islamic women's history. The waqfiyyat provide the most comprehensive information about the women whose lives I am attempting to recover. They reveal such personal information about the donor as sexual and marital history, examine the relationships within a family and *bayt* (household), and give detail about the donor's property. When considered collectively, the waqfiyyat of eighteenth-century Egyptian women tell us much about how women amassed the property they endowed and how they used the waqf system to control and protect their property and to provide them with an income during their lifetime.

The relationship between elite women's property and their position within the household was crucial. Women's ownership, inheritance, and management of property as well as the importance of marriage alliances and concubinage enhanced a woman's status within the household, demonstrating that women were not peripheral members of the household, as they supplied cohesion, stability, and continuity that were crucial to its reproduction. Women's importance in eighteenth-century elite households is a corrective to the historiography of Ottoman Egypt, which has either ignored women entirely or considered them inconsequential or irrelevant to the household system of politics that dominated the period. Thus, a historical study that uses gender as its primary mode of analysis not only allows us to retrieve the historical experiences of women but also challenges us to revise our understanding of the Ottoman Egyptian household in several significant ways.

THE WAQF AS a way of protecting and passing down property is ideally suited to the neo-Mamluk system of Ottoman Egypt and to the economic needs of women. A waqf is the alienation of income-producing property in perpetuity to benefit, although not always immediately, a religious or pious cause. According to Islamic tradition, the idea of waqf can be traced to Abraham, who spent his wealth in acts of charity, including the construction of the foremost altar in Arabia, the Ka'ba at Mecca. However, the view Muslims most commonly hold is that waqf was unknown in pre-Islamic times but was instituted through the prophet Muhammad's authorization.[3]

Jurist Abu Yusuf (d. 798) formulated the legal doctrines related to waqf. He established the fundamental principle that a waqf was valid only if it were irrevocable and made in perpetuity, and developed the legal precedent that allowed the creation of the *ahli* (family waqf) in addition to the *waqf khayri* (pious waqf). The difference between the two is that the pious waqf immediately benefits religious institutions or such pious causes as providing bread to the poor, whereas a family waqf allows the donor to receive the income of the endowment during her lifetime and her heirs to receive it after her death. Once there are no more heirs of the donor to claim an income from the waqf, the revenues the property generated revert to the religious or pious causes the donor stipulated. The family waqf also allows the donor to name herself the administrator (*nadir*) of her waqf, giving her control of the endowment.

Although Islamic law guarantees women's right to own property, the waqf gives additional legal sanction and protection to women's property ownership and control because Islamic law regulates it and it comes under Islamic court authority. Alienating property in waqf has short-term and long-term benefits for both women and men. The donor of an endowment can alienate her entire estate and is not limited to one-third, the maximum allowed for legacies or testamentary gifts. This permits the donor to designate heirs to the income of the waqf after her death without regard to Islamic law, which stipulates how the estate of a deceased Muslim should be divided and apportions a greater share to males. In addition, property endowed in this manner is not subject to taxation.

The pattern that emerges from a reading of eighteenth-century women's waqfiyyat is that most women founded family waqf and named themselves the beneficiaries of the income from their waqf during their lifetime and administrators of their own waqf. Thus, women used the endowment system as a court-sanctioned trust fund from which they derived an income and over which they exerted control. By endowing a waqf, women were able to safeguard their property from predatory relatives, benefit from its income during their lifetime, ensure their right to manage it, and pass it on to their designated heirs. But women were also members of their society and were making waqf for reasons linked not only to their gender but also to their class and in response to the social and economic conditions of the time. Like men, they undoubtedly saw the institution of the waqf as a way to protect and pass on property during a particularly tumultuous period in Egyptian history.

THE RECORDS OF the Ministry of Awqaf (waqf) show a total of 3,316 entries related to waqf cases during the entire Ottoman period. The ministry's index includes various transactions associated with waqf, including additions, deletions, and changes, as well as the establishment of new waqf. However, the ministry's index records only those waqfiyyat housed in its archives. Additional waqfiyyat as well as records of transactions involved in the establishment of a waqf can be found in other collections, including the national archives, the Dar al-Watha'iq al-Qawmiyya.

The ministry's index lists 496 new waqf founded in the eighteenth century, which 393 men and 126 women endowed.[4] That women founded approximately 25 percent of these waqf is consistent with results other researchers obtained for both the Arab provinces and Anatolia during the Ottoman period.[5] Of the women's waqf of eighteenth-century Cairo, ninety-seven were established by women individually, seven with other women, sixteen with husbands or male relatives, and six with unrelated men. Of the waqf founded by men and women together, fourteen were established by husbands and wives; one by a woman, her husband, and her brother; and one by a mother and her son. One male and three female freed slaves, fifteen amirs and two female freed slaves, and a woman and her guardian founded three of the waqf by unrelated men and women.

The kind of property women endowed can be described broadly as urban commercial, residential, and agricultural, and included shops, workshops, warehouses, living units in apartment houses, tenements or apartments often found over wakala, as well as mills, waterwheels, watering troughs, springs, courtyards, gardens, coffeehouses, a public bath, and productive agricultural land. In short, women owned and endowed all manner of income-producing property, including an enterprise where the bodies of dead Muslims were prepared for burial.[6]

The most problematic investment from the perspective of the historian is the *makan*, another kind of property women endowed, which means "place, site, spot, [or] location."[7] Although we cannot be certain of the value of a makan because of the ambiguous meaning of the term itself, we do know that women who endowed them were well-off because they represented a quarter of a middling merchant's estate.[8] My analysis of the Egyptian waqf shows that the majority of women's waqf (56 percent) were either middling or large, having multiple assets, while a minority (44 percent) had only one or a share in one unit of property. Occasionally, that asset was a *manzil* or *dar* (a dwelling); infrequently, it was a shop; most often, it was a makan. More women endowed all or part of one or more makan — 60 out of 104 women — than any other type of property. For the majority of women (more than 75 percent), a makan was among a number of properties endowed; fewer than a quarter of the women surveyed owned only a single makan or a unit in a *rab'* (tenement or apartment).

The waqf of eighteenth-century women exhibit a pattern very different from the one Carl Petry discerned of medieval women.[9] As shown above, women acting as individuals, not in partnership with spouses, male relatives, or immediate families, established the vast majority of women's endowments in the eighteenth century using the property they had accumulated. Waqfiyyat clearly show that women owned the property endowed. Additionally, the stipulations that they made ensured their right to manage and benefit from the waqf they created by naming themselves the administrator of their own endowment and the beneficiary of the income. Rather than seeing autonomous economic behavior as a Western phenomenon, as Petry does, we should locate the difference between elite women of the medieval and Ottoman periods in the political, economic, and social changes that took place during the transition from independent sultanate to imperial province.

TO EVALUATE THE property ownership of these women and to assess their economic activity, it is necessary to consider them in the context of the eighteenth-century Egyptian economy. Egypt was the hub of a network of long-distance trading routes extending into Asia, Africa, and Europe. In its commercial economy, the largest fortunes were made in trading coffee, spices, and textiles. Textile production and export was of secondary importance, although its production was the most important artisanal activity of the eighteenth century. Thus, women who invested their capital in wakala, *khan* (similar to a *wakala*), rab', warehouses, and shops of various kinds behaved like rational economic actors in the context of the trade economy and in the ways available to men and women to invest their capital productively.

Given Egypt's position as an entrepôt in the international transit trade, one of the foundation stones of the country's economy was the wakala, which served three purposes: warehouse, retail sales, and residence. On the ground floor were the warehouses, where owners stored goods before redistribution inside the country or reexportation outside of Egypt, shops for retail sales, or artisanal workshops. The residential units, which owners rented to merchants, looked out over the interior courtyard (*hawsh*) from the upper floors. The value of a wakala depended on its size and location. The price of the property could surpass 1 million *paras*, a sum that significantly exceeded the value of any other economic investment in Cairo.

Besides the makan, shops, and land, more women endowed all or part of a wakala than any other kind of property. Thus, women not only owned the most lucrative property but also, as owners, managed an investment of considerable complexity. Owners rented the various units of a wakala to merchants, shopkeepers, and artisans. Of the eleven women investing in wakala, five owned the entire property and six endowed shares in it. Five of the women endowed all or part of the rab' on top of the wakala. For one of the women, the structure was the only property endowed in her waqf, and for another woman, her waqf consisted entirely of shares in a wakala. For the other nine, the wakala was only one of several properties they owned and endowed.

Women invested in the same mix of urban commercial real estate as merchants. In 1755, for example, 'A'isha Hanim, daughter of the amir Radwan Agha, endowed all of a wakala in Bulaq in addition to water-wheels, a baking oven, a mill, and an unspecified number of makan.[10] Zaynab Khatun, freed slave of the deceased amir Ismatil Bey, endowed considerable property, including three wakala, a courtyard, a workshop for the making and selling of bread, a one-quarter share in a shop, a coffee-house, four makan, and two shops. The makan she owned were in two of the most prestigious neighborhoods in Cairo: one on the east bank of Elephant Lake (*birkat al-fil*), inhabited only by beys (high-ranking Mamluks), and the other west of the city's main canal, a residential district for Mamluks of middle rank.[11] These examples show that the women buying, selling, and endowing property were making two decisions: first, to invest their capital, and, second, to invest it in lucrative income-producing properties. Both decisions indicate that women understood the economy and through their investments and endowments were active participants in it.

THE POSITION OF elite women in eighteenth-century Egyptian society is attributable not only to Islamic law, which gave women property rights, but also to the system of household politics, which gave women status as wives and/or concubines as well as certain avenues for achieving and enhancing their autonomy, influence, and power. Historically, elite women have benefited from the fact that power was located in households rather than in the more formal mechanisms and structures of the centralized, bureaucratic state. In eighteenth-century Egypt, there was a state, the Ottoman, that increasingly had become unable to exercise authority so that real power became lodged in the households of the Mamluk grandees. Since the last quarter of the seventeenth century, the resurgent Mamluks successfully had challenged Ottoman control of Egypt.

The Mamluk revival began among the beys, who took control of the major positions in the Ottoman hierarchy, such as the amir of the annual pilgrimage to Mecca and the vice governor, as well as the lucrative tax farms. The *ojaqs* (military corps), which the Ottomans created after the conquest to provide security and protect Ottoman interests in the country, controlled the urban tax farms, including the customs houses. Eventually, the beylicate absorbed the military corps, giving the beys command of the regiments as well as most of Egypt's revenues. As Ottoman power waned, Mamluk rivalry became increasingly acute as their households and factions fought each other and the representatives of the Ottoman state for control of Egypt's wealth. Capturing the revenues of the country was crucial to the power and success of a household, as they were necessary to purchase Mamluks and to support an entourage of Mamluks and manumitted Mamluks who fought other households for dominance and the forces of the Ottoman administration.

In the second half of the eighteenth century, one household, the Qazdughli, and its most powerful leader, 'Ali Bey al-Kabir, consolidated power by the ruthless suppression of his rivals. The dominance of the Qazdughli beys did not bring the internecine struggles to an end. These continued under 'Ali Bey's successors after his death in 1773 until Napoleon's invasion in 1798, which took Egypt into a new phase in its political history.

Women were caught up in the political maelstrom of the times, as illustrated in this incident recounted by the foremost chronicler of the period, al-Jabarti. It occurred when 'Ali Bey al-Kabir, in a purge of his rivals, ordered 'Abd al-Rahman, the *agha* (highest-ranking officer) of the Janissaries (a military corps), to put to death Isma'il Agha, an officer who had been exiled to Lower Egypt but had returned to his house in Cairo:

> When he [Isma'il Agha] saw 'Abd al-Rahman and his entourage in front of his house, he knew he had come to kill him, and he refused to show himself and closed the door of his house. 'Abd al-Rahman began to shoot. Isma'il Agha had only a musket and a rifle and with him only his Turkish concubine. She fired one of the two guns while he used the other. The fight lasted two days. Many of the men of 'Abd al-Rahman fell, struck by Isma'il's bullets. Finally, he ceased firing on his enemies: his powder and his shot were gone. 'Abd al-Rahman promised him safety. Having faith in this promise, he descended the stairs, but one of his enemies ambushed him there and ran him through with a saber. All the others fell on Isma'il and decapitated him.[12]

Al-Jabarti does not relate what happened to Isma'il's concubine. However, this incident demonstrates how the Mamluk resurgence, characterized by factionalism, rivalries, and internecine conflicts, periodically pitted household against household and master against Mamluk in armed combat.

IN ADDITION TO their endemic instability, another similarity between the classic Mamluk and neo-Mamluk system is their slave origins. In Arabic, Mamluk means slave. The system of enslaving non-Muslim men, training them for service in the military or the state administration, and then manumitting them goes back to the Abbasid period and Caliph al-Mutasim (833–842), who began to recruit mainly animist Turks from the Central Asian steppe as soldiers for his army. This form of slavery has sometimes been called "oriental slavery" to distinguish it from the plantation-based, agricultural slavery of the West.

As Mamluks, young boys underwent military training as well as schooling in language, literacy, and administrative skills, which would equip them to occupy the highest military and bureaucratic posts. After they completed their training and converted to Islam, they would be manumitted and assigned to a post in the ruler's service. In fact, a Mamluk's service as a soldier in an elite unit or as an imperial guard was an enviable first step in a career that opened to him the highest state offices.

While scholars have focused primarily on the young men who were bought and trained as military slaves for the Mamluk households during the classical and neo-Mamluk periods, they have paid scant attention to women who, not surprisingly, were enslaved as well. We know substantial information about the training male slaves received, the positions they occupied in the state administration and the military, and the salaries and allowances they received, but we know much less about the fate of the women after their arrival in Cairo. Although we know women were destined to become concubines and wives of the Mamluks, we are not aware of the kind of training they received in the households that acquired them.

The female elite in eighteenth-century Mamluk households are immediately recognizable as slaves or former slaves by their names, such as Al-Sitt Mahbuba Khatun bint 'Abd Allah al-Bayda ma'tuqat mawlana al-Amir Ibrahim Bey al-Kabir wa zawjat Ismatil Bey Kashif mattuq Ibrahim Bey al-Kabir (Lady Mahbuba Khatun, daughter of the servant of Allah, the White, freed slave of the esteemed Amir Ibrahim Bey and wife of Isma'il Bey, the freed slave of Ibrahim Bey).[13] The patronymic Bins 'Abd Allah, which female slaves used after their conversion to Islam because they did not have a Muslim father, identifies Mahbuba Khatun as a former slave-concubine. Mahbuba's name also reveals that her master was the amir Ibrahim Bey, that he manumitted her, and that she was the wife of one of his freed slaves, Isma'il Bey. The words "al-Bayda" or "the White" identify her as a Caucasian.

The slaves of the neo-Mamluk period came primarily from Georgia. A stipulation from the waqf of Khadiga Qadin Bint Abd Allah, freed slave and wife of the amir Ahmad Katkhuda of the Janissaries and the Qazdughli household, shows that Mamluks shared an ethnic identity and consciousness that contributed to the cohesion of the household in a perilously unstable system.[14] Khadiga stipulated that the administrator of her deceased husband's waqf go to Georgia and purchase a female slave of Georgian nationality who would become the administrator of Khadiga's own waqf after her death. Khadiga specified the character traits and behavior that the woman had to exhibit: she had to be honorable and conduct herself properly in religious practice and in everyday life. If the woman displayed these characteristics, Khadiga stipulated, then the administrator who purchased her had to manumit and marry her. If, on the other hand, the slave showed any character defects, she was to be sold or, if married, driven away. This story illuminates the importance of ethnicity and marriage in the creation of strong bonds among the members of a household. Belonging to a household as a slave or client did not ensure loyalty and fidelity; the link was stronger if there were shared ethnicity and marital ties.

SCHOLARS GENERALLY HAVE overlooked the importance of marital and nonmarital (concubinage) alliances to the cohesion, continuity, and stability of the neo-Mamluk system. Instead, they have focused on the factors contributing to its instability and tendency to fragmentation.[15] The death of 'Uthman Katkhuda, the master of Shawikar Qadin, is an example of the fierce and bloody struggles that marked the period. In this incident, a request by a provincial governor to be elevated to the rank of bey led to a murder plot which resulted in the deaths of eleven high-ranking amirs, including 'Uthman Katkhuda. But this concentration on instability, factionalism, and violence in the historiography of Ottoman Egypt overlooks the roles women played in households and the various ways they contributed to its cohesion, stability, and continuity. Marital and nonmarital unions strengthened the links among men; women legitimized the succession of men to power, and women's property ownership added to the overall wealth, prestige, and power of a household. The integration of women into the history of the household and the Mamluk system reveal the countervailing forces that acted to mitigate the tendency toward fragmentation and instability and, thus, the crucial role women played in this process.

On one level, marriage served to strengthen links between men, thereby making the household more cohesive. It was common for a master or head of household to intensify ties between himself and a manumitted Mamluk by arranging a marriage between his Mamluk and one of his female slaves. Such was the case with the amir Ibrahim Bey, cited above, who undoubtedly arranged the marriage of his freed slaves Mahbuba Khatun and Isma'il Kashif.

On another level, marriage served as an instrument of political legitimacy for the resurgent Mamluks. Shawikar's life illustrates this point. Following 'Uthman's murder, Sulayman Jawish, his freed slave, seized his former master's estate from the designated heir, 'Abd al-Rahman Jawish, the son of 'Uthman's former master, Hasan Jawish.[16] After seizing the estate, Sulayman manumitted and married Shawikar. Subsequently, Sulayman became *sirdar* (commander) of the troops guarding the pilgrimage caravan to Mecca. Accompanying him was his wife, Shawikar. En route to Mecca, he died, possibly from syphilis. Immediately after his death, the highest-ranking Mamluk officer designated 'Abd al-Rahman Jawish the heir to the deceased and turned over to him the keys, trunks, boxes, and pavilion that were part of the trappings of office. 'Abd al-Rahman also inherited Sulayman's tax farms and married Shawikar.

Shawikar's concubinage and marriages show how women added an important element of continuity to a household and the neo-Mamluk system generally. By the time Shawikar registered her waqfiyyat, she had been married and widowed at least three times, the last to Ibrahim Katkhuda al-Qazdughli (d. 1754), regarded as the architect of Qazdughli ascendance to power. Shawikar's life spanned three generations of Qazdughli leaders and encompassed the household's rise to prominence and domination. As the concubine of 'Uthman and wife of Sulayman and 'Abd al-Rahman, she was connected to the founders of the Qazdughli household, Mustafa Katkhuda and Hasan. As the widow of Ibrahim Katkhuda, she served as a link between the founding generation of the Qazdughlis and the third generation, represented by 'Ali Bey al-Kabir, Ibrahim's favorite Mamluk, who built on the foundation laid by his master to consolidate Qazdughli power. Thus Shawikar, similar to other

Mamluk women, through longevity and marriages provided important elements of cohesion and continuity within the household.

Because of their need to legitimize themselves as well as to provide continuity and cohesion within the household, the neo-Mamluk grandees, unlike their predecessors of the medieval period, did not allow their women to become dowagers. Petry describes medieval women as "living symbols of stability who might survive several generations of men cut down in their prime" and who often presided over their houses as dowagers.[17] Such women as Shawikar also became living symbols of lineage continuity but did not remain widows very long. As her life illustrates, when a Mamluk grandee died, his successor seized or inherited not only his predecessor's rank and title but also his widow.

THE INSTABILITY OF the neo-Mamluk period created a paradoxical situation for women. On the one hand, the political importance of marriage deprived women of autonomy in the marital and sexual spheres. The weight of the evidence suggests that women had little choice in the matter of whom or whether to marry. But the importance of marriage alliances and women's role in legitimizing the succession of men to power enhanced women's position in the household. In addition, a woman's rank, status, and access to wealth derived from her membership in a Mamluk household and her relationship to a Mamluk grandee. Thus, she may have been reluctant to decline marital unions that would maintain or enhance her status and power.

In the economic realm, on the other hand, women possessed a great deal of autonomy. As their waqfiyyat demonstrate, they used their position in rich and powerful households and access to wealth to accumulate assets independently of their husbands or male relatives. Indeed, women utilized the waqf institution as a court-supervised trust to secure an income for themselves during their lifetime, as well as to ensure their right to manage their own property.

Women had more autonomy in the economic than in the sexual or marital realm. A woman's sexual autonomy could have been more of a threat to the household than her economic activity. For example, if a household's political strategy dictated a certain marriage or if a woman's remarriage would have taken her and the property she owned or controlled out of the household and into a rival's, her independence in the sexual/marital sphere potentially would have posed a threat to the house-hold's stability. However, a woman's ownership of property or management of another's property as an administrator would add to the house-hold's overall wealth and power.

In addition, women's property ownership did not threaten male control of the major sources of revenue, primarily the urban and rural tax farms and salaries for the soldiers in the military garrisons. Under the medieval Mamluk sultanate, the sultan granted land to his followers in feudal tenure as *iqta'*. The Ottomans abolished this form of land tenure after their conquest of Egypt and eventually replaced it with tax farms. The Mamluk resurgence in the late seventeenth century was based not only on the beys capturing the major posts in the Ottoman administration, but also on their taking control of the rural and urban tax farms and placing their manumitted slaves into the military corps. Thus, beys took the tax revenues that were supposed to pay the salaries of Ottoman administrators and soldiers in Egypt and to fill the Ottoman treasury in Istanbul and used them to finance the Mamluk revival.

Manumitted male slaves received salaries on the basis of their rank in the Mamluk hierarchy. To be a Mamluk meant to be a man, specifically a manumitted male slave. In the sources, the word Mamluk is not used to describe a woman. She is either a *jariyya* (slave-concubine), *ma'tuqa* (freed slave), or *zawja* (wife). The property available to women, as well as merchants and all non-Mamluks, for purchase was urban commercial and residential real estate or agricultural land that was not tax farmed.

The property rights and economic autonomy of women allowed them to purchase not only the kinds of urban real estate and agricultural land they endowed as waqf but also male and female slaves. Evidence of women's ownership of slaves comes from the chronicles of the period and also women's waqfiyyat; it was customary for them to name their slaves among the heirs to their waqf income. I have already shown how Khadija Qadin stipulated the purchase of a female slave, who would become her waqf administrator after her death, and set aside money in her endowment for that purpose. However, women purchased slaves not just to fill certain positions in their households. They also constructed patronage networks of their own that paralleled the ones men created.

In his obituary of Jalila Khatun, al-Jabarti observed that "most of the women of the amirs were among her slaves."[18] Women similar to Jalila Khatun placed their freed slaves in Mamluk elite households and arranged their marriages. As a patroness, a woman had a continuing claim to the loyalty of her former slaves. Women at the head of a network of freed slaves enhanced their standing in their own households in part because they were privy to information their former slaves relayed to them about their current husband or master. Thus, the patroness could inform her husband about activities in various households and could use her information to arrange marriages that would expand her own influence as well as the power of her husband's household.

Keeping in mind the coercive nature of slavery, even in its more benign "oriental" form, women could and did use their position in the household and their wealth to benefit their freed female slaves. In addition to naming them as heirs to waqf income or employing them in their household administration, women named freed slaves as administrators of their waqf. Shawikar, for example, stipulated that after her death, her children and then her grandchildren should assume the post and after their deaths, her freed slave, Mahbuba Bint 'Abd Allah al-Bayda. A note in the margin of the waqf deed shows that Mahbuba eventually did assume this post, acting as the administrator in the legal exchange of a piece of property from Shawikar's waqf. Shawikar's waqfiyyat provides the additional evidence that women used waqf to enrich and empower other women and that women, in addition to founding waqf, had administrative authority over them.

FROM 1777 TO 1778, the French traveler C. S. Sonnini visited Egypt, and in his travel journal, published two years later, he described the harem of a bey "taking an airing," accompanied by a eunuch "of a mean but fierce countenance." Sonnini wrote: "It is to be presumed that this was the cavalcade of beauty. But these charmers were masked with thick veils, and so wrapped up in various kinds of drapery, that neither feature nor form could be seen of any one of them, and they appeared only like so many shapeless figures."[19] The Comte de Volney, who visited Egypt a couple of years before Sonnini, described the women of the Mamluks as "rigorously sequestered from the society of men. Always closed up in their house, they communicate only with their husbands, their father, the brother and their first cousins; carefully veiled in the streets, scarcely daring to speak to a man, even about business. All must be strangers to them: It would be indecent to look at them and one must let them pass as if they were contagious." Volney betrays his ignorance of Islam and Egyptian society by claiming that the degraded condition of women was due to the Qur'an, which "does not do them the honor of treating them as part of the human species." He also blamed the government for depriving women of all property and personal liberty, making them dependent on a husband or father, which Volney calls "slavery."[20]

Presenting a distorted and one-sided picture of "oriental" women, this common and remarkably tenacious view was propagated by the predominantly male travelers to Turkey, the Levant, Egypt, and North Africa in the eighteenth century. It emphasized the sexual sphere by portraying the harem as a virtual prison where masters or husbands kept women to satisfy their voracious sexual appetites. At the same time, it ignored or misrepresented the rights women had and exercised in the economic sphere.

As I have shown, the sexual and marital autonomy of elite women was constrained in order to create the marriage alliances that were crucial to the survival and reproduction of the neo-Mamluk system and to enhance its political legitimacy. However, the harem was not a prison; it was instead the family quarters of an upper-class home which became exclusively female space when men not related to the women were in the house and whose entry into the harem was forbidden. Women, heavily veiled, could and did leave their home. They visited the tombs of their dead on Fridays, visited the baths, and regularly were entertained in the homes of other women, especially on occasions such as the birth of a child. Also, women were present at such public, ceremonial occasions as the opening of the main Cairo canal at the peak of the annual Nile flood or accompanying a bride through the streets to her new husband's home. Women were not imprisoned in the harem or in the veils and cloaks that concealed their bodies and faces on the street, but both customs were important signifiers of women's lack of sexual autonomy and of men's control over the selection of women's sexual and marital partners.

In the economic sphere, however, women had a great deal of autonomy. Islamic law grants women property rights and acknowledges women as legal persons, allowing them to be party to a contract, a necessary precondition for the exercise of property rights. Legally empowered, women could buy and sell property, make a will, or endow a waqf. The waqfiyyat of the eighteenth century provides evidence of women's independent economic activity and the accumulation of assets that in some cases rivaled the estates of the wealthiest merchants.

Therefore, the eighteenth-century Egyptian household should be seen not as the site of unrelieved oppression of women but in terms of asymmetries of power between men and women. Michele Rosaldo argued almost twenty years ago that although sexual asymmetry is universal, its form is context-dependent. Scholarship, by examining context, must determine how gender acquires meaning through concrete social interactions. Eighteenth-century Mamluks maintained gender hierarchy in several ways: by making military training and service, from which they excluded women, the primary path to power; by maintaining male control over the most lucrative sources of wealth; and by controlling female sexual autonomy and directing female sexuality toward approved marital unions. Women, however, could and did exercise agency through their legal right to own property. This allowed them to amass estates of income-producing urban and commercial real estate as well as agricultural land, and through their purchase and manumission of slaves to create a network of clients that strengthened their position in the household.

Notes

1. Waqf no. 921, Ministry of Awqaf, Cairo.

2. John Esposito, *Women in Muslim Law* (Syracuse: Syracuse University Press, 1982).

3. John Robert Barnes, *An Introduction to Religious Foundations in the Ottoman Empire* (Leiden: E.J. Brill, 1986).

4. There are a total of 519 donors and only 493 waqf because some waqf have multiple donors.

5. Gabriel Baer, "Women and *Waqf*: An Analysis of the Istanbul Tahrir of 1546," *Asian and African Studies* 17 (1983): 9–28; Haim Gerber, "The *Waqf* Institution in Early Ottoman Edirne," *Asian and African Studies* 17 (1983): 29–45.

6. Waqf no. 2238, Ministry of Awqaf.

7. Hans Wehr, *A Dictionary of Modern Written Arabic*, ed. J. Milton Cowan (Beirut: Librarie du liban, 1980), 847.

8. Andre Raymond, *Artisans et Commerçants au Caire au XVIIIe Siècle*, 2 vols. (Damascus: Institut Français de Damas).

9. Carl F. Petry, "Class Solidarity versus Gender Gain: Women as Custodians of Property in Later Medieval Egypt," in *Women in Middle East History: Shifting Boundaries in Sex and Gender*, ed. Nikki R. Keddie and Beth Baron (New Haven: Yale University Press, 1991), 133–134.

10. Waqf no. 2441, Ministry of Awqaf.

11. Waqf no. 509, Ministry of Awqaf.

12. 'Abd al-Rahman al-Jabarti, *'Aja'ib al-Athar fi al-Tarajim wa al-Akhbar* (Cairo: Lajnat al-Bayan al-Arabi, 1959), 2: 390.

13. Waqf no. 3131, Ministry of Awqaf.

14. Waqf no. 134, Ministry of Awqaf.

15. For example, Michael Winter, *Egyptian Society under Ottoman Rule, 1517–1798* (London: Routledge, 1992).

16. Al-Jabarti, *'Aja'ib al-Athar*, 2: 57–58.

17. Petry, "Class Solidarity," 125.

18. Al-Jabarti, *'Aja'ib al-Athar*, 1: 382; translation by Mary Ann Fay.

19. C. S. Sonnini, *Travels in Upper and Lower Egypt* (1800; reprint, London: Gregg International Publishers, 1972), 451–452.

20. Constantin Francois Chasseboeuf and Comte de Volney, *Voyage en Syrie et en Égypte pendant les anneés 1783, 1784, 1785* (Paris: Chez Dugour et Durand, 1799), 95, 441–442; my translation.

Adele Perry

Reproducing Colonialism in

British Columbia, 1849–1871

Within settler colonies, which were based on the occupation of land alienated from indigenous peoples, reproduction was central to the construction and maintenance of imperial authority. Demographic change, gender ratios, and the relative size of white and nonwhite populations worried colonial administrators and theorists of colonization, such as Edward Gibbon Wakefield, who elaborated complex schemes that aimed to create stable and prosperous colonies that improved on inherited European social structures. In many colonies, however, including the case of British Columbia explored here, interracial relationships were common during the early stages of colonialism and hybrid communities flourished. This essay examines the prominent place of mixed-race families in the development of the colony and the ways local realities subverted idealized visions of empire building propagated in the distant imperial center.

The nineteenth-century British empire was a mire of contradictions. It promised to transform indigenous people into modern citizens and indigenous peoples into modern nations but delivered what John Comaroff calls a "racinated world of ethnic subjection."[1] It spoke of the unity of all that was British, but produced and managed, with varying degrees of success, a set of overlapping, many-leveled hierarchies that ranked and arranged natives, settlers, nations, citizens, colonies, and subjects. The preponderance of metaphors of family in discourses of empire reflects an obvious attempt to manage these contradictions by linking them to an institution that was not only ubiquitous but presumed to be simultaneously — and, not incidentally, justly — hierarchical and communal. The colony of British Columbia, explained its governor in 1859, was "the youngest child" of a "Mother country."[2] This logic, like so much else, could be easily turned back on its purveyors. Children, after all, eventually become adults, and colonials demanded to be citizens and colonies to be nations.

The contradictions inherent in empire and the inability of familial and developmental metaphors to effectively manage them evoke some of the connections between reproduction and the local colonial state that this essay reckons with. The subject is the state of empire in one local colonial context: British Columbia between the years 1849 and 1871. Here, Britain repeatedly and ultimately unsuccessfully struggled to create and sustain a state that matched its expectations of the sort of government fitted to a white settler colony. These plans were disturbed by, among other things, the very process of their implementation.

British Columbia was the product of three sometimes conflicting manifestations of mid-nineteenth-century colonialism: the fur trade, the gold rush, and the British tradition of settler colonies. North America's northern Pacific Coast and Columbia Plateau were densely populated by linguistically, culturally, and politically diverse aboriginal peoples — now, in contemporary Canadian public discourse, self-identified as First Nations — reliant on various combinations of foraging, hunting, and fishing. Eighteenth-century exploration, trade, and reportage put Vancouver Island within the orbit of European imagining and geopolitics.[3] Such activity and representation laid the framework for the establishment of formal colonial authority in 1849, when Vancouver Island was made a British colony.

LONDON INTENDED THAT this colony — and the various colonies that followed it — be settler colonies. One observer summarized Vancouver Island's imperial mission by saying it was to become "a Settlement of resident Colonists, emigrants from the United Kingdom or other British Dominions."[4] This was an apt enough summary of the idealized vision of this and other British settler colonies: colonists and residents are one and the same, they are British, or at least from other settler colonies, and, most telling of all, aboriginal people's presence is categorically negated.

Settler colonies were distinguished by their exact method of dispossession, which tended to focus on alienating aboriginal land instead of appropriating aboriginal labor. They were also marked by what we might see as their particular reproductive regimes. Most colonies had admittedly small and overwhelmingly male imperial populations that were reproduced largely through migration, whether voluntary or forced. Children born of relationships between migrant men and local women wore away at the distinction between settlers and natives, and for that, this "unofficial reproduction" was increasingly regulated during the nineteenth century.[5] Settler colonies, on the other hand, aspired to large colonial populations reproduced locally, preferably by European women. In settler colonies, the politics of what Anna Davin so aptly labeled imperial motherhood was thus central and, indeed, literal.[6]

The continuing scarcity of European women and the continuing presence of mixed-race relations and children suggested how settler colonies' reproductive politics produced their own contradictions. Rather than construct and appropriate indigenous structures, the state worked to deny their existence by deeming territory *terra nullus* and / or extinguishing aboriginal title through treaties. Rather than administering "native tradition," the settler state worked to recreate the institutions of metropolitan Britain, including offering limited manhood franchise and, to a greater or lesser extent, parliamentary institutions. This recreation was never strictly literal, and settlers would bristle at Britain's unwillingness to accord them the full rights and privileges promised to European men by discourses of citizenship. The state valorized colonial residents of European descent as whites and colonizers, but failed to fully deliver on the promises this identity conferred. Aboriginal peoples, for their part, refused to disappear, and their continuing presence was an even stronger indictment of the settler colony's implicit promise to remake England anew.

Thus, a number of profound and vexing contradictions lay at the heart of the settler colony's project. Its settlers had to be white, but could not really be so. Its native people supposedly did not exist, but obviously did. The settler population was supposed to reproduce itself, but often created hybrid local populations instead. These contradistinctions played out in a particular way in mid-nineteenth-century British Columbia, as they did in other settler colonies. Britain colonized Vancouver Island in spite of its declining interest in North America, and disinterest would characterize its formal and informal relationships with the colony. London wanted a political and military foothold on the west coast of North America but wanted it on the cheap. It initially tried to achieve this by granting the Hudson's Bay Company (HBC) proprietorial rights to the Island, as they had done previously in the Caribbean. In exchange for exclusive trading privileges, the fur trade company promised to fund and coordinate European settlement. The HBC looked to the ideas of colonial theorist Edward Gibbon Wakefield to do so. Colonies troubled Britain's claims to a monopoly on social truths by presenting examples of life lived differently. Wakefield's response was to devise schemes to reassert British social organization in unfamiliar soil. Property and marriage were two important tools. Wakefield argued that relatively expensive land prices would create a landless proletariat and mandatory marriage would ensure that "each female would have a special protector from the moment of her departure from home" and "no man would have an excuse for dissolute habits."[7] The HBC followed some of this advice by adopting relatively expensive land prices (£1 an acre) in an effort to deflect poorer migrants into the local labor pool and by requiring purchasers of one hundred or more acres of land to "take out with them five single men, or three married couples, for every hundred acres."[8] In these ways they worked to create a settler colony in northern North America that recreated the central fractures and divisions of the metropole.

The HBC's efforts to reconstitute norms of gender and the family were sundered both by the prevailing patterns of migration and labor and by local practices of sexuality and domesticity. The European population remained small and, visions of happy families aside, overwhelmingly male. When a census was taken in 1855, there were 265 settler women to 509 settler men. This small settler population was dwarfed by roughly 25,873 aboriginal people.[9] European men continued, as they had from the outset of the fur trade, to form relationships with local women. In 1851, naval official Fairfax Moresby suggested that the HBC import married rather than single servants from Britain, as "single men scattered amongst an Indian population will cause results not necessary to dilate on."[10] Efforts to recreate British class relations through high property prices were premised on the presence of agricultural land, a steady flow of wealthy migrants, and the presence of landless workers willing to do wage work, three factors that did not prevail on Vancouver Island. Walter Colquhoun Grant wrote that the biggest difficulty facing the settlers who, like him, were not connected to the HBC was the difficulty retaining white labor, or as he put it, "securing the services of the rascals." Grant, like other Island farmers, relied on the labor of aboriginal women and men instead, whom he found willing to "work for a week for the remuneration of 'A shirt,' an article which they prize more than all European Gold and Silver."[11] White labor, more than being expensive, possessed the dangerous ability to use the language of race and rights in their own interests. Andrew Muir, a Scottish collier, revolted against the HBC and was put in irons for his trouble. "In a British Colony Governed by English laws," he wrote, "it is a disgrace to talk of slavery being abolished here it reigns in full force."[12]

The HBC's stewardship was deemed a failure by critics who argued that the fur trade company was a private enterprise with little or no interest in colonizing the Island, and perhaps specific interests in failing to do so. Critics painted the HBC as refusing to adequately embrace the proper and presumably noble mission of Britain overseas. Colonization should be motivated by a higher racial calling, but the HBC was self-interested and arbitrary. Imperialism should create and foster racial separation and hierarchy, yet the HBC did the opposite by depending heavily on aboriginal labor and allowing its servants and officers alike to form families with aboriginal women. Instead of supplanting aboriginal society and economy with European, they were creating dangerous hybrids. Creolization was a sign of imperial administration gone awry, and for this and related sins the HBC grant was revoked in 1859.

The specific form of British Columbia's colonial project shifted in response to the perceived failure of the HBC and to new imperial opportunities. Britain's civil authority on Vancouver Island was shored up throughout the mid-nineteenth century, and between 1849 and 1863 the colony acquired all the constitutional mechanisms usually accorded settler colonies, namely, a governor and a bicameral legislature. The discovery of gold on the mainland's Fraser River in 1857 fundamentally shifted the character and form of British Columbia's colonial project. It precipitated the creation of a massive mainland colony called British Columbia. This was, according to imperial opinion, destined to be a major colony of settlement. "Never did a colony in its infancy present a more satisfactory appearance," remarked one Anglican cleric. But, by the mid-1860s, "those who once entertained most extravagant expectations began to despond."[13] There were fewer than one thousand settlers in 1855 and only over ten thousand in 1871. White women remained a telling minority of between 5 and 35 percent of the settler population. Never did the settler population rival the aboriginal, which, despite massive depopulation caused by European disease and dispossession, likely hovered around the forty-five thousand mark in the early 1870s. Settlers were more than bodies. They defined the settler colony's project and indeed were, according to one governor, "the bone and sinew of the state."[14] What happened when a settler state had so few settlers to support it and be governed by it?

THE PROFOUND CONTRADICTIONS that lay at the heart of settler imperialism in British Columbia was literally personified in the experiences of its governors. Mark Francis's analysis suggests how colonial governors were expected to not only protect Britain's interests locally but to personify operative definitions of morality and leadership.[15] Catherine Hall's treatment of the controversy surrounding Governor Eyre's response to the Morant Bay uprising in Jamaica alerts us to the centrality of race and gender to colonial administration and suggests how debates about imperial governance were very much debates about the character of English middle-class masculinity.[16]

The definitions of bourgeois masculinity were difficult to sustain in local contexts. Richard Blanshard, Vancouver Island's first governor, lasted only seven unhappy months. An Oxford-educated barrister who had traveled widely through Britain's possessions in India and Honduras, Blanshard was a colonial administrator from central casting. His first posting to the new colony of Vancouver Island would prove a disappointment to both himself and London. He arrived in Victoria in the spring of 1850, a human symbol of Britain's reasserted authority over the territory. Such symbols were supposed to inspire earnest mimicry, but Blanshard merely seemed anomalous and more than a little sad. HBC physician and colonial politician John Sebastian Helmcken remembered that "Blanshard was really and truly a gentleman — with a military moustache and fine features — but he was out of place."[17]

Blanshard's prosaic mission was as troubled as his symbolic one. As governor, he was daunted by the extent to which the HBC not only rivaled but outmatched the imperial state's effective authority, by the small numbers of settlers, and by what he deemed the colony's poor prospects as an agricultural settlement. In effect, he suggested that Vancouver Island, with an overbearing merchant presence, a tiny European population, and a large aboriginal one, was hardly a settler colony at all. The Colonial Office staff deemed his performance "very uninspiring" and accepted his resignation in November 1850.[18]

Blanshard was unable to reconcile the vision of empire he was charged with enforcing with the local practice of colonialism on Vancouver Island. The Colonial Office responded to Blanshard's defection by appointing James Douglas governor. Douglas was the chief factor of the HBC, and by augmenting his considerable mercantile powers with those of the state the Colonial Office effectively admitted that the local, for the time being, had effectively trumped the metropolitan. As much as Blanshard represented the visions of empire nurtured and elaborated in the center, Douglas personified its refraction through diasporic colonial practice. Douglas was born in 1803 in Demerara, British Guiana, the son of a Scottish sugar merchant and a woman variously described as "creole" and "Free coloured," one of three children produced by an unchurched union that persisted after his father took a Scottish bride in a Christian ceremony.[19] Neither Douglas nor his brother would inherit their father's sugar interest, but they would receive a "place," although in another, suitably distant outpost of empire. After receiving a basic education in Scotland, sixteen-year-old Douglas was apprenticed as a clerk to the North West Company, the Montreal-based fur trade operation.[20]

Douglas, the son of British imperialism in the Caribbean, would spend the rest of his life in northern North America. After violence and competition led to the merger of the HBC and the North West Company, Douglas worked for the HBC at various locations throughout the northwest. In 1828, while posted at Fort St. James, he married Amelia Connolly *à la façon du pays*, or by the custom of the country, the fur trade marriage rite that blended European and aboriginal tradition. Connolly's father was Douglas's direct superior and a British fur trader, and her mother was Cree. The Connolly-Douglas family was, by mid-nineteenth century, a penultimate example of how empire bred, literally and more figuratively, hybridity. It was also an example of how such hybridity could persist in the face of the nineteenth century's increasing commitment to racial classification, separation, and hierarchy. In a period when fur traders increasingly abandoned their aboriginal families in bids for upward mobility, Douglas bucked the trend: he and Amelia married by Anglican ceremony in 1837. Amelia bore thirteen children, of whom six survived. Douglas would cast a disapproving eye on his colleagues who abandoned their local families in pursuit of status.[21]

As governor, Douglas utilized local practices and power structures to maintain or advance Britain's claim to British Columbia. When gold was struck on the mainland in 1857, Douglas, acting quickly and without

Colonial Office permission, proclaimed British authority over the territory. London followed his lead and created the colony of British Columbia in 1858. Douglas was appointed governor of the new colony as well.
Local hagiography celebrates Douglas's upward mobility as a marker of
his exceptional, self-made character, but it was really a signal of the Colonial Office's willingness to work with practices of empire that departed so
substantially from dominant conventions of it. Correspondence between
London and British Columbia treats Douglas's familiarity with North
American languages and peoples as strengths rather than problems. Here,
the imperial state functioned not by supplanting indigenous society, as
the settler state promised to, but by working with it. In Douglas's estima-
tion, the primary role of the colonial state was to manage indigenous
people and serve as an intermediate between them and the politically
dubious settler population.

Douglas's administration represented the disciplining of empire to
local conditions to an extent that was perhaps unusual within the British empire. Creole governors were certainly an exception: by the mid-
nineteenth century the upper ranks of the colonial service had been essentially professionalized and drew almost entirely from the British gentry
and bourgeoisie.[22] Douglas's creole persona was obviously tolerated by
London, but not without reservation. In private conversation, Lord Bulwer Lytton, secretary of state for the colonies in 1858 and 1859, told
British Columbia's Anglican Bishop George Hills that "he appointed
Gov. Douglas on account of his great influence with the Indians yet
he received his dispatches with reserve."[23] The Colonial Office worked
hard—as best they could, given the six months it took to correspond
between London and Victoria—to school Douglas in the formal disciplines of imperial administration both big and small. They corrected the
manner in which he wrote his dispatches. They intervened when Douglas
committed especially outlandish acts of patronage, as when he appointed
his brother-in-law, a sugar estate administrator from Demerara with no
legal training, chief justice of the colony and worried about the number of
Douglas's sons-in-law appointed to the colonial service.[24] That Douglas
was knighted in 1863 suggests that, for London, the practical advantages
of what we might call creole administration outweighed such misgivings.
With his peerage, a man of African and Scottish heritage who had spent
the bulk of his life in North America became Sir James Douglas and his
half-Cree wife Lady Douglas.

Douglas's unavoidable hybridity meant different things in British Columbia than it did in London. The Douglas-Connolly family was not, of course, alone. They had obvious parallels with elite Eurasians in the Dutch and French empires and local equivalents in the handful of prominent fur trade families who possessed major land holdings around Victoria. In the British territories to the east, people of mixed aboriginal and European heritage would form a self-identified Métis nation rooted in economy, society, and, as the Red River Resistance of 1869 made clear, political grievance with Canada.[25] In British Columbia, racial formation took a different trajectory. Conjugal and domestic relationships between First Nations women and European men were crucial to the fur trade and remained significant into the settlement era. Yet they were not uncontested. In the 1860s, missionaries, journalists, colonial officials, and self-appointed do-gooders constructed mixed-race relationships as both indicative and constitutive of British Columbia's failure as a colonial society. Observers constructed First Nations women as threats to white men's racial identity and, via that, to colonial society as a whole. This discourse racialized and damned both European men and aboriginal women — the latter as "squaws" and the former as "squaw men" — for their violation of racial boundaries and gendered conventions. Reformers responded to the apparent threat of mixed-race relationships by working to reconfigure them along the lines of European marriages, laboring to discourage them altogether or, more radically, attempting to racially segregate urban, colonial space.[26]

Class privilege insulated the Douglas-Connolly family from the most violent manifestations of this changing racial politics, but it could not and did not spare them altogether. Early records make clear claims to Douglas's African heritage. George Simpson, governor of the HBC, called him "a Scotch West Indian" in 1832, and a decade later, Letitia Hargrave, the English wife of a fur trader, referred to Douglas as "a *mulatto* son of *the* renowned Mr Douglass of Glasgow."[27] Such racial designations ceased as Douglas rose in the HBC ranks and as local and global changes made it increasingly difficult to be simultaneously mixed-race and respectable. The Douglas-Connolly family dealt with this quandary in the obvious way: they constructed themselves as white. The Census of 1870 enumerated the entire family as "White," and later head counts rebaptized Amelia "Irish."[28] Agnes Douglas Bushby, James and Amelia's daughter, apparently told local historians that her father had been born in Lanarkshire, Scotland.[29]

The Douglas-Connollys' racial self-fashioning involved literal reclassifications and a more generalized embrace of key symbols of British gentility. The youngest children, Martha and James Jr., were sent to England to be educated. Both ultimately opted to subvert their special places in the family's self-fashioning project, albeit in different ways. James Jr. proved a discipline problem who died at the age of thirty-two. Martha, like her sisters, confirmed the family's status among the local elite by marrying a white engineer. Yet she registered a quiet ambivalence with her family's half-century of whitening by publishing a slim work of amateur ethnography called *Story and Folklore of the Cowichan Indians* in 1901. In it, Martha Douglas Harris does not identify as being of mixed heritage, but she does insert herself in local *métissage* by translating oral narrative from Chinook jargon, the flexible language that was born in the fur trade and nurtured in cross-cultural communication throughout nineteenth- and twentieth-century British Columbia.[30]

It is undoubtably correct to identify stories like the Douglas-Connollys' as evidence for the immense flexibility of racial categories and identities. What historians once assumed were permanent, obvious, and transparent we now know to be fictive and elastic. The racial identities both attributed to and adopted by the Douglas-Connollys were local and particular. That Amelia's aboriginal background loomed larger than James's African heritage suggests that the famed "one drop" rule of racial provenance was not as universal in North America as is sometimes assumed. Racial discourse around the Douglas-Connolly family changed over time as well. Douglas was rarely identified as part-African after midcentury. When he was, it was done covertly. A missionary-turned–travel writer describing "remarkable matrimonial alliances to be met with" to his British readers remarked, "A gentleman of large property, reported to be of Mulatto origin, is married to a half-breed Indian" but went no further.[31]

While the criteria changed, Douglas's pedigree, and thus that of the imperial state he locally personified, remained in question. Critics instead turned to his lack of British identity, arguing in effect that Douglas was insufficiently acquainted with the metropole to govern on its behalf. Annie Deans, a poor white settler, tried to explain the political quagmire that was Vancouver Island in 1854 to her family in Britain. She related it to the governor's experience and his wife's racial identity: "For the Governor of Vanc[o]uvers Island has been in the Company out here ever since he was a Boy about 15 year[s] of age and now he is a Man upwards of 60 now — so you may say he has been all his life among the North American indians and has got one of them for a wife so how can it be expected that he can know anything at all about Governing one of England[']s last Colony's in North America."[32]

Life in North America and marriage to a North American had unfitted the governor for governing. What good was a representative of empire who could not move smoothly around the center? Edmund Hope Verney, a naval officer well-connected to British missionary circles, informed his family at home that Douglas planned to visit England on his retirement in 1864. "I hardly think he will remain long in England," he predicted, "as he will find himself such a stranger, and so utterly lost in the crowd."[33] The discourse of origins had been eclipsed by the discourse of culture, but Douglas's status as an outsider remained essentially unchanged.

As Deans's biting and jumbled reportage indicates, Douglas's dubious racial identity was thought to flow, in part, from his wife's. This reflected a staple of local colonial discourse, namely, that racial contagion flowed especially quickly from women to men. The notion that white men were effectively deracinated by their attachments to First Nations women had some important political ramifications for the administration of colonialism in British Columbia. Imperialism bore a familial face, and observers of colonial British Columbia were not sure if the face of the Douglas-Connollys was the right kind. Sophia Cracroft, niece and traveling companion of Lady Jane Franklin, found the domestic hospitality of the Douglas-Connolly family a far cry from what she expected from a colonial governor in 1861. She was slighted when an invitation to stay at the Douglas residence was not forthcoming and linked this social breach with Amelia Connolly Douglas's aboriginality and hybridity. She explained that the governor's wife "keeps very much (far too much) in the background . . . partly because she speaks English with some difficulty; the usual language being either the Indian, or Canadian French wh is a corrupt dialect." She watched the Douglases' daughters carefully for apparent signs of their First Nations lineage, seeing the width of their faces and the cadence of their speech as indisputable signs of their mixed parentage. Cracroft concluded that they had done remarkably well given the awesome weight of backwardness they labored under. "Considering the little training of any kind these girls can have had, it is more wonderful they shd be what they are, than that they should have defects of manner. They have never left Northern America, nor known any society but such as they now have," she judged.[34]

Cracroft regarded the Douglas-Connolly family much as she did her African American landlady in Victoria, with the mixture of condescension, fear, and enthusiasm for the Other and its particularities that is perhaps unique to the traveler. Local whites could be less forgiving, seeing hybridity not as local color but as a telling indictment of the colonial project writ large. Verney thought that Douglas's family and tolerance for sexual nonconformity rendered him unsuitable for the position of governor. He found him kind but deemed him "a great drag on the colony" and explained to his father why: "A refined English gentleman is sadly wanted at the head of affairs: a man who is perhaps living with a woman who is not his wife may be seen in intimate familiar conversation with the Governor, or even met at his table: then, really, for Mrs. Douglas and her daughters, the less said the better: I do not conceive that I can do any good by recounting instances of their ignorance & barbarism."[35]

Verney relied on the language of genteel imperialism—the "refined English gentleman" versus those who consorted with the unwed and unmarried and reproduced the ignorant and the barbarous—to condemn the Douglas administration. Others used democratic reform discourse to similar ends. In 1860, Jane Fawcett, a white woman settler, complained bitterly about the colony to her sister: "A more ignorant self interested, crawling administration could not be anywhere, they pretend to administer English laws, but they are so twisted and altered to suit each one's interests, and ignorance—that I think we might as well have no government as the present one; and the Governor with his Squa[w] wife, and half breed daughters, and those under him."[36] As did reformers elsewhere in Britain's North American empire, Fawcett traded on the association of femininity and family with political corruption. For her, as for the critics of HBC rule in Vancouver Island and Rupert's Land, this was about race as well as gender. The illegitimate authority of the local "family compact" cannot be severed from its illegitimate connections to local peoples. Settlers like Fawcett defined themselves in the name of England and the rule of law and in opposition not only to untrammeled private interests but to métissage.

The shifting swirl of opinion and gossip surrounding the racial identities of the Douglas-Connolly family confirms that race and racial identity were indeed constructed and reconstructed. But it also suggests some of the limits on that process, at least for individuals. The Douglas-Connolly family worked hard to fashion themselves as white and brought considerable economic and political clout to the process. But the Douglas-Connollys' adherence to conventions of British respectability and considerable wealth and power did not stop settlers and visitors alike from remarking on what they saw as fixed racial attributes. The specific character of these racial attributes shifted measurably over time and across space. Surely Douglas's creole heritage would have been a bigger issue in the British Caribbean; in British Columbia, it was a minor point in comparison to the fact that his wife was part Cree, which in turn was conditioned by the fact that this racial identification tied her to Plains nations instead of local, coastal peoples. But however flexible and variable, race revealed itself as tenacious in particular locations. People could not opt in and out of it as they saw fit. Race was socially and historically constructed, but the Douglas-Connollys' case reveals that it was not individually constructed. James Douglas's career as governor similarly suggests the powers and limits of the imperial state's capacity for working with the particularities of colonialism not as it was imagined, but as it was constructed on the ground in colonial space.

THE MID-NINETEENTH-CENTURY British imperial state was willing to accommodate, incorporate, and sometimes yield to local practices that differed from and challenged its putative aims. In British Columbia, the British imperial system had to allow for flexible and seemingly arbitrary codes of authority; it had to make copious room for local economies, whether foraging or the fur trade. It also had to find a way to live with local practices of conjugality, most notably in relationships and families forged between settler men and aboriginal women, and the politics of identity that flowed from them.

Yet we would be mistaken if we read this grudging accommodation for acceptance. That colonial officials in London were hardly enthusiastic about the disciplining of the imperial to the local is made clear by their quiet discomfort around Douglas, a discomfort that, though never entirely muted by their enthusiasm for his cost-effectiveness, was palpable. It is affirmed by ongoing, if never particularly successful, efforts to regularize the smaller details of the imperial state in British Columbia.

It is not incidental that these efforts multiplied after Douglas retired in 1864. He was replaced on Vancouver Island by Arthur Edward Kennedy, who probably would have fulfilled Verney's request for a proper English gentleman and thus imperial administrator. A former army captain, Kennedy had served in Ireland and had been governor of Sierra Leone and Western Australia.[37] He was unable to manage the colony's fractious settler politics, but he proved a dab hand at imperial spectacle. He created the colony's first Government House, hosted grand social events, and mobilized an image of bourgeois conjugality by putting his wife and daughters to work in the business of representing empire. While the local press found his political performance wanting, they were careful to pay the Kennedy family "a proper tribute to the many virtues that have adorned their private life, the exercise of which have endeared them to the hearts of all who have enjoyed the pleasure of their acquaintance."[38]

Kennedy worked to remold Vancouver Island's state along the lines of respectability that he also aimed to personify. He was aghast at both the state of society and the state that governed it in Vancouver Island. "The present Indian Settlement at Victoria, is a disgrace to humanity," he reported to the Colonial Office soon after taking office, "and I cannot learn that any effective measures have been taken to prevent the shameless prostitution of the women and drunkenness of the men who live mainly by their prostitution."[39] Kennedy also shared these opinions with relevant aboriginal authorities when, in his inaugural address to the "Indian Chiefs," Kennedy took it upon himself to distance his imperialism from that practiced by settlers. "I would here warn you," he said, "that all white men are not alike; there are those unhappily among us, who encourage these vices to satisfy a base cupidity, and I hope for the co-operation of all honest Indians in bringing them to justice."[40] Kennedy pledged to reform the administration of empire and, in doing so, to create a colonial society based in firm lines between European and Native.

Kennedy worked toward this goal by ridding the local state of officials too obviously associated with métissage and the rough ways of the backwoods. He found local policemen so wanting that he requested Irish ones be sent to replace them.[41] When the Colonial Office failed to grant his request, Kennedy's staff began routing out police officers with public connections to local women. Frederick Turner was sacked when he was found "living with an Indian Woman at Sooke, and cultivating a tract of land."[42] Turner was officially dismissed for spending too much time away from his post, but the real reason behind his firing became clear when Kennedy approved a new regulation that specified that "the practice of

Constables in out-lying districts living with Indian women will not be tolerated."[43] Colonial officials too closely associated with the rough pastimes of the backwoods as well as with local women would find their status challenged. Richard Gollenge, an old HBC servant, was the gold commissioner for the Sooke Mines, where he carried out the functions of the state in a region newly colonized by gold miners. Kennedy suspended him when he heard that Gollenge "was leading an intemperate and disreputable life — addicted to drink and prostitutes."[44] At a special meeting of the Colony's Executive Council, a series of witnesses were called to testify not only to Gollenge's penchant for drink, but to his relationship with a known prostitute and cross-dresser named Fanny Clarke.[45] Drinking, gambling, gender inversion, and a casual familiarity with the sex trade may have been common coin in the rough homosocial culture forged by white, working-class men around British Columbia's gold mines, but they had no place in the offices of the British empire.

The alterations in the small administrative practices of the colonial state were suggested by larger ones at work. Kennedy's final act as governor was to lay the framework for the reformation of British Columbia's state to better reflect what London saw as its lackluster performance and diminished potential. In 1866, the two colonies were merged, retaining the name of British Columbia but the Island capital of Victoria. Frederick Seymour, appointed governor of the mainland in 1864, assumed control over the enlarged jurisdiction. Like Kennedy, Seymour was a professional colonial administrator who had served as assistant colonial secretary of Van Dieman's Land and lieutenant-governor of British Honduras. Unlike Kennedy, he was a bachelor.[46] He, too, would struggle to reconcile British Columbia's colonial practice with the putative aims of empire, especially by working to reconstitute the administrative practices of the local state and, in doing so, revise the colonial government's relationship to its subjects.

Administration mattered to empire, and especially to the imperial state. Scott argues that the modern state was in effect made possible by mechanisms of categorization and enumeration.[47] Certainly the imperial state was profoundly invested in the related acts of naming, recording, and counting. By amassing a paper empire, Thomas Richards suggests, Britain signaled its discomfort with the fundamental unknowability of its possessions.[48] But the practice of administration also worked to make the unknown known and thus amenable to rule. Numbers, writes Arjun Appadurai, were "part of the enterprise of *translating* the colonial experience into terms graspable in the metropolis."[49]

Numbers were empowered by their ability to translate but were disempowered by the difficulty of counting colonial life. Blue Books were the standardized registers that all British colonies were expected to fill out and submit to London. Blue Books thus sought not only to transfer information from periphery to center, but to do so in a way that minimized the colony's difference not only from Britain but from each other. Vancouver Island did not submit any Blue Books until Kennedy was appointed governor. When they were submitted, the Blue Books for the colony were inevitably partly completed and accompanied by apologetic remarks that "In the present state of the Colony it is not practicable to afford the particular information herein required under the different heads."[50] Local officials tried to modify the forms to make room for local knowledges and structures, rejecting, for instance, the Colonial Office's bifurcated racial categories (white and colored) in favor of a scheme that categorized people as either white, native, colored, or Chinese. But it was hard to reconcile the practice of British Columbia with the theory of empire implicit in the Blue Books. Even when officials were willing to hazard some guesses about the number of people, their racial identity and gender, they felt compelled to remind the Colonial Office that the colony was at heart unknowable to the state. "The returns," explained one, "are made by the magistrates, but as these officers are stationed in some instances more than 100 miles apart, it is evident that in so vast an extent of territory as that comprised with the Colony of British Columbia with a population scattered throughout its length and breadth there must be a large number of persons for whom the magistrates can have no knowledge."[51] Here officials articulated what Philippa Levine calls "a common European complaint about the promiscuous Indigenous masses: there was simply too many of them to count,"[52] buttressed by the belief that North American geography was additionally and almost intentionally uncooperative.

It was not simply the number of the people nor their location across space that rendered them incompatible with the techniques of the colonial state. Their unknowability was also attributed to their basic character as aboriginal peoples and as settlers committed to hybrid, local lifeways. In 1865, Governor Seymour attempted to pass what was commonly called a "census law" mandating the registration of births, marriages, and deaths. But the census law was dropped on the grounds that the colony was too confusing to count and classify. Seymour, referring to "the futile attempts I had made on two occasions" to pass a census law, plainly explained that the colony's racial and gendered character rendered it fundamentally incompatible with modern state information gathering: "I really do not know how a general system of Registration could be worked satisfactorily here. The population is greatly scattered. The majority are Indians whom we could hardly expect to register any one of the great events of life. Many of the white men are living in a state of concubinage with Indian women far in the Interior. They would hardly come forward to register the birth of some half breed."[53] The Colonial Office forwarded a copy of Ceylon's Ordinance for inspiration, but if the colony could not adequately fashion itself after the center, it could also not remold itself along the lines of another colony. No full census was ever taken of colonial British Columbia, and no system of mandatory registration was ever adopted.[54]

Efforts to reconstitute how the colonial state regulated and enumerated its citizens were as unsuccessful as they were revealing. They were only a small part of the reason why Seymour, like other governors before him, deemed his administration of British Columbia a failure. "It would be difficult to imagine a post more hard to fill than I now occupy," Seymour explained in a confidential memo to the Colonial Office. The apparatus of the colonial state reflected a hope that British Columbia would become a populous and self-sufficient settler colony. "But for a white population now probably less than ten thousand," he continued, "had been established the Government required for the expected one hundred thousand."[55]

After he died unexpectedly in 1869, Seymour was replaced by Anthony Musgrave, recently governor of Newfoundland. The Colonial Office made clear that Musgrave should deal with the colonial state in British Columbia by encouraging it to shift its very form and join Canada, the self-governing settler colony created by the confederation of the British North American colonies in 1867. That he did, and British Columbia joined Canada as a province in July 1871. London had solved the problem of maintaining an imperial presence on the edge of America without spending very much money. Empire's history was generated in practice rather than in theory, and in that practice something of a theory was born and undone at the same time. The particularities and problems of administering colonialism did not sunder empire, but they did force its transformation.

THE FRAGILE, HYBRID, and forever disappointing character of the state in British Columbia bears witness to the significance of the local in creating the imperial and, ultimately, in challenging it. Wolfe, among others, has noted that scholars of imperialism remain heuristically dependent on the alleged opposition between Europe and colony and between the ideal and the material. These linked oppositions, he rightly points out, mask the facts that consciousness is inseparable from practical activity and that Europe and not-Europe coproduced each other.[56] The point is thus not that colonial theory and colonial practice were polar opposites: the point is that they made and ultimately unmade each other. Britain aimed to bring hegemonic definitions of racial and gendered respectability to its administrators and administration in British Columbia but often found itself forced to work with local practices that were themselves created by the practical administration of empire in this context. Visions of the settler state were modified and sometimes thwarted by the contradictions encoded within the very structure of imperialism. Britain was neither very interested nor very able to render this edge of empire into a respectable white settler colony. British Columbia and its state could not be remade along the lines of Britain because it was not and could not be Britain. In this equation lay an obvious revelation about the colonial experience and a quiet but damning challenge to empire and, ultimately, to Britain itself. What good, after all, was a mother country that could not reproduce?

Notes

1. John L. Comaroff, "Reflections on the Colonial State, in South Africa and Elsewhere: Factions, Fragments, Facts and Fictions," *Social Identities* 4, 3 (October 1998): 8.
2. James Douglas to Edward Bulwer Lytton, 2 July 1859, Original Correspondence, British Columbia, [hereafter CO 60], Public Archives of Canada, [hereafter PAC], MG 11, CO 60/4, Mflm B-80.
3. See Daniel W. Clayton, *Islands of Truth: The Imperial Fashioning of Vancouver* (Vancouver: University of British Columbia Press, 2000).
4. W. Murdoch and Alexander Lord to Herman Merivale, 19 January 1853, Colonial Office, Original Correspondence, Vancouver Island [hereafter CO 305], CO 305/4, University of British Columbia Library [hereafter UBCL], Mflm 288:3.
5. See, for instance, Ann Laura Stoler, "Rethinking Colonial Categories: European

Communities and the Boundaries of Rule," *Comparative Studies in Society and History* 31, 1 (January 1989): 134–161; Sylvia Van Kirk's seminal *"Many Tender Ties": Women in Fur Trade Society in Western Canada, 1670–1870* (Winnipeg: Watson and Dwyer, 1980).

6. Anna Davin, "Imperialism and Motherhood," *History Workshop* 5 (spring 1978): 9–66.

7. Edward Gibbon Wakefield, "A View of the Art of Colonization: With Present Reference to the British Empire: In Letters Between a Statesman and a Colonist," in *The Collected Works of Edward Gibbon Wakefield*, ed. M. F. Lloyd Pritchard (London: Collins, 1968 [1849]), 972.

8. See Hudson's Bay Company [HBC], *Colonization of Vancouver Island* (London: Horace and Sons, 1849).

9. W. Kaye Lamb, ed., "The Census of Vancouver Island, 1855," *British Columbia Historical Quarterly* 4, 1 (1940): 51–58.

10. Fairfax Moresby, 7 July 1851, UBCL, CO 305/3, Mflm R288:1.

11. See Walter Colquhoun Grant to Brodie, 29 August 1848, in James E. Hendrickson, ed., "Two Letters from Walter Colquhoun Grant," *BC Studies* 26 (summer 1975): 7–9.

12. Andrew Muir, "Private Diary, 9 November 1848–5 August 1850," BCA, transcript, Add Mss E/B/M91A, 102

13. Henry Wright, *Nineteenth Annual Report of the Missions of the Church of England in British Columbia for the Year 1877* (London: Rivingtons, 1878), 16–17.

14. James Douglas to Duke of Newcastle, 24 August 1860, PAC, CO 60/8, Mflm B-83.

15. Mark Francis, *Governors and Settlers: Images of Authority in the British Colonies, 1820–1860* (London: Macmillian, 1992).

16. Catherine Hall, "Competing Masculinities: Thomas Carlyle, John Stuart Mill and the Case of Governor Eyre," in *White, Male, and Middle Class: Explorations in Feminism and History* (New York: Routledge, 1992).

17. Dorothy Blakey Smith, ed., *The Reminiscences of Doctor John Sebastian Helmcken* (Vancouver: University of British Columbia Press, 1977), 135.

18. Undated note from EG, en verso to Richard Blanshard to Earl Grey, 15 June 1850; and Richard Blanshard to Earl Grey, 18 November 1850, CO 305/2, UBCL, Mflm R288:1.

19. See Kaye Lamb, "Some Notes on the Douglas Family," *British Columbia Historical Quarterly* 17 (1953): 41–51.

20. See Dorothy Blakey Smith, *James Douglas: Father of British Columbia* (Toronto: Oxford University Press, 1971); Derek Pethick, *James Douglas: Servant of Two Empires* (Vancouver: Mitchell, 1969).

21. See Sylvia Van Kirk, "Tracing the Fortunes of Five Founding Families of Victoria," *BC Studies* 115/116 (autumn/winter 1997–1998): 148–179; Constance Backhouse, *Petticoats and Prejudice: Women and Law in Nineteenth-Century Canada* (Toronto: The Women's Press, 1991).

22. John W. Cell, *British Colonial Administration in the Mid-Nineteenth-Century: The Policy-Making Process* (New Haven: Yale University Press, 1970).

23. George Hills, "Diary, 11 June–31 December 1863," transcript, Anglican Church of

Canada, Archives of the Diocese of New Westminster/Ecclesiastical Province of British Columbia, Vancouver School of Theology, 129.

24. See note en verso from Lord Palmerston, 21 August 1854, CO 305/5, Mflm R288:3; Hills, "Diary 1863," 108.

25. Gerhard Ens, *From Homeland to Hinterland: The Changing World of the Red River Metis in the Nineteenth-Century* (Toronto: University of Toronto Press, 1996).

26. See Adele Perry, *On the Edge of Empire: Gender, Race, and the Making of British Columbia, 1849–1871* (Toronto: University of Toronto Press, 2001).

27. See Simpson's "Character Book," reprinted in Thomas Thorner, *"A few acres of snow": Documents in Canadian History, 1577–1867* (Peterborough, Ontario: Broadview, 1997), 304; Letitia Hargrave to Mrs. Dugald Mactavish, December 1842, in Margaret Arnett Maclead, ed., *The Letters of Letitia Hargrave* (Toronto: Champlain Society, 1947), 132, emphasis in original.

28. See Vancouver Island Police and Prisons Department, "Charge Book, 1862–1866," BCA, GR-0428 for the census, and Van Kirk, *"Many Tender Ties,"* 237.

29. See Lamb, "Some Notes on the Douglas Family," 43.

30. Martha Harris Douglas, *Story and Folklore of the Cowichan Indians* (Victoria: The Colonist, 1901).

31. Matthew Macfie, *Vancouver Island and British Columbia: Their History, Resources, and Prospects* (London: Longman, Green, Longman, Roberts and Green, 1865), 379.

32. Annie Deans to Brother Sister, 29 February 1854, "Annie Deans Outward Correspondence," BCA, Add Mss E/B/D343A, transcript.

33. Edmund Hope Verney to Harry Verney, 2 May 1864, in *The Vancouver Island Letters of Edmund Hope Verney, 1862–1865*, ed. Allan Pritchard (Vancouver: University of British Columbia Press, 1996), 202. Lamb, "Some Notes" discusses Douglas's year in England.

34. Dorothy Blakey Smith, ed., *Lady Franklin Visits the Pacific Northwest: Being Extracts from the Letters of Miss Sophia Cracroft, Sir John Franklin's Niece, February to April 1861 and April to July 1870* (Victoria: Provincial Archives of British Columbia Memoir No. XI, 1974), 22–23.

35. Verney to Harry Verney, 16 August 1862, in Pritchard, *Vancouver Island Letters*, 84.

36. See Jane Fawcett to Emma, 24 June 1960, "Extracts from Letters and Diary," BCA, Add Mss 1963, transcript, 91–92; emphasis in original.

37. See G. P. V. Akrigg and Helen Akrigg, *British Columbia Chronicle 1847–1871: Gold and Colonists* (Vancouver: Discovery Press, 1977), 294.

38. "The Departure of Governor Kennedy," *Colonist*, 24 April 1864.

39. Arthur Kennedy to Edward Cardwell, 1 October 1864, CO 305/23, Mflm B-246. Also see Arthur Kennedy to Edward Cardwell, 7 July 1864, CO 305/22, NAC, Mflm B-246.

40. "The Governor's Address to the Indians, Victoria August 22nd, 1864," in Arthur Kennedy to Edward Cardwell, 23 August 1864, CO 305/23, NAC, Mflm B-246.

41. See Arthur Kennedy to Edward Cardwell, 7 July 1865, CO 305/22, NAC, Mflm B-246.

42. Phillip Hankin to Acting Colonial Secretary, 1 April 1865, BCA, "Colonial Correspondence," GR 1372, File 1395, Reel B-1357.

43. Note signed AK, 16 May 1865, on Phillip Hankin to Acting Colonial Secretary, 16 May 1865, BCA, "Colonial Correspondence," GR 1372, File 1396, Mflm B-1357.

44. Arthur Kennedy to Edward Cardwell, 30 November 1864, CO 305/23, NAC, Mflm B-246.

45. See "Vancouver Island, Extract from Minutes of Executive Council, 23nd November 1864," in Arthur Kennedy to Edward Cardwell, 30 November 1864, CO 305/23, NAC, Mflm B-246.

46. Akrigg and Akrigg, *British Columbia Chronicle*, 295.

47. James C. Scott, *Seeing Like a State: How Certain Schemes to Improve the Human Condition Have Failed* (New Haven: Yale University Press, 1998).

48. Thomas Richards, *The Imperial Archive: Knowledge and the Fantasy of Empire* (London: Verso, 1993).

49. Arjun Appadurai, "Number in the Colonial Imagination," in *Orientalism and the Postcolonial Predicament*, ed. Carol A. Breckenridge and Peter van der Veer (Philadelphia: University of Pennsylvania Press, 1993).

50. Vancouver Island, Blue Books of Statistics &c 1863, BCA, Mflm 625A, 222–223.

51. British Columbia, Blue Books of Statistics, 1867 &c, BCA, Mflm 627A, 140–141.

52. Philippa Levine, "Orientalist Sociology and the Creation of Colonial Sexualities," *Feminist Review* 65 (summer 2000): 9.

53. Frederick Seymour to Duke of Buckingham and Chados, 11 August 1868, CO 60/33, BCA, GR 1486, Mflm B-1444.

54. See James E. Hendrickson, ed., *Journals of the Colonial Legislatures of the Colonies of Vancouver Island and British Columbia 1851–1871.* Vol. 4, *Journals of the Legislative Council of British Columbia, 1866–1871* (Victoria: Public Archives of British Columbia, 1980), 207–209.

55. Frederick Seymour to Duke of Buckingham and Chados, 17 March 1868, CO 60/32, BCA, GR 1486, Mflm B-1442.

56. See Patrick Wolfe, "History and Imperialism: A Century of Theory from Marx to Postcolonialism," *American Historical Review* 102 (April 1999): 389.

Lucy Eldersveld Murphy

Native American and Métis Women as "Public
Mothers" in the Nineteenth-Century Midwest

*Using the category of colonization to describe the historical conditions under
which Native American and Creole communities lived in the nineteenth-
century American Midwest, this essay skillfully excavates evidence of indigenous
and hybrid practices from a variety of primary sources. The focus on "public
mothers" enables us to see with particular vividness how Anglo "pioneers" constructed, and often pathologized, locally powerful Creole women with whom they
came into contact on their way westward—leaving behind an archive that we
can now read critically for what it can tell us about a variety of gendered
practices. As healers, hosts, midwives, and entrepreneurs, Métis women negotiated the colonial encounter in ways that demonstrated both their autonomy and
their authority in their own communities. Marinette Chevalier, Thérèse Marcotte Schindler, and Theresa Rankin Lawe are just a few of countless such women
appearing in immigrants' accounts who remind us of the many untold individual stories at the heart of the global imperial experience that American frontier
expansion represents.*

On the northwestern shore of Lake Michigan's Green Bay,
where the Menominee River flows into the lake along an old
fur trade route, there is a city straddling the border of Wisconsin and Michigan. This city and the county that surrounds it are named
for a woman of color: she was Marinette Chevalier, and the place-name
is Marinette. A Menominee, Ojibwe, and French Métisse (mixed-race
woman) related to a prominent Ojibwe family, she married one fur
trader, separated from him, and then married another according to "the

custom of the country," working side by side with each husband at the mouth of the Menominee River, a region in which many Indians spent part of their year.[1] She eventually separated from her second husband, took over the management of the trading post with the help of her children, and became extremely successful in business and in cultivating warm relationships with the Indian people living in the area, many of whom were her kin.

When she was in her twenties, the War of 1812 clamped U.S. sovereignty onto this northern borderland region, and the Native people and fur trade families were colonized by the United States. The conquering army built new forts and fortified older ones, enforcing control to be administered by a new judicial and legislative system. Although Marinette Chevalier and most of the other residents spoke French and/or Indian languages, the United States imposed English as a new court language. Waves of immigrants from the eastern United States and even some from Europe swarmed into the Midwest, bringing different ideas about race, class, and gender. Before long, such people as Marinette Chevalier were minorities in their own communities. Yet, when English-speaking immigrants began to move into the Menominee River area, they, like the local Indians and Métis people, became her customers, neighbors, and friends.

Although Marinette Chevalier's experiences were notable, they were not unique. Many other women whose lives spanned the transition to U.S. control of the Midwest worked to mediate between cultural groups, as did some of their brothers, sons, and husbands. During the nineteenth century, as the newcomers were changing the region's economy, landscape, and government to the detriment of many Creole people, some of these women created connections and even transcended the prejudices of the Anglo "pioneers" to gain the praise of their neighbors.

Although many members of the old fur trade families were what Canadians would call "Métis," that is, people of mixed Indian and white ancestry, others were not. Residents of these communities, such as Green Bay and Mackinac, also included Indians, whites, and people with African backgrounds. Rather than having an identical *ancestry*, they had in common a *culture* born in the Midwest, one that was in place before the United States took control of the region. For this reason, the word "Creole" is used here as a general term to describe the culture and the people who created it, with the understanding that it may refer to any of the long-time residents connected to the old fur trade culture who were Métis, Indian, Euro-, or African American. This essay discusses the roles of Creole women in multiethnic and changing communities. Some of them, I argue, found ways to mediate between cultural groups by negotiating overlapping ideals of womanhood common to both Anglos and Native-descended people, serving their communities in roles as "public mothers."

In many ways, Creole women's experiences in the American Midwest resembled those of women facing colonization in other parts of the world. For example, during the eighteenth and nineteenth centuries, West African coastal women, often operating as traders, served as social and cultural intermediaries, helped to create networks linking people of different ethnic groups, and facilitated cultural fusion in changing communities. In Senegal, African women traders married European men and helped to create a hybrid society in Saint-Louis and Gorée; their Euro-African daughters might be political as well as economic and social mediators. In Sierra Leone, women traders facilitated cross-cultural contact both as travelers and as vendors in the great markets. Their roles and activities, however, were frequently overlooked or misunderstood by foreign observers.[2]

CREOLE FAMILIES IN the American Midwest were initially formed when, during the seventeenth and eighteenth centuries, French Canadian and French fur traders traveled into the Great Lakes region in increasing numbers and married into Indian customers' families and communities. These mixed couples raised biracial children in bicultural households. Many of these mixed families eventually moved from the Indian villages into their own fur trade towns and developed hybrid societies. Over fifty Creole communities were founded during the eighteenth century in the western Great Lakes and upper Mississippi Valley by Francophone men who married Indian women and raised Métis children. At least ten to fifteen thousand people called these communities home by the late 1820s, according to historian Jacqueline Peterson's conservative estimate.[3] Quite possibly, the number was much higher.

Marinette Chevalier usually spent part of each year in the fur trade town of Green Bay, known in French as La Baye. Like her, thousands of people lived in culturally mixed communities and shared a syncretic culture. These people spoke French and various Indian languages, dressed, farmed, traveled, and celebrated in unique ways, and were not particularly loyal to the United States of America. People who had been born in the Great Lakes region, residents of towns such as Green Bay, Prairie du Chien, St. Louis, Vincennes, Detroit, and Mackinac, included French and Anglo-American fur traders and related workers, Indian wives, and some of their kin, and a wide variety of young and old Métis people, with a few African Americans.

It is important to understand these people in the context of colonization, as residents who lived in this part of the Midwest before it was annexed by the United States. During the eighteenth century, they had created communities with a regional culture that was a distinctive mix of their varied cultural heritages. Although they were not indigenous in the same sense that Indian peoples were, they were residents with a culture that was specific to the region and strongly related to Indian culture. Their history parallels that of the Spanish-speaking Californios, Tejanos, and Hispanos of the nineteenth-century Southwest, people who were also colonized by the United States in the nineteenth century.[4] The people of midwestern fur trade communities thought of themselves in cultural rather than racial terms, and they were keenly aware that they were being invaded and dominated by the culturally different Anglos of the United States. Both they and the Anglos understood them to be an ethnic group that predated U.S. hegemony. In the early nineteenth century, the word "Creole" was used in the Mississippi Valley to convey this sense of a culture group created in the previous colonial era (although the word had other meanings in other contexts).[5] Other, somewhat misleading terms — such as Canadians, French people, and half-breeds — were sometimes used.

Creole culture combined Native American and Euro-American elements as mixed families negotiated lifeways and selected ideas and practices from their collective traditions. Wives' Indian kin connections linked traders to friends and customers during the fur trade era. Children tended to speak both French and at least one Native language. Native wives, who had grown up in societies that regarded farming as women's work, often continued to be very active in growing food, while white or Métis husbands might raise livestock, a practice that was not customary in Indian communities. Dairying might be unpopular with Creole wives, but Indian maple sugaring expeditions became part of their Lenten season.[6]

Creole culture was also complex and variable: the people who lived and created it were often bi- (or even tri-)cultural; they might be Ojibwe, Dakota, Potawatomi, Sauk, Pawnee, or members of other Native tribes, French, Scottish, English, African American, or any combination of the above. Practices and beliefs varied from one community or family or individual to another; there was change over time, presenting a real challenge to historians. The variety and historical change are circumstances that parallel those of other cultures, however.

THE COLONIZATION OF the Midwest by the United States and the immigration of large numbers of Anglo-Americans chiefly from New England and the Mid-Atlantic states caused profound social change. Such people as Marinette Chevalier faced a new political reality that altered membership of society's elite class, imposed new ruling families, and worked to demote many previously elite Creoles. The transition to Anglo hegemony had the potential to constrict women's rights and to stigmatize and marginalize Creoles, possibilities that had implications particularly for elite women of color. The newly dominant society not only brought different gender ideals, but also tried to enforce those values with a legal system that constricted the rights of wives and rigidified the concept of marriage. Whereas the *coutume de Paris* as applied in New France (including the Midwest) had allowed wives to be co-owners of a couple's property and guaranteed widows at least half of the estate, U.S. hegemony imposed coverture on wives and did not protect widows from creditors. Local norms recognized marriages that had been contracted "according to the custom of the country," but under the new regime these marriages were sometimes considered illegitimate, and in at least one instance, a new magistrate charged couples in such partnerships with adultery and fornication.[7] Marinette Chevalier's second husband was one of thirty-six men charged with fornication by a new judge in nearby Green Bay because the couple had not formalized their union according to the legal system of the United States.[8]

In addition, Creoles experienced both cultural prejudice and racism on the part of the colonizers. Anglophone immigrants referred to themselves as "settlers," and would later call themselves "pioneers." They arrived intending to build farms, towns, and businesses, bringing with them cultural baggage that included ethnocentrism and devotion to a social hierarchy based on race. Most wanted to believe that they were creating a new society where none had existed before, so they wrote essays for their "pioneer societies" congratulating themselves for having brought "civilization" to the "wilderness." In their letters and memoirs, they often felt the need to denigrate the established populations of Indians and Creoles.

One would expect, of course, that the writings of the colonizers would privilege their own people and minimize and marginalize those they colonized, and in fact, most of the Anglo writers followed this pattern. Their own people appear in their letters and memoirs as energetic and progressive civilizers, while Creoles and Natives appear as primitive, backward, and unambitious. In many cases, however, Anglos' accounts are our only written sources for knowing about Creole women. They reveal much about both what the women did and how the Anglos viewed them.

Creole women's activities reveal clear patterns of intercession during the nineteenth and into the twentieth century, particularly in roles that might be described as public mothering. In particular, elite Creole women — that is, those who were prominent, wealthy, and/or well-connected — seem to have taken on activities related to charity, hospitality, healing, and midwifery. They nurtured their neighbors, newcomers, travelers, kin, and fellow clan and tribal members. They came from Native and Creole traditions in which women's roles, particularly those of elite women, could be at once public and private, social and political. Although political and economic roles for Creoles under the new regime were being constricted and the Anglo gender system being imposed was more restrictive than the systems of Creoles and Native Americans, some Creole women maintained quasi-public roles in transitional communities because they were perceived by the newcomers as praiseworthy females doing motherly work. Although there are many instances of elite Creole men making connections and laboring to smooth intercultural relations, the role of Creole mediator is perhaps most evident in the actions of women — actions most often reported by Anglos.

SOME CREOLE WOMEN reached out to their communities as healers, a role women could hold in Native communities, and as midwives, a trade women monopolized among Indians. Native and Métis women brought their knowledge of medicine, midwifery, and nurturing to the service of their neighbors; it is likely that bicultural women drew on multiple medical traditions, making their range of treatment options greater than those available to people with access to only a single medical tradition. Creole women healers were appreciated enough to have been mentioned in Anglo memoirs and newspaper accounts. Their efforts frequently brought them into the homes of neighbors who were culturally different, creating ties of respect and affection and sometimes enhancing the healer's status and authority.

One such woman was Marianne LaBuche Menard, Prairie du Chien's midwife and healer, "a person of consequence," according to an 1856 pioneer writer who knew her in the early nineteenth century. She was a woman of French and African descent, a native of New Orleans who had thirteen children by three husbands. "She was sent for by the sick, and attended them as regularly as a physician, and charged fees therefor[e], giving them . . . 'device and yarb drink' [advice and herb drink]. . . . she took her pay in the produce of the country, but was not very modest in her charges." After the U.S. army brought in a physician who would attend to civilians, many still preferred "Aunt Mary Ann," as she was called, and she sometimes cured people despaired of by the army doctor.[9]

During the mid-nineteenth century, an Ojibwe Métisse from Detroit came with her husband, Louis Demarie, to Chippewa Falls, Wisconsin. An Anglo neighbor wrote about Madame Demarie in 1875: "She was a woman of uncommon natural abilities, and with education and culture would have graced a high social position in any community. She was a born physician, and for many years the only one in the valley; and in making a diagnosis of disease, and her knowledge of the healing proper- ties and proper application of many of the remedies used in the Materia Medica, exhibited extraordinary insight and skill in her practice. She was frequently called to attend upon myself and family, and her prescriptions were simple, natural, and always efficacious."[10] Similarly, Josette De- Rosier Duvernay Moon Robinson, another Ojibwe Métisse, cared for the sick and pregnant of Oceana County, Michigan, during the second half of the nineteenth century and delivered hundreds of babies.[11] At the time of her death in 1904, an obituary in the Hart *Journal* stated, "Perhaps no other woman of Indian blood has been more respected and generally beloved than was Mrs. Robinson. . . . A woman of no literary education, yet she possessed much wisdom. . . . The sick and suffering always desired 'Grandma' Robinson as nurse, and she was never known to refuse aid whenever it was possible for her to render it. Every home in the township of Elbridge has welcomed her at their firesides and her death has caused more than usual mourning."[12] Josette's daughter, Sarah Moon, also con- tinued as a midwife.

Like Indians, Creoles expected prominent families to offer hospitality to travelers, particularly their own, but also to miscellaneous strangers. In doing so, they became the strangers' patrons but also served their communities by supervising the outsiders' behavior. Marguerite LePage LeClaire, for example, was a Métisse related to a prominent Mesquakie (Fox) family and married to Potawatomi Métis interpreter Antoine LeClaire, who was stationed for many years at Rock Island. She received a substantial land grant at the request of her Indian relatives at the time of the removal treaty of 1832, a grant that helped her family to become wealthy and prominent as founders of the city of Davenport, Iowa.[13] Afterward, according to a local historian in 1910, "delegations of the Sac and Fox Indians visited her place every year, where they were always made welcome, entertained as long as they wished to remain, and when leaving, always carried away as a free gift what necessaries they required — corn, flour, etc."[14] Anglo uneasiness about having Indians in town might be calmed by knowing that they were associates and relatives of Marguerite LePage LeClaire and that she was keeping an eye on them. Many other Creole women remained in touch with distant Indian communities, and welcomed, fed, and sheltered visitors. Some, such as Hononegah Mack, a HoChunk (Winnebago) woman married to an Anglo fur trader, moved out of their own homes and into the guests' wigwams during the visits.[15]

Creoles frequently offered hospitality not only to Native but also to non-Indian travelers and newcomers. Elizabeth Baird was one of Green Bay's hospitable Métisses six years after moving to Green Bay and experiencing a warm Creole welcome. When Juliette Kinzie and her husband visited the town in 1830, according to Kinzie's 1856 memoir, a party was thrown for them. "Every body will remember that dance at Mrs. Baird's. All the people, young and old . . . were assembled. . . . Everybody was bound to do honor to the strangers by appearing in their very best [clothing]. It was to be an entertainment unequalled by any given before."[16] It is interesting that Kinzie remembered this party as being at *Mrs.* Baird's rather than as at the Baird home or Mr. Baird's. Furthermore, the hostess evidently succeeded in making Kinzie feel well-honored.

Creoles adopted the Native sense of elite obligation, extending to neighbors the generosity they showed visitors. Marinette Chevalier, for example, "had been looked to as a mother by all the early settlers and Indians" because of her charity and comforting neighborliness. Marguerite LePage LeClaire, too, was extremely generous not only to her

Mesquakie relatives, but also to her church and "any public or philan-thropic enterprise."[17] Similarly, Hononegah Mack was known in north-ern Illinois for her hospitality and charity to everyone. When she died in 1847, her Anglo husband wrote: "In her the hungry and naked have lost a benefactor, the sick a nurse, and I have lost a friend who taught me to reverence God by doing good to his creatures. . . . Her funeral proved that I am not the only sufferer by her loss. My house is large but it was filled to overflowing by mourning friends who assembled to pay the last sad du-ties to her who had set them the example how to Live and how to Die."[18] After her funeral, one Anglo man remarked to his neighbors, "The best woman in Winnebago County died last night." In later years, a forest preserve was named for her.[19]

A Trempealeau County, Wisconsin, pioneer in 1886 recalled a woman who, during the 1850s, epitomized for him the "twin traits [of] generosity and hospitality," one of James Reed's three invisible wives (probably Arch-ange Barret). "Squaw though she was, she was an angel of mercy to the residents of Reed's Landing and Montoville. How distinctly I recall her commanding figure — going from house to house — not with words, for few could understand her broken French and native tongue — but with well filled basket, and ready hand — tender as only a woman's is — to cheer the sick."[20] Although this Anglo writer racialized her as a "squaw," he viewed Archange Barret Reed's actions as appropriate, gendered behavior.

IN THE EASTERN United States, changes in social relations since the mid-eighteenth century had altered some Anglo behaviors and expectations, while creating in many people a sense of nostalgia for colonial-era hospi-tality, communalism, and perceived idealism.[21] In the colonial era, charity had been one of the fundamental virtues expected of women, particularly elite women, but as the economy and society changed in the northeast during the early national period, new gender ideals were being created.[22] Many people were ambivalent about the new individualism touted as appropriate for men, mourning the loss of the communalistic ideal. Ideals for women, therefore, came to encompass the old communalism: the selflessness, empathy, and concern for the well-being of one's neighbor.[23] Charity continued to be seen as a positive attribute for women.

In the meantime, women's roles in childbirth and healing were chang-ing. Before the early nineteenth century, communities typically included a number of women with healing skills, but male doctors increasingly took over midwifery and healing work, administering new therapies and gradually closing women out of a professionalizing medical field, a change that must have made many people uneasy.[24] Creole women healers probably reminded emigrants of doctoring women and midwives in the preprofessional traditions. Kinship terms brought them into the family sphere and distanced them from "modern" professionals.

Anglophone emigrants to the Midwest were people dissatisfied enough with their lives in older communities to leave them behind. Many had been displaced by an evolving market economy and its attendant social disruptions. They frequently had mixed feelings about changes in their home societies: on the one hand, they looked back nostalgically to the old communalism and hospitality of days gone by; on the other hand, they tried to recreate many innovations of the changing societies they had left. For example, community studies of places such as Sugar Creek, Illinois, and Trempealeau County, Wisconsin, emphasize the ways Anglophone "pioneers" idealized "good neighborship."[25]

The Creoles seemed weird and exotic to these emigrants who would come to call themselves pioneers. Creoles spoke different languages, practiced a different religion, dressed oddly, had people of color among their elites, tolerated uppity women, and farmed differently. The pioneers might have trouble waxing enthusiastic about Marinette Chevalier's success as a businesswoman. They might be unwilling to designate James Reed's wife Archange Barret as a "first permanent settler" with her husband. They might try to persuade young Métis women that they could better serve a Protestant God as domestic servants than as religious leaders. But the pioneers were comforted by women of color who looked after their neighbors. This was appropriate behavior for women, even for women of color. They seem to have lauded Marinette Chevalier, Archange Barret Reed, and other Creole women for their nurturing, mother-like behavior, as they understood the concept, and the ways that this activity corresponded to their ideals.

The Creole women serving as public mothers succeeded in gaining the appreciation of the pioneers and Creoles because their actions corresponded to congruities in the two groups' value systems. But the ideals of these two groups did have significant differences, and women could behave in ways that seemed appropriate to the Creoles but peculiar or even scandalous to the pioneers. Although Creole gender ideals varied from family to family and region to region and evolved during the course of the nineteenth century, as a whole they differed in significant respects from those of Anglo-Americans. In particular, Creoles approved of women's activism in a wide range of areas, including economic management and innovation, political participation, and social network building. Even within local Catholic communities, some women played dynamic roles as they found ways to make the institution of the Catholic Church and belief system enhance their authority. Like Native women, many Creole women — even wives — could own, control, and convey property and manage independent businesses. In other words, they had the undisputed right to make economic decisions and often had a substantial amount of both personal autonomy and authority within their Creole communities and among the tribes of their Native kin.[26]

Indian traditions strongly influenced Creole ideals because Creole women were usually either Native or part-Native. From the mid-eighteenth century onward, multicultural and multiracial families had been negotiating gender-role differences. Whereas Europeans and Euro-Americans tended to believe that families should be patriarchal, that men should farm and take over leadership in government, religion, and commerce, Indian women played more active roles in politics, religious leadership, and the management of many forms of production. Creole couples' and families' compromises fell in between these traditions.[27]

Creoles valued public mothers because their actions reinforced many of the ideals and values of their own culture. The multiethnic nature of Creole families and communities meant that mediation and negotiation were fundamental to human behavior. Women were at the nexus of Creole families, as scholars of the fur trade era make clear, linking immigrant men to large family, clan, and community networks. Women learned and taught their husbands and Native relatives about each others' languages, customs, beliefs, values, and expectations. They interceded with each side on the others' behalf, translated, and negotiated local and family economic matters, contributing to the creation of syncretic cultures. They and their husbands raised multicultural, multilingual children who continued to have ties to both Indian and Creole communities, and they taught their daughters and sons to honor intermediaries.[28]

Creole peoples' values were distinctly communal: they built their homes close together, valued friendly cooperation, and scorned people who were argumentative. Historian Carl Ekberg argues that Creole communities were more socially cohesive than those of Anglo-Americans, that Creole people strongly valued congenial social interaction with their neighbors, reflected in their closely spaced village settlement patterns. In addition, he suggests that this dedication to the community, based on communal agricultural practices, created an aversion to violence, in marked contrast to frontier Anglos.[29] Jacqueline Peterson similarly argues that they "valued harmony and unanimity over competition; leisure over excess productivity; family and clan over economic interest and class; hospitality over exclusivity; generosity over saving; and today over tomorrow." These values, she suggests, were linked to Creoles' Native American influences.[30]

Because Creoles valued women and men who were community-minded, they appreciated that public mothers did more than create personal links between themselves and other individuals. These women's actions had specific meaning for the community as a whole: their efforts served social welfare and educational functions, facilitated social control, provided intergroup diplomacy, promoted peace, and served to acculturate and assimilate newcomers into the community. Many of these functions of public mothering are evident in two different sources: a Creole woman's memoir and an English traveler's narrative. One Métis woman responded to colonization by writing a memoir of life in Creole towns and changing times, an account published serially in a Green Bay newspaper in the 1880s. Elizabeth Thérèse Fisher Baird's reminiscence gives us glimpses of women in these communities from a point of view different from the pioneer narratives. Two incidents from the memoir, in the context of arrivals, can help us to understand Creole women's actions in the early-nineteenth-century Midwest.

The western Great Lakes had long been a region where people were in motion: Native Americans migrated seasonally and traveled widely, as did fur traders. The earliest Anglos came into the area as explorers, surveyors, soldiers, and officials, all of whom traversed the region more or less continuously, as did Anglo lead miners after 1822. Even the earliest judges and lawyers representing the U.S. government rode circuit. Their entrances into Creole towns were frequently facilitated by Creole women, as the following examples from Baird's memoir make clear.

One July day in 1820, a family arrived in a birch bark canoe at Mackinac Island and pitched their wigwam near the shore. With an infant only a few days old, the couple and their three other children were soon visited by Thérèse Marcotte Schindler, a forty-six-year-old Métisse and member of an elite fur trading family living in Creole Michilimackinac. Schindler (Elizabeth Baird's grandmother) extended a customary welcome and took them under her wing. She spoke fluent Ojibwe to mediate a separation between the quarreling husband, John Tanner, and his Ojibwe wife and became a patron to the Ojibwe woman (who appears in the memoir under the nickname "La Sateuse").[31] Schindler and her adult daughter, Mary Ann Lasallière Fisher, helped La Sateuse find a house nearby and become economically self-sufficient and encouraged her conversion to Catholic Christianity. Thus, La Sateuse followed the path that Indian women such as Schindler's Odawa mother had taken in joining the mixed-race fur trade society of the Midwest seventy years earlier.[32]

In 1824, four years after La Sateuse moved to Mackinac, Schindler's granddaughter Elizabeth Baird moved to Green Bay as the fourteen-year-old wife of a Scots-Irish lawyer. When she and her husband arrived, two elite Métis women and their husbands welcomed them to the community. Baird did not yet speak much English, but Catiche Caron Grignon put her at ease by speaking the Ojibwe language with her. Theresa Rankin Lawe's clothing reminded Baird of her grandmother and great aunt. She later wrote, "Mrs. Lawe was one of the best of the earth, and as she wore the Indian dress, that at once endeared her to [me]." Creole women in these communities often maintained multiethnic identities, evidenced in their clothing, language, tribal affiliations, and names. Baird's Green Bay hosts made no effort to deny their Native heritage; in fact, their Native dress and use of Indian languages facilitated the creation of ties to Baird, and no doubt to others. Her grandmother's biculturalism likewise created ties to La Sateuse and to other Native, Métis, and Euro-American people.[33]

Clearly, they intended (whether consciously or not) to create bonds of affinity and mutual obligation between their own families and kin networks and the families and kin networks of those they assisted. They were also doing what they had been taught was the right thing for people to do, "to reverence God by doing good to his creatures," as Stephen Mack interpreted the labors of his wife, Hononegah. The alliances they sought were not just for themselves and their families, but for the good of their communities. As such, they were very public actions.

Elite Métis women in Baird's account — Thérèse Marcotte Schindler, Catiche Caron Grignon, and Theresa Rankin Lawe — reached out to newcomers and to those in need, creating ties of affection accompanied by bonds of obligation, integrating outsiders into their communities in ways that minimized socially disruptive alienation. In greeting the newcomers, these elite Creoles gained information about them, then became their patrons and/or mentors, providing social welfare functions such as foster care and vocational training and mediating marital disputes. Some of these activities, such as Marguerite LeClaire's hosting visiting Mesqua-kies, served as a form of social control. At both the personal and in-tergroup levels, public mothers promoted peace. Furthermore, public mothering was educational in that it facilitated cross-cultural learning, as both helpers and helped gained knowledge from their contacts with each other. Contacts among Creole healers, hostesses, and charity workers, and their beneficiaries, could dispel suspicion, ignorance, and intoler-ance. In addition, some Creole women educated their neighbors in re-ligious traditions: Schindler, her daughter, and her sister Madeleine La-Framboise taught Catholicism to their female neighbors, as did many other Métis women.[34]

The Métis women helping new arrivals in Baird's account were clearly negotiating social and even economic connections, but they could also facilitate diplomatic alliances. Although he did not understand what he was seeing, a traveling Englishman who published under the pseudonym "A Merry Briton" in 1841 happened upon the home of Nancy McCrea and her husband, Augustin Grignon, at a fur trade center on Wisconsin's Wolf River consisting of a house and garden (including several acres of corn), with a number of Indian lodges nearby. The traveler entered the house uninvited and observed that "sundry pigeon-toed squaws, and mild-looking, half-breed girls, were busy preparing victuals about an immense fire-place." Meanwhile, Augustin Grignon and another Creole man sat by a window working on account books, while "several Indians and half-breeds lounged about in various attitudes . . . smoking their tomahawk pipes." The Briton was greeted by Grignon, who made him welcome.[35]

At dusk, the Menominee chief Oshkosh, a kinsman of the Métis hostess Nancy McCrea, arrived with a number of companions and was warmly greeted by the family and other guests. After a meal consisting of "wild-duck stew, tea, and cakes," Oshkosh stood before the fireplace to make a long and formal speech in the Menominee language to the sizable crowd. A member of the Grignon family translated the half-hour-long presentation for the Briton. "The speech, from first to last, was in the declamatory style, and against whisky," he wrote. Another speech was clearly called for, and Nancy McCrea Grignon spoke up in the Menominee language. "Anon, old mother Grignon, a squaw of high and ancient family, with a crucifix round her neck, replied, in a nasal, whining voice: her speech was listened to with great attention." Unfortunately, we do not know what she said, as the Briton dozed off during the oration.[36]

McCrea ("old mother Grignon"), the fur trader's wife, was clearly a person who connected people of different worlds. The daughter of a woman from an elite Menominee family and a Scottish fur trader, she spoke French and Menominee and probably several other Indian languages.[37] Her role as public speaker in the simultaneously public and private arena of her home and the rapt attention of her family and guests testify to her significance in smoothing relations between the fur traders and their Indian customers, between Creoles and Menominees, and between the extended Grignon family and the clan of Oshkosh.

In the old French Canadian fur trade regions, such women combined social, political, and economic roles as they created and enhanced relationships, facilitated communication, and helped negotiate intercultural relations. The diplomacy evident in Nancy McCrea Grignon's oration took another form in the actions of Thérèse Schindler and any of the other public mothers mentioned by the pioneer writers. They adapted patterns of intercultural relations to the new waves of colonization. During the fur trade era, the connections had been between Native peoples and members of the Canadian fur trade world. After the War of 1812, the challenge was to adapt mediation skills in order to smooth relations with the Anglos and European immigrants.

Marriage had been one way to create ties. Indian peoples in the Midwest had approved of—and even encouraged—intermarriage. Although Native women who married Euro-Americans during the fur trade era smoothed personal and economic relations between the two groups, after the War of 1812, Indian and Métis wives often mediated among three cultures: Indian, Creole, and the conquering Anglophone newcomers from the United States. Many wives served as translators and cultural interpreters for neighbors, husband, kin, and whole communities. Some Creoles created links by promoting and arranging marriages between their children and Anglo immigrants. These marriages honored the Indian custom of incorporating outsiders into families and communities through marriage, and mirror the historical experiences of some Spanish-speaking families in California and Texas during the transition to U.S.

hegemony around the time of the Mexican War.[38] But a look at 330 recorded marriages in Crawford County, Wisconsin, where Prairie du Chien is located, shows that exogamous marriage (marriage to someone of another ethnic group) was declining as a proportion of all marriages, from 32 percent in the 1820s, to 24 percent in the 1830s, to 14 percent in the 1840s.[39] The relative decline in exogamy reduced opportunities for people to gain linguistic and cultural tools needed to create alliances. Even so, many Creoles responded to colonization by continuing to mediate, not only between Indians and Creoles, but also between these two groups and the immigrants. Indeed, the decrease in intermarriage in the face of surging Anglo immigration created a greater need for informal mediation within a community; public mothering thus seems to have created other bonds, and it is no mere coincidence that the pioneers sometimes referred to the public mothers in kinship terms.

If creole women were doubly oppressed — as women and as minorities — were they doubly sensitive? As people living in fur trade communities founded expressly to link indigenous and alien cultures, they had been reared observing negotiation and mediation, hearing it praised, perhaps even trained in it. When the balance of power shifted as the United States colonized the region, the roles of both women and people of color became increasingly at risk. Creoles' history suggested that these issues might be negotiable, as they had been during the fur trade era.

THE BEHAVIORS OF Creole public mothers, and the extent to which their efforts were appreciated and even valorized, teach us that they actively reached out to their communities, and that in doing so, they found a middle ground among the various ideals of womanhood held by the region's people. The fact that they found this intersection testifies to the continuation of Creole traditions of mediation. For the Creole people of the Midwest, the nineteenth century was a transitional era, and they experienced the imposition of increasing restrictions on women and people of color. As mediators, many Creoles responded to changes brought by Anglo immigration by continuing activities of negotiation, learning, and adapting. A decrease in exogamy reduced one tool of mediation, but Creoles explored others. Some Creole women expanded the roles available to them by their matrifocal culture, in which women's activities could be at once public and private, concerned with family and household while also for the benefit of the community. In the actions of hostesses, midwives, healers, and other caring neighbors, we see Creole communalism expressed by mature elite women creating and extending matrifocal networks. Their new Anglo neighbors — people who themselves had emigrated from transitional cultures — were particularly receptive to these women of color, whose actions conformed to their evolving feminine and communalistic ideals.

These Indian, Métis, and even African American women nurtured their neighbors, acting as public mothers to mediate among disparate groups in multiethnic regions. Their actions were in the best traditions of Native American, African American, Euro-American, and Creole women's activism. Although Creoles were frequently scorned for their cultural, ethnic, racial, and economic differences, some Creole women succeeded in reaching across the barriers by navigating the intersections of cultural ideals.

Notes

1. The terms "Native American," "Native," and "Indian" are used interchangeably in this essay, following American Indian studies conventional usage.
2. George E. Brookes Jr., "The *Signares* of Saint-Louis and Gorée: Women Entrepreneurs in Eighteenth-Century Senegal," in *Women in Africa: Studies in Social and Economic Change*, ed. Nancy J. Hafkin and Edna G. Bay (Stanford: Stanford University Press, 1976), 19–44; E. Frances White, *Sierra Leone's Settler Women Traders* (Ann Arbor: University of Michigan Press, 1987).
3. Jacqueline Peterson, "The People in Between: Indian-White Marriage and the Genesis of a Métis Society and Culture in the Great Lakes Region, 1680–1830" (Ph.D. diss., University of Illinois at Chicago, 1981), 133, 136.
4. Rodolfo Acuña, *Occupied America: A History of Chicanos* (New York: Pearson Longman, 1988).
5. Les Rentmeester and Jeanne Rentmeester, *The Wisconsin Creoles* (Melbourne, Fla.: Privately published, 1987), v–iii; Mary Gehman, *Women and New Orleans: A History* (New Orleans, 1988), 10; "Creoles," *Iowa Patriot*, 6 June 1839.
6. Peterson, "People in Between"; Lucy Eldersveld Murphy, *Gathering of Rivers: Indians, Métis and Mining in the Western Great Lakes, 1737–1832* (Lincoln: University of Nebraska Press, 2000), 45–76.
7. See, for example, Allan Greer, *The People of New France* (Toronto: University of Toronto Press, 1997), 69–71.
8. Beverly Johnson, *Queen Marinette* (Amasa, Michigan: Whitewater Associates, 1995), 32–33.
9. James Lockwood, "Early Times and Events in Wisconsin," *Collection of the State Historical Society of Wisconsin* 2 (1856):125–126.
10. Thomas E. Randall, *History of the Chippewa Valley* (Eau Claire, Wisc., 1875), 17–18.

11. *Oceana County History*, 1990, 1: 425; Paula Stofer, "Angels of Mercy: Michigan's Midwives," *Michigan History* 73, 5 (1989): 46.

12. "Mrs. H. L. Robinson Dead," *The Journal* (Hart, Mich.), 22 April 1904, 1. Typescript copy in the possession of Susan Russick.

13. "Memoir of Antoine LeClaire, Esquire, of Davenport, Iowa," *Annals of Iowa* (1863), 1: 144–147; Harry E. Downer, *History of Davenport and Scott County, Iowa* (Chicago: S. J. Clarke, 1910), 394–405.

14. Downer, *History of Davenport*, 400.

15. David Bishop and Craig G. Campbell, *History of the Forest Preserves of Winnebago County, Illinois* (Rockford, Ill.: Winnebago County Forest Preserve Commission, 1979), 35; Elihu B. Washburne, "Col. Henry Gratiot—A Pioneer of Wisconsin," State Historical Society of Wisconsin, *Collections* (1888), 10: 258; Walter O'Meara, *Daughters of the Country* (New York: Harcourt, Brace and World, 1968), 297.

16. Juliette M. Kinzie, *Wau-Bun: The "Early Day" in the North-West* (1856; Urbana, 1992), 19.

17. Downer, *History of Davenport*, 400.

18. Stephen Mack to H. M. Whittmore, Pecatoni, Oct. 8, 1847, quoted in Bishop and Campbell, *History of the Forest Preserves*, 35.

19. Bishop and Campbell, *History of the Forest Preserves*, 35.

20. John McGilvray to B. F. Heuston, June 18, 1886, Heuston Collection, Murphy Library, University of Wisconsin, La Crosse, Wisconsin State Historical Society.

21. Rhys Isaac, *The Transformation of Virginia, 1740–1790* (Chapel Hill: University of North Carolina Press, 1982), 71, 302–305.

22. Laurel Thatcher Ulrich, *Good Wives: Image and Reality in the Lives of Women in Northern New England, 1650–1750* (New York: Knopf, 1982), 59–65.

23. Barbara Welter, "The Cult of True Womanhood: 1820–1860," *American Quarterly* 18 (1966): 151–174; Mary P. Ryan, *Cradle of the Middle Class: The Family in Oneida County, New York, 1790–1865* (New York: Cambridge University Press, 1981), 210–218.

24. Laurel Thatcher Ulrich, *A Midwife's Tale: The Life of Martha Ballard, Based on Her Diary, 1785–1812* (New York: Vintage Books, 1990), 62, 254–261; Gerda Lerner, "The Lady and the Mill Girl," in *The Majority Finds Its Past* (New York: Oxford University Press, 1979), 15–30.

25. Merle Curti, *The Making of an American Community* (Stanford: Stanford University Press, 1959), 114–116; John Mack Faragher, *Sugar Creek; Life on the Illinois Prairie* (New Haven: Yale University Press, 1986), chap. 14.

26. See, for example, Rebecca Kugel, "Re-Working Ethnicity: Gender, Work Roles and the Redefinition of the Great Lakes Métis," in *People of Persistence: Cultural Change in the Great Lakes Region*, ed. R. David Edmunds (Urbana, Ill., forthcoming).

27. Kinzie, *Wau-Bun*, 48; Donald Jackson, ed., *Black Hawk, an Autobiography* (Urbana: University of Illinois Press, 1990), 104; Roger L. Nichols, *Black Hawk and the Warrior's Path* (Arlington Heights, Ill.: H. Davidson, 1992), 89; David Lee Smith, *Folklore of the Winnebago* (Norman: University of Oklahoma Press, 1997), 155–157; Norman Gelb, ed., *Jonathan Carver's Travels through America, 1766–1768* (New York: Wiley, 1993), 69, 70.

28. Peterson, "People in Between"; Sylvia Van Kirk, *Many Tender Ties: Women in Fur Trade Society 1670–1870* (Norman: University of Oklahoma Press, 1983); Jennifer S. H. Brown, *Strangers in Blood: Fur Trade Company Families in Indian Country* (Vancouver: University of British Columbia Press, 1980); Kidwell, "Indian Women as Cultural Mediators"; Susan Sleeper-Smith, *Indian Women and French Men: Rethinking Cultural Encounters in the Western Great Lakes* (Amherst: University of Massachusetts Press, 2000); Murphy, *A Gathering of Rivers*.

29. Carl Ekberg, "Agriculture, *Mentalités*, and Violence on the Illinois Frontier," *Illinois Historical Journal* 88 (summer 1995): 101–117.

30. Jacqueline Peterson, "Goodbye, Madore Beaubien: The Americanization of Early Chicago Society," *Chicago History* 9 (summer 1980): 101.

31. La Sateuse means "the Ojibwe woman." John Francis McDermott, *A Glossary of Mississippi Valley French, 1673–1850* (St. Louis, 1941), s.v. "Saulters," 136.

32. Elizabeth Baird, "O-De-Jit-Wa-Win-Wing," Henry S. Baird Collection, Box 4, folder 9, State Historical Society of Wisconsin, Madison, ch. 17; John E. McDowell, "Therese Schindler of Mackinac: Upward Mobility in the Great Lakes Fur Trade," *Wisconsin Magazine of History* 61, 2 (1977–78): 125–143; Susan Sleeper-Smith, "Women, Kin, and Catholicism: New Perspectives on the Fur Trade," *Ethnohistory* 47 (spring 2000).

33. Baird, "O-De-Jit-Wa-Win-Wing," chaps. 7, 10, 11. Although some sources spell the maiden name Marcot, Elizabeth Baird gave Marcotte as the spelling. "Memoranda," Box 4, folder 1, Baird Collection, State Historical Society of Wisconsin, Madison.

34. Baird, "O-De-Jit-Wa-Win-Wing"; Samuel Mazzuchelli, *The Memoirs of Father Samuel Mazzuchelli* (Chicago: The Printing Press, 1967).

35. *A Merry Briton in Pioneer Wisconsin* (1842; Chicago, 1950), 69.

36. Ibid., 71–72.

37. Virginia G. Crane, "A Métis Woman of the Fox River Frontier: The Two Cultures of Sophia Grignon Porlier," paper presented at the conference "Women of the Midwest: History and Sources: A Women's History Outreach Conference," Madison, Wisc. 13 June 1997.

38. Darlis Miller, "Cross-Cultural Marriages in the Southwest: The New Mexico Experience, 1846–1900," *New Mexico Historical Review* 57 (1982): 335–359; Antonia Castañeda, "Presidarias y pobladoras" (Ph.D. diss., Stanford University, 1990); Douglas Monroy, *Thrown among Strangers: The Making of Mexican Culture in Frontier California* (Berkeley: University of California Press, 1990).

39. Hansen, "Crawford County, Wisconsin Marriages 1816–1848," *Minnesota Genealogical Journal* 1 (May 1984): 39–58.

Mrinalini Sinha

Britishness, Clubbability, and the Colonial Public Sphere

European clubs were historically elite white male preserves in Britain, and even more so in India, where they functioned as islands of Englishness in a sea of "natives." Over the course of the nineteenth and twentieth centuries, as educated Indian men sought inclusion in the imperial nation-state through both political and social means, the racial exclusivity of English clubs became more and more apparent. But the prejudices that marked "clubland" in both the United Kingdom and its empire were not merely a matter of race or even class, but of gender as well. This essay reveals the ways in which the spaces of relaxation and recreation that clubs provided to a certain elite segment of the colonial public tried to prevent certain bodies from coming into contact, notably, those of white English women and Indian men of all classes. Not only were white women not deemed "clubbable," that is, capable of that male-defined collegiality that was thought to underwrite English national character, they also had to be protected from the presumptively sexual interests of "native" men. Elite Indian women, equally determined to enter politics, proved some of the fiercest critics of clubland, though the persistence of a club mentality in postcolonial India testifies to the capacities of "natives" to appropriate and transform even the most exclusive symbols of Raj power down to the present.

The ubiquity of the European social club in the European empires in the nineteenth and early twentieth centuries has been widely recognized in both popular and academic writings on European, and particularly British, imperialism. Although each individual club often catered to a very different and distinctive clientele among elite Europeans in the empire, "clubland" as a whole served as a common ground where elite Europeans could meet as members, or as guests of members, of individual clubs. These clubs represented an oasis of European culture in the colonies, functioning to reproduce the comfort and familiarity of "home" for Europeans living in an alien land. The cultural values that the club represented were understood as transplanted to the colonies. In the words of H. R. Panckridge, "It is the practice of European peoples to reproduce as far as possible in their settlements and colonies in other continents the characteristic social features of their natural lives. . . . For more than a century no institution has been more *peculiarly British* than the social club."[1]

Scores of British memoirs about India testify to the centrality of the club in the lives of the British in India. As Leonard Woolf has noted, the club, indeed, was "the center and symbol of British imperialism . . . with its cult of exclusiveness, superiority and isolation."[2] These often racially exclusive institutions were equally the object of "native" desire and resentment. Thus George Orwell in *Burmese Days* wrote that "in any town in India the European Club is the spiritual citadel, the real seat of British power; the Nirvana for which native officials and millionaires pine in vain."[3] The imperialist British historian Valentine Chirol went even further in reducing the cause of the "Indian Unrest" in the early decades of the twentieth century to the racial exclusivity of the social clubs in India. "A question which causes a good deal of soreness," he wrote, "is the rigid exclusion of Indians from many Anglo Indian [British] clubs."[4] What marks the European social club in India as a quintessentially imperial institution is neither its origin as a metropolitan extension nor its representation as an island of exclusive "Britishness" in India. It is, rather, as a privileged site for mediating the contradictory logic of Eurocentrism in the creation of a distinctive colonial public sphere that the European social club acquires its centrality as an imperial institution in colonial India.

EXCEPT FOR A few descendants of the old coffeehouses, the new, luxurious, and exclusive clubs were creations of the nineteenth century. The heart of this clubland culture was located in central London in St. James's Street and Pall Mall. The clubs on St. James's Street had their origins in the "aristocratic" eighteenth century and had a clientele drawn mainly from the British aristocracy, and the clubs on Pall Mall were mainly nineteenth-century creations and their membership was predominantly middle class. Membership in particular gentleman's clubs became a passport for entry into the culture of the ruling elites in Britain and helped to sustain an elaborate system of old boys' networks. By midcentury, these private gentleman's clubs, whose function was to mediate and distribute elite power, had, like the Great English Public Schools and Oxbridge, become naturalized as important, and seemingly timeless, monuments of national English culture.

The popularity of clubs in India was in part a response to the particular demographic challenges of the overseas European population in India.[5] There was, for example, a heavy preponderance of single British men, or married men living singly in India, especially in the early decades of colonial rule. Even as late as 1921, however, the total European population in India comprised approximately 45,000 women and some 112,000 men. Moreover, there were always relatively few elderly persons and children in the overseas European community. In addition, a great deal of mobility was required of at least the officials of the colonial government. It was in this context that the clubs became popular for providing boarding and lodging for a transient elite white male population; they set apart chambers for the members residing permanently in the city and for those making only a short stay. This "domestic" function of the club is emphasized by H. R. Panckridge, a former secretary of the Bengal Club in Calcutta: "The idea of the club makes a special appeal to the large number of men, who are compelled by circumstances to be separated from their wives and families for longer or shorter periods. . . . [The clubs] offer a welcome solution of a difficult problem to the many bachelors with a distaste for housekeeping."[6] The control and management of Anglo-Indian domestic life, implied by the rapid rise and popularity of European social clubs in India, served to reproduce the desired forms of private as well as public life for Anglo-Indians.[7]

Even after the arrival of a larger number of white women in India, the clubs continued to play an important role in integrating the private "domestic" and public lives of the Anglo-Indian community abroad. By the end of the century the clubs had become the center of European social life in India. In the words of Lieutenant General Reginald Savory, who served in India from 1914 to 1947, "If you didn't belong to the Club you were an outcast. . . . Either you were a rebel, and a rather courageous rebel, who didn't belong to the club, or else you were a social outcast who wanted to belong to the club and couldn't get in."[8] The "rebels" were to be found mainly among European missionaries, single women, and independent-minded intellectuals who were self-conscious about rejecting the norms of Anglo-Indian social life. The centrality of the club in European social life in India put pressure on the incorporation of white women in clubland. For, as W. O. Home, a civil servant in turn-of-the-century Madras, feared, white women, if left on their own in India, would lower the prestige of the ruling race and "let down the side."[9] This ensured that the European social clubs in India became immediately more vulnerable to the "infiltration" of women than their counterparts in Britain.

When J. H. Rivett-Carnac, of the elite Indian Civil Service (ICS), arrived in India in 1856, he noted that most local European clubs in India already had their "special ladies' quarters."[10] By midcentury the dingy *moorghi khanna* or henhouse for white women had become standard in most city clubs in India. Although backcountry station clubs held out a little longer, they ultimately proved even more vulnerable to the entry of white women. In the smaller up-country or *mofussil* towns, women were often allowed even into the main club buildings, with only the bar carrying the warning: "Women not allowed beyond this point." The club, in particular the club veranda, came to serve as "a sort of get together place for the women folk."[11] These clubs, having been forced to accept the intrusion of women, even carried advertisements for the sale of "prams, ponies, sewing machines etc. on their notice boards."[12] To be sure, the "domestic atmosphere" that permeated many of the station clubs was the source of much complaint among die-hard masculinist members.[13] Even as late as the 1920s the presence of a white woman who, having lost her way, had strayed into the premises of the United Services Club in Simla to ask for directions created quite a stir. Sir Henry Sharp recalls that the "vision of female form profaning this sacred precinct" so alarmed another member of the club that "with commendable tact and presence of mind . . . [he] snatched a notice from the wall and holding it in front of him, barred further progress to the intruder. The notice ran 'Dogs and other noxious animals are not allowed in the Club.' "[14] White women, indeed, were seldom allowed unrestricted use of the club premises. Although they had been incorporated grudgingly into clubland, they had no official standing in the clubs and their names seldom appeared in the list of members. Yet clubland in India, in response to its particular colonial location, was already more of a "domestic" institution than it ever became in metropolitan Britain.

When in the interwar period the issue of admitting Indians (especially those in the elite all-India services) acquired great urgency, Anglo-Indian segregationists cited the presence of white women in the clubs as the grounds for their reluctance to allow native members or guests in the clubs. White segregationists argued that the Indians were as yet "unclubbable" because "they would not bring their wives [to the club], but hang around English ladies, for whom, it was well known, Indians held lascivious yearnings."[15] H. T. Wickham, who was the superintendent of police at Bishraw in 1921, recalled the debate over allowing Indians to join the local club: "The Club was a purely private club supported by subscriptions from members who had to be elected, and when the question of permitting Indians to join arose a large number of the members didn't like it. Their chief objection was the fact that the Indians, if they joined the Club, would consort with the female members of the club, while their own female members were prohibited from coming, because they would be in purdah and could not therefore mix with people unveiled."[16]

On the one hand, white women were grudgingly accorded the status of being clubbable to prevent them from getting into trouble if left on their own. On the other hand, the alleged protection of white women from the unprovoked attention of Indian men also made them crucial determinants in the "unclubbability" of Indians. The clubland of colonial India was thus not so much a "hothouse" import from a sealed-off national British culture as a response to the particular demands of its colonial location. More generally, the European social clubs in India formed part of an elaborate set of mechanisms that articulated the legitimate boundaries of an acceptable image of "whiteness." Through gendered, raced, and class-specific assumptions, the concept of clubbability rendered whites "visible in a certain way" in the colonial domain.[17] The clubs, by their very nature as self-selecting institutions, confined their membership to "select people": mainly elite European bureaucrats, military officials, and nonofficials (those who were not in the employ of the government). Through such institutions as the clubs, this select group of people was able to sustain a certain lifestyle that corresponded to the politically desirable self-image of a ruling white population in India. For most of the nineteenth century nearly half the European population in India consisted of "poor whites." These poor whites posed an obvious challenge to the racial self-image of the white community. By the end of the century, therefore, many of these poor whites had been shipped back to Britain, while even more — nearly six thousand — had been taken off the streets and confined in workhouses, where they were simultaneously "invisible" and "useful."[18] Nonetheless, there was always a sizable population of "lower-class" Europeans in India, most notably British soldiers, who were excluded from the contours of whiteness represented by clubland. The clubs, indeed, functioned in complementary ways with such institutions as the workhouses for the poor, the military cantonments for the soldiers, and the Railways Institutes for the Eurasians in setting the limits of, as well as determining the visibility of, whiteness as such in colonial India. The clubland, which was never coextensive with the European population in India, was thus implicated in dramatizing a very specific and limited construction of whiteness in India.

The clubs also served to provide private European economic firms in India direct access to the representatives of the colonial government, thereby contributing to the exclusive European control over the economy and the gradual decline of native economic competitiveness in the nineteenth century, especially in Bengal. To be sure, as Charles Allen reminds us, membership in individual clubs was based on occupation, and there was general discrimination against Europeans in "technical work" and against "counter-jumpers" (people who worked in shops).[19] Yet clubland, both through the system of reciprocation among major clubs and the provision for entertaining European guests on club premises, provided easy access between different sections of the Anglo-Indian elite. Even the Bengal Club, one of the most exclusive clubs of Anglo India, had relaxed its rules about guest nights in 1872, enabling members to invite guests any night of the week so long as the name of the member and his guest was entered in the dinner book the previous evening.[20] Several Anglo-Indian memoirs, indeed, testify to the advantages of the ties that were forged between official and nonofficial sections of the European population in the clubs.

It was these "clubland ties" that gave nonofficial Europeans in India their edge over rival Indian economic competitors in the colonial political economy. Official and nonofficial members were able to settle business matters on a friendly and informal basis in the clubs. For example, a case in the Calcutta High Court over a dispute concerning land in the Port Canning area was amicably discussed by the two parties concerned over a friendly dinner at the Bengal Club. The civil servant representing the Bengal government in this case wrote that "the counsel for the plaintiff was a friend of mine, and after we had been served with notice of appeal I spoke to him about the case one day at the Club." The conversation ended with a remark from his friend: "You must not betray my after-dinner confidences."[21] The premium associated with club membership is further brought out in a trial in 1927 of a young Bengali man who, on the strength of some stolen stationery from the United Services Club in Calcutta, could pass himself off as an Anglo-Indian and defraud several European firms in Calcutta. The clubs, indeed, were an important instrument in the European stranglehold of the colonial political economy.

The "gentlemanly obligations" of club membership also enabled these institutions to serve as a mechanism for reconciling Anglo-Indians to decisions affecting sections of the population differently. The stormy relationship between the official and nonofficial sections of the European population was frequently mediated through the protocol and etiquette of club membership. In 1836, for example, the Bengal Club was rocked by a controversy that almost threatened the existence of the club. J. H. Stocqueler, the founder of the popular European daily in Calcutta, the *Englishman,* had severely criticized certain measures taken by Mr. Lumley as adjutant general on behalf of the Bengal government. Lumley filed a defamation case against Stocqueler in the High Court. Stocqueler's decision to attack publicly the official action of a fellow member of his club raised questions about the proper ethics of club membership.[22] The subsequent move to expel Stocqueler led to a schism that almost brought about the dissolution of the club. The smooth functioning of the club, as the Stocqueler-Lumley episode reveals, required a certain degree of civility between members of a club whatever their political differences.

In the 1860s, the divisions within the Anglo-Indian community, this time over the indigo disturbances or the "blue mutiny," surfaced once again in the activities of the Bengal Club.[23] The well-meaning translation of the vernacular play *Nil Darpan* (by a clergyman, Reverend Long) drew attention to the wretched condition of native indigo cultivators in the European-managed indigo plantations in Bengal. Subsequent government action regulating the planters and protecting indigo cultivators was greatly resented by powerful sections of the nonofficial European population. Morduant Wells, of the Calcutta High Court, who was also president of the Bengal Club, was involved in the trial of Reverend Long for libel. Sir Henry Cotton, an ICS officer and member of the Bengal Club, recalled that during the disturbances, "It was the practice to blackball an official at the Bengal Club . . . merely because he was an official."[24] The potential of schism within influential sections of the Anglo-Indian community was often contained within the contours of clubland.

Although the various European agents of colonialism in India continued to have contradictory priorities, clubland came to represent the powerful voice of Anglo-Indian public opinion. Government officials, in fact, looked on club membership as a means of keeping a finger on the pulse of popular Anglo-Indian opinion in the province. As one European civil servant wrote, "It was interesting, though not always satisfactory, to know what non-officials thought of official proceedings; and opinions were expressed [in the Club] with very considerable freedom."[25] It was thus that officials were expressly enjoined to play an active part in the club life of their station. The assistant collector's manual in Bombay, for example, clearly defined participation in the clubs as an official duty: "Even though you may be shy of thrusting yourself among comparative strangers, make a practice of going to the clubs regularly, it will probably rub off some unsuspecting corners of your personality to your lasting benefit. Even if you should find the society of the club uninteresting, you have, in virtue of your position, to fill a place in the social life of the station, and to do your part to amuse and entertain the other residents, who may not have your resources of culture and interest. Golf, tennis, etc. are valuable aids to getting to know your fellows."[26]

It was as a public space that the clubs, especially in isolated up-country stations, served the function of fashioning Anglo-Indian public opinion in India. The efficacy of this strand of public opinion was especially felt in the political controversies of the second half of the nineteenth century. The conditions for the cohesion of Anglo-Indian public opinion were created in part by the rebellion of 1857, which had heightened white anxieties about Indian hostility. Furthermore, the growing challenge posed by middle-class Indian nationalists to exclusive white privileges fostered further the need for greater Anglo-Indian cooperation as well as the desirability of internal mechanisms to resolve differences within the Anglo-Indian community. The role of the clubs in representing Anglo-Indian public opinion was especially marked during the "white mutiny" of 1883–1884, when pressure from official and nonofficial Anglo-Indian opinion forced the viceroy and his law member to modify drastically a bill that would have granted Indian civil servants the right to exercise criminal jurisdiction over nonofficial Europeans in the small up-country stations in India. The clubs, where official and nonofficial Anglo-Indians gathered together, orchestrated the massive opposition to the government-sponsored measure. Clubs all over India were at the center of Anglo-Indian opposition to the bill; in remote country stations, for example, protest meetings of Anglo-Indians were held in the club reading rooms. The members of the Byculla Club in Bombay, contrary to the tradition of that club, refused a proposal to entertain the viceroy on his way home to Britain. Anglo-Indian clubland, especially in Bengal, became the backbone for the opposition against the bill.

The members of the Bengal Club, whose honorary patron was the viceroy of India, used the controversy to spearhead the formation of the European and Anglo-Indian Defence Association (EAIDA), which would henceforth monitor any infringement of the privileges of the white population in India. The need for an organization with such an explicit political aim had been broached first in a letter from a member of the Bengal Club. The anonymous letter writer wrote that "the Bengal Club by no means answers the purpose. It is a somewhat dull and decaying institution, but whether it might not be galvanized into new and vigorous life by being placed, in commemoration of these events, on a political basis, it is for its managers to decide."[27] Mr. J. J. J. Keswick, a senior partner in the firm Jardine, Skinner and Company and the president of the Bengal Club, along with other prominent members of the Club Committee, pioneered the creation of the notorious EAIDA as a separate political arm of clubland opinion in India. The close ties between the two institutions continued well into the 1920s, when Panckridge, as secretary and historian of the Bengal Club, also served as paid secretary for the EAIDA.[28]

The point, of course, is not that there were unified interests shared even among elite Anglo-Indians in India. It is rather that the clubs themselves produced and represented what counted as Anglo-Indian public opinion in India. The *Pioneer*, almost the semiofficial newspaper of the British in India, defended the role of the clubs during the controversy: "We are . . . inclined to think that the inherent justice or injustice . . . of political measures is what dictates the opinion of men — not so much that opinions spring from the fortuitous gathering of them together in a club."[29] Colonial clubland, however, was itself clearly instrumental in fashioning Anglo-Indian opinion. It is interesting to note, for example, that at the general meeting of the Bengal Club on 27 November 1912, the members decided to give the club vote in the elections for municipal commissioner representing Ward 16 in Calcutta to an Anglo-Indian over an Indian candidate. The decision apparently required no discussion among the members on the individual merits of the two candidates. Colonial clubland, despite the arguments of its apologists, had long become implicated in constructing and maintaining the boundaries of a particular representation of "whiteness."

IN THE 1860s Mr. James Hume, then the chief magistrate of Calcutta, together with some Indian friends, tried to promote the establishment of the Cosmopolitan Club for Indians and Europeans alike. Accounting for its eventual failure, one Anglo-Indian paper wrote, "The idea was in advance of its age and collapsed in a few years."[30] The India Club, established in 1882 under the patronage of the Maharaja of Cooch Behar, was one of the more durable of subsequent experiments along these lines. It provided the model for several "native" clubs that were set up by Indians in the smaller mofussil towns in Bengal and, later, in other parts of India. The entrance fee for the India Club when it started was only 5 rupees (as compared to the 200 rupees at the Bengal Club and the 100 rupees at the United Services Club in Calcutta) and there was a monthly subscription of 2 rupees. The object of the club was "to supply a place where gentlemen, both native and European, could freely mix, independent of their social, political, and religious differences."[31] The list of some of the early Indian patrons of the India Club included prominent Hindu, Brahmo, Muslim, Parsi, and Christian men of Calcutta. In the first year the club had a membership of 200, and by 1890 it had increased to 435. The Bengal Club for approximately the same time period had a membership of just under 800.[32] The India Club, however, never became very popular with its European members. When Wilfred Scawen Blunt, a member of Parliament, visited India in the 1880s, he wrote of his experience at the India Club that "the bitterness of feeling is now so great that, with the exception of two or three secretaries in attendance on Indian princes I was the only Englishman present."[33]

In patronizing tones, the Anglo-Indian press had been predicting the dissolution of the India Club from the very outset. According to the *Englishman,* the failure of such mixed experiments raised doubts if there were "clubbable men . . . to be found amongst the natives of India."[34] The

Pioneer pointed to the lack of solidarity among "native" club members; it noted that the India Club was "proof that natives cannot utilize the club system of Europe for . . . marshaling and centralizing opposition, [or] as a means of inspiring its peculiar press."[35] This was in response to a scene that had allegedly taken place in the club on 20 March 1883. Raja Shib Prasad, a member of the Viceroy's Council, was reported to have been harassed by the Indian members of the club for his unpopular stand on the criminal jurisdiction bill of 1883–1884. The India Club, however, outlived the gloomy predictions of the Anglo-Indian press and continued to be patronized by the leaders of Indian public opinion. It entertained the delegates of the second annual conference of the Indian National Congress held in Calcutta in 1886. In 1901 the India Club was still being patronized by Indian National Congress delegates. During the 1901 Calcutta Congress the Congress stalwart, Gopal Krishna Gokhale, and his as yet relatively unknown apprentice from South Africa, M. K. Gandhi, enjoyed the hospitality of the India Club.[36]

Despite the success of such individual experiments, however, colonial clubland not only consisted primarily of European social clubs, but the private gentleman's social club never became a dominant institution in the emergent Indian counterpublics under the Raj. The endless deferral in the acknowledgment of Indians as properly clubbable always marked the experience of even sufficiently Europeanized Indians in colonial clubland. Brajendranath De, a Cambridge-educated Indian who was among the early generations of Indians to enter the ICS in the 1870s, experienced the limits of such assimilation. His commissioner refused to let him use the local station club in Hooghly because his wife was still in purdah (seclusion). The *Ananda Bazar Patrika,* a vernacular newspaper of Bengal, was clearly skeptical of such excuses: "A native may adopt English customs, wear the English dress, change his paternal name, and move in English society with his wife, yet nothing can lead the Englishman to think that a native is his equal."[37] The colonial expression of clubbability functioned precisely to ensure that the colonizer was seen as unique and exceptional, on the one hand, and that the colonized was seen as perpetually still-to-be redeemed, on the other.

The slow and painful process by which Anglo-India was forced to accept the "Indianization" of elite government services in the 1920s and 1930s, however, brought considerable pressure to bear on the ban against Indians as members or as guests of Anglo-Indian members in the European social clubs in India. By the interwar period, especially in the country stations, many of the formerly whites-only clubs had granted Indian officials at least honorary membership. Christopher Masterman, who, as member of the Board of Revenue, had an opportunity to travel extensively in the various districts in Madras during the 1940s, noted the extent to which the "color bar" had disappeared from the small station clubs in Madras. According to Masterman, status, and not color, now determined entry into clubland.[38] When Dharam Vira, who joined the ICS in the post–First World War period, was appointed district magistrate and collector in Bareilly in the United Provinces, he found that as district magistrate he was also ex-officio president of the local club. Although he was an Indian, he could not easily be refused admission to the club.[39] Alakh Kumar Sinha, who would become the first Indian to be appointed inspector general of police, was already in 1928 a member of the Executive Committee of the Bankipore Club in Patna, once the exclusive citadel of Anglo-Indian planters and officials in Bihar. Several other Indians who served in the ICS and other elite services in the last decades of the Raj also testify to the gradual opening up of the local European clubs.[40] Yet clearly, the politically charged issue of allowing Indian members and Indian guests in a European club had not been entirely resolved because Indian entry continued to be implemented unevenly, especially in the major city clubs. Dorothy Ganapathy, a graduate of Durham University, found that when her husband, an officer of the Indian Medical Service, was posted to Madras, they were not allowed to fraternize with her husband's colleagues at the local Adyar Club.[41] Similarly, as late as December 1945, the Calcutta branch of the European Association (formerly the EAIDA) was still debating the desirability of Indian membership, and the introduction of Indians as guests, in the leading clubs of Calcutta.[42] Well up to the end of colonial rule and beyond, some clubs, most notably the Bengal Club, maintained their character as whites-only institutions.

The changing imperatives of the colonial situation, however, had made the concept of clubbability ever vulnerable to the selective incorporation of "proper sorts" of Indians — especially Indians in elite government services and business firms as well as the rajas and maharajas of quasi-independent princely states — into the formerly whites-only institutions. It is significant that some of the most successful initiatives at setting up mixed clubs in the interwar period came from senior Anglo-Indian officials themselves, many of whom could scarcely be accused of otherwise harboring "liberal" sentiments of Indian equality after having failed to persuade several existing European clubs to permit Indians. Lord Willingdon, who was exceedingly popular with the Anglo-Indian community, became most active in promoting mixed clubs in Bombay, Madras, and Delhi after his experience as governor of Bombay, when he was unable to entertain Indian maharajas as his guests at the Royal Bombay Yacht Club.[43] The creation of the Willingdon Clubs, for both Europeans and Indians, in Bombay and Delhi was the product of a new political expediency demanded by a reconstituted imperial order. The price of retaining the color bar now could often mean the loss of official patronage for the club.

The popularity of mixed clubs in late colonial India, however, was not so much a repudiation of the colonial elaboration of the class, gender, and racial assumptions of clubbability as its fulfillment. The Calcutta Club, established as a mixed institution in 1907 by then viceroy Lord Minto, was a case in point. As a mixed institution, the Calcutta Club contained special stipulations in its charter for the use of its ladies' annex. The members of the club and other guests could be invited to the annex, but no man whose wife was in purdah was to be permitted access. In this way, such institutions as the Calcutta Club both incorporated select Indians into the culture of clubland and perpetuated notions about the unclubbability of Indians. It is no wonder that Raj Chatterjee of the Imperial Tobacco Company and a member of a mixed club in Delhi in the 1940s recalls that Europeans still remained so fearful that Indian men might "ogle" white women that most Europeans held their more intimate social gatherings in their homes or in the remaining whites-only clubs.[44]

By the final decades of the British Raj, the particular dramatization of whiteness in the clubland was already being rendered obsolete. So, for many of the Europeans arriving in India during the Second World War, a great number of whom were quite diverse in their background and in their political orientation, the "stuffy clubs" of Anglo-India held less and less attraction. The Fategarh Club, as recalled by the Indian ICS officer N. B. Bonnerjee, offers a telling example of the growing obsolescence of colonial clubland in late colonial India. The Anglo-Indian collector's wife banned the books of H. G. Wells from the club library on the grounds that they were too iconoclastic to be suitable for its Anglo-Indian members![45] Many of the Indians who were now eligible for club membership, moreover, were equally disenchanted by colonial clubland. In the new racially mixed clubs, as Bonnerjee complained, any intelligent political discussion was virtually impossible: "A casually adverse remark against the Secretary of State for India, for example, which would have met with approval in the National Liberal Club [in London] under Gladstone's life-size portrait, could be cause of pained looks and embarrassed silence in the lounge of any club in India."[46] The new Indian members of colonial clubland were equally sensitive to any signs of patronage or humiliation in the predominantly European social clubs. Rajeshwar Dayal, who entered the ICS in the 1930s, writes that "one was not expected to be hobnobbing with the notables of the town by joining their club, except for going to play a game of bridge, because in bridge you don't have to make any conversation or establish any personal rapport with anybody. But at the same time, we were not admitted, at least in the United Provinces, to the service club as full members. We could only become honorary members; and we Indian officers thought that it was infra dig to accept that sort of situation."[47] Similarly, General Palit, then a junior officer in the Indian Army, wrote, "We joined the Club, of course, but we only went there for games. I never once saw an Indian officer share a table with a British officer or his wife."[48]

Some of the Indian women who gained access to the European social clubs by virtue of their husband's position became some of the strongest critics of the gendered construction of whiteness in colonial clubland. Renuka Ray, the wife of an ICS officer and herself a member of the Central Legislative Assembly in India, found that her involvement in public politics came in the way of her enjoyment of typical Anglo-Indian club life: "I did go to the Club, and I knew how to play tennis and bridge and all the rest of it. But could not tolerate some of the things they started saying, and I used to have long and bitter discussions with them. Eventually, I decided not to meet them too much, because they didn't like me."[49] Dhanvanthi Rama Rau, the wife of another ICS officer and herself an activist in the women's movement in India, was particularly dismayed by the attitude of the typical Anglo-Indian *memsahib* (white woman) in the clubs. The average club-going memsahib, as Rama Rau quickly discovered, either knew very little about or was expressly hostile to struggles for women's suffrage, whether in Britain or in India.[50] The dilemma for the few single women professionals, such as Cornelia Sorabji, was even greater: "The Bengal and United Services Clubs have Ladies Annexes but for English folk only. The Calcutta Club is for Indians and has an annex and I suppose a library but spinsters may not join."[51] Colonial clubland came under increasing siege from within precisely because of the limits of its own rigid gendered and racial elaboration of whiteness.

Furthermore, the intimate identification of colonial clubland with whiteness made the clubs seem increasingly the bastion of an outdated social order. It was as such that clubland became clearly marginal in the emerging national "Indian" counterpublics in late colonial India. Colonial clubland, in fact, became the target of widespread nationalist Indian criticism. With the transformation of the nationalist movement into a mass movement, the clubs became increasingly identified as the last vestiges of an outmoded system of power and privilege in colonial India. The clubs were especially vulnerable to revolutionary "terrorist" attacks from the extremist wing of Indian nationalists. In 1908, for example, young Bengali terrorists gunned down two Europeans outside the Mozuffarpur Club in an assassination attempt aimed at the newly appointed sessions judge of Mozuffarpur.[52] For Preeti Waddadar, a young female terrorist who led a raid on the Pahartali Railway Club in 1932, the club seemed to symbolize exclusive European privilege.[53] The most ironic reversal of colonial clubbability, however, came from the growing mobilization of elite and middle-class Indian women themselves, who, in their own pursuit for women's rights, overturned the underlying assumptions of its particular colonial elaborations. When a group of Indian women invaded the inner sanctum of the all-male Bengal Club in 1936, they used the logic of clubbability to devastating effect. The aim of the women's group was to convince the British legislators residing in the club of the fallacy of their argument that Indian women were not ready to be enfranchised because so many of them were still in purdah. The women argued that men, who themselves practiced seclusion in their clubs, could ill afford to pass judgment on the seclusion of Indian women. That at least some of the so-called new women in India had begun to find a home in international women's clubs that had burgeoned in the first half of the twentieth century — the most famous of which was the Lyceum Club in London — was, perhaps, the final coup de grâce to a colonial elaboration of clubbability that frequently invoked the prevalence of purdah among certain classes of women in India as justification for the exclusion of all Indians from the clubs.

At the same time, however, the subsequent transformation and resilience of clubland in independent India stands as a testimony to that other, more universal dimension that was also always part of the colonial elaboration of clubbability. A journalist, writing some years after Indian independence, comments on the peculiar phenomenon of the "brown sahibs," or the thoroughly Europeanized natives, who find themselves completely at home in the clubs: "In any officer's mess in South Asia, you can meet a Brown Sahib playing the blimp, imitating and caricaturing his predecessors in the colonial armies. He is recognizable, too, in social and sporting clubs: the made-over Englishman bemoaning the passing of the Empire with the arrogance and nostalgia of the Daily Express."[54] The club survives in independent India, however, not merely as sentimental nostalgia for the British Raj. Its survival owes as much to the selective reappropriation by Indians of the ever-present tension in colonial clubbability: the potential clubbability of the Indians themselves. In this context, then, the subsequent proliferation and transformation of clubland in independent India is not so much a site for uncritical Raj nostalgia as a multilayered space for the articulation and mediation of the interests of specific elite formations in India. It was precisely the colonial legacy of clubbability, both specific and universal, that enabled, eventually, the appropriation of clubbability in the service of a new elite in independent India.

Notes

1. H. R. Panckridge, *A Short History of the Bengal Club, 1827–1927* (Calcutta, 1927), 1, emphasis added.
2. Quoted in Roland Hunt and John Harrison, *The District Officer in India, 1930–1947* (London, 1980), 127–128.
3. Quoted in Charles Allen, ed., *Plain Tales from the Raj: Images of British India in the Twentieth Century* (New York, 1976), 99.
4. Valentine Chirol, *Indian Unrest* (1910; reprint, New Delhi, 1979), 290.
5. See Dennis Kincaid, *British Social Life in India, 1608–1937* (1938; reprint, New York, 1971), 281.
6. Panckridge, *A Short History,* 1.
7. *Editors' note:* "Anglo-Indians" refers to the British community in India.
8. Quoted in Allen, *Plain Tales,* 100.
9. W. O. Home, *Work and Sport in the Old ics* (London, 1928), 23.
10. J. H. Rivett-Carnac, *Many Memories of Life in India: At Home and Abroad* (London, 1910), 15.
11. Allen, *Plain Tales,* 99.
12. Cited in Margaret Macmillan, *Women of the Raj* (New York: Thames and Hudson, 1988), 160–161.

13. For a sample of some of the complaints against the presence of women in the clubs, see Boxwallah, *An Eastern Backwater* (London, 1916), 45, 55, 275.

14. Cited in Sir Henry Sharp, *Goodbye India* (London, 1946), 137–138.

15. See Michael Edwardes, *The Sahibs and the Lotus: The British in India* (London, 1988), 226.

16. Quoted in Allen, *Plain Tales,* 103.

17. Satya Mobanty, "Kipling's Children and the Colour Line," *Race and Class* 31, 1 (1989): 37.

18. Ibid., 30.

19. Allen, *Plain Tales,* 101–102.

20. Club Committee Meeting, 7 November 1872, Committee Proceedings of the Bengal Club, 1869–1888, Bengal Club Archives, Calcutta, India, 68.

21. Ex-Civilian, *Life in the Mofussil or the Civilian in Lower Bengal* (London, n.d.), 2: 253.

22. Panckridge, *A Short History,* 17.

23. For a history of the indigo disturbances, see Blair Kling, *The Blue Mutiny: The Indigo Disturbances in Bengal 1859 1862* (Philadelphia: University of Pennsylvania Press, 1966) and Ranajit Guha, "Neel Darpan: The Image of a Peasant Revolt in a Liberal Mirror," in *Peasant Resistance in India, 1858–1914,* ed. David Hardiman (Delhi: Oxford University Press, 1992), 1–60.

24. See Sir Henry Cotton, *New India or India in Transition,* rev. ed. (London, 1909), 62–63.

25. Ex-Civilian, *Life in the Mofussil,* 1: 51.

26. Quoted in Hunt and Harrison, *District Officer,* 12.

27. *Englishman,* 8 March 1883, 2.

28. See Raymond K. Renford, *Non-Official British in India to 1920* (Delhi, 1932), 335.

29. *Pioneer,* 28 April 1883, 1.

30. See Ranabina Ray Choudhury, ed., *Calcutta: A Hundred Years Ago* (Bombay, 1988), 46.

31. *Statesman,* 24 March 1882, 3.

32. See Bengal Club Annual Accounts Book 1860–1890, BCA, Calcutta, India.

33. Wilfred Scawen Blunt, *India under Ripon* (London, 1909), 115.

34. Quoted in Choudhury, *Calcutta,* 46.

35. *Pioneer,* 28 April 1883, 1.

36. See M. K. Gandhi, *An Autobiography: The Story of My Experiments with Truth,* trans. Mahadev Desai (Boston, 1957), 229.

37. Ananda Bazar Patrika, 9 April 1993, 167, in *Report on Native Papers Bengal Presidency* (January–December 1883), no. 16.

38. Cited in Hunt and Harrison, *District Officer,* 127–128.

39. Dharam Vira, *Memoirs of a Civil Servant* (London, 1975), 16–17.

40. See, for example, K. P. S. Menon, *Many Worlds: An Autobiography* (London, 1965), esp. 89–147.

41. Cited in Zareer Masani, *Indian Tales of the Raj* (London, 1987), 53.

42. Cited in Rajat Ray, *Urban Roots of Indian Nationalism* (New Delhi, 1979), 231–232.

43. The incident involving Willingdon is mentioned in Humphrey Trevelyan, *The India We Left: Charles Trevelyan, 1826–1865, Humphrey Trevelyan, 1929–1947* (London, 1972), 112–113.

44. Quoted in Masani, *Indian Tales,* 52.

45. Cited in N. B. Bonnerjee, *Under Two Masters* (Calcutta, 1970), 117–118.

46. Ibid.

47. Quoted in Masani, *Indian Tales,* 16. *Editors' note:* "infra dig" means "beneath one's dignity."

48. Masani, *Indian Tales,* 25.

49. Ibid., 55.

50. See Dhanvanthi Rama Rau, *An Inheritance: The Memoirs of Dhanvanthi Rama Rau* (London, 1977), 99–100, 119.

51. See letter from Sorabji to Elena [Alice Bruce] Richmond, dated 24 February 1926, in "Cornelia Sorabji Papers: Correspondence and Private Papers," January–April 1926, India Office Library and Records, London, folder no. 40.

52. See report of the incident in Renford, *Non-Official British,* 309–311.

53. See the recollection of this episode in Kalpana Dutt, *Chittagong Armoury Raider's Reminiscences* (1945; reprint, New Delhi, 1979), 40–44.

54. Varindra Tarzie Vittachi, *The Brown Sahib* (London, 1962), 10.

Patrick F. McDevitt

Muscular Catholicism: Nationalism, Masculinity, and Gaelic Team Sports, 1884–1916

The Gaelic Athletic Association brought Irish men's bodies into rough, though disciplined, contact through the games of hurling and football in ways that created community and helped to challenge British cultural, if not political, dominance in Ireland. Both games had histories before the nineteenth century, when they became symbols of a certain kind of Irish manliness in the face of claims that the (Catholic) Irish should be subject to British (colonial) rule because of Irish men's incapacity for self-governance. Part of a general end-of-the-century Gaelic renaissance, these activities sponsored new playing fields and arenas of competition and accomplishment that had more than symbolic value; the collision of bodies helped to produce and sustain a form of Irish nationalism that could not find expression in other spaces of Irish life. Though not totally gender-segregated, Irish sports did underscore the separate-sphere ideology that undergirded Irish society and even progressive Irish nationalism.

S panning four decades from the 1880s through the 1910s, a diverse movement that came to be called the "Gaelic Renaissance" sought to create an Irish nation by emphasizing a living Irish language, a national theater, and a native Irish culture. This movement gained particular prominence in the twenty-five years between the death of home rule leader Charles Stewart Parnell in 1891 and the Easter Rebellion of 1916. During this period there seemed to be a retreat from explicitly political agitation in favor of the ideological work of building a nation from the bottom up. The period after 1891 was characterized by a "shift of interest from Westminster to Ireland, from the source of constitutional reform to the breeding-ground of rebellion."[1] The revival of the Gaelic games was a hallmark of the Gaelic Renaissance and a strong pronouncement of Irish nationalism, but the highly gendered nature of this experience has been largely ignored by scholars.

Two such games, hurling and Gaelic football, produced an image of Irish masculinity of which the nationalist community could be proud. The random violence of the earlier games was nominally replaced with order and virtuous manliness. Although it may seem commonsensical that sports are related to masculinity, the connection should not be taken as a given. The means through which sports have come to be instantly associated with manhood and the manner in which this connection works in colonial and gender discourses must be probed. To a greater degree than commentary on many other games, the everyday coverage of Gaelic sports was couched in gendered language, and the issues surrounding Irish "manhood" implicitly and explicitly dominated the commentary. Gaelic games, while culturally importing much of their foundation from the British, provided the Irish with a novel form of self-expression through which they were able to foreground the differences between themselves and the British and to fashion a masculine identity that they viewed as uniquely "Irish."[2] Founded by Michael Cusack in 1884, the Gaelic Athletic Association (GAA) and its supporters could be said to have fashioned a philosophy of "muscular Catholicism" to counter the doctrine of "muscular Christianity" that was the driving motivation behind the development of modern sport in England.

IRISH MEN SOUGHT to distinguish themselves from the British through anti-imperialism, Catholicism, Irish culture, egalitarianism, and fraternal solidarity; these marks of distinction coexisted with an emphasis on morality, codification, and competition that was shared with the British. Distinct images of manhood were created: a British version based on Protestant elitism and class, and an Irish version dominated by Catholic communalism.[3] For men, one of the most readily accessible manners of defying the British and celebrating one's Irishness was participation in Gaelic games. Sport can be viewed as a medium for self-expression in many ways; impressions of the self and the other are linked inextricably in the evolution of sport in a given locality and society.[4] For the men of the nationalist community, the concepts of manhood, patriotism, and resistance were so interconnected as to be almost conflated, and these three ideals of nationalist philosophy are drawn together most dramatically by the national pastimes.

The games provided Irish nationalists with a symbolically defiant act broad enough to encompass aspects of ritual, nostalgia for a legendary Irish past of united independence, physicality (with its attendant discipline and ordered violence), and strict differentiation of gender roles. The athlete's beautiful, healthy, and vigorous Irish male body counteracted the Victorian English characterizations of the Irish as either simian, drunken ruffians or effeminate and feckless, childlike inferiors in need of Anglo-Saxon domination.[5] The athletic bodies produced and displayed in hurling and Gaelic football also provided muscular counterimages to the memory of weak and emaciated Irish Famine (1845–1847) victims. This was a profound moment of self-definition: first and foremost, the English and Anglo-Irish were excluded and thereby deemed "un-Irish"; second, Irish men were distinguished from Irish boys; third, Irish women were excluded from the centers of action and power. If communities, whether nations or fraternities of sportsmen, are symbolic constructs created via cultural imaginings, then the example of hurling and Gaelic football allows us to see this cultural imagining in its making and in its most naked and powerful form.[6]

The history of hurling stretches back into the time of Irish legend and was intimately connected to warfare and warriors. While infinitely safer in its modern form than in its folk and ancient forms, hurling is still perhaps the most hazardous game in the Western world and has been described as "the nearest approach to warfare consistent with peace."[7] The modern game entails thirty men running around swinging heavy wooden clubs at a small hard ball flying through the air at distances up to one hundred yards. Cusack argued that "the game was invented by the most sublimely energetic and warlike race that the world has ever known. . . . It teaches the use of arms at close quarters . . . [and] it gives its votaries that courage which comes from a consciousness of having in one's hand a weapon which may be used with deadly effect."[8] Neither hurling nor Gaelic football allows tackling in either the rugby or soccer sense; however, both incorporate a large amount of physical contact, and hurling allows for vast "incidental" contact between one player's caman (the stick used in hurling) and another's body. The games required a certain degree of fearlessness in the men who played them.

This vigorous image of Irish games and men was constantly held up in contrast to the weakened and stunned apathy of the country between the Great Famine of 1845 and the founding of the GAA in 1884. It is estimated that, out of a pre-Famine population of just over 8 million, nearly 1.5 million people emigrated and over 1 million died of famine-related disease and starvation between 1845 and 1850. The effects of the Famine were felt for decades after the restoration of the potato crop. The *Celtic Times* reported in 1887 that "it would be idle to deny that a considerable section of Irishmen is thoroughly demoralized."[9] In addition to drawing together the Irish present with a Golden Age of united independence, the promoters of the games sought to regain the pre-Famine confidence and optimism associated with Daniel O'Connell's movement in the 1840s to repeal the Act of Union between Great Britain and Ireland. The banishment of the image of weak Irish men produced by the Famine was a prerequisite for national autonomy, and the advent of the GAA was the first step in this process for many nationalists. Cusack, it was said, "was content to re-endow his compatriots with the qualities of Strong-men, [and] assumed that in God's good time they would reach the status of Freemen."[10] In this way, the revival of ancient traditions was in fact part of a modernizing mission to bring Ireland into the community of independent nations.

By creating the GAA, Irish men were performing a deliberate act of heresy in the face of the cultural imperialism and political domination of Great Britain. Rather than standing as an institution against orthodoxy, Gaelic team games came to represent a new orthodoxy. One observer, criticizing half-hearted support of hurling and football, stated that the true Gael "cannot be orthodox today and unfaithful tomorrow: Non-Gaelic on Saturday and Ultra-Gaelic on Sunday."[11] Other peoples in the British empire subverted English sports by beating the British at their own games; the Irish blasphemed in a different manner. By repudiating the central rituals of the British imperial religion, they rejected the tenet that team games were symbolic of the superiority of British manhood. The creation of the "antirituals" of their own games became the most visible, viable, and successful pillar of the Irish cultural renaissance.

Gaelic sports were not isolated from the rest of the revival movement; rather, GAA promoters surrounded the games with festivals, music, and oratory that explicitly rejected the imperial creed implied in the "foreign" games. During the third quarter of the nineteenth century, the Irish Catholic Church underwent a "devotional revolution" characterized by a dramatic increase in the number of vocations and the resurrection, accentuation, and reestablishment of many long-forgotten and half-remembered rituals. In the period from 1850 to 1875, the upper clergy of Ireland transformed the casual, personal Catholicism of the pre-Famine era into a highly codified, ritualistic, and institutionally centered religion.[12] The centralization of the Church in these years helped to enable the population of Ireland to conceive of themselves in national rather than parochial terms.[13] In a similar manner, Gaelic games and the Irish language, which had fallen into disuse, were revived and propagated on a national and centralized level. These cultural artifacts were not simply recovered but reconstructed. Both hurling and football needed to be organized and standardized in order to coexist with the self-perception of Irish men as civilized counterparts to their Anglo-Saxon overlords, despite British claims to the contrary.

The nationalist community was not monolithic, and images of masculinity were not limited to the participants in the Gaelic games. The nationalist movement ranged from radical republicans who sought complete independence to moderate home rulers who advocated remaining part of the British empire with local self-governance. However, the nationalist movement was, through the sheer number of adherents, the dominant force in Irish life in this period, and it was from this community that Gaelic games drew their support.[14] In addition to the many shades of independent nationalism, other political ideologies existed, and different groups had contrasting conceptions of manhood that were not affected by Gaelic sports, including masculinities molded by English sports then being played in Ireland. Irish members of the Crown Forces offer one example of Irish men who did not hold that participation in Gaelic games was a central requirement for Irish manhood. Soon after its founding, the GAA instituted a policy known as "The Ban," which forbade the participation of soldiers, sailors, and members of the Royal Irish Constabulary (RIC) in Gaelic games. This policy was in actuality enforced with varying degrees of strictness throughout the period. The RIC's organ, the *Constabulary Gazette*, decried The Ban as "outrageous" and "narrow-minded, unsportsmanlike, un-Irish, unmanly. . . . The R.I.C. embraces the finest specimens of muscular manhood in or out of Ireland, and they are to a man the product of this country."[15] Despite the fact that the RIC was at this point still made up overwhelmingly of Irishmen, the GAA would argue that it contained not a single Gael, and thereby offered nothing to

Gaelic games. On the other hand, although the article rejected The Ban and the authority of the GAA to define Irish manhood, its purpose was to encourage the removal of The Ban and allow the participation of Crown Force members in Gaelic games.

Masculinity is connected to Gaelic games in several significant ways. First, there were "civilizing" tendencies which sought to remove the violence and brutishness inherent in earlier versions of the games. Repeatedly, discipline and control of violent impulses were praised in participants and upheld as a benefit of the games. Here we see that although Gaelic games were a reaction to the British, there were also many areas of overlap between British and Irish games philosophy. Irishmen wanted to demonstrate that they were not naturally unruly and that organized team games did not correspond to British superiority. Simultaneously, they incorporated similar civilizing goals as British games and relied on the imposition of a formal set of rules and regulations to order and enforce these notions of civilization. Second, in opposition to the civilizing trends and creating a running tension for the games, hurling and football were tied to militarism through descriptive metaphors and the organization of training and tactics, and through a huge overlap in membership between the GAA and the various sectarian militias. Third, the games helped to define separate spheres for men and women within the nationalist movement, reserving the most active and prominent duties for the men. According to the GAA's *Annual* for 1907–1908, "The ideal Gael is a matchless athlete, sober, pure of mind, speech and deed, self-possessed, self-reliant, self-respecting, loving his religion and his country with a deep restless love, earnest in thought and effective in action."[16] Hurling and Gaelic football required dedicated men motivated by a republican brotherhood. The games inculcated and cultivated these coveted values, whose presence was proven by success. Victorious team members were the pride of Gaeldom and role models for younger men and boys, and thus perpetuated the games, their political ideology, and a Gaelic conception of masculinity.

THE PROPAGATION OF the highly gendered English sporting philosophy to the empire was to some degree an attempt to control the minds of colonials *through* their bodies rather than simply in addition to them. English games, most notably cricket, rugby, and soccer, were actively disseminated throughout the empire by the hundreds of public school–educated teachers, missionaries, and administrators; these games were seen as one of the best ways to transmit the values of British society to the collaborating colonial classes.[17] Once hurling and Gaelic football were enlisted to combat that corporeal colonialism, the body became the battle ground for an imperial confrontation. It was not by any means predetermined that the Irish would choose to propagate these "native" games as a means of national reinvigoration. In addition to the British sports, which some Irishmen favored adopting as a means of literally beating the English at their own games, there were other options as well, including German-style gymnastics, cycling, baseball, and Australian rules football. However, it was Gaelic football and hurling that were chosen and that excited massive participation nearly instantaneously; other sports then being played in Ireland did not. Both the games themselves and their accompanying rhetoric welded them to Irish notions of manhood, of the body, of the community, and of their relation to the land. These aspects of Gaelic games made them unique for the Irish.

With a founding motive of improving the musculature of Irish manhood, a nationwide movement was born which, by the eve of the First World War, was rivaled only by the Catholic Church as the most powerful organization in the country.[18] As with nearly every modern sport, the spectacle of physical strength, grace, and beauty was central to the success and popularity of Gaelic games. However, a mind/body symbiosis was still held to be of cardinal importance. Watching a game on a typically cold Irish winter day, one priest observed "two or three dozen young fellows with naked arms, naked heads, naked feet, and clad only in a light silken jersey and drawers. . . . Our young men stripped and fought fiercely for victory, utterly heedless of cold or danger."[19] The weekly display of healthy, muscular, and vigorous male bodies provided by hurling and football worked not only to define masculinity but also to illustrate Irish attitudes toward the male body and to act as propaganda for the Irish-Ireland movement which sought to "de-Anglicize" Ireland. First, the strength and dominance of rural teams underscored the enduring image of the manly and virile Gaelic body as rooted in a flourishing and fertile rural landscape. Second, the active Gaelic athletes were a reproach to those who were not participating because of their alleged sloth. Third, the will to continue playing despite physical hardships highlighted the manner in which mental and spiritual qualities allowed the men to convert physical ability into victory. Fourth, the triumph of the Gaelic athletic movement was viewed as a resounding rebuttal to the anguish caused by the Famine and British policies that protected financial interests of land-lords at the cost of suffering among the Irish people. The spiritual aspects of Gaelic games were considered partial compensation for lack of Irish independence in the present, and the physical benefits were viewed as guarantors of that independence in the future.

The GAA produced nothing less than a social revolution in parts of rural Ireland. Many areas had not held games or festivals in over fifty years, nor witnessed large crowd gatherings since O'Connell's mass repeal meetings in the 1840s. T. F. O'Sullivan, the first historian of the GAA, believed that the "dull monotony of Irish rural life [had been] dispelled forever [with the advent of the GAA]. A new spirit had been created in the country."[20] Whether this social revolution was bona fide or not, it was portrayed at the time as genuine, and the GAA did create strong rural networks of likeminded Irishmen. The *Democrat* reported in 1893 that before the GAA had revitalized the area, the men spent their time drinking and gambling, while "their physique in general had deteriorated and . . . the young men walked with stooped shoulders and a shambling gait. A couple of years of hurling and football soon changed this and the athlet-icism which permeated every nook and corner of the South Midlands and the West of Ireland during the years 1886 to 1890 brought forth myriads of athletes."[21] In this way, Gaelic sports fortified the belief that the true Ireland of past greatness was waiting to be resurrected and that the nation would rise and take its independence once the men of Ireland recovered their lost physical prowess.

Gaelic games were also intimately tied to Irish Catholicism, both philo-sophically and through the one-parish–one-club organizational ethos. Gaelic sports complemented their Catholic environment when contrasted with Protestant English games. Unlike many Protestant churches, which had been stripped of representations of the body, Catholic churches were full of images of embodied religious figures in paintings, statues, and stained glass, suggesting less of a mind/body separation in Irish Catholic culture than in Protestant cultures. The overemphasis on physicality al-legedly propagated by "foreign" games was held up in contrast to the mutuality of mind and body in the Irish case. P. J. Devlin wrote: "The exultation of mere bodily grace and virility is fundamentally pagan, basi-cally carnal and foreign to all our historical conceptions of perfect man-hood . . . spiritual qualities long survived the memories of their bodily vigor."[22] Thus, cleverness of play evidenced spiritual advancement by exhibiting the ability of Irishmen to transcend the purely physical and leave the realm of the grossly material behind.

Despite a wariness of overt brutishness, participants in Irish games still came to equate muscularity with manly action and slenderness with neutered apathy. In a scathing attack leveled by the *Celtic Times* at some of the citizenry of Kilkenny, where the GAA had not taken off with the same vigor as in other parts of the country, Cusack contrasted the "fine, strapping men" of the GAA to "a score of pale, emaciated figures, seeming engaged in criticizing the dress and motions of everybody moving past them. . . . Another crowd of persons, who probably call themselves men, was slothfully reclining with their faces towards the sun."[23] The notion that males who are not part of the movement cannot legitimately be considered "men" is emphasized here, as is the contrast between the ideal bodies of the Gaels and the undernourished bodies of nonparticipants. In a land haunted by memories of the Famine, laziness and inactivity led, in the Irish symbolic universe, to emaciation and thinness, not slovenly corpulence, as in more affluent societies. The athletic physiques of the GAA men also offered a vivid contrast to the fleshy image of John Bull, who had grown corpulent feasting on profits reaped from the misery of Ireland's poorest. Moreover, in addition to a lack of strength and industry, the highly gendered pastimes of catty gossip-mongering and concern with fashion are ascribed to the non-GAA men.

Gaelic games were seen by large numbers of Irishmen as antidotes to the sickly national body. In the article that officially called for the formation of the GAA, Cusack argued that a "rot" which began in urban centers and had spread across the country could be remedied only by Gaelic games.[24] The organic imagery of a rot spreading visibly across the land clearly equates British culture with the blight that was responsible for the failure of the potato crop in the 1840s. It was not enough that the games promoted healthy, muscular men, as nearly any sport would have done that. By standing in opposition to Anglican games, Irish nationalists could further nationalist as well as sectarian agendas while creating sports that more closely resembled their concerns and views. The success of hurling and Gaelic football rests in part on their ability to speak to national memories of the pre-Famine era as well as hopes of a post-British future.

Male supporters of Gaelic games often connected images of British men with those of women or neutered men. The effeminization of the enemy here displays male Irish attitudes not only toward British men but also toward women and themselves. If the most pejorative label one man can place on another is that he is emasculated, that is, "made like a woman," the level of equality available to women in that society is necessarily low. Likewise, compliments that stress manhood by definition demean women and feminize those who do not succeed, thus associating failure with the feminine. The phrase "worked like men" was often used to describe a particularly diligent side.[25] At times, this was in reference to schoolboys, who, though male, were not adult men; at other times, it was applied to men's teams. In this context, all males (even all adult males) are not "men" unless they follow certain preordained behavior patterns. Messner and Sabo argue that "sports suppress natural (sex) similarities, construct differences, and then . . . weave a structure of symbol and interpretation around the differences which naturalizes them."[26] In this case, the physicality and brutality of the games accentuated differences in favor of men and then claimed that artificial advantage as evidence of male superiority.

The concept that men are not always men allowed players to step outside their socially dictated roles and behave otherwise at other times. Although they may "work like men" on the field, perhaps they get to "play like boys" at the pub afterward. The increase in traveling and use of the railroads precipitated by the games made many matches holidays in themselves. Although spectators traveled to games, often on specially chartered trains, expenses dictated that usually only the players and perhaps the male supporters would go.[27] The camaraderie generated on trips "with the lads," away from the stresses of work and families, included restaurants and pubs with their attendant drunkenness, singing, and gaiety. The games reinforced the image of political unity, namely a brotherhood of Gaels which, with their women in concomitant subordination, would reclaim their lost nation from a feminized oppressor.

Participants and administrators of the game had little difficulty reconciling the incredible violence involved in hurling with their desire to portray the Irish man as peaceable. The *Gaelic Athletic Annual* stated that "the hurler who would raise a caman to strike another player is unworthy to use it. The caman is not a weapon of offense—amongst Gaels at least. . . . [Those who] decry hurling as a dangerous brutal game . . . have acquired the instinctive dread of the 'Anglo-Saxon' for manly vigor."[28] Statements of civilizing nonviolence notwithstanding, the practitioners of the Gaelic games, especially hurling, clearly associated them with violence and violence with manhood. Any fear of bodily harm was deemed a sign either of encroaching British influence or of effeminacy.

The connection between English males and unmanliness dates to the very inauguration of the association. In a letter accepting the invitation to become a patron of the GAA, Archbishop Croke of Cashel penned what was for many years considered the charter of the association. Urging the public to support the new organization, he derided the manner in which, along with importing England's manufactured goods, the Irish had taken to imitating English fashions, mannerisms, accents, and "such other effeminate follies as she may recommend."[29] Croke was not alone in equating English activities and fashions with dandyism and other womanly affectations. Cusack argued in 1887 "that as the courage and honesty and spirit of manhood grow, the hurling steadily advances on the domains of football."[30] That is, as the number of Irish males who are truly masculine grows, the unmanly British games will naturally wither away because of lack of participation. Cusack argued that by joining a Gaelic sports team an Irish man not only became more manly but also contributed to the removal of British domination.

Cultural awareness, anti-Britishness, and fluency in the Irish language were highly regarded nationalist credentials for both sexes in Ireland. As mothers, women played an active role in the propagation of a nationalist ideology within the household.[31] In 1902, female members of the Gaelic League devised a less violent version of hurling and called it camogie.[32] The efforts of these nationalistic women who took to the playing fields with camans in hand were not warmly received by the sporting community and were largely ignored by the press and the GAA. The perceived newsworthiness of sports furthered the gendering of sports and national identity.

Even before the invention of camogie, women were not excluded from the carnival of Gaelic games, and their presence was often noted. Before the mid-nineteenth century, folk games of any sort throughout Europe were not events in themselves, but rather were part of festivals and fairs in which whole communities participated. This inclusiveness had changed by the late nineteenth century for most of the world, as games became reasons in themselves to gather. For at least their first two decades, however, Gaelic games were often surrounded by Gaelic festivals (formal or informal), which included contests or exhibitions of Irish music, dance, and speech making, all of which involved women in pivotal roles. In describing the spectacle of one day's matches, which were preceded by a Mass and a parade, a newspaper praised the young women of the town as "typical Irish cailini, fine Irish speakers, and Irish singers and dancers, and able helpers of the boys, [who] are well worthy of their country too."[33] Although female participation was welcome and widespread, the gender hierarchy remained firmly in place. Men held center stage while the women were assigned supporting roles of muse-like encouragement. When discussing the sorry state of traditional pastimes in his inaugural letter, Archbishop Croke referred to the "sour humiliation . . . of every genuine son and daughter of the old land." He went on to discuss the "ball-playing, hurling, football-kicking . . . and all such favorite exercises and amusements amongst men and boys."[34] So, although the shame of national subjugation was felt by all, only the males were able to avenge this directly. Although there were Gaels of both sexes, their paths to that status were defined by the larger bifurcation of Irish society into spheres of activity that overlapped but were viewed as largely distinct.

Both Gaelic masculinity and femininity had the stereotypes of their British and Anglo-Irish counterparts against which to define themselves. Criticizing the rigid qualifications for amateurism for Irish athletes as governed by loyalists, Cusack stated, "For years . . . clubs excluded . . . people who are vulgar enough to be muscular and would give a daddy-long-legs . . . no chance in the presence of his wasp-waisted sweetheart."[35] Archbishop Croke echoed the popular dichotomy between virile, poor Irishmen and effete, well-off Anglo-Irish when he contrasted the "youth-ful athletes . . . bereft of shoes and coat, and thus prepared to play" to the "degenerate dandies . . . arrayed in light attire . . . and racket in hand."[36] The repetitious labeling of the British as effeminate spoke as much to the Irish fear of themselves becoming effeminate as it did to a concern over the status of British men. Distinctions between manly Irish and effemi-nate British reassured Irish men that political and economic subjugation did not mean a loss of sexual power. The conception of a feminized oppressor was unusual, and represented an inversion of the more com-mon representation of a feminized colonial subject.

Class cannot be separated from the anti-British and antiloyalist senti-ment and perceptions of gender. The gentry of Ireland and the absentee landlords in England were forever tied to Ireland's greatest tragedies, Cromwell's brutal conquest of Ireland in the seventeenth century and the Famine, which together were seen as completely robbing the Irish of their own land. The influence and involvement of aristocracy, who previously had sponsored almost all nineteenth-century athletic contests in Ireland in the form of estate cricket and gentlemanly races, were vigorously opposed in Gaelic games.[37] The strict financial and social requirements of much Anglo-Irish sporting activity also contributed to Irish resentment. For example, the Cork Drapers Association was denied affiliation with the Irish Rugby Union because of their profession.[38] In an editorial deriding upper-class women who participated in that most English of sports, fox hunting, a writer asked, "Can anyone even pretend to imagine that such a woman [could] possibly be a good wife or mother, or have sympathy with sorrows and the sufferings of others. . . . How many ladies of rank and leisure and means, either in the city or country, help to teach catechism in our churches on Sunday?"[39] The Gaelic woman was above all a working- or middle-class mate and nurturer who was actively religious and morally unquestionable. Here once again, the valued status of Irish women's reproductive ability is highlighted. Men were consistently defined as independent actors, while women were most often defined as relational objects, as the mothers, daughters, sisters, and wives of men.

Upper-class women also represented independence of action for women. Women who possessed the free time to go on fox hunts were not working from early morning to late at night running a household. In the same vein, Irish women who strayed beyond the boundaries of the domestic sphere received little encouragement from the sporting community. At one match there were "several ladies with collecting boxes in aid of the rifle fund for the Irish Volunteers [who] reaped a rich harvest; a strong contrast to the cold reception given to the few ladies soliciting support for the Women's Suffrage cause."[40] This discouragement of women as equal partners by spectators of Gaelic games mirrored women's relegation to the background by the games themselves, through both the physicality of the games and the symbolism surrounding them that demarcated the proper roles of the sexes.

DISCIPLINE WAS OF primary importance to the promoters of the games. In fact, one prominent writer stated his belief that "the creation of proper control was the first and most important task" of the GAA.[41] Few reports passed up the opportunity to comment on the exemplary behavior of the players and crowds. One team was described as having "Celtic faces [which] were the faces of well-schooled, well-disciplined men, full of enthusiasm but also full of self-control. Enthusiasm dominated by self-control!"[42] The unending parade of compliments and emphasis on good behavior would seem almost comic were it not so seriously offered. Rhetoric aside, it seems that, as the winning of games became more closely tied to the honor of the parish or county, tempers often did flare. The rough play of one man was blamed for the early termination of a game in 1906, when his use of foul language and deliberate kicking of opponents were described as "ungaelic."[43] Likewise, the employment of questionable tactics in a game in 1889 was termed "unmanly."[44] While the ethics of the games revolution in both Britain and Ireland demanded sportsmanlike conduct, Gaelic games produced an atmosphere where infractions of rules, or even the spirit of the rules, were interpreted as betrayal of one's race, nation, and gender, not simply of a mechanistic code.

Despite the emphasis on skill on the field, neither the physicality of the players nor the military benefits of disciplined men were ignored. The highly integrated and open playing style forced teams to train more. In this way, the move away from preeminent physicality made ties between the games and military potential paradoxically closer. P. J. Devlin observed that GAA patron and Fenian leader John O'Leary "knew that it was manpower that fought battles, and that only disciplined manpower could win them."[45] As the games evolved, the image of an ideal Gael as a prepared Gael became more axiomatic. However, it was incessantly reiterated that this manly and military vigor must be kept under control. The ritualization of violence surrounding modern Gaelic games was aimed at promoting a martial image. The *Freeman's Journal* described how, after one match in 1888, the teams "were marshaled . . . in military fashion [and] ordered to fall into lines." The team "captain" gave the order "Right About!" and the men, victors and vanquished together, paraded through the town.[46] Even though a martial, and therefore inherently violent, performance was enacted, the imitation of the military kept that violence within disciplined ranks. Because controlled and organized violence was, in fact, much more powerful than its disorganized counterpart, the advent of the GAA and modern Gaelic games increased the potential for violence in Irish society. The greater number of men participating in these games enlarged the portion of the population that was directly involved in activities requiring physical force. Here, then, we see that a transformation rather than reduction of violence characterized the evolution of modern Irish sport.

The connection between training for sport and training for revolt was not left unstated, but was continually enunciated by players, administrators, and commentators. For example, the caman has long held symbolic value as a substitute for a rifle. The men of the GAA marched at the funerals of prominent statesmen and association figures with camans draped in black and carried on the shoulder in a rifle-like manner, thereby doing little to ease the minds of Dublin Castle, the administrative headquarters of the British government in Ireland, that they were not an army in training.[47] Although the GAA as an organization maintained strict neutrality during the Home Rule Crisis of 1913, the pro–Sinn Fein views of most GAA members were easily discernible, and a marked decrease in the number participating in the games ensued as militia ranks swelled.[48] One writer proclaimed that "the Gaelic body, be it club or council, that puts camans into the hands of boys can do as much for a future Ireland of ideal dreams as those who would arm a battalion in the same area."[49]A rally speaker stated, "When the time comes, the hurlers will cast away the caman for the sharp bright steel that will drive the Saxon from our land."[50] The conflation of sport and militarism seemed to suggest that, if Gaelic athletes could conquer and defend the borders of the playing fields of Ireland from the imposition of British institutions, surely it was only a matter of time before the same was done for the nation.

The growth of hurling and Gaelic football as propagated by the GAA was instrumental in the restructuring of an Irish nationalist manhood. The power to oppose British games and reclaim independence of action one sphere at a time marked the first dramatic steps toward greater freedom from English control. Because these endeavors took place within the highly gendered and male-dominated world of sports, they affected the construction of gender roles in the wider community. While masculinity is never a static entity and its characteristics evolve over time, the period from 1884 to 1916 is clearly distinguished by the development of a distinct conception of masculinity in the Gaelic community that bound together manhood and nationalism in the context of active participation in Gaelic sports. Being born male in Ireland was not equivalent to being an Irish man; Gaelic masculinity was the product of a dynamic cultivation of physical and mental qualities that distinguished the Irish man from both women and British men.

The games' dynamic was in large part dominated by tensions that molded and distorted the meanings of the games and their relations to

Irish society. The games were characterized by dichotomous conflicts between civilizing tendencies and violent content; between a desire to be viewed as peaceable and disciplined and a determination to present an impression of incipient revolution; and between the paramountcy of muscular stature and the ascendancy of intellectual control. Like their British counterparts that sought to reconcile Christianity with social Darwinism, Gaelic sports fed on the tensions produced by these varying objectives competing for dominance. In this way, the games reflect the fortunes of the Irish nationalist movement itself, which wavered between parliamentarianism and military defiance and between conciliatory home rule and republican separatism. Through the process of revamping the games, new sports were born that shared ideals and goals with the community's conceptions of a nationalist manhood and that came to symbolize the Irish struggle with the English while simultaneously participating in that struggle.

Notes

1. Nicholas Mansergh, *The Irish Question 1840–1921* (London: George Allen and Unwin, 1975), 243–246.
2. Ashis Nandy examined similar issues in an Indian context in *The Tao of Cricket: On Games of Destiny and the Destiny of Games* (New Delhi: Penguin Books, 1988), xi, 1–4.
3. Although Roman Catholicism and the GAA were intimately tied, the association's relationship with the clergy was often stormy in its first decade because of clerical opposition to the Irish Republican Brotherhood. See James O'Shea, *Priest, Politics and Society in Post-Famine Ireland: A Study of County Tipperary 1850–1891* (Dublin: Wolfhound Press, 1983), 150, 171–176.
4. Nandy, *The Tao of Cricket*, 1–4.
5. See L. Perry Curtis Jr., *Apes and Angels: The Irishman in Victorian Caricature* (Washington, D.C.: Smithsonian Institution Press, 1971).
6. Benedict Anderson, *Imagined Communities: Reflections on the Origin and Spread of Nationalism* (New York: Verso, 1983).
7. *The Gaelic Athletic Annual and County Directory* 1910–1911, no. 3 (Dublin: Cahill and Co., 1911), "Compiled and Edited by Gaels for Gaels," 58.
8. *Celtic Times*, 26 February 1887.
9. Ibid.
10. P. J. Devlin, *Our Native Games* (Dublin: M. H. Gill and Son, 1935), 14.
11. Ibid., 48.
12. Emmet Larkin, "The Devotional Revolution in Ireland, 1850–1875," *American Historical Review* 77 (1972): 625–652.

13. Donal McCartney, *The Dawning of Democracy: Ireland 1800–1870* (Dublin: Helicon, 1987), 207–208.

14. This community also comprised the Gaelic League, with its Irish language movement, and the Abbey Theatre of Yeats, Gregory, and Synge. For an interesting reaction by this community to a divergent presentation of Irish gender roles in Synge's play *Playboy of the Western World* in 1907, see James Kilroy, *The "Playboy" Riots* (Dublin: Doleman Press, 1971).

15. Devlin, *Our Native Games*, 20.

16. John Sugden and Alan Bairner, *Sport, Sectarianism and Society in a Divided Ireland* (Leicester: Leicester University Press, 1993), 29.

17. See J. A. Mangan, ed., *"Benefits Bestowed"? Education and British Imperialism* (Manchester: Manchester University Press, 1988).

18. W. F. Mandle, *The Gaelic Athletic Association and Irish Nationalist Politics, 1884–1924*, 221.

19. *The Gaelic Athletic Annual* 1910–1911, 18.

20. Marcus de Búrca, *Michael Cusack* (Dublin: Anvil Books, 1989), 120, and Marcus de Búrca, *The GAA: A History* (Dublin: Cumann Lúthchleas Gael, 1980), 28.

21. Quoted in Fr. Michael Gilsenan, S.S., C.C., *Hills of Magheracloone 1884–1984* (Monaghan, 1985), 19.

22. Devlin, *Our Native Games*, 62–63.

23. *Celtic Times*, 16 April 1887.

24. *United Ireland and the Irishman*, 11 October 1884, as quoted in de Búrca, *Michael Cusack*, 96.

25. *Irish Daily Independent and Nation*, 7 November 1904.

26. Michael A. Messner and Donald F. Sabo, *Sex, Violence and Power in Sports* (Freedom, Calif.: Crossing Press, 1994), 96.

27. Although women often attended matches, it would more likely be the men alone who would travel to see the games. *The Gaelic Athletic Annual* 1910–1911 reported: "Half the male population of the kingdom [Co. Kerry] must have traveled to Tipperary on that day" (14).

28. *The Gaelic Athletic Annual* 1908–1909, 45.

29. Mark Tierney, *Croke of Cashel: The Life of Archbishop Thomas William Cooke* (Dublin: Gill and Macmillan, 1976), 195.

30. *Celtic Times*, 26 February 1887.

31. Carol Coulter, *The Hidden Tradition: Feminism, Women and Nationalism in Ireland* (Cork, 1993), 9–18.

32. de Búrca, *The GAA: A History*, 93.

33. *United Irishman*, 29 July 1905.

34. Tierney, *Croke of Cashel*, 195.

35. *Shamrock*, 24 January 1884, as quoted in de Búrca, *Michael Cusack*, 83.

36. Quoted in Padrig Griffin, *The Politics of Irish Athletics* (Ballinamore, Ireland, 1990), 16.

37. See Kevin Whelan, "The Geography of Hurling," *History Ireland* 1 (1993): 28–31.

38. *United Irishman*, 18 March 1899, as cited in Tom Graven, *Nationalist Revolutionaries in Ireland 1858–1928* (Oxford: Clarendon Press, 1987), 67.

39. *United Irishman*, 19 August 1905.

40. *Irish Independent*, 19 October 1914.

41. Devlin, *Our Native Games*, 12.

42. GAA 1915: *Yearbook* (Dublin: Gaelic Press, 1915), 39.

43. Gilsenan, *Hills of Magheracloone*, 127.

44. *Clare Journal*, 14 October 1889, quoted in Tim Moloney, ed., *The Claret and Gold: A History of the Tulla Henley Club, 1887–1987* (Ennis: Clare Champion Printers, 1987), 58.

45. Devlin, *Our Native Games*, 21.

46. *Freeman's Journal*, 3 April 1888.

47. de Búrca, *The GAA: A History*, 62.

48. *Editors' note*: Sinn Fein ("Ourselves Alone") is an Irish nationalist group founded in 1905.

49. de Búrca, *The GAA: A History*, 124–127.

50. Devlin, *Our Native Games*, 56.

Elisa Camiscioli

Reproducing the "French Race":
Immigration and Pronatalism in
Early-Twentieth-Century France

As with discourses of travel, nation, and progress, debates about immigration and labor in modern Europe were carried on through reference to female bodies and their reproductive capacities. In turn-of-the-century France, where an influx of all manner of "foreign" bodies was accompanied by a crisis of depopulation among the "native-born," public concern about reproduction was influenced by anxieties about racial purity and the fate of the civilized nation. This essay focuses on the link between productivity and racial order by analyzing the role of the National Alliance for the Increase of the French Population in shaping national discussions of immigration (by both colonial peoples and Poles, Italians, and Spaniards). Made up of doctors, industrialists, and social scientists — and predominantly Catholic — the Alliance offered a number of powerful diagnoses and prognoses about the future of France if it failed to guard its borders, both literal and metaphorical. Its paranoia about infiltration and its emphasis on keeping the body politic racially pure enables us to see connections between depopulation and fascism elsewhere in Europe, as well as to appreciate how constitutively concerns about race and gender helped contribute to the character of reactionary politics in the interwar years.

The immigrant question of early-twentieth-century France was formulated with reference to both the labor power and reproductive value of potential foreigners. Politicians, industrialists, social scientists, and racial theorists agreed that the "demographic crisis" had created a shortage of citizens as well as workers, and thus immigrants who came to work in France must also be assimilable and able to produce indisputably French offspring. The new emphasis on assimilability was a reflection of the widespread panic created by depopulation, as social critics with pronatalist convictions lamented the steady drop in French births and the "individualistic" nature of French men and women that, in their view, had encouraged stringent reproductive practices. They argued that depopulation had social as well as economic consequences, evidenced by the lack of husbands for French women, young men for the army, and children for the future labor force. Despite the pronounced nationalism of the pronatalist movement, its leaders therefore conceded that to mitigate the effects of the demographic crisis on the labor market and the French family, the importation of foreign workers was a necessary, though temporary, solution.

No European nation experienced demographic decline more acutely than France, and the casualties of the First World War, added to an already low birthrate, exacerbated French anxieties. From 1911 to 1938, the French population increased by only 2 million inhabitants, despite the addition of 1.7 million people from Alsace and Lorraine.[1] On the eve of WWI, the average French family was composed of two children, and, in 1926, only three families out of ten could claim three or more! In fact, French demographic growth in this period was largely due to immigration. The 1931 census counted 808,000 Italians, 508,000 Poles, and 352,000 Spaniards, to name the most numerous groups. In the interwar period, nearly 3 million foreigners resided in France, and three-fourths of all demographic growth could be attributed to immigration.[2]

The debate on fecundity and assimilability, however, was carried out in a particular racial order. Although family immigration also occurred in this period, foreigners to France in the early twentieth century were overwhelmingly young and unmarried men. Male foreigners were, in many regards, particularly welcome: the catastrophic loss of French men in the Great War had created a shortage of husbands for French women while exacerbating the effects of depopulation. The demographic crisis thereby forced hybridity on the nation; intermarriage with "racially" appropriate foreign men was encouraged, as it was necessary for the rebuilding of the national body. Participants in the immigration debate conceived of the "French race" as a dynamic construct with the ability to incorporate select elements into its fold. In consequence, the dominant racial metaphor of this period was one of judicious mixing rather than an appeal to "racial purity." The sanctioning of prescribed forms of racial mixing, however, did not refute the logic of biological essentialism. Only "compatible" blood was to be combined with that of the French, in order to sustain, or even regenerate, the race.

Moreover, the surplus population of Africa and Asia and, specifically, the potential labor source of the French colonies had to be dismissed as a possible remedy for depopulation in the metropole. Although Africans and Asians had immigrated to France before, during, and after the First World War, the pressing need to reconstitute French families in the interwar years reframed the immigrant question. As assimilability and the ability to reproduce French offspring became the most salient criteria by which foreigners were to be judged, the evaluation of simple labor power no longer sufficed. Pronatalists therefore cautioned against the importation of nonwhite workers, arguing instead that the Italians, Poles, and Spaniards were the most viable candidates for naturalization. This amounted to a repudiation of the universalist vision of the Enlightenment and the Revolution which, in its purest form, viewed all bodies, whether white or of color, as essentially the same.[3] Instead, in the historically specific political economy of mass immigration and colonialism, the possibility of assimilation — and hence citizenship — was closed to those whose difference was deemed immutable.

IN SEVERAL IMPORTANT demographic studies of the late nineteenth and early twentieth century, depopulation was theorized in terms of the relationship between civilization and birthrate. For example, liberal economist Paul Leroy-Beaulieu of the College de France juxtaposed the depopulation of northern Europe and North America with escalating birthrates in the African and Asian world, and argued that as a nation modernized, achieving a higher standard of living and increased industrial production, its birthrate necessarily fell.[4] This was, of course, a dramatic refutation of Malthusian doctrine, which prophesied an exponential increase in human populations and thus a depletion of global resources. After approximately 1860, Malthusianism fell out of favor, and demographers focused instead on the trend toward fertility decline or, in the words of Leroy-Beaulieu, the "true law of population among civilized people."[5] Hoping to attain a greater level of material comfort, even the "humblest of citizens" began to postpone marriage, limit births, and opt for an "individualistic" existence that, according to the pronatalist position, blatantly ignored the collective concerns of the nation.[6]

A society's birthrate could therefore be expressed as inversely proportional to its level of "civilization." According to Leroy-Beaulieu, civilization was composed of an urbanized society with a democratic government and a developed middle class in which education, affluence, and leisure had been extended to the majority of the population. Despite the virtues of the civilized state, depopulation was the necessary outcome: "In recent and present times, the diminution of fecundity among the civilized nations . . . can be considered a general, if not universal fact."[7] Demographers explained that while the state of civilization facilitated global predominance and justified European expansion overseas, it was a double-edged sword, bringing degeneration and depopulation in its wake. Ironically, the march of progress ultimately compromised the power of "civilized" nations, now confronted with the demographic superiority of less developed societies.

In Africa and Asia, where the colonial project was to transport civilization to "savage" and "barbarous" lands, birthrates were high despite substantial mortality rates. Demographer and physician Jacques Bertillon succinctly explained: "The most ignorant countries are also the most fecund ones."[8] The anticlerical and socialist-leaning demographer Arsène Dumont echoed the conservative Bertillon's position, claiming that "those who absorb no part of civilization, like the poor in France and barbarians worldwide, conserve their high birthrates, while those who absorb much of civilization ultimately die as a result."[9] Demographers hypothesized that as African and Asian societies modernized, embracing industrialization, hygienic practices, and democratic values, they too would begin to limit their births. But in the meantime, with African and Asian populations growing unchecked while birthrates in most European nations dwindled, the fertility of nonwhite people was perceived as a threat to white hegemony worldwide.

Opponents of nonwhite immigration therefore insisted that it was the duty of the entire Occidental world to form a united front against immigrants of color.[10] According to this view, Malthusianism among Europeans was nothing short of race suicide, a myopic practice that amounted to an abdication of the white mission to civilize the globe. If strength was in numbers, as pronatalists argued, Europeans and North Americans must not remain passive while nonwhites propagated at their expense. In the words of Auguste Isaac, the Catholic deputy named minister of commerce in 1919, father of eleven children and founder of the pro-family lobbying group La Plus Grande Famille (the Largest Family): "If the white race restrains [its births], who will guarantee us that the yellow race will follow its example? Who will assure us that the black race will sacrifice the fecundity which, to cite but one example, is a cause of anxiety for whites in the United States?"[11]

Depopulation was thus characterized as a "general phenomenon . . . which one could note among all people of the white race," now menaced by the fecundity of the Asian and African world.[12] Around the turn of the century, high Asian birthrates in addition to several important examples of Asians asserting themselves against white nations — such as the Boxer Rebellion, the Russo-Japanese War, and the founding of the Congress Party — aided in the construction of the phantasmic "Yellow Peril."[13] The possibility of Chinese or Japanese expansion heightened Europe's wariness with regard to population increases outside of the Western world. Prominent pronatalist Fernand Boverat explained: "Among the colored races, and the yellow race in particular, birthrates remain formidable. Japan will see its population rise by one million people per year. For a country like France, which has a great colonial empire . . . this demographic disequilibrium is particularly serious."[14]

Thus, in France, pronatalist concerns were not galvanized by German demographic strength alone. Instead, a vision of colonial imperialism and a "Europe submerged" by nonwhites intensified French anxiety. Only white immigration could provide assimilable labor power while counteracting the demographic might of Africans and Asians. While it met French requirements for foreigners to serve as both workers and citizens, it also allowed members of a transnational white polity to secure themselves against the fertility of the non-Western world. Foreign labor would therefore have to be recruited among European countries with surplus populations. The partially modernized and demographically prolific nations of southern and central Europe constituted an intermediate category between the depopulation of northern Europe and the fecundity of Africa and Asia.

Because the economic development of nations like Italy, Spain, and Poland could not accommodate the size of their populations, many workers opted to immigrate to depopulated and industrialized states. Not only could the Italians, Spaniards, and Poles fill shortages in the fields and factories; they could also reproduce with native women without substantially changing the "racial composition" of the French people. According to demographer Arsène Dumont, it was best to seek out immigrants like the Italians who had not yet "broken their ties with their native land," as they retained high fertility rates and the values that promoted large families.[15] Demographers agreed that the state of civilization brought with it many consequences, and that nations like Italy, Spain, and Poland had retained the best of the preindustrial world: prolific birthrates, a commitment to hard work, a strong sense of family, and, a value praised by some but not all pronatalists, a more pious Catholicism. In turn, these traits were reinforced by traditional conceptions of masculinity and femininity which, by preserving the "innate" distinction between the sexes, promoted fertility and a devotion to family life. In contrast, social critics like Leroy-Beaulieu noted that in modernized nations like France, the boundaries between women and men had been blurred, and the feminist movement, which sought to make women identical to men, was largely responsible for depopulation. He wrote: "The masculinisation of women is, from all points of view, one of the grave dangers facing contemporary civilization. It is a *facteur dessechant et sterilisant* [a desiccating and sterilizing factor]."[16]

By the turn of the century, the connection between depopulation and feminism had been firmly established, and as one further manifestation of the "individualist virus," feminism was said to have encouraged French women to abandon their prescribed role as mothers and homemakers. Similarly, pronatalists called into question the virility of the nation and its male citizenry, conflating the frailty of a depopulated France with the effeminacy of French men. In this context Fernand Boverat, the most prominent figure of the pronatalist movement, warned that for nations as well as men, to be "afflicted with a pernicious anemia" rendered them vulnerable to outside attack.[17] Immigration was to reinvigorate the national body by introducing young and robust male elements from Europe into an anemic population further debilitated by the casualties of the Great War. In the context of a biological understanding of degeneration and revivification, then, foreigners were frequently described as the "blood transfusion" necessary to curtail or even reverse the effects of national decline. Albert Troullier of the Alliance argued that the nation should select its immigrants like a physician preparing for a transfusion, "[choosing] an individual without physiological flaws, with blood *compatible* to that of the person requiring the transfusion. . . . There exist actual blood types and one cannot, without great danger, mix the blood of different and *incompatible* groups."[18]

Unmarried foreign men, however, were widely considered to be promiscuous, dissolute, and unstable. Social commentators claimed that foreign bachelors were more prone to alcoholism, criminality, and venereal disease, and without wives to persuade them to settle in one place, they wandered France in search of work or returned to their native land, thus mitigating their contribution to the national economy. The "excess virility" of male immigrants was therefore to be tempered by marriage, with their sexuality channeled through the conjugal union in the interests of repopulating the French nation. For this reason, pronatalists encouraged both family immigration and the marriage of male immigrant workers shortly after their arrival in France. Thus, once again, the pronatalist position on immigration mirrored its entreaty to the French nation as a whole, exalting marriage, fecundity, and procreative sex enacted within the confines of traditional gender roles.

Linking the problem of reproduction to the racial order of the early twentieth century, pronatalists conveyed white demographic panic while condemning the existing gender order. In reconstituting the citizen body, both the labor power and reproductive value of potential foreigners would be considered. On each count, the contribution of white Europeans was deemed far superior to that of Africans and Asians. Specifically, pronatalists held that an immigration of Latin and Slavic elements could supply qualified labor without recourse to Chinese and colonial workers. According to the monthly journal of L'Alliance Nationale pour l'Accroissement de la Population Francaise (the National Alliance for the Increase of the French Population): "After having been flooded during the war with Kabyle street sweepers, Annamese stokers, Negro dockers, and Chinese laborers, whom we had to import because it was the best we could get, we were forced to send the majority of these worthless immigrants back to their faraway homelands. They were more disposed to pillage and thievery than serious labor. The re-establishment of the peace has permitted us to replace these 'undesirables' with our usual immigrants, the Italians and the Spaniards."[19]

The Alliance was France's largest and most influential pronatalist movement, which by 1939 could claim over 25,000 members. Its presence in the depopulation debate was enduring, determined, and obstreperous. Founded in May 1896 by demographer Jacques Bertillon, Drs. Charles Richet and Emile Javal, civil servant Auguste Honnorat, and Catholic statistician Emile Cheysson, the Alliance was initially composed of secular and socially conservative patriots, most of them bourgeois businessmen, industrialists, doctors, and lawyers. However, its blend of antiindividualism, antifeminism, and nationalism permitted ties with Catholics as well as those sympathetic to the populationist policies of Nazi Germany and fascist Italy. The Alliance led a widespread propaganda campaign that included the publication of pronatalist brochures, periodicals, films, demographic statistics, and proposals for legislative action, and its lobbying efforts had a direct effect on postwar legislation such as the 1920 law repressing propaganda for contraceptives, the 1923 law aimed at increasing prosecutions for abortions, and the granting of family allowances for dependent children. Its members held that depopulation was largely the fault of the Third Republic's institutions and policies, as they promoted individual rights at the expense of collective duties. Alliance members viewed depopulation as the result of a "liberal and individualistic political and economic order that disproportionately rewarded the childless." Demographic decline, they claimed, could be reversed only if liberal institutions like the tax system, military, civil service, and perhaps even the wage system were reworked to favor prolific fathers.[20] At annual congresses and in its journal, members of the Alliance frequently debated questions of assimilation and naturalization. They held that the stability of the family was the key to social peace but, paradoxically, found among foreigners some of the best examples of strong and unified households. First and foremost, depopulation had to be rectified internally, by French men and women, with the support of the state. In the meantime, however, immigration would serve as a stopgap measure replenishing the anemic French population. While the Alliance claimed that unassimilated, nonnaturalized foreigners were a potential danger to the "French race," its members had little sympathy for the harshest French critics of immigration. Auguste Isaac explained: "Those who complain the most about the intrusion of foreigners are generally not those who make the most personal efforts or sacrifices to change the state of affairs. The same pens warning of social ills are often used to propagate the very ideas that foster them: the love of material well-being, the right to happiness, the glorification of pleasure, and distaste for the family."[21] Naturalization was, of course, the bona fide emblem of citizenship, and because the Alliance wished to see a clear increase in French population statistics, it demanded that assimilable foreigners be naturalized quickly, without complications or delays.

The Alliance also framed the problem of immigration and depopulation in terms of white demographic panic. In its official publications, references to the Yellow Peril were abundant, depopulation was repeatedly described as the "plague of the white race," and low European birthrates were explained through recourse to the rhetoric of degeneration. In numerous articles and speeches, President Fernand Boverat hierarchized foreigners according to their assimilability and potential for citizenship. He explained that although Belgium and Switzerland had furnished assimilable workers in the nineteenth century, shrinking birthrates in those nations made it necessary to evaluate other sources. Boverat insisted that the only countries able to supply France with both labor power and assimilable immigrants were Italy, Spain, Czechoslovakia, Poland, and Romania. As for the Greeks, "Levantines," and Kabyles of North Africa, he continued, these populations were, "with some exceptions . . . second-rate immigrants that no country is actively seeking out, and which we have no interest in attracting to France." While this group was not classified among the assimilable, and in all likelihood was not recognized as fully white, its difference was less weighted than that of Asians and other Africans who, according to Boverat, should under no circumstances be permitted to enter France in large numbers. He wrote: "Despite the dangers of depopulation we must carefully avoid the mass immigration of men of color, at the risk of witnessing the development of racial conflicts on French soil, the disastrous consequences of which we have already seen in the United States."[22]

While the Alliance conducted a parliamentary and legislative assault on behalf of the pronatalist cause, one of its most successful popularizers was author Ludovic Naudeau. As an international correspondent for the Paris newspaper *Le Temps*, Naudeau had earned his journalistic reputation with his eyewitness accounts of the Russo-Japanese War and the Bolshevik Revolution, having been detained in Japanese and later Bolshevik prison camps for his efforts. Returning to Paris after the First World War, he was employed by the popular weekly review *L'Illustration*, publishing accounts of his travels to various European countries as well as books on modern Japan and Russia, both of which were awarded prizes by the French Academy. In addition to his acclaimed exposés of the rise of fascism and Nazism, Naudeau turned his flair for travel writing infused with political analysis on his native France. After a two-year journey through twenty French departments to document the gravity of depopulation, in

1929 and 1930, his findings were printed as a serial. This dense, meticulous, and highly subjective work is indicative of the shift in the 1930s toward an increased public awareness of the populationist platform: its publication generated passionate responses from readers, including a barrage of letters to the author, debates in provincial newspapers, and the undertaking of several local monographs further investigating the depopulation problem.[23] In 1931, Naudeau's study was reprinted as a best-selling book entitled *La France se regarde: Le problème de la natalité* (France confronts itself: The birthrate problem).[24]

Naudeau also held that despite the potential dangers of immigration, it was the necessary first step in combating depopulation. Following closely the demographic arguments of Bertillon, Leroy-Beaulieu, and Dumont, he concurred that French depopulation was a reflection of the relationship between fertility and civilization. Moreover, he agreed that the pernicious "individualism" of the French had produced a population more interested in pursuing pleasure than fulfilling its collective duties to the nation. French women, in particular, were guilty of this charge, as Naudeau claimed that the female gender was most easily seduced by the desire for luxury and material comfort. Even before the First World War, it was widely accepted by republicans, Catholics, and socialists alike that French women, in their quest for economic independence and sexual freedom, had abandoned the obligations of social citizenship, namely, motherhood and care of the domestic sphere. The charge that "female individualism" engendered depopulation and other social ills had become, by the interwar years, a ubiquitous criticism of the perceived gender order.[25]

Naudeau began his study with the uncompromising stance that France had always been, and must remain, a white nation. Despite the magnitude of French demographic decline, he explained, the "integrity of the white race" was a value he planned to uphold. Employing contemporary metaphors that invoked the unity of metropolitan France and its colonial empire, Naudeau expressed disdain for those who envisioned a "greater France," composed of "one-hundred million Frenchmen." In his view, colonial immigration would blur the boundaries between the ruler and the ruled, compromising the safety of French possessions, and promoting hazardous forms of racial mixing. He wrote: "I affirm that we will not sustain our place in the world if we do not remain what we have always been: a white nation. Our colonial empire is guaranteed by the strength of the metropole."[26]

Naudeau therefore called for the immigration of the transition populations of Europe. At the end of his long tour of the French departments, he concluded, without hesitation, that no immigrants were better candidates for assimilation than the Italians. He described them as diligent, fertile, and simple people who flourished in the countryside and maintained a strong commitment to family life. Because the Italians had not yet fallen victim to the potential ills of modernity, Naudeau portrayed their immigrant communities as idyllic havens brimming with the most wholesome of preindustrial values. In contrast, the French family, which had once possessed such admirable traits, was currently falling into a state of degeneration. Thus, when relaying his visit to the Lot-et-Garonne (a department in southwestern France), Naudeau praised the Italians as passionately as he excoriated the French. He began his cautionary tale by explaining that throughout this department, there were numerous cases of impoverished Italian families arriving with no money but many children. While sons were hired out as agricultural laborers and daughters sent to work as maids in neighboring villages, the family, as a unit, cultivated their land. Because family members were "numerous, hardworking, frugal, and humble in their desires," the land was paid for in the course of a few years. Meanwhile, the former proprietor of the land, an "old, solitary, hunched up Malthusian," has retired to the city to "sadly vegetate" while paying an enormous rent. Naudeau concluded: "The simple power of fecundity and labor produced the buying power sufficient for [the Frenchman] to be evicted and effaced. Having all his life sought out too many material pleasures, too many egotistical satisfactions, this Frenchman, at the end of his life, is nothing but a lugubrious island, a *deraciné* [uprooted individual], and . . . a vanquished man."[27]

Naudeau's trenchant observations illustrate how strongly he believed civilization was a double-edged sword that, while ushering in progress, had also undermined paternal authority, work discipline, and a sense of civic duty. Because the French placed material comfort and a higher standard of living before the good of the national community, the birthrate was rapidly declining, the countryside had been left fallow, and society was becoming dangerously atomized. Although Naudeau echoed the familiar conviction that the state of "primitive life" conformed best to high fertility rates, he too called for a reconciliation of fecundity and civilization. Because all societies would eventually undergo the shift to modernity, the state must correct the social ills this transition had engendered:

"When, through the inevitable workings of civilization, [the state of primitive life] is dispelled, it is necessary to substitute powerful social and sanitary organizations, as we must not leave uprooted proletarians to fend for themselves. In short, civilization must remedy the ills that it causes."[28] Thus, like other pronatalists, Naudeau called for government-sponsored social reform to counteract the dangers of too much civilization.

Because the Italians lived "close to nature" and subordinated all other desires in order to acquire property for cultivation, they reminded Naudeau of a France that had disappeared several decades earlier. He repeatedly called for the French to imitate Italians' diligence and sobriety and the simplicity of their lives. Moreover, he invoked the probity of Italian women in an effort to further vilify *la femme moderne*, whose selfish and pleasure-seeking nature was evidenced by her refusal to produce children for the nation. So monstrous were French women who abandoned their maternal role that Naudeau was forced to look abroad for examples of feminine virtue. Faced with the high fertility rates of Italian families, he demanded: "Is it not because [Italian women], known for the simplicity of their attire . . . and paying little mind to fashion, content themselves with being mothers, as did our French women, one hundred years ago?"[29]

Naudeau saw in the Italians those rooted, conservative, family-oriented values the French once possessed. However, he understood all too well that if the French had something to learn from the Italians, this greatly complicated the assimilation process. If the pronatalist crusade was primarily about changing the mores and values of the degenerate French, it follows that little was to be gained in making the Italians resemble the French too closely. His greatest fear was one that was echoed in a number of pronatalist circles: What if the Italians, as they assimilated, developed the same Malthusian practices so dear to the French? How could social critics argue for the need to turn immigrants into French men and women if, at the same time, they were insisting that French mores had to change? Could the fecundity of less "civilized" people be harnessed without their constituting dangerous, unassimilated pockets of foreigners in the midst of French territory? It was possible, Naudeau hypothesized, that first-generation Italians would remain prolific because they brought with them from Italy a strong work ethic, a commitment to family life, a disdain for luxuries, and a disposition that allowed them to be content with little. However, the need to assimilate the Italians, while simultaneously benefiting from their particular national character, led him to fear the worst. He asked: "Will they remain fecund once they have assimilated our mores? Will the second and third generation be even more prolific, or will they conform to the milieu that surrounds them? If we are to assimilate them, is that not because we want to make them resemble us?"[30]

Pronatalism, immigration, and assimilation were three inseparable components of the early twentieth century's demographic calculus, with the integration of appropriate foreigners as one part of a broader project seeking to remake the French family. Meanwhile, because countless French men and women had ignored their civic obligation to procreate, assimilable foreigners could gain access to the nation by displaying the qualities pronatalists believed to have once been intrinsically French: a love for the countryside, a commitment to family, and a collectivist vision of civic life. Pronatalists had long advocated that, in exchange for their patriotism, large French families be rewarded with family suffrage, monetary allocations, a reduction in military service, and the like. The extent to which they were willing to extend these privileges to foreign families that fulfilled their reproductive obligation to the state greatly complicates our understanding of the movement's nationalism.

IN THEIR EFFORT to reinvent the French family and redefine the practice of citizenship, pronatalists invoked the categories of gender, race, and reproduction to define the stakes of the immigrant question. The language in which they discussed degeneration and national renewal was to be echoed in the political and social hygienic discourse of the Vichy state, whose impulse to regulate reproduction, marriage, and domestic life had its roots in the populationist politics of the Third Republic.[31] Under Pétain, prominent pronatalists like Boverat, Haury, Duval-Arnould, and Mauco would continue their efforts to revive the traditional family, along with its high birthrates, cultural conservatism, and strictly segregated gender roles.[32] With the Occupation serving as further evidence of the wounded virility of French men, the selfishness of French women, and the perils of depopulation, the Vichy state (1940–1944) was to both amplify and institutionalize the natalist familialism of the interwar years.

Pronatalist ideology was a vital part of the political culture of the French Third Republic, and for this reason, any study of immigration to France must reckon with its position on foreigners, citizenship, and nationhood. Ultimately, the impulse to hierarchize immigrants according to their productive and reproductive value was a rejection of the Revolutionary doctrine of universal humanism, which, in its capacious understanding of community, heralded the abstract sameness of all beings. Similarly, pro-natalist discourse on immigration severely undermined the republican and assimilationist model of nationhood, according to which any foreigner willing to assume the French cultural patrimony would be granted access to the citizen body. Instead, the abstract egalitarianism of the "French citizen" was repeatedly confronted with the intractable problem of differ-ence, an unsurprising consequence of the grounding of citizenship rights in patriarchy, bourgeois individualism, and hierarchical racial difference. In this manner, the nation's hopes and anxieties were deflected onto those who had come from beyond its borders, as the Italians, Poles, and Span-iards were to assist in restoring the racial and gender order.

Notes

1. Francoise Thebaud, "Le mouvement nataliste dans la France de l'entre-deux- l'Al-liance National pour l'Accroissement de la Population Francaise," *Revue de l'histoire moderne et contemporaine* 32 (1985): 276. All translations from the French are Elisa Camiscioli's.

2. Gerard Noiriel, *Population, immigration, et identite nationale en France, 19e–20e siecle* (Paris, 1992), 53.

3. Maxim Silverman, *Deconstructing the Nation: Immigration, Racism, and Citizenship in Modern France* (London, 1996), 19–27.

4. Paul Leroy-Beaulieu, *La question de la population* (Paris, 1913).

5. Ibid., 237.

6. Mario Gianturco, "Le probleme international de la population," *Revile politique et parlementaire,* 426 (1930): 225–226.

7. Leroy-Beaulieu, *La question de la population,* 184.

8. Dr. Jacques Bertillon, *La depopulation de la France: Ses consequences, ses causes: Mesures a prendre pour la combattre* (Paris, 1911), 130, 128–137.

9. Dumont, *Depopulation et civilisation: Étude démographique* (Paris, 1890), 241.

10. See, for example, Jean Pluyette, *La doctrine des races et la selection de l'immigration ex France* (Paris, 1930), 140.

11. Auguste Isaac, "Discours," Congres National de la Natalité, *Compte rendu,* 1922, 19.

12. Tournaire, *La Plaie française* (Librairie-Bibliotheque Auguste Comte, 1922), 231.

13. *Editors' note:* "Congress" refers to the Indian and African National Congresses, bodies representing anticolonial nationalism. "Yellow Peril" means the threat to West-ern civilization said to arise from the power of Asiatic peoples.

14. Fernand Boverat, "La denatalité, ses causes et les mésures à prendre pour l'enrayer," *Le Musée social,* 1 (1936): 4.

15. Arsène Dumont, "Demographie des etrangers habitant en France," *Bulletin de la Société d'anthropologie de France* (1894): 425.

16. Leroy-Beaulieu, *La question de la population*, 270–273.

17. Boverat, "La denatalité," 4–5.

18. Albert Troullier, "Immigration — Demographie," *L'Economie nouvelle* (June 1928): 314; emphasis in the original.

19. "Immigration et naturalisation," *Revue de l'Alliance Nationale Pour l'Accroissement de la Population Française* (hereafter *Revue*), 134 (1923): 279.

20. Susan Pederson, *Family, Dependence, and the Origins of the Welfare State* (Cambridge: Cambridge University Press, 1994), 61.

21. Auguste Isaac, "Discours," Congres National de la Natalité, *Compte rendu*, 1926, 13.

22. Boverat, "Il faut à la France une politique d'immigration," *Revue*, 129 (1923): 119–120.

23. Robert Talmy, *Histoire du mouvement familiale*, 2: 220 (Paris, 1962).

24. Ludovic Naudeau, *La France se regarde: Le problème de la natalité* (Paris, 1931).

25. Joshua H. Cole, *The Power of Large Numbers* (Ithaca, N.Y., 2000), 197.

26. Naudeau, *La France se regarde*, 8.

27. Ibid., 68; see also 39, 66.

28. Ibid., 116.

29. Ibid., 66.

30. Ibid., 54, 154–155, 333–334.

31. Miranda Pollard, *Reign of Virtue: Mobilizing Gender in Vichy France* (Chicago, 1998), 3, 40.

32. *Editors' note*: Henri-Philippe Pétain (1856–1951): leader of the French army in World War I and head of the Vichy government of France during World War II (1940–1944).

Fiona Paisley

Race Hysteria, Darwin 1938

Anxieties over racial and gender boundaries have been frequently sexualized, particularly on imperial frontiers, where the drama of cross-cultural contact played out within the uneven power relations that characterize colonialism. The story of Packsaddle (or Too Put Ah Malay), an Australian Aboriginal man who was charged with the attempted sexual assault of a white woman in Darwin in 1938, not only encapuslates the concerns about sex and violence that were so prominent in many colonies, but also reveals key assumptions about the gendered nature of sexuality in both white and Aboriginal society. This essay examines the ways these assumptions were articulated and fiercely contested as various settler and indigenous commentators responded to Packsaddle's trial and the "race hysteria" it triggered. In its careful delineation of the cultural fissures that were present in Australia's Northern Territory, where Italian, Greek, Malay, and Chinese communities existed alongside Anglo settlers and a range of Aboriginal peoples, it also underscores the ways demography and the organization of social space shape cross-cultural interaction even in small cities like Darwin.

In March 1938, an Aboriginal man was found guilty of attempting to sexually assault a white woman in the Northern Territory coastal city of Darwin. Contemporary accounts of his trial provide us with a remarkable record of one Aboriginal man's agency in the face of police, judge, local population, the Northern Territory Aboriginal Ordinance, and the Protection Board. Brought to trial on circumstantial evidence and a purported admission of guilt, he subsequently retracted his confession, claiming police coercion. His story powerfully illustrates the ways the historical overlap between criminal justice and Aboriginal administration in Australia has impacted individual Aboriginal lives. Although the circumstances of his arrest and trial drew the ire of a variety of indigenous and nonindigenous critics, the accused was found guilty and sentenced. As one leading commentator remarked, his case ignited unprecedented hostility among Darwin's white residents, hostility verging on race hysteria.[1]

While his right to a fair trial was supported by many individuals and organizations from around Australia, protests to the federal government concerned not only court procedure but also wider debate about Aboriginal men's sexual agency in cross-cultural and interracial contexts. Letters to the Department of the Interior, responsible for the administration of Aboriginal people in the Northern Territory (which had been under federal control since 1911), identified a range of race relations issues raised by the case, particularly Aboriginal masculinity. Arguments for or against the assailant were about not only justice and punishment, but also race, identity, and sexuality as they occurred in urban Darwin in the late 1930s.

ACCORDING TO POLICE, on the morning of Thursday, 3 March 1938, an Aboriginal man working as a delivery "boy" entered a white home in a better part of town. He surprised the woman of the house in her bedroom, throwing her to the ground, hitting her about the face, and biting her neck, "like a madman."[2] Her cries alerted a female neighbor, who was also knocked down and received blows to the face as the assailant fled. Neither could provide a clear description but agreed their attacker was dark-skinned, well-built, dressed only in a pair of dirty white shorts and that he parted his hair "like a white man."[3] As far as the white community would be concerned, the first of these two assaults was attempted rape.

When news broke, relatives of the two women, their husbands "almost demented with rage," joined in the search.[4] Darwin police called in Constable McNab and his Aboriginal tracker, Charlie. Usually McNab worked outside of Darwin, but his knowledge of local Aboriginal people and his general "astuteness" concerning Aboriginal men were considered invaluable by authorities.[5] Charlie's skills as a tracker were equally evident. Viewing the scene of the crime, Charlie identified a footprint belonging to a Melville Island man called Packsaddle. His narrow foot, Charlie later stated in court, was as clearly identifiable as a "white man's signature."[6]

Some days later, the Darwin administrator would assert that Packsaddle had been suspected of having "these tendencies" for some time, but perhaps McNab and Charlie were drawn to their conclusions because he was not only one of a number of Aboriginal men delivering letters in the area for a Chinese merchant, Yam Yan, but had been at the house in question on the morning of the attack.[7] Nonetheless, a lengthy process of rounding up and interviewing all Aboriginal men ensued, beginning with those who had criminal records, then those on work permits, and, last, all Aboriginal men in town.

Knowing where Aboriginal people were and who they were with was extremely important to administrators of Aboriginal people and to towns-people. Concerns about opium use, leprosy, and venereal disease among the Aboriginal population politicized their social and sexual interactions. Further, Aboriginal people in Darwin were subject to the Aboriginal Ordinance, which restricted their movement, their employment, and their relationships according to their status as "half-caste" or "full-blood." Half-caste children were removed from their parents and placed under the guardianship of Chief Medical Officer Cecil Cook, the girls to be absorbed into the white population through enculturation and marriage to white men. In practice, sexual relations between Aboriginal women and white men were tolerated (despite contravening the Aboriginal Ordinance), but white men who lived with Aboriginal women were derided. Few marriages between half-caste women and white men actually took place. Aboriginal men who were half-caste were expected to marry Aboriginal women on settlements or missions. Packsaddle was among the full-blood Aboriginal male population in Darwin, administered separately from half-castes. Employers in the town applied for permits to employ Aboriginal men like Packsaddle. Prohibited from the town precincts after dark, he and his peers were under curfew at night, locked in the Aboriginal Compound between 9 P.M. and 8 A.M.

As an adjunct to permits, compounds, and curfew, the chief protector of the Northern Territory and chief medical officer, Cecil Cook, had instituted the fingerprinting and medical examination of all Aboriginal people, who were then issued a tag worn around their neck to facilitate their identification, the infamous "dog tag" system. Men like Packsaddle were to be isolated from half-castes as they were from whites because biological assimilation demanded they marry into the full-blood community. They were permitted into Darwin for their casual labor.

When McNab decided to make a raid on the compound a few days after the reported assault it was to confront a group of five or six Melville and Bathurst Island men already on his list of likely suspects. Packsaddle was among this group. That he backed away and looked worried was represented in court as indicating his guilt. When interrogated, however, Packsaddle readily cooperated, agreeing that he had delivered a letter to the house that morning, but denying that he was the assailant. While fixing the chain on his bicycle, he said, he had seen another Aboriginal man leaving the scene but could not provide his description.[8]

Several days later, having no other leads, McNab accosted Packsaddle in town after the Saturday football game and took him to the hospital where the women were recovering. Neither identified him as their assailant, saying he was not tall enough. Handcuffed to McNab, Packsaddle was taken to the scene of the crime, where he was led through the same muddy patch of ground where the first footprint had been found. Charlie declared that the footprint he made was the same as the original. According to newspaper reports, when interrogated Packsaddle confessed, saying he had hit the missus, he had gone a bit silly. Or, as the prosecution would elaborate later for the benefit of the court, he had seen her in light clothing and he had wanted her.[9] Back at the hospital, the first woman confirmed that Packsaddle had delivered a letter to her house before the attack. Later that day, he signed a full confession at the police station with his fingerprint and a cross. In his cell under police guard that night, he repeated his guilt to Chief Protector Cook as required under the Ordinance to protect Aboriginal people from misinterpretation or police influence resulting in false confession. It seemed that the culprit had been caught.

During the initial hearing of his case, however, Packsaddle (who informed the court that his "blackfella" name was Too Put Ah Malay),[10] gave a quite different account of his arrest and conditions of confession. Handcuffed to McNab sitting on one side and with Charlie on the other, he was quiet in court until it was asserted that the identifiable footprints were sufficient evidence of his guilt. Speaking in pidgin through Charlie, Packsaddle remonstrated that although he had been at the house earlier in the day, he had only confessed to the assault out of fear for his life. When McNab led him through town to the crime scene, they had stopped at the Greek grocer, where McNab had remarked that either he would get the truth or Packsaddle would get a bullet. When at the house, and in front of Charlie and several other Aboriginal men (termed "police boys"), he had again been threatened and bashed and then forced to repeat McNab's account of the crime. Even a visit from Chief Protector Cook in his cell later that day did not cause him to retract this account. Although he knew Cook was there to protect his interests, he told the judge, he had been afraid there was a policeman standing behind him. None of the witnesses, neither Vaginis Kyriakos, the Greek grocer, nor the Aboriginal "boys," Toby and Sugarbag, supported his story. His own brother, Butcher, among those at the house during his questioning by McNab, gave evidence that he had advised Packsaddle to confess, as the footprint was his.[11]

DURING THESE YEARS, Darwin was undergoing considerable demographic, cultural, and economic changes, changes that exacerbated anxieties about race relations in town. By the late 1930s, Darwin's largely masculine population was becoming increasingly Europeanized. Comprising Anglo-Australians, Europeans (including Greeks and Italians), non-Europeans (predominantly Chinese and Malays), and Aboriginal mainland and islander peoples, the percentage of Anglo-Australian males in Darwin was increasing from the 65 percent of earlier in the decade. As this influx of white settlers was attracted by new suburbs and urban infrastructure, the proportion of white women rose steadily from its 1933 level of 36 percent. Darwin's population doubled in these years, reaching over 3,600 by the late 1930s. But despite the obvious attraction of urban living in the north, unemployment remained at about 20 percent. By the late 1930s, European unemployment and the greater presence of white women no doubt focused hostility on Aboriginal people employed in the town.

Of non-Europeans in Darwin, Koepangers were single men from Southeast Asia indentured to work on Japanese pearling boats off the coast of Darwin.[12] They, along with their employers, were considered outside the bounds of Darwin society, renowned for their violent exchanges with Aboriginal men over the barter of Aboriginal women and for infecting them, and potentially the wider population, with venereal disease. Darwin members of the Women's Christian Temperance Union complained to the minister of the interior in the 1930s that Malays, Koepangers, and Japanese were spreading venereal disease to half-caste Aboriginal women in town and should be brought under stricter control.[13] Almost half of non-Europeans were Chinese and a quarter were

Chinese women, making the Chinese, unlike other non-Europeans, a relatively gender-balanced group engaged in various forms of family migration and business. Concern about the presence of Aboriginal people in Chinatown no doubt reflected broader anti-Asian sentiment among Europeans, but it also indicates that the two groups were in considerable daily social interaction and may have had personal ties, including those between Aboriginal women and Chinese men.

Biological assimilation policies distinguished between half-caste Aboriginal populations and full-blood Aboriginal people no longer living in a traditional way. Numbers of these "detribalized" men in Darwin, Packsaddle among them, came from islands off the coast. They spent months at a time on their island homes, where the only whites were settlement managers and missionaries. Like half-castes, detribalized men were thought to be highly influenced by either the worst or the best elements of white society. It was seen as the paternal duty of the state to protect them from the former. When in town, these men were doubly segregated, housed and administered separately from half-castes, most of whom were Aboriginal women domestic servants. "Tribal" men and women, those who had almost no contact with whites, were to be "preserved" through isolation from the white community. Half-castes were to be absorbed through their biological and cultural mergence into the white community. But detribalized men were black men living among whites. They were outsiders within, offered little hope of settlement or worthwhile employment. Although they had grown up under traditional law, as adults they worked for at least some of the year doing menial tasks for whites, considered alienated not only from most of Darwin, but also increasingly from their tribal life.

Other Aboriginal people in town included "police boys" or native trackers. These men were often recruited from among Aboriginal prisoners and chosen for their traditional enmities with local groups. In Victoria, for example, the recruitment of Aboriginal men as Native Police provided a quasi-military front line in the process of nineteenth-century colonization. Being a member of the Native Police did not supersede Aboriginal men's involvement in tribal politics. The former often proved an advantage to the latter.[14] Similarly, hostilities between different Aboriginal groups were regularly exploited on stations by northern pastoralists, who promoted particular Aboriginal people to control or discipline others. It is not surprising, then, that tracker Charlie was reportedly pleased with the outcome of Packsaddle's trial—he was described as a tribal enemy of the accused.[15] We can only guess at the hostility between Charlie and Packsaddle and the part this played in the trial.

THE PRACTICE AMONG some Aboriginal groups of loaning women to men from other groups, including to settler men, earned strong disapproval from settlers (this despite their ready utilization of Aboriginal women as a sexual resource of the frontier). In line with evolutionary thinking, Aboriginal men were seen as "savages" in their dealings with their own women and were considered an inherent danger to white women. When Aboriginal men were tried for the rape of white women in mid-nineteenth-century Queensland, their alleged savagery provoked a level of hostility disproportionate to the number of cases, because white women were considered the sacred possessions of the colonizers and reproducers of the white race: "The rape of a white woman by a black man was regarded by the dominant ideology . . . as an assault on the supremacy of the white race."[16] During the trial of a mission-educated Aboriginal man accused of raping a white girl in Victoria in 1897, the judge was quick to attribute the attack to the assailant's savagery, regretting that even the best influence of mission life had been unable to civilize him.[17] Arguably, Aboriginal men's sexual violence threatened nineteenth- and early-twentieth-century assumptions that colonization would "civilize" them.

Perhaps the savagery argument was preferable to evidence that Aboriginal men were motivated to take revenge on white colonizers by sexually assaulting their women. In the 1870s, for example, an Aboriginal outlaw declared that he would treat white women in the same way white men treated Aboriginal women.[18] The prospect of Aboriginal women's sexual agency has been considered along different lines. Aboriginal women throughout this period were represented as amoral or immoral. This view worked to absolve white men's brutal behavior toward them and in turn has helped to establish their predominantly victim status in Aboriginal history. Against the assumption that Aboriginal women were utterly oppressed by white men's colonization, Ann McGrath has used oral histories to argue that an Aboriginal woman could possess a degree of agency in her relations with a white man, including through her own sexual desire and through "economic rewards for the family."[19]

If the possibility of Aboriginal women's agency confounds history's representation of colonial race relations, the possibility of white women's desire for Aboriginal men appears equally contradictory. Yet, gendered histories of colonization have pointed out that white women occupied an ambiguous status, policing boundaries between the races but criticized for inciting new forms of interracial conflict. The vestiges of this paradoxical position can be seen in Darwin in the 1930s, when white women were needed for settlement but their presence seemed to call for harsher race management in town. They were new to the north and seen as "inexperienced" in their relations with Aboriginal men, who worked around their homes or made deliveries during the day, when white men were not present. In an interview some decades after the Packsaddle case, Cecil Cook asserted that it had been well-known that the woman attacked had treated the Aboriginal man working at her house like a "pet pussycat."[20]

Various, often contradictory accounts of Aboriginal masculinity were put forward by contemporaries in their responses to the Packsaddle case. From the outset, Judge Wells was seemingly convinced of Packsaddle's guilt. Several years earlier, when presiding over a case involving Tuckiar, an Aboriginal man accused of murdering a white man, the judge had earned his reputation for hostility toward Aboriginal people who accused police of brutality or of forcing confessions. Southern humanitarians were outraged when Tuckiar, who claimed self-defense, received the death penalty despite the clear evidence of police brutality toward those Aboriginal witnesses who testified against him. Their intervention led to a retrial in the High Court, which overturned Wells's decision; Tuckiar was given a prison sentence.[21] During Packsaddle's trial, Wells showed that he had not modified his position in the preceding years. At the initial hearing of the case, Wells was quick to assert that the defendant was clearly a "cheeky" native and therefore undoubtedly a liar. Even without a confession, he stated, Packsaddle was obviously guilty and the trial should proceed.[22] Wells then used the ensuing trial and media attention to reiterate his long-held views that Aboriginal men in town were becoming increasingly dangerous to the white community.

Not only was the Aboriginal Ordinance not being properly enforced, Wells complained, but its administration had been weakened by southern-based anthropologists and missionaries whose influence on the federal government had resulted in the "petting" and "pampering" of Aboriginal people. Allowing Aboriginal men to work as delivery boys was a case in point. Through this means, they came into contact with white women when they were alone in their homes and, as they moved around the town, they accosted white women and children on lonely bushtracks. Nor was the existing punishment of a jail term sufficient deterrent. According to Wells, Aboriginal prisoners grew fat on regular rations and regarded jail as a holiday. They returned heroes to their communities, while time away from their culture further diminished the control of their elders. Recent assaults on white women were the result of an urban Aboriginal population not kept under appropriate control. Charged with intent to commit rape, Packsaddle could be jailed for up to seven years, but not flogged. Flogging was outlawed under the Aboriginal Ordinance. Wells considered that only an amendment to introduce flogging for attempted rape could reverse this decline toward anarchy.

But such a move raised the specter of white masculinity being itself undercivilized, overly reliant on brute force to maintain its ascendancy over "natives." Although flogging or whipping was on the books for a number of crimes in Australia, the question of government legislation to flog natives was of a different order, raising comparisons with discredited colonial regimes such as that of the Germans in New Guinea. In particular, the reputation of Darwin as a modernizing township was at stake, and government officials were concerned to maintain the city's attraction as a destination for white settlers. In an early report to the secretary of the Department of the Interior, Carrodus, Darwin administrator Abbott concluded that press reports of the white community taking the law into its own hands in the Packsaddle case had "unquestionably a bad effect upon the reputation of the Northern Territory and is not deserved."[23] In front of the few police and press present in the closed court during the hearing of the case, the senior magistrate, G. Piggott, had called on the citizens of Darwin to remember they were members of a "civilised race."[24] And John McEwen, minister of the interior, hurriedly issued press releases from Canberra discounting the veracity of press reports about vigilantism.[25]

Representatives of the federal government seemed more concerned that their policies were not blamed for the crime, and that Aboriginal masculinity remained amenable to the existing regime of surveillance and casual employment. They hoped to silence Wells's criticism of their policy and administration but were less interested in debating the future of detribalized men in Darwin. Prompted by Frank Brennan, a Labour member of the New South Wales parliament, who wanted to know if press reports that Wells favored flogging were accurate, Acting Attorney

General Robert Menzies tersely reminded Wells that the judiciary was supposed to stay out of political debate.[26] Ultimately, Wells would fail in his attempt to influence the minister to endorse an amendment of the Ordinance; the Aboriginal threat in Darwin was not considered serious enough to warrant further action.

BY THE LATE 1930s, it appeared as if the federal government might be moving to ameliorate Aboriginal conditions in the Northern Territory. In 1928 the Queensland chief protector, J. W. Bleakley, reported that 170 Aboriginal men employed in Darwin were housed in the compound, originally located at some distance from the town. But Darwin suburbs had rapidly expanded, making it difficult, as Bleakley advised, to protect these "simple people" from large numbers of aliens and itinerant white men. A chief concern of residents, he noted, was the Aboriginal clinic within the compound; whites feared that venereal and other diseases would spread to the general population through the "agency of Aboriginals going backwards and forwards to employment." Bleakley proposed a new clinic attached to the white hospital and the appointment of "some religious body" to organize services and social events and to educate the natives, whose "absolute ignorance places them at great disadvantages in their simple trade transactions." The occasional breaking of curfew was inevitable, he concluded: "As . . . nothing is done to relieve the monotony of the hours at night, it would not be surprising if the native, having once tasted the pleasures of town, and unable, like his white brother, to occupy his leisure time with reading or music sometimes stayed out at night."[27]

Ten years later, the Aboriginal compound was relocated four miles outside the expanded town limits, but none of Bleakley's suggestions had been implemented. In response to reports of problems with Aboriginal behavior in town, the chief protector had been sending increasing numbers of Aboriginal men to the compound. He suggested that this strict application of the Ordinance had produced the very outcome whites feared: boredom and the lack of a teacher at the compound were directly linked to the attacks on white women. Similarly, administrator Abbott noted that Aboriginal men were excluded from meaningful work by the Northern Australian Workers' Union.[28]

The idea that Aboriginal people needed education, training, and useful employment, however, did not sit well with white concerns about the Aboriginal presence in town, particularly their frequenting of the Chinese quarter, where gambling was common. One of the first acts taken after the assaults was to ensure that no Aboriginal people were breaking curfew in the Chinese quarter. Their presence in movie theaters was considered another example of laxity, although Aboriginal people could attend only with the permission of the chief protector, who previewed films to make sure they were suitable. Bleakley recommended in 1928 that the compound have its own cinema, as this "ban" was a "sorepoint" among Aboriginal people.[29] No doubt this recommendation was considered by locals to be yet another example of "southern-style" pampering.

Humanitarians advocated the care of Aboriginal people rather than control over them, arguing that they could and did take their place among other Australians if given the opportunities of education, work, and citizenship as well as marriage, family, and community life. Reading reports of this case in the press, humanitarian and Aboriginal organizations from around the nation responded in two ways. First, they questioned whether the right man had been accused, denouncing Wells's "anti-native" bias, and rejecting the introduction of flogging. Aboriginal activist William Cooper of the Australian Aborigines League called for the removal of Judge Wells and the retrial of the case.[30] Second, they explicitly situated the case as evidence of the urgent need for a more progressive policy toward Aboriginal people, for greater funding rather than greater controls and more brutal punishments. Alongside these criticisms, they expressed concerns about the racial implications attributed to the assaults. Reverend Burton, of the local Australian Methodist Mission Society, and Aboriginal activist John Patten, of the Aborigines Progressive Association, each asserted that one man's actions should not be interpreted as characterizing the degeneracy of a whole race. "Even if aboriginal," warned Burton, "the assailant was not necessarily typical of his race."[31] White and Aboriginal were not so different and should not be treated differently for sexual crimes.

But how civilized was the white man? Would flogging an Aboriginal man result in the degeneracy of the white race in Australia? Would a civilized society flog its indigenous people? The Kurri Kurri Dole Workers and Unemployed Association declared that support for flogging revealed that the people of the Northern Territory were incompetent to make decisions about "natives." Surely modern Darwin no longer resorted to such treatment of its criminals, and certainly not of its native criminals, for that was how an enlightened society measured its own advancement and white masculinity could be measured above "savagery." J. Boocker, honorary secretary, advised that the association had resolved that Aboriginal people deserved equality and citizenship. He continued, "The urge to hang and flog aborigines, after they have been detribalised and demoralised by the white man, denotes a low state of culture. . . . The problem of how to deal justly with the aborigines is largely how to overcome the brutality of the white man." He asked, would the government flog all the "Whites and Asiastics who sexually violate, and fill with venereal disease, all the young aborigine girls and women?"[32]

Similar themes concerned the Women's Auxiliary of the Australian Workers Union and the Women's Non-Party Association of South Australia. Each advised the minister that flogging merely brutalized both those flogged and those doing the flogging. The Auxiliary argued, "Such punishment degrades both the giver and the receiver of it, and according to modern psychology, does far more harm than good."[33] The same law should apply to native men as to white men who assaulted Aboriginal women. Sadly, they noted, the widespread abuse of Aboriginal women by white men did not spark similar public outrage. Aboriginal activist William Ferguson regretted that the far more disturbing issue of white men's assaults on Aboriginal women hardly raised a murmur in the white community: "For every case of a black man assaulting a white woman there are 10,000 cases of white men assaulting black women. . . . These assaults by aborigines are entirely the fault of the Government in keeping aborigines in ignorance and depriving them of the rights of citizenship."[34]

But the morality of white men and their laws had been the subject of considerable public debate over previous years. As numbers of women's organizations, humanitarian groups, and even some official accounts of race relations in the outback (such as Bleakley's 1928 report) had for some time argued, lack of sexual restraint shown by white men had resulted in great injustice toward Aboriginal women, not only in the violation of their bodily rights but in the loss of their mixed-descent children to authorities. National and international Anglo-Australian women's networks in the 1920s and 1930s promoted a widely publicized campaign to change Aboriginal policy in Australia. Their campaign asserted that existing settler culture was anachronistic, its brutality combining with unjust policies to limit the great potential of Aboriginal people to live successfully in two cultures, their own and that of whites. At the core of their vision for settler colonialism was the end of the sexual excesses of white settler masculinity, an issue that gained headlines in Australian and English press in the mid-1930s. Enforcement of existing legislation that prohibited such "cohabitation" through the reform of the Aboriginal Board and the appointment of women protectors would show that governments around Australia were serious about protecting Aboriginal women.

Throughout these years, Chief Protector Cook resisted the appointment of women protectors, citing lack of suitable medical facilities and transportation in the outback. But Cook also revealed that he considered it ultimately impossible to control white men's behavior toward Aboriginal women: "It is not practicable to impose morality by regulation. The result would be to increase the number of technical offenders without diminishing the evil."[35] The idea that white men couldn't change was anathema to women activists, who argued that every person, people, and race could either uplift themselves or be uplifted by socially responsible government. Thus, Aboriginal culture would also have to change and Aboriginal men would no longer be permitted to treat their women as property. While they were critical of white men and tribal Aboriginal men, these women activists were largely silent on the question of single Aboriginal men living in urban centers among the white community. Leading activist Mary Bennett considered that Aboriginal women similarly employed as domestics in white homes were not only vulnerable to sexual assault but were wrongly isolated from the emotional and spiritual support of their own people and country.

AS THE PACKSADDLE case reveals, among humanitarians in the 1930s at least, eighteenth- and nineteenth-century images of sexually predatory Aboriginal men had been overturned by twentieth-century assertions that the good white woman had always been treated with affectionate respect by Aboriginal men and continued to be safe from assault. To make this argument, historical incidences of the sexual assault of white women by Aboriginal men had to be carefully forgotten. Several critics of the Packsaddle case even went so far as to assert that there had never been a sexual assault by an Aboriginal man of a white woman and that white women alone on stations had never been in danger from Aboriginal men. They insisted that self-control was inherent to Aboriginal masculinity and that sexual aggression was absent from the Aboriginal man's makeup. White man had to catch up to Aboriginal man, as neither self-restraint nor absence of sexual aggression yet characterized his dealings with Aboriginal women. On behalf of the Aborigines Protection League, Dr. Charles Duguid declared, "It is still true that in 150 years of contact between the aborigines and whites no instance has occurred of a native man attempting a sexual offence on a white woman." To legalize flogging would "result in a fresh series of atrocities" by whites and would bring Australia "into disrepute throughout the civilised world."[36]

Reverend Burton gave his own version of this argument. The Packsaddle case was an isolated example resulting from the loss of tribal laws experienced by detribalized Aboriginal men. Rather than blaming the Aboriginal people, Europeans should realize that "The primitive mind comprehends the simple, often animal, vices of civilisation much more readily than its complex virtues."[37] For many, including government officials, however, the cunning of the assailant raised questions about his Aboriginal identity. Their assumption of passive and childlike Aboriginal masculinity seemed to preclude in their minds the level of violence present in the assault and in Packsaddle's apparent capacity to mislead investigators. In his first report to the minister, Darwin administrator Abbott advised that the assailant was thought to be a Keopanger, or colored man employed in the pearling industry. Once Packsaddle was arrested and assumed guilty, his "unusual" behavior as an Aboriginal man continued to puzzle journalists, who noted that he had used his fists to make his getaway; when under suspicion, he had not run away; and once interrogated, he had cunningly misled police investigations. One critic went so far as to suggest that the assailant was a white man who had pretended to be an Aboriginal man in order to direct suspicion toward the Aboriginal population. Angered by the Darwin Returned Services League's call for stronger measures to control Aboriginal men, Aboriginal activist Pearl Gibbs, vice president of the Aborigines Progressive Association, wrote about the case to Dame Enid Lyons, the prime minister's wife. She called for British justice and a fair trial for Packsaddle, the same as "white men who attack women, small girls and boys." She pointed out that, after all, Aboriginal men had fought on the side of the "white diggers" during the Great War. As she struggled to find a motive for the crime, Gibbs wondered if Packsaddle had been ill-treated by the woman in question or her husband. If not, given the existing racial tension in Darwin, perhaps the assailant had been a white man "blackened" to look like an Aboriginal man.[38]

For others, Packsaddle's behavior might be explained by his physique. From the prosecution's perspective, the defendant's face and build were important because they might lead to a positive identification. He would argue that Packsaddle's confidence during the trial came from knowing that his attack had been too swift for the women to get a good look at him. Mobilizing a racist logic of the homogeneity of Aboriginal appearance, Constable McNab dismissed the lack of positive identification: as the assailant had changed his clothes before the attack, "it would be difficult for an inexperienced white person to recognise the black again."[39] But even when he was "caught," Packsaddle's body was fetishized. He was described variously as tall and powerfully built, of medium height, well built, or wiry. Beyond the problematic gender and race relations of urban Darwin, of course, a strong Aboriginal physique was to be admired. In his 1928 report, J. W. Bleakley described Melville Island Aboriginal people as "of a splendid type and worth preserving."[40] But in Darwin, and in the context of a sexual assault, such an Aboriginal man assumed the specter of a hybrid masculinity, powerfully full-blood yet able to use white cunning. Thus, Packsaddle occupied a contradictory identity. He was a Darwin "boy" working at menial tasks among white women, but he was also an island man, "roaming the bush" half the year. His tribal marking provided condemning evidence both of his latent savagery and his hardy masculinity. As the *Melbourne Herald* informed its readers, on his chest "deep gashes have been self-inflicted with a knife and the wounds filled with hot ashes."[41] Disturbingly, Packsaddle appeared neither assimilable nor fully under the control of his elders. He parted his hair like a white man, suggesting assimilation, yet his clothes merely veiled a savagery lying underneath. In contrast, tracker Charlie was one of the "better class of natives," ready to help in the case. He lived in two worlds also, but in ways that benefited white power in Darwin.

Detribalized Aboriginal masculinity was thus a dual or hybrid identity, recognizable as a product of colonization even to contemporaries. According to Michael Sawtell of the Association for the Protection of the Native Races, dual existence was crucial to understanding Packsaddle's crime. Assaults on white women were always committed by "detribalised and demoralised natives who had lost their own tribal laws and could not understand the white man's moral laws. In their contact with white men they assimilated all that was bad and received very little that was good."[42] Taking this argument one step further, John Patten of the Aborigines

Progressive Association told the *Sydney Morning Herald*, "Similar assaults are perpetrated in the cities by white men, who are regarded as criminals or lunatics, and are tried as individuals, not as representatives of the white race. In the name of justice, we appeal that the act of one lunatic or sexual pervert be not deemed sufficient to damn the whole native race."[43]

A. P. Elkin, president of the Association for the Protection of the Native Races and chair in anthropology at Sydney University, agreed that the Packsaddle case could best be understood in terms of the universals of psychology. Elkin attributed the reported increase of sexual assaults by Aboriginal men in Darwin to their restricted environment. Given appropriate living conditions, including interactions with Aboriginal women (rather than being locked up with other men in the compound), Aboriginal men would not behave abnormally toward white women: "Aborigines do not normally accost white women and children. Apparently there is something unsatisfactory about the organisation of life, work, pleasure, and association of the sexes in Darwin Compound . . . [it is] education and a life of useful and healthy interests which alone will prevent [their] recurrence." Jail did not provide education and "respect for our ways." As Aboriginal justice was built on physical punishment in any case, flogging would not have the desired impact: "Moreover, it is doubtful whether the flogging of a coloured offender by a white authority is in the best interests of the latter. In any case, there would be a very great and righteous protest if authorities instituted corporal punishment of aboriginal offenders for accosting white females, unless similar punishment was made the penalty for white men who accost either full-blood or half-caste native women and girls. In the matter of sex offences, the native race is more sinned against than sinning."[44] Interviewed by the *Sydney Morning Herald* two weeks later, he warned against "race hysteria" over the case and looked to individual psychosis or political motive (that is, attributing the crime to either universal or specific, but not racial, factors) for understanding the crime. Accepting that the assault was an attempted sexual assault and that the assailant was an Aboriginal man, Elkin advised: "We must treat the matter as we would treat similar incidents in our own society [that is, by finding out why it happened]. . . . The individual [in this case] might be mad; or he might have been impelled by tribal authorities to take revenge for interference by whites with native girls."[45]

Widely differing views about the significance of racial difference to masculinity existed in the late 1930s in Australia, regarding not only Aboriginal masculinity but also white masculinity, the very lens through which Aboriginal masculinity appeared as normal or abnormal, universal or racialized, manageable or unmanageable. This suggests that ideas about the interstices between gender and race relations were undergoing a period of flux. If sexual violence was masculinity's most disturbing aspect, it was also one that was routinely attributed to the lower or more primitive impulses in man's nature, impulses usually thought to be controlled by the influence of civilization. When this model of higher and lower faculties was projected cross-racially, the capacity of men from the "lower races" to control their instinctive needs was considered self-evidently less evolved. In the Packsaddle case, questions about the mutually corrupting effects of culture contact were resolved by resorting to this far simpler explanation. Already of the opinion that Aboriginal people treated incarceration as a holiday, Wells was sympathetic to defense appeals for a comparatively light four years' hard labor. According to counsel H. J. Foster: "As far as the offence is concerned, it is not one for the maximum sentence. The accused was evidently taken by some sudden passion. After all, he is a half-savage and that should be taken into consideration. If the same offence had been committed by a white man, it would be much more serious, but by a half-savage it is not quite as bad."[46] Elided from this account of the evolution of masculinity along racial lines was the unavoidable fact that white men in the outback had long since betrayed their "civilized" status through their treatment of Aboriginal women. But for the north to be successfully settled, more white women were needed and the white frontiersman would have to become the Darwin suburbanite, building a house, bringing a wife, and settling down. Government assimilation of the detribalized man paralleled the white man's in Darwin — both were to be achieved culturally. As the frontier became urbanized and feminized, each was to learn self-control.

FINALLY, THE PACKSADDLE case reminds us that race and gender must be read in spatial as well as historical, social, and cultural terms. When Packsaddle's defense claimed that only a physical assault had taken place, Judge Wells countered that entering a white home without knocking was in itself evidence of intent to rape.[47] In his mind, sexual intent was already present when an Aboriginal man invaded white domestic space. Perhaps Darwin's hostile response to this case finds its present-day equivalent in support for mandatory sentencing in the Northern Territory. Echoing the

1930s, late-twentieth-century Darwin underwent rapid expansion and suburban development. In a move designed to appeal to white suburban voters, the Northern Territory government passed amendments to the Northern Territory Sentencing Act and the Juvenile Justice Act in March 1997 to provide for draconian mandatory sentencing on property offenses, including unlawful entry. Criticism from southern Australia only hardened Territorian resolve. Of little consequence to the crime rate, in its first year mandatory sentencing succeeded in increasing the incarceration of Aboriginal people by nearly 60 percent, its greatest impact felt among young Aboriginal men living in Aboriginal communities. The Packsaddle case suggests that the gender and race impacts of such legislation have a considerable and complex history.

Notes

1. *Sydney Morning Herald*, 7 March 1938.
2. *Sydney Morning Herald*, 4 March 1938.
3. *Melbourne Herald*, 4 March 1938.
4. *Sydney Morning Herald*, 4 March 1938.
5. Darwin Administrator C. L. A. Abbott to J. A. Carrodus, Secretary, Department of Interior, National Archives of Australia, 8 March 1938.
6. *Sydney Morning Herald*, 20 April 1938.
7. Ibid.
8. *Northern Standard*, 13 April 1938.
9. Ibid.
10. This is his name as it appears in newspaper reports. That its Chinese or Malaysian appearance was not commented on by contemporaries suggests a far more complex history of Aboriginal/Asian connections in Darwin than it is possible to investigate in this essay.
11. *Northern Standard*, 13 April 1938.
12. The name "Koepanger" was derived from Kupang in present-day West Timor.
13. Ann McGrath, *"Born in the Cattle": Aborigines in Cattle Country* (Sydney: Allen and Unwin, 1987), 87.
14. Marie Hansen Fels, *Good Men and True: The Aboriginal Police of the Port Phillip District 1837–1853* (Melbourne: Melbourne University Press, 1988), 103.
15. *Melbourne Herald*, 7 March 1938.
16. Carmel Harris, "The 'Terror of the Law' as Applied to Black Rapists in Colonial Queensland," *Hecate* 8, 2 (1982): 25, 44.
17. Bain Attwood, *The Making of the Aborigines* (Sydney: Allen and Unwin, 1989), 124.
18. Patricia Grimshaw et al., *Creating a Nation* (Ringwood, Australia: McPhee Gribble, 1994), 149.

19. McGrath, *"Born in the Cattle,"* 89–90.

20. Ann McGrath, "Mirror of the North," in *Australians 1938*, ed. Bill Gammage and Peter Spearitt (Sydney: Fairfax, 1987), 41.

21. Andrew Markus, "'The Impartiality of the Bench': Judge Wells and the Northern Territory Aborigines 1933–38," in *Law and History*, ed. Diane Kirkby (Bundoora, Australia: La Trobe University Press, 1987), 109–122.

22. *Northern Standard*, 13 April 1938.

23. Abbott to Carrodus, Department of Interior, National Archives of Australia, 8 March 1938.

24. *Sydney Morning Herald*, 8 March 1938.

25. Press release, Department of Interior, National Archives of Australia, 4 March 1938.

26. Frank Brennan to Menzies, 4 August 1938; Menzies to Wells, letter dated 27 January 1939, Department of Interior File, "Flogging of Natives: Remarks by Judge Wells," National Archives of Australia (NAA), A432/81, 38/755.

27. "The Aboriginals and Half-castes of Central Australia and North Australia," report by J. W. Bleakley, Chief Protector of the Aboriginals, Queensland, 1928, *Commonwealth Parliamentary Papers*, session 1929, 2:21, 12–14.

28. Abbott to Carrodus, National Archives of Australia, 5 March 1938.

29. Bleakley, *Commonwealth Parliamentary Papers*, 14.

30. Andrew Markus, ed., *Blood from a Stone: William Cooper and the Australian Aborigines' League* (Melbourne: Monash Publications in History, 1986), 2.

31. *Sydney Morning Herald*, 5 March 1938.

32. Kurri Kurri Dole Workers and Unemployment Association to McEwen, 20 April 1938.

33. Joyce Payne, honorary secretary of the Women's Auxiliary, Australian Workers Union, to Federal Attorney General, 28 June 1938.

34. *Melbourne Herald*, 4 March 1938.

35. Letter dated 11 June 1929, Department of Interior, "Suggested Aboriginal Protection Policy, N.T.," NAA A431, 46/3026.

36. *Northern Standard*, 17 May 1938

37. *Sydney Morning Herald*, 5 May 1938.

38. Heather Goodall, "Pearl Gibbs: Some Memories," *Aboriginal History* 7, 1 (1983): 20–22.

39. *Sydney Morning Herald*, 7 March 1938.

40. Bleakley, *Commonwealth Parliamentary Papers*, 34.

41. *Melbourne Herald*, 7 March 1938.

42. *Melbourne Herald*, 4 March 1938.

43. Ibid.

44. *Sydney Morning Herald*, 21 February 1938.

45. *Syndey Morning Herald*, 7 March 1938.

46. *Northern Standard*, 13 April 1938.

47. Ibid.

Heidi Gengenbach

Tattooed Secrets: Women's History in

Magude District, Southern Mozambique

Forms of bodily adornment and decoration have frequently assumed a central position in cross-cultural encounters and understandings of gender. Arguing that women in southern Mozambique have historically used tattoos (tinhlanga) both as a way of responding to social change and to express the importance of female affiliations in a male-dominated world, this essay charts the transformation of "traditional" practice and the heightened significance of tattooing for women adversely affected by colonial rule. The persistence of tinhlanga challenged Portuguese colonial and missionary efforts to reform local customs and cultivate "civilization" through the propagation of new standards of feminine beauty and bodily adornment. The ensuing struggle over women's bodies reveals the gendered meanings of racial difference and the limits of European power in colonial Mozambique, reminding us that the cultural projects of colonialism frequently focused on practices that embodied identity and affirmed the "traditional" bonds of community.

The Lenge and the Tsopi women have the story of their lives
written on their own flesh. — E. Dora Earthy, *Valenge Women: The
Social and Economic Life of the Valenge Women of Portuguese Africa*

Some of the most innovative work in African history in recent years
scrutinizes the body — the gendered, dark-skinned body — as text,
social object, and field for the inscription and operation of colonial
power. Focusing on the range of practices through which African bodies
were disciplined and commodified by European regimes, this literature

has paid particular attention to the role of Christianity, clothing, and biomedicine in the transformation of African lifeways between the late nineteenth century and today.[1] Discussions of colonized bodies also spring from, and flow into, wider debates about colonialism itself, prodding us to rethink European conquest of Africa as an intervention of the most intimate kind, an embodied experience where power engages even "private" identities, behaviors, and affections.

Writing the history of colonial bodies has necessarily involved new kinds of evidence as well as novel approaches to conventional sources. Advertisements, letters, gossip, household objects — all have been mined as texts that reveal the corporeal meanings of colonization for the men and women who were its victims, and in some cases, its agents. Conspicuously absent in this literature, with its emphasis on the unstable quality of the colonized body politic, is interrogation of the historical meanings etched on African bodies unclothed, above all, the signs of personhood worn in the form of body markings or tattoos on men's and women's skin. This essay argues that the body markings of women in southern Mozambique are indispensable sources for understanding women's experiences of Portuguese colonialism and a vital form of evidence for African colonial history more broadly.

Reading history from women's body markings is not as strange a proposition as it might appear. There is a thin trail of documentary evidence of tattooing in southern Mozambique, beginning around 1800, when European visitors to the busy port town of Delagoa Bay caught sight of tattooed men and women in and around the Portuguese settlement. European ivory hunters and explorers similarly noted the decorative scars on "native" skin as they roamed the region in the turbulent nineteenth century, especially after the conquest of much of this area by the Gaza Nguni in the 1820s, and as imperial competition for the territory heated up from 1880 on. The spread of Swiss Presbyterian missionaries from the Transvaal into southern Mozambique during the 1880s and Portugal's defeat of the Gaza king Ngungunyana in 1895 ushered in the period of formal colonization and stimulated a flurry of reports detailing "native customs and traditions" among the "Tsonga." In these texts, too, *tinhlanga* attracted European attention, but by this time, the majority of men in southern Mozambique were migrating to work in South Africa and had begun to abandon the habit of body marking. Tattooing became, in European eyes, a frivolous if intriguing feminine practice, a holdover from the "primitive" past, though one that showed a curious persistence throughout the colonial period.

If two hundred years' worth of written evidence is available, why focus on body marking as a source for colonial history? Interviewees' stories about tinhlanga expose some of the most intimate — and ambitious — reaches of Portuguese colonialism in Mozambique; while other invaders and immigrants reacted to local habits of body marking, only the European colonizers (and, revealingly, their African "middles") turned the elimination of women's tattoos into a near-religious crusade. Yet the intensity of this struggle was due less to a priori colonial determination than to women's awareness that their efforts to "make themselves beautiful" were as threatening to European power as they were precious to the women themselves. Memories of tinhlanga center the colonial moment, in other words, because colonialism simultaneously undermined and encouraged women's tattooing. Tinhlanga may have predated and outlived European rule, but it was the European presence that cast their gendered value in sharp relief.

Tattooing was valuable to women for two reasons. First, tinhlanga provided an idiom both for mediating androcentric social structures and for asserting female-centered networks of affiliation, whether in the private spaces of friendship, the uneven playing field of patrilineal kinship, or the high-stakes realm of colonial race relations. In the waves of crisis and conflict that swept the region after 1800, women used their skin to map a social world in which boundaries of belonging were rooted less in ascribed familial or ethnic identity than in shared feminine culture, bodily experience, and geographic place. Under the mounting pressures of the twentieth century, "blood ties" forged through tattooing — more flexible and inclusive than those dictated by birth or marriage — became an important resource for women in need.

Second, tinhlanga offered women a bold yet "secret" (*xihundla*) voice for telling history, a silent yet visible language for commenting on social change — for a strictly female audience — in a context where oral traditions did not take women's perspectives into account, and where women were often not supposed to put their feelings into words. The secrecy of tattooing took on dangerously subversive implications during the colonial period, as colonizers strove to implant "civilization" and commodity capitalism in part by forcing women to adorn their bodies in "white" (*xilungu*) ways. But if colonizers insisted that what women did to their skin was a mark of civilization's progress, women insisted in turn that they could use their bodies to define identity themselves, not by shrugging off white standards of beauty but by renegotiating, through tinhlanga, the frontier between "white" and "black" (*xilandin*) ways, incorporating colonial things into what they continued to call a "traditional" practice.

My methodology here combines oral history with the insights of feminist archaeologists who have teased out women's pasts from the tracks of social and spatial relationships embedded in feminine material culture.[2] Grounding my arguments in the interface of memory and cultural production, I interpret transformations in women's body marking in the context of mission Christianity, schooling, migrant labor, Portuguese racial ideologies, and increasing marriage and family pressures during and after the colonial period. Significantly, women said very little about reasons for changes in tattooing; in fact, it is difficult to periodize this history from women's memories alone, which speak in a uniformly ahistorical voice. Yet women's insistence on the atemporality of their tattoos in fact exposes one of tinhlanga's boldest claims: that Portuguese colonialism had little if any impact on rural women; that despite the aggressive presence of xilungu attitudes and ways, daily life in the countryside — at least for women — remained essentially the same.

WILLIAM WHITE, A British merchant who visited southern Mozambique in 1798, published one of the first comments on body marking among local men and women: "They are all tattooed, some down the middle of the forehead, and point of the chin . . . and of their temples, of this shape X: their bodies are so likewise, particularly on the chest, but none of them are exactly alike; those, however, of the same family, are tattooed very nearly in the same manner."[3]

The tension here between White's recognition of the uniqueness of an individual's tattoos and his belief that tattoos showed "family" resemblances prefigures the central problem with European writings about tinhlanga from 1800 on. Europeans presumed that Africans were divided along "tribal" lines, with ethnicity and its subcategories (for example, clan or lineage) determining how people decorated their bodies — even when decorative marks did not follow such divisions perfectly. Thus, in the early nineteenth century, when European traders met travelers with tattooed faces and chests hailing from anywhere between the Limpopo

River and Delagoa Bay, they took it for granted that these men belonged to a single ethnic group, labeled by historians later as "proto-Tsonga." This correlation of particular decorative markings with people known as Tsonga-Shangaan hardened from the 1840s on, when Portuguese hunter and slave trader João Albasini was joined at his military stronghold in the northern Transvaal by refugees from southern Mozambique who bore large keloid scars on their noses and cheeks — described as "knobs," "lumps," "warts," and "buttons" — which earned them the epithet "Knob-nose" from residents of the Zoutpansberg.[4]

After midcentury, European writings began to include more elaborate descriptions of "native" practices of bodily adornment, from tattooing to teeth filing, lip piercing, jewelry, and dress. These commentaries also became more openly concerned with distinguishing dark-skinned "savages" from light-skinned bearers of "civilization." Reading tattoos as a "marker of the primitive," imperial observers believed that differences in personal ornamentation reflected Africans' position on the evolutionary hierarchy, and ranked "tribal" groups according to their cultural resilience in the face of pressures for change.[5] In these discussions, the Tsonga appear to have an unusually plastic ethnic identity. According to Henri Alexandre Junod, a Swiss missionary and prolific writer on the Tsonga, keloid facial tattooing had "ancient" roots in the coastal lowlands around the Save River. When proto-Tsonga groups invaded this area in the fifteenth century, their subjects ridiculed the "flat noses" of their conquerors so relentlessly that the latter adopted facial tattooing themselves. With the Nguni invasions of the early nineteenth century, these markings assumed heightened political significance when Zulu armies sent in pursuit of the rebel Nguni leader Soshangane targeted men with no "buttons on their face," and many Nguni soldiers decided to "submit to the operation." By the 1860s and 1870s, however, when British explorers were criss-crossing southern Mozambique, "knobnose" tattooing had become a scorned sign of inferiority among subject peoples and was being supplanted by the style of ear piercing popular among the Nguni elite. As Europeans saw it, this transformation in body marking signaled a wholesale acceptance of assimilation into a conquering tribe. St. Vincent Erskine summed up the prevailing view when he wrote in 1868 that "Knob-nosed Caffres" had "amalgamated with the tribes of Manjaje and Umzeila. . . . In a few years knob-noses will be as extinct as pig-tails."[6]

Yet amalgamation with respect to tattooing was a distinctly gendered process: not only were women decorating their skin more extensively than men at this time, but they also continued doing so even after men adopted plain-skinned Nguni, then European, fashions of bodily adornment. By the early twentieth century, ear piercing was the only form of body marking. Extant among men, yet women's bodies displayed a "bewildering" variety of scars. Surprised that this practice was not disappearing with the "evolution of costume," colonial commentators were nonetheless certain that the once "deep" ritual meanings of tinhlanga had "disappeared"; women's tattoos were now merely "ornamental mutilations" connected with "nubility" or marriage, a way, Junod scoffed, "to make themselves prettier . . . as they think!"[7]

Not even missionary-ethnographers such as Junod or Emily Dora Earthy deemed it necessary to look more closely into the stubborn persistence of tattooing among women, or at the meanings of the tattoos themselves. Women, they assumed, were marginal members of patrilineal kinship groups, their body markings passively derived from the clan or tribe into which they were born. Yet Earthy acknowledged that women's tattoos also followed "particular fashions of certain districts," and that by the 1920s, tinhlanga depicted an increasingly diverse range of objects: plants, birds, insects, reptiles, seashells, astral bodies, arrowheads, musical instruments, but also scissors, keys, watches, and waistcoats.[8] Although Earthy's informants told her that they obtained these markings to "do honour to their bodies, to make them beautiful," the inclusion of elements of a masculine foreign world in their tinhlanga repertoire, alongside images from the landscape of women's everyday life, suggests that rather more was going on. Scissors, keys, watches, waistcoats — for rural women, these items may have represented the gendered materialities of colonialism as it infiltrated the countryside through Portuguese administration and commerce and South African mining capital. Scissors are a labor-transforming household technology; keys stand for new concepts of privacy, property, and residential space; watches serve as status symbol and keeper of industrial time (the clocks that keep husbands from home); and waistcoats are the archetypically ornamental component of a "civilized gentleman's" wardrobe, a metonym for the prodigal, yet necessary, expense of a European-style three-piece suit.

Women's desire to appropriate the symbolic power of these goods is evident from the following testimony, quoted by Earthy: "If we see any object which particularly pleases us, we go home and have it tatued on our bodies — but if other people envy us, and want to make incisions like ours, we do not reveal where we have seen the object — for the spirit . . . of the thing remains with her who has made a representation of it on her body."[9] It is this expressive comment that leads Earthy to characterize women's tattoos as "the story of their lives written on their own flesh" — yet her analysis of tinhlanga stops abruptly here. For Earthy, as for earlier European commentators, tattooing may have been "ancient," but it was certainly not historical. Its value lay in its status as a vanishing "custom," not in its social dimensions as a living practice among women who were determined to continue "making themselves beautiful" in this particular way.

WOMEN IN MAGUDE tell the history of tinhlanga very differently from European accounts, and their recollections challenge ethnographic stereotypes on every front. No interviewee gave ethnic or clan identity as the reason for her tattoos, and no two women from the same ethnic group or clan had identical sets of scars. Nor did they portray tinhlanga as aimed primarily at transforming girls into sexually desirable wives. While many women laughingly confided that tattoos "make your husband happy" because when a man strokes a woman's scarred body he instantly "wakes up" (that is, achieves erection), interviewees clearly linked heightened male excitement with their own sexual satisfaction: tinhlanga not only induced a man to spend more time caressing his wife during foreplay, but they also helped to ensure that he "woke up" (when his penis "rested" against her abdomen or thighs) for a second round of intercourse. Perhaps more telling, many women had their first tattoos cut long before puberty, and some went on accumulating them through adulthood, even after a failed marriage had convinced them to live without men. While the desire to be attractive to men certainly mattered, and other divorced or widowed women who added to their tinhlanga did so in part for this reason, women's raucous stories about husbands' comically slavish attention to tattooed wives (or mistresses) represent male pleasure as an ancillary effect of tinhlanga. One woman who was not tattooed at all challenged me to deny that a man "needs more than that little hole" to enjoy intercourse.

The emphasis in oral narratives on the "secrecy" surrounding the act of "cutting" tattoos also troubles the assumption that body marking was a rite of initiation girls endured under the supervision of female elders. Tinhlanga, according to interviewees, were always done "in the bush" (*nhoveni, khwatini*), so that no one would "see all that blood." Small groups of girls would "invite one another" and make clandestine arrangements to meet at dawn the following day, having prepared what they needed for the operation (cloth to staunch the bleeding, for example) the night before. They would sneak off in the morning without telling anyone where they were going. The discretionary nature of tattooing was also reflected in memories of how the tinhlanga economy functioned. If a girl wanted to be "cut," she went to the tattoo artist (*mutlhaveli*) of her choice, whether a relative, a neighbor, or a stranger with a reputation for not "hurting" too much or causing infection. The mutlhaveli could be of any age, from an "old woman" (*xikoxana*) to a slightly older girl, and the most skillful among them had "lines of girls" requesting their services. Unless the mutlhaveli was a relative, girls were expected to compensate her with a gift, such as a few hours of work in her fields, a load of water or firewood, a tin of corn, a bead bracelet, or a safety pin to "wash her eyes" because she had seen so much blood. In rare instances, they might give her a small amount of money, but interviewees declared unanimously that cash presents were never a payment (*hakelo*) — tattooing, they insisted, was not a commercial transaction.

When asked to explain why they cut tattoos, interviewees' most common first response was "to make myself beautiful," "to beautify [*kuxongisa*] my body." Beauty is, of course, historically specific, constituted by ideals shared among people with a sense of common social location and cultural identity. Indeed, the relational content of tattooed beauty in Magude was clear in the comment that usually followed women's first response: "Well, I saw what my fellow girls had, and me, I longed for it too." By "fellow" (*kulorhi*), women meant other females in their age group (*ntangha*), with divisions based on puberty, marriage, and motherhood. However, the fellowship of tattooing was also contingent on shared geographic place. Interviewees recalled women of all ages wandering quite freely across the agrarian landscape, their horizons of mobility defined formally by the *tiko* (chieftaincy) where they resided but shaped informally by paths traversed with female peers or relatives for long-distance visiting and trade. During the colonial period, as the Portuguese administration tightened its grip and male migrancy took its toll on the countryside, girls and women may have begun traveling more out of need than recreation; but whether motivated by sociability or survival, their overlapping movements enabled them to create new networks of female "fellowship" through the crossing of physical and visual paths beyond the confines of home.

Whether at home or on the road, the key site of female connection was at the river's edge, where girls and women went to draw water, wash clothing, and bathe every day. Like the bush, "at the river" (*combeni*) was a pivotal location in tattooing stories, the place where fellow girls and women compared the beauty of one another's tinhlanga and where tattoo-based friendships were negotiated and sealed. Indeed, as Albertina Tiwana explained, the imperatives of friendship left many girls feeling they had little choice where tinhlanga were concerned: "Don't I long for what my friends have? When we're swimming around in the water, they show each other, 'Eh, look at my tattoos!' 'Eh, look at mine!' Well . . . when I see that woman is cutting tattoos again, shoo! I go." The desire to belong to communities of female friendship (*xinghanu*), whose boundaries were marked by shared standards of tattooed beauty, was just as compelling when young women moved to their marital home (*vukatini*), typically some distance away from where they had grown up. Anxious to shed newcomer status and forge affective bonds beyond the precarious circle of her in-laws, a bride often found that tinhlanga were an effective means of laying the groundwork of friendship among women with whom she might have nothing in common besides the geography of virilocal marriage.[10] That tattooing was perceived as one constituent of gender identity is implied more directly in some women's recollection that they were called "men" until they were tattooed. Yet, here again, oral accounts make clear that painfully inscribed standards of feminine beauty were targeted more at a female than a male audience.

The central feature of every tinhlanga story was a graphic description of the "suffering" the operation entailed. In voices that ranged from melodramatic whisper to comic shriek, women narrated how their skin was "stabbed" and "chopped," how their "blood ran everywhere," how they thought their "bowels were coming out," how some girls had to be held down by their friends so that their squirming would not "spoil" the scars. Girls who sat through the process stoically were considered "strong" or "steady" (*kutiya*) and "courageous" (*kutimisa*); women who were cut repeatedly wore on their skin permanent proof that they had no "fear" (*kuchava*). In a context where menstrual blood is believed to endanger the health of men and cattle, where menstruating women are considered so "taboo" (*kuyila*) that they are denied not only sexual access to men but also physical contact with anything that might touch and so "pollute" men, interviewees took almost defiant pride in their willingness to shed nonmenstrual blood in copious quantities. The prominence of this image in oral narratives suggests its centrality to the meaning of tinhlanga for women and invites a closer look at the gendered symbolism of blood (*ngati*) in these circumstances.

According to these sources, nonmenstrual blood possesses a number of contradictory powers. A metaphor for both the deepest obligations of kinship and the effort required to fulfill one's goals in life ("There is no tattoo without blood," that is, no achievement without struggle), blood is a positive force, a substance that guarantees personal well-being just as it heals illness, misfortune, or spirit possession when spilled through animal sacrifice or consumed as part of a ritual cure. Yet blood is also the most treacherous of the body's fluids: the loss of blood saps one's physical and moral strength (someone who is corrupt or cowardly is said to have "weak blood"); blood that has fallen on the ground must immediately be covered with sand because "wizards" might use it to make deadly "charms" (called *tingati*, the plural for "blood"); and life-sustaining liquids such as milk and beer can be made life-threatening by being magically transformed into blood.[11] With these apparently contrary meanings in mind, women's panegyrics about voluntary blood loss take on complex importance. Being tattooed means giving up one's blood and allowing it to fall freely on the ground, which makes one vulnerable to supernatural, physical, and social threats of all kinds. However, blood shed to obtain tinhlanga brings valuable rewards: new bonds of kinship (a kind of "blood sisterhood"); proof of nerve and bravery; and, ironically, a kind of dually regendered prestige, for if tattooing contributes to the making of girls into women, it does so in part by mimicking the battlefield heroics of men.

In other words, the experience of being tattooed was just as crucial to its social and historical meaning for women as the tinhlanga themselves. The essence of this experience was a test—a trial by ordeal—undertaken and judged by a circle of female peers. Aimed both at marking girls' bodies feminine and at demonstrating that femininity was a quality girls had to achieve through their own strength and suffering, the operation generated shared memories that, like shared tinhlanga designs, transformed peer pressure and competition into bonds of intragenerational female community.

Tinhlanga were a medium of feminine connection that refused to obey or perpetuate other kinds of social boundaries. Shared notions of tattooed beauty often crossed generational lines, because older *vatlhaveli* influenced girls' choice of designs, and because girls "looked over" the bodies of senior women for inspiration as well. One of the tinhlanga Rosalina received in Chibuto, for example, was identical to a tattoo worn by her mother and a paternal aunt, which they had obtained some thirty years earlier. More surprising is the eliding of ethnic differences in women's selection of tinhlanga. Lucia Ntumbo, who identifies herself as Nguni, had her tattoos done by her maternal grandmother's sister, Qimidzi Mandlaze, an Ndau woman from north of the Save River and a popular mutlhaveli, in whose household in Chaimite (Gaza province) Lucia spent her adolescence. Qimidzi, Lucia remembers, learned her repertoire of tattoo designs from other vatlhaveli in the predominantly Shangaan communities of Chaimite. Lucia's daughter, in turn, has different tattoos from her mother "because she was born in Xitezeni [in northwest Magude], and cut tinhlanga there."

WHILE INTERVIEWEES' RECOLLECTIONS of tattooing were vividly detailed, women had little to say about how or why tinhlanga changed over time. Yet a history of change was visible in their body markings, which were patterned in conspicuous if not immediately comprehensible ways. Tinhlanga, in fact, speak with a "voice" all their own, and the story they tell casts startling new light on rural women's engagement with, and understanding of, Portuguese colonialism. As women struggled to hold their own against colonial power, tattooing remained an activity defined through and for intragenerational female relationships. However, it also underwent a multilayered shift, from a painful and bloody process that utilized mainly indigenous materials and that was oriented in part to enhancing relations between the sexes, to one that involved less physical discomfort, the use of mainly xilungu materials and designs, and a concern with interracial rather than intergender contests.

Certain kinds of tinhlanga followed a straight trajectory of decline during and after the late nineteenth century. As European commentators noted, keloid facial scars had largely disappeared from the region by the 1920s. Keloid tattoos on women's shoulders and backs were widespread until the 1920s, but became less common after the 1930s, as did the most extreme form of cicatrization on the lower abdomen, pubic area, and thighs, which sometimes produced scars over half an inch in diameter.[12]

Not one of the interviewees, nor any of their daughters, had acquired a pubic tattoo (*vusankusi*) after around 1950. This dorsal and hypogastric tattooing, which women described in especially gory detail, was done by lifting the skin with a fishhook, thorn, or the fingers, and then slicing across it with a razor blade or broken glass. A mixture of ground charcoal or ash and castor oil or red ochre was then rubbed into the wounds to darken the scars. Normally, these marks would be recut and -colored at least once to heighten the tattoo's visibility and ensure it would last. More painful, more bloody, and more susceptible to infection than other types of tattoos, these tinhlanga were also preeminently tactile in nature and most closely associated with male sexual interest. Another name for the dorsal tattoo, *xikhoma nkata* — to "clutch your darling" — makes this meaning explicit.

Incised scarification of women's epigastric area, though, remained more or less constant during this period (late 1910s–1950). All interviewees bore some version of an incised design referred to as *nxurhana* (a geometric pattern consisting of triangles and parallelograms) and/or the *xilova* (sets of parallel and oblique lines). These tinhlanga were made by "drawing" the desired pattern on the skin with charcoal or a stick and then making small cuts along the lines, coloring the scars in the manner described above. Nxurhana tattoos range from simple designs based on four or five lines to expansive networks of geometric shapes that wrap around the woman's torso on both sides. In addition, many interviewees also had one or more smaller tattoos incised on their stomach or sides, and these tinhlanga were much more diverse. About one-quarter of the group had a tattoo they called *xinkwahlana*, a type of lizard. Katarina Matuka, who was born around 1910 and spent her youth near the heartland of the former Gaza state, had a tinhlanga representing the Nguni warriors' oval shield (*xitlhangu*) on her side. Women in their eighties from the western border region of Magude recalled girls there tattooing their "bellies" with images of flowers and shrubs; two slightly younger women from Facazisse, the community near Magude town where I resided during fieldwork, had a chevron pattern that, according to Earthy, represented an arrowhead or snake, and one of these two women also had a tattoo she called a *ximusana* (small wood pestle). In another trend reminiscent of Earthy's findings, several women who had grown up near Magude town had a symbol they called *xikero*, or scissors, on one or both sides.

Between the 1920s and the 1940s, depending on the area, a dramatic shift occurred in female tattooing: the introduction of a new method of producing scars using bunches of needles instead of sharp-edged cutting tools. Less painful, messy, and dangerous, needle tattooing also produced much less tactile, and more narrowly visual, transformations of the skin, and seems to have had no overtly sexual implications; at least, no interviewee mentioned male sexual interest when talking about these tinhlanga. This revolution in tattoo technology led to critical changes not only in tattoo aesthetics but also in the social relations of body marking. By the mid-1920s near Magude town and the mid-1930s further out in the countryside, women remember younger and younger girls, "even children," using needles and ash to give one another a new style of facial tattoo known as *swibayana*, which consisted of clusters of three or four small round scars on the cheeks, forehead, and chin. More revealing still, women who grew up near the Swiss Mission station at Antioka (Facazisse), where the Swiss and their African evangelists had been proselytizing since the 1880s, recall a popular fad among young girls in the 1920s: having one's European first name "written" on the right forearm, and one's clan name (or the name of "the boy you loved") on the left. In the hands of older girls and women, needles were used to create more complex patterns representing objects from the agrarian landscape, such as women's trusty iron hoe (*xikomu*).

By the 1940s, needle tattooing had encouraged an even more radical departure in women's body marking, especially in the villages ringing Magude town. Older girls and women began to acquire needle-cut tinhlanga on their chest, arms, and thighs; these designs represented objects of European origin, incorporated new xilungu materials such as ink and shoe polish, and in nearly every case were tattooed onto women by men. Migrant workers who returned home from South Africa or Swaziland with "notebooks" of tinhlanga styles popular among women in their place of employment, these men offered their services to female kin and neighbors whose memories of this event stress the excitement of choosing among a wealth of new tattoo possibilities on the basis of what "the girls had over there." The most common male-cut tattoos among interviewees were images of factory-made flowerpots, bevelled diamonds and stars, and a cross-like design representing the trademark of Blue Cross condensed milk. Occasionally, the mutlhaveli would also include signs of the xilungu identity he had acquired while working away from home: his European name, and sometimes the year the tattoo was done.

In a society with stringent controls on male access to women's bodies, where it is still taboo for a woman to bare her thighs in public, the fact that some women permitted men who were not their husband to have intimate contact with their body demands explanation in itself. Changes in tattoo technology, then, were interwoven with both changing gender relations and an expanding notion, at least for some women, of the social and cultural world to which they belonged. As conventional boundaries between the sexes were being crossed for the purpose of making women beautiful, so were boundaries among women — in this case, political, ethnic, and geographic boundaries — breaking down as they looked farther afield for models of beauty to make their own. Riverside appraisals, motivated by conflicting desires to imitate, outdo, and claim affinity with prospective "fellows," had moved from a local to an international stage, with tattoos still as powerful a medium as ever for building and broadening feminine communities through the changes of the mid-twentieth century.

To understand these transformations in tinhlanga practice, we need to look at the context in which tattoo styles waxed and waned and at the changing social complexion of the tattooed population. At the same time as girls and women were adopting new methods of body marking, they were also confronting new, sometimes violent pressures to cease decorating their bodies altogether. Lise Nsumbane was born around 1910 near the Antioka mission station and remembered that at the mission school, "Oh, we hid these things, you know! From the teacher. We hid them, or he beat us, there at school. . . . When . . . your friends, they cut tinhlanga, he beat them. He says, 'What's that? Say, are you cutting one another?' . . . Those things, they forbade them! You were beaten for them, truly." When I asked why, she replied, "Ah, they say they're for heathens."

Women who attended the Portuguese Catholic mission school in Magude town in the 1920s told similar stories of freshly cut girls being beaten by priests and African teachers. As Christianity presented a new physiology of the human body as God's creation, as the "temple of the Holy Ghost" — a vessel not one's own and not to be "disfigured" in any way — church girls ironically risked corporal punishment by European mission personnel or their African evangelists, lay leaders, and teachers if they were caught with tinhlanga. Women's stories often allude to this theological conflict, which swirled as much around meanings of blood and bleeding as around contending ideas about the body itself. For the missionaries and their converts, "finishing" one's blood for the vain purpose of physical beauty not only defied the will of God (who "doesn't want you to change the body He gave you") but also mocked Christianity's symbolic equation of blood loss with sacrifice, redemption, and the gift of everlasting life. Faced with the threat of harsh punishment, some church girls decided not to be tattooed, especially when they hoped to marry a boy from a prominent Christian family. Yet, evidence from Magude suggests that these girls formed a very small minority; adolescence in the countryside rarely entailed the luxury of bodily privacy, and peer ridicule was less easily avoided — and sometimes more cruel — than disciplinary sanctions girls encountered in the public domain.

Other girls, however, rejected tinhlanga not because of religion but for reasons they presented in terms of ethnicity or "race" (*muxaka*). Sara Juma, born in 1942 to a Shangaan woman and her *mestiço* husband, refused to be tattooed because "I wasn't . . . of that race, those Shangaan people":

> I was different, I was — those Shangaan things, I didn't follow them well, because I didn't know anything Shangaan. . . . Because I didn't want that . . . well, there were these things, eh, cutting tinhlanga, I don't know what else. Now I, no. [laughs] Even my mother didn't want that. I wasn't one of these people to go around doing tinhlanga. Mmm. My mother didn't want me to follow those *xilandin* [black] ways. [HG: Why not?] Ah, it's my mother who didn't want it, because I wasn't . . . of that race, for me to run around, to know things that those people were doing. My sisters, those daughters of my [mother's] sister, *they* went, but I went to watch, what they were doing there! [laughs] They went to do those tinhlanga, to cut them. . . . I went to watch, truly. They beat me! They always chased me away. When you don't go there to do it, they don't allow you to watch there. They *beat* me. . . . Well, when I reach [home], I say, "I saw her! They're cutting each other!"

For Sara, tinhlanga were the principal metonymic differences separating her from the embellished bodies of her "black" mother and sisters. Sara's mother's desire to define her mixed-race daughter as "white," a status she was not entitled to in colonial law, may have been shaped by her own upbringing on the grounds of the São Jerónimo mission station in Magude town, and would certainly have been reinforced by Sara's attendance at the Catholic primary school in the late 1940s.

Indeed, women's narratives suggest that by this time the place of female body marking in mission Christianity's definitions of sin and heathenism had converged with Portuguese colonial discourses vaunting the benefits of assimilation while articulating the differences between civilized and native in increasingly racialized terms. In the aftermath of the 1928 Indigenato labor code—a bundle of laws designed to maximize state control over African labor by formalizing the distinction between (white) "citizens" and (nonwhite) "subjects"—*assimilado* status was regarded by most Africans, according to historian Jeanne Penvenne, as "the best of a bad deal."[13] Available only to those Africans who were literate in Portuguese, had traded tribal for European culture, and were engaged in the colonial economy as artisans, traders, or skilled workers, assimilation promised all the rights enjoyed by Portuguese citizens, including exemption from forced labor. Although these opportunities were meaningless for the vast majority of the African population, it appears that the shadow of this legislation had fallen on Magude by midcentury, so that "white" was a condition to aspire to and "black" was one to be discarded or despised. Thus, for many interviewees who had contact with mission schools or colonial urban centers in their youth, tinhlanga embodied all that civilized women were supposed to abandon; whether for God or the myth of attainable whiteness, black female skins were to remain smooth and unmarked.

These disincentives were compounded by the seductive pressures of South Asian ("Banyan") shopkeepers who vigorously promoted xilungu dress in Magude from the early 1900s on. Yet even women who fondly recalled the rare occasions when they purchased a blouse or *capulana* (length of cotton cloth) insisted that tattoos remained an essential method for beautifying female bodies. In fact, perhaps the greatest irony of tinhlanga politics in the colonial period is that the very clothing civilization required African girls to wear made it possible for them to conceal the tattoos European dress was supposed to be replacing.

How should we interpret girls' and women's determination to go on cutting themselves through this period? Rosalina Malungana offered a cynical reading of Christian elders' efforts to throw the weight of a sternly judgmental God behind what was, on one level, a battle for control over how women made themselves pretty: "Eh! They say . . . it was a sin. 'These things, they're for heathens.' . . . Ah, but that's just politics. God, what does he know of these things? What he wants, God wants a person to have a good soul. What you do with your body, he doesn't care about that." Few interviewees voiced such bold skepticism; their tinhlanga, however, sketch a similarly defiant, though complicated, story. In the thinly settled cattle country of western and northern Magude district, most girls and women went on being tattooed, following the trends described above, through the 1940s and 1950s. Yet, contrary to my expectations, tattooing began to decline earlier in these areas than in communities closer to Magude town and other colonial urban centers. Moreover, the shift to needle tattooing did not make as significant an impact in these more remote areas. In fact, women's enthusiasm for the xilandin practice of body marking — and, paradoxically, their incorporation of xilungu materials and methods — seems to have increased in proportion to their exposure to colonial influences. Nearer mission stations and towns, women were more likely to replace tinhlanga acquired through "suffering," blood loss, and "strength" (tattoos aimed, in part, to attract male sexual interest) with tinhlanga that were less physically risky, more technically sophisticated, and more beautiful in appearance than to the touch. The "ancient custom" of women's tattooing, in other words, became both more popular and more "modern" — and less oriented to marriage — as the forces of Portuguese colonialism and mission Christianity stepped up their efforts to anchor their authority in the countryside. This simultaneous reversal and confirmation of European predictions about the "evolution" of African fashion was accomplished by girls and women who were fully aware that their bodies were not only a critical site for the construction of feminine community, but also a key terrain in a colonial contest in which fellowship among rural women was more necessary than ever before.

This awareness intensified as the twentieth century progressed, as male migrancy, taxation, forced cash crop production, and ecological crises sapped the agrarian economy and required women to extend affective networks across as wide an area as possible. Women in southern Mozambique had long been using their skin to mediate the exclusionary claims of a dominant culture, but the power to decide how women would make themselves beautiful assumed much higher stakes under Portuguese rule. Tattooed beauty was no longer just about making friends, attracting husbands, or proving one's capacity for masculine valor; under colonialism, it became both part of women's response to the ailing institution of rural marriage and an optic for defining what was civilized and what was not.

Such definitions had consequences — for marital options, economic prospects, relations with Europeans — even among women who could never hope to qualify for assimilated/civilized status themselves. Yet precisely because the legal privileges of whiteness were beyond their reach, relinquishing blackness was not a desirable option either. Under these circumstances, tinhlanga offered a medium for women to conduct their own debate about the dividing line between white and black ways. Just as Ntete Khosa, the daughter of one of the African pioneers of the Swiss mission at Antioka, waged a personal campaign to translate the lessons of mission schooling into a new tinhlanga style, women of all ages used tattooing to appropriate elements of the changing world around them without sacrificing the most crucial features of the practice. A woman who had tinhlanga, then, was still xilandin, and enjoyed the wide-ranging webs of feminine connection that tattooed female blackness entailed. Yet because her tinhlanga could include timeless images from the agrarian landscape *and* writing, flowerpots, and condensed milk, her body proclaimed — with a defiance she could not safely utter aloud — that she was civilized and xilungu too.

By the late 1960s, tinhlanga were falling out of fashion in the Magude area. Interviewees explained that girls began to "abandon" tattooing because xilungu schooling and improved state medical services had convinced them that tinhlanga were dangerous to a woman's health. Frelimo's (Front for the Liberation of Mozambique) ideological campaigns after independence contributed to the devaluation of tribal practices that were inconsistent with the Marxist-Leninist government's push for national unity and modernization, and the havoc of the Renamo war made tattooing an indulgence few could afford. Yet, in postwar Magude, the stirrings of a tattoo revival confirm the vital role that body marking has historically played for rural women. In 1996, when I interviewed Unasse Sitoi, a former war captive in her seventies who was still living at Ngungwe, the Renamo base camp that occupied the western fringes of Magude and Moamba districts, she mentioned that she had begun tattooing younger female captives in the early 1990s as a way to obtain water, firewood, and help in her fields. When Mozambique's national elections in 1994 instilled a sense of stability even in this state-forsaken corner of the countryside, the girls of Ngungwe, according to Unasse, began walking back and forth across the South African border to visit relatives living in the refugee communities of the Transvaal. When they came back, newly conscious of their status as members of transnationally scattered families, many of whom would like to relocate permanently in South Africa, they told Unasse that "over there, the girls, they don't cut tattoos. And we, we won't cut tinhlanga now either."

In Magude town, the situation was different. In the periurban settlements where displaced women of all ages and points of origins were still crowded in ramshackle shelters, supporting children and parents and, often, unemployed husbands through backbreaking work in borrowed fields, survival depended on one's ability to court extensive networks of friends and kin. Here, tinhlanga were staging a much discussed comeback, and mothers had begun to watch their daughters for signs of cutting when they returned home from the Nkomati River. Conversations about tattooing in these two distant points of the district in the mid-1990s oddly echoed the reminiscences of women who beautified their bodies with tinhlanga during the colonial period. Future research may find that their repertoire of designs and instruments have changed with the reconfigured identities of the postwar world, but what stood out at the moment of tinhlanga's resurgence in Magude was their enduring value as a means of feminine outreach and historical remembrance, an ineffable record of women's experience in a land still trying to recover from the "scars" of European rule.

WOMEN IN THE Magude area have used tattoos to re-"write" boundaries of difference — most strikingly, ethnic and racial difference — and build ever wider female communities throughout the nineteenth and twentieth centuries. Yet, it was the transformed meanings of female beauty in the colonial period that most dramatically highlighted the contradictory powers of tinhlanga for rural women. Surrounded by Christian discourses, Portuguese notions of racial identity, and the battery of practices — literacy, commodified food, potted plants — through which colonialism sought to enact its authority, girls and women used tinhlanga to claim more inclusive grounds of common experience and affiliation. Their efforts, preserved in personal narratives and in the scars themselves, manifest four important tensions in women's lives under Portuguese rule. First, while the cutting of tattoos was shrouded in secrecy, and civilized dress supplied a useful layer of concealment for illicitly tattooed bodies, tinhlanga were intended to be seen, their assertions of history and xilandin identity bolder — because more permanent — than the disposable accessories of xilungu culture. Second, perhaps because of the very boldness of tattooing's claims, women's stories about tinhlanga are wrapped in secrecy of another kind: an unwillingness, or inability, to articulate their full historical significance. Reticent when asked to explain changes documented in plain view on their skin, women preferred to use the inscribed memories of tinhlanga to prove the strength of their bodies and the resilience of traditional practices in the face of colonial pressures to become civilized and modern.

And yet, third, in the most telling irony of all, if the persistence of tattooing exposed the incompleteness of European power, it was the female casualties of colonial society who drew most extensively on xilungu materials and designs, engaging and adapting colonial culture as they transformed the practice of tattooing to preserve its place — and theirs — in a changing world. Finally, if the ultimate value of tinhlanga lay in their role as a medium for girls and women to forge chains of feminine fellowship that transcended boundaries of clan, marriage, class, ethnicity, race, even nationality, how do we explain the memories of competition, envy, and ridicule motivating the decision to be cut? Why, indeed, go to such painful lengths for the sake of beauty and friendship at all? Perhaps the bonds formed through suffering are truer, and more potent, because of the self-sacrifice they entail; perhaps the price of female community is so high because of the centrifugal forces against it in a male-dominated world, or because the price of living without it is comparably great. Either way, tinhlanga represent a hard-won feminine victory, a declaration that the respect and approval of one's fellows are more enduring than individual fear, colonial power, or the desires of men. Exhibiting tattooed skin as evidence that they are anything but victims, the women of Magude embody truths of Mozambique's colonial history — truths we would not have access to any other way.

Notes

1. For example, Hildi Hendrickson, ed., *Clothing and Difference: Embodied Identities in Colonial and Post-Colonial Africa* (Durham, N.C.: Duke University Press, 1996).
2. Janet Spector, *What This Awl Means: Feminist Archaeology at a Wahpeton Dakota Village* (St. Paul: Minnesota Historical Society Press, 1993).
3. William M. White, *Journal of a Voyage Performed in the Lion extra Indiaman, from Madras to Colombo and Da Lagoa Bay . . . in the Year 1798* (London, 1800), 27.

4. *Editors' note*: A keloid is a growth of dense fibrous tissue that develops over the site where skin is punctured or otherwise damaged.

5. Jane Caplan, "'Speaking Scars': The Tattoo in Popular Practice and Medico-Legal Debate in Nineteenth-Century Europe," *History Workshop Journal* 44 (1997): 107–142.

6. H. A. Junod, *La Tribu et la Langue Thonga* (Lausanne, 1896), 16–17; H. A. Junod, *Life of a South African Tribe* (2nd ed., London, 1962), 1: 178–179; St. Vincent Erskine, "Journey of Exploration to the Mouth of the River Limpopo," *Journal of the Royal Geographic Society* 39 (1869): 238.

7. H. A. Junod, *Life of a South African Tribe* (1st ed., Neuchatel: Attinger Frères, 1913), 1: 180.

8. E. Dora Earthy, "On the Significance of the Body Markings of Some Natives of Portuguese East Africa," *South African Journal of Science* 21 (1924): 573–587.

9. Ibid., 577–578.

10. *Editors' note*: in virilocal marriage, the husband and wife live with the husband's kin after marriage.

11. Junod, *Life of a South African Tribe*, 1: 201, 2: 360, 416, 489, 512.

12. *Editors' note*: cicatrization refers both to the ritualistic scarring of the body through the creation of elaborate patterns and the actual biological process of scar formation.

13. Jeanne M. Penvenne, *African Workers and Colonial Racism: Mozambican Strategies and Struggles in Lourenço Marques, 1877–1962* (Portsmouth, N.H.: Heinemann, 1995), 467.

III

THE MOBILITY OF POLITICS AND

THE POLITICS OF MOBILITY

Carter Vaughn Findley

An Ottoman Occidentalist in Europe:

Ahmed Midhat Meets Madame Gülnar, 1889

Ahmed Midhat was an Ottoman traveler who "returned the gaze" by subjecting the customs of the West to the kind of scrutiny it reserved for non-Western peoples and societies. A critic of unreflective Westernization, he used his travel writings as an opportunity to survey the symbols of European modernity — among them, the international congress and the industrial exhibition. In the process, he provided a rare and remarkable ethnography of Western "civilization." His astonishing encounter with Madame Gülnar, an accomplished Russian noblewoman and Turkophile, and their travels together set in motion a running critique of Western civilization. As Ahmed Midhat presents it, this combines male and female, Ottoman and Russian points of view to compare Europe with Russia and the Ottoman Empire in terms of such major themes as the state of progress, dress and deportment, women's status, family, and society. Throughout, he develops the image of Madame Gülnar as a new modern woman, honorable not just for her irreproachable morality but also for her talent and achievement. An "Occidentalist," or purveyor of knowledge about the West, in an age of Orientalism, Ahmed Midhat offered Ottoman readers (and now us) a dually gendered, dually cultured outsider's view of Europe, a view also rich in implications for the construction of Ottoman modernity.

In the modern era, Europeans constructed a new image of themselves, defined in opposition to images of an external Other, often identified with the "Orient," starting with the end of the Orient they knew best: the Middle East and North Africa. What was at stake was not just Europeans' cognitive control of the Orient or the colonial world generally but European elite males' cognitive control of all their Others, domestic and foreign, as defined by gender, class, religion, ethnicity, or any combination of traits.[1] The simultaneous acceleration of both technological advance and imperial expansion produced a rapid growth of techniques for ordering information and tangibly representing visions of the Other in ways that viewers expected to find borne out when they traveled to the places depicted. Not only museums and zoos but also congresses of scholars and diplomats and — most distinctive of the period — world's fairs and exhibitions all asserted such visions and helped to establish their credibility. Inventions such as telegraphy and photography enhanced the effect of immediacy, while the railroad and steamship hastened travel between the "represented" and the "real." The impact of the exhibitions began to wane after 1900; yet, for a time, the world came to be "experienced as though it were an exhibition."[2]

Visitors from the Orient joined the throngs at the exhibitions. One thoughtful observer who traveled from the Middle East to late-nineteenth-century Europe was the Ottoman author Ahmed Midhat. His *Avrupa'da bir Cevelan* (*A Tour in Europe*, 1889) recounts his journey to a scholarly congress of orientalists in Stockholm and his subsequent travels, including a visit to the World Exhibition in Paris. Now largely forgotten but pivotal to his career, the book shows how two examples of "the world-as-exhibition" looked to a self-described Occidentalist.[3]

THE LATE OTTOMAN Empire was doubly imperial. On the one hand, it remained a formally independent, multinational empire. On the other hand, it lost territory to separatist nationalisms and to great-power imperialism, and it slipped into economic and political dependence. Under the circumstances, Ottoman society produced a "segmented bourgeois class formation," including an Ottoman-Muslim bureaucratic intelligentsia with vital interests in preserving and modernizing the empire, and an ethnically divided, non-Muslim commercial bourgeoisie that became identified with separatist nationalisms and dependent integration into the world economy.[4] The elite defined itself not by ethnicity but by state service and assimilation of the Ottoman-Islamic imperial culture. Over time, the Ottoman elites differed over redefinition of their collective identity and over choices between the Ottoman-Islamic and the Western. In general, they clung to Ottomanism as long as there was an empire to cling to and, as rulers of a partly European empire, became increasingly European-oriented.[5]

Ahmed Midhat, for his part, was exceptionally interested in fashioning a modern Ottoman culture that was "nevertheless not Western."[6] A man of humble origins who rose by his own talents, Ahmed Midhat (1844–1912) became a successful writer and publisher, a literary jack-of-all-trades. One Ottoman intellectual who was not actually an official, he personified an emerging Ottoman print capitalism. For years, he edited and largely wrote the newspaper *Tercuman-i Hakikat* (Interpreter of truth). An unabashed popularizer and encyclopedist who often cribbed from European sources, he authored some 150 books of several genres, serializing most in his newspaper. Translations of European novels had appeared before, but he became the first Ottoman novelist. Because widespread illiteracy still limited readership for works in Ottoman Turkish, he also wrote plays in order to reach a wider audience.

His works fed a keen hunger in a society where modern print media had developed only lately and where contacts with the outside world were fast intensifying. He was not always a careful stylist, yet his best writing still appeals, and some of his novels are avant-garde in technique. Once dubbed a "forty horsepower writing machine," he enjoyed a popularity comparable to Charles Dickens's or Mark Twain's. Ahmed Midhat's popularity partly derived from his exuberant nature and communitarian view of society. It was hard to leave Istanbul, he said, because he was a father figure to sixty or seventy families with over three hundred members.

Collaborator and publicist of Sultan Abdülhamid II (r. 1876–1909), Ahmed Midhat is easily branded a conservative, yet he had progressive traits. In contrast to the progressive ideologues who took constitutionalism as their "symbol of Western modernity," he, while sharing some of their positivistic and Social Darwinist ideas, believed social, economic, and cultural change should come first. Not a religious conservative at all, on balance he favored Westernization. Like many other Ottoman writers, he criticized excessive, superficial Westernization, a danger personified in his works by playboys whose rootlessness brought them to bad ends. Much more than other writers, however, he examined both Ottoman and European cultures minutely to distinguish good and bad points in each. As a result, he advocated change in many domains, from table manners to social roles. While championing the "patriarchal life" of the Ottoman household, he became a pioneer author of books for and about children and a precursor of change in gender relations.[7]

Ahmed Midhat found that one fruit of the sultan's favor was his selection to represent the Ottoman Empire at the Eighth Congress of Orientalists in Stockholm. He spent seventy-one days in Europe, visited the Exposition Universelle in Paris and other sites, and then wrote a book that opened a new phase in his career.

He had published books since 1870, a major goal always being to make Europe known to the Ottomans. His earlier books had been "mental journeys" based on reading, however, whereas this thousand-page travel narrative recounted a "real journey." Ahmed Midhat stated that he would speak only from observation and not swell his book with things from guidebooks. In fact, compilation was essential for his fast-paced encyclopedism. Yet, if his "Tour in Europe" resulted in part from pedestrian information gathering and writing strategies, this did not preclude his pursuing ambitious literary ends. His artistry becomes clear from the way he combined translation and compilation with descriptive and novelistic passages, including moments of rhetorical eloquence, dialogue, stage setting, and character development. Beyond that, two traits stand out.

Near the end of his book, Ahmed Midhat relates a conversation in Vienna in which the Ottoman ambassador there suggested evaluating Europe's progress in terms of the "material" and the "moral." In fact, Ahmed Midhat had already made this contrast his leitmotif, developing it in much earlier discussions. One reason for this emphasis may have been that the moral-material duality paralleled Sultan Abdülhamid's view that Western civilization consisted of "technique" and "idea," the former helpful, but the latter more likely dangerous, to ill-educated peoples who still needed paternalistic rule. Ahmed Midhat's use of this dichotomy gave his work more than a kind of political correctness. Applying the moral-material dichotomy to the Other implied applying it to the Self. This turned his trip to the realm of material progress into a reflection on the spiritual realm in which a modern Ottoman culture might be created.

Ahmed Midhat's itinerary took him by ship from Istanbul to Marseille, by train to Copenhagen, and on by steamer and train to Stockholm. Given the political configuration of Sweden-Norway, the orientalist congress convened in both Stockholm and Christiania, as Oslo was then known. Thereafter, he traveled with one or more of the Russians he had met at the orientalist congress to Berlin (three days' stay), Paris (twelve days), across Switzerland to Vienna (five days), and back by train to Trieste and steamer to Istanbul.

Ahmed Midhat used his travel narrative as a means of Occidentalist empowerment. Much as Europeans demonstrated their command of practicalities in their travel books — a literary form dependent in turn on many other technologies of travel — he sought to convey his mastery of the requirements for a successful journey across Europe. Ever methodical, he saw his trip as one big tour made up of smaller ones, using the same term *cevelan* for all. Using guidebook, map, and compass to plan and follow his routes, he organized his book as a day-by-day account, inserting descriptions of sites and events. As he planned his outings, he perfected a method of studying his map and listing the streets he wanted to follow. He liked to start the day early with a walking tour planned the night before, returning to the hotel to meet his travel companions. They would then devote the rest of the day to major sites. At night, they would go to the theater, spend the evening over dinner, or retire early to sleep or write. Occasional references to writing articles for his newspaper or keeping a journal imply regular attention to these pursuits. It is hard to see how he could have written his book so quickly otherwise. The "little museum" of brochures and catalogues that he collected also helped.[8]

In addition to guidebooks and maps, the Ottoman traveler confronted endless complexities of a world culturally polarized between *alafranga* and *alaturka*[9] and had to negotiate transitions from one to the other in matters ranging from clocks and calendars to the intricacies of dress and deportment, sources of fascination to Ahmed Midhat. To deal with such matters, he advocated "researching the country," adding that he had done so for fifteen years to learn about Europe before going there. Prior study of guidebooks enabled one to make the most of one's time and to know things even the locals did not. Occidentalist empowerment thus included power over Europeans, at the price of mastering European ways. Travelers dependent on human guides were prisoners in their hands. Baedeker was right about this: travelers owed their freedom to him. Local guides spouted misinformation, led travelers to brothels, and took those who wanted to shop to stores that gave the guides kickbacks. An explorer in red fez rather than pith helmet, Ahmed Midhat showed such people that he was in control. He did not fault natives for staring as he studied fine Parisian buildings with binoculars in one hand and guidebook in the other; he persisted because he had to try to memorize everything he saw.

The smart Ottoman traveler, moreover, knew the advantages of travel by train or ship, preferring the latter to avoid the smoke, coal dust, and uncomfortable motion. Ahmed Midhat planned unavoidable train trips in short stages, preferably at night, so as not to lose days. He knew to telegraph ahead for hotel reservations. Aware of the dangers of European cities, he knew that the police would respond to travelers' complaints, especially in Germany and Switzerland. He understood the importance of maintaining his health and acted accordingly. Ahmed Midhat did not have to tell his readers that no Ottoman traveler could manage without knowing at least one European language, preferably French. Implying his own mastery, he related an impassioned speech that he allegedly made at the congress, extemporaneously in French, on Muslim women. He recounted the speech in Ottoman as a polished composition, enough so to make one wonder if he could have delivered it with the same panache in French. How much confidence his readers gained from this picture of prowess is uncertain.

Ahmed Midhat also did not need to tell his readers that the unaccompanied Ottoman Muslim traveler had to be male, but some of his references to gender issues reflected that fact. His warnings about European prostitutes conflated otherness, femininity, and sexual danger in a way that turned the tables on European Orientalism and attitudes toward "oriental" women. This conforms to a larger pattern in Ottoman Occidentalism: figuring the West as feminine and its greatest danger to the East as its libidinousness. Moreover, a traveler as gregarious as Ahmed Midhat could not be expected to travel alone. He never did for long, even though he presents himself as the lone delegate from Istanbul at Stockholm. Then as now, exhibitions and congresses not only projected visions of the world but also created settings for unexpected meetings among people of diverse backgrounds. So it was for Ahmed Midhat, especially at the congress. There he befriended numerous delegates, including Egyptians and Russians. Perhaps, then, his most important travel skills were his social ones.

One of the gala events in Stockholm was a reception at the Grand Hotel, an occasion featuring waiters clad in Egyptian costumes and entertainment provided by the opera orchestra and ballet. For Ahmed Midhat, this spectacle was quickly eclipsed by an astonishing introduction to a "polyglot" Russian noblewoman, who immediately began talking to him in Ottoman and gave her name as "Gülnar" (Rose). When he expressed admiration but pointed out that this beautiful name was not proper to her nationality, she handed him her card, with the name engraved on it in Arabic calligraphy. The name he needed to know, she said, was Gülnar.[10] Ahmed Midhat thus began his acquaintance and friendship with one of three Russian travelers. His interest in Madame Gülnar and later her compatriots may seem surprising, given the history of Ottoman-Russian enmity. Yet, because he was an author approved at the highest level, Ahmed Midhat's attitude of fascination toward these travelers cannot be considered accidental; it matches other signs of circumspection in Ottoman policy toward Russia at the time. He justified his view with interesting blurrings of orientalist distinctions: the Russians' customs are like the Ottomans'; the French say that if you scratch a Russian, a Tatar emerges, and the same is true of an Ottoman. The Russians had started accepting European civilization before the Ottomans and had gone further, but they had not lost their Asian manners and customs, and so on. When the Russian physician Dr. Boris Yanpolskii, whom he met through Madame Gülnar, treated both of them for colds, Ahmed Midhat compared the Russians' humaneness to the Ottomans' generosity. He added the Social Darwinist note that such qualities were greater among peoples who, like them, were still on the lower rungs of civilization. He also valued his colloquies with the Russians as a way to learn about Russia's Tatars; he did not protest that Russia ruled the Tatars.

Through Madame Gülnar, Ahmed Midhat met not only Dr. Boris, as he called him, but also an old man, whom he called Professor Goldwald (the real name, Gottwald, might have had off-color associations in Turkish), and his daughter. They traveled together to Berlin, from which the professor and his daughter returned to Russia. Ahmed Midhat and Madame Gülnar went on to Paris and visited it together. Parting from her there, Ahmed Midhat went to Switzerland, joining Dr. Boris and traveling with him as far as Vienna. Ahmed Midhat depicts memorable scenes with all three of the Russians, including a moving talk in Stockholm with the old professor, who urged Ahmed Midhat to work hard to show the wisdom of Islam to Europe, which had made progress in industry and science but not in wisdom. But the person at the congress who most intrigued Ahmed Midhat was Madame Gülnar. It did not take long to learn her real name and that she was a countess, but she asked him not to use her real name in his book. He promised, referring to her first as Madame Gülnar, eventually just as Gülnar—appellations that concede a Turkish identity while maintaining her liminality.

Was he as interested in manipulating her image as she was? Olga Ser-geyevna Lebedeva (1854–?) by her right name, she impressed him first by the quality of her Turkish. She explained that she was from the Kazan region, where her family employed Tatar workers and had relations with notable Tatar families, that she had long known Tatar, and had begun to learn Ottoman when she went to Petersburg. She also knew numerous European languages and enough Arabic and Persian for use in Ottoman; in addition, she played the piano and painted. An admirer of Ottoman customs, she wore Turkish clothing at home and put fezes on her children. Madame Gülnar showed Ahmed Midhat a manuscript of a book that she had translated from Russian into Ottoman, and he noted with surprise that the translation hardly needed correction. When he asked for a copy to publish in Istanbul, she simply gave him the manuscript. In another ap-praisal of her written Ottoman, Ahmed Midhat wrote that it was not inferior to that of the newspaper *Tercüman* (The interpreter), published by the noted Crimean Tatar intellectual Ismail Gasprinski (1851–1914).

Later, as traveling companion, Madame Gülnar displayed behavioral traits not unknown in other accomplished, upper-class, nineteenth-century ladies. In contrast to Ahmed Midhat's energy and early starts, she needed more sleep, often felt ill, and spent some days without leaving the hotel. While she showed surprising stamina for things she wanted to do, such as visiting the Louvre, on balance her sightseeing was limited. While Ahmed Midhat often felt homesick, if she felt similar feelings, he did not report them, not until she got a letter in Paris, informing her that her mother would shortly arrive with Madame Gülnar's nine-year-old son, Sasha, who had a chest ailment and needed to travel. After the old countess and the boy arrived, Ahmed Midhat was startled at Madame Gülnar's childlike submission to the will of her mother and her absent husband. For example, when Ahmed Midhat invited Madame Gülnar to visit the Père Lachaise cemetery, her mother forbade it, saying, "The weak nerves of women are affected by such sights."[11] After a century, it is hard to know which of Madame Gülnar's idiosyncrasies were hers alone and which resulted from then prevalent factors of gender, class, or ethnicity. In 1889, the nature of women's dress might explain her inability to keep up with Ahmed Midhat or her wish not to go out some days.

What mattered to Ahmed Midhat was that he found in Madame Gül-nar a Turkophile, companion, and intellectual counterpart. He stressed how much more he learned from outings when she went along. At art museums, her knowledge was so valuable that he was all ears from head to toe, he wrote, clinging to her words as if they were his very life. All finery and diamonds at the reception where they met, she had not cared about such things or about how the other women were turned out; she had talked to him about intellectual matters. "Truly, it is a strange coincidence that two minds could be so compatible."[12] On their last night in Paris, Madame Gülnar presented to him her plan to translate literary works from Ottoman into Russian and from Russian into Ottoman, seeking his help. Despite fear that his own work would keep him from following through, he could not refuse; Ottomans and Russians were neighbors, he wrote, who, while both borrowing from Europe, had remained strangers. Moreover, women who attracted attention by their genuine, fine qualities achieved the honor (*şeref*) of belonging to "the most beautiful, refined, and sacred part of humanity."[13]

Madame Gülnar thus not only introduced into the narrative a third subject position between Self and Other, a role that the two Russian men helped play, she also became a prototype for the "new woman." Signs that Ahmed Midhat later grew disillusioned with her suggest that her usefulness as an embodiment of this image proved short-lived. However, the idea of the new woman was destined for great and lasting importance. Muslim Ottomans were still unaccustomed to women whose honor could be a şeref won by achievement as well as one dependent on chaste behavior (*iffet, ismet*). In Ahmed Midhat's narrative, Madame Gülnar becomes, in fact, a surprisingly early evocation of the desexualized, high-achiever image that entered mainstream nationalist discourse decades later to justify the movement of women into public life under the Turkish republic.

IF THE STOCKHOLM congress was a culturally multivalent event, where the official program could not control every visitor's experience, the Exposition Universelle of 1889 in Paris was more so. No one observer could take it all in; some facets could not even be mentioned in a work that had to pass Ottoman censorship. At one and the same time, this *Exposition tricolorée* celebrated the centennial of the French Revolution (Ahmed Midhat certainly could not mention that), it asserted France's reconsolidation under the Third Republic, it dramatized the European powers' dominance over their colonies, it displayed the latest advances in art and technology, it fostered internationalism by bringing together visitors and exhibitors from many countries, and it served as an amusement fair for 32 million visitors. The exhibition occupied a huge site, with a long tract running from the Trocadero to the far end of the Champ de Mars, a shorter tract consisting of the Esplanade des Invalides, and a narrow strip connecting these two along the Quai d'Orsay. The exhibition thus covered some of the most important open spaces of Paris with buildings and exhibits, mostly intended as temporary. The exhibition's structural highlights were the Eiffel Tower and the Palace of Machines, a futuristic structure of iron and glass. The grand plan, materializing a binarist orientalism, assigned the largest, finest spaces to display Europe's progress and the remaining spaces to show the rest of the world as bizarre and picturesque.

A purposeful observer, Ahmed Midhat still could not absorb everything. One would never know from him that Buffalo Bill's Wild West show was in town or that some exhibits of Asian cultures might move creative artists, such as Paul Gauguin and Claude Debussy, "to push their own . . . culture to one side to embrace another."[14] Ahmed Midhat took no interest in the re-creations of colonial villages. Showing no solidarity with colonial peoples, he was nearly as ready to laugh at them as were the Europeans. For him, this was not so much a world exhibition as a Social Darwinist yardstick for measuring Europe's progress and the Ottomans' standing compared to it.

What impressed Ahmed Midhat most positively was the Palace of Machines. In what would be called "the last great engineering experiment to appear at an exhibition,"[15] this structure had its roof supported by arches, each made of two curved iron girders, pivoted where they touched the floor and where they met each other, forming a record-breaking span of 110 meters. With a length of 420 meters, the building enclosed a vast space for the display of machines of all sizes, even locomotives. Electric generators provided power for the machines. Spectators could observe from "rolling bridges" mounted on overhead rails and powered by rotating shafts, which also distributed power from the generators to the machines by means of belts. Equipped with elevators and lit with both electricity and gas, the Palace of Machines epitomized advanced technology. The whole exhibition, in fact, was illuminated by both electricity and gas, including such novelties as electric lights built into the fountains to color the jets of water and the nocturnal spectacle of the Eiffel Tower lit from top to bottom while tricolored spotlights played over the city from its top.

At the Palace of Machines, what fascinated Ahmed Midhat was not the structure, although the rolling bridges were impressive, but the "miraculous" machines, especially small ones usable in Ottoman manufacturing. He focused on machines for working with silk and other fibers, for knitting, embroidering, sewing, shoemaking, printing, and performing household tasks. Characteristically expressing his economic outlook, he noted how a 1,000 franc tape machine could support a family. If only Istanbul craftsmen had been sent to Paris, what machines they could have bought to revitalize Ottoman industry.

IN THE PALACE of Machines as elsewhere, Ahmed Midhat's assessment of Europe's moral and material progress dominated his narrative. Evaluating the European Other in terms of moral versus material implied reflecting on the Ottoman-Islamic Self in the same terms, most likely with different values assigned to corresponding categories. In an Occidentalist narrative on Europe, could the idea of "moral progress" in fact prove meaningful? Ahmed Midhat's treatment of several themes helps to answer these questions.

Ahmed Midhat explained Europe's material progress in many fields, from the drains that kept streets free of mud to electric lights. Often, as in discussing railroads and printing presses, he evaluated how up-to-date the Ottomans were. Yet his focus remained on Europe. His assessment seemed to gel in Paris, when he returned from the Palace of Machines to tell Madame Gülnar that Europe's progress went beyond what he had realized and that the machines at the Palace were its greatest proof. Knowing his propensity to identify Europe with material progress and moral decay, she reminded him that he had earlier approved of the big buildings, boulevards, parks, and extraordinary orderliness. He admitted admiring Europe's general prosperity, but only the machines merited true envy.

On other occasions, he praised Europeans' observance of the law. Repeatedly, he praised the cleanliness and efficiency of European waiters and waitresses; in contrast, Istanbul had few eating places that would not disgust a person of taste. On the steamers plying the Bosporus, he added satirically, passengers seemed to think that the signs saying "Il est défendu de parler au capitaine" meant it was forbidden for the captain to talk, but anyone else might talk to him. Touring the Ringstrasse in Vienna, Ahmed Midhat felt stupefied, not just by the colossal buildings between the university and the art museum but by the whole conception of structure and space, all put in place within a few decades. But his greatest amazement came in Paris when, asking where he could buy the catalogue of the Bibliothèque Nationale, he learned that a commission had been working on it for thirty-five years but was still not through, and that it would eventually be published in many volumes. To identify all such elements as "material" progress was to stretch that category. Still, Ahmed Midhat cautioned that Ottomans must *not* emulate Europe's "moral progress." A further look at elements he placed under that label will amplify what he meant.

Having to negotiate nineteenth-century European expectations about dress and deportment, Ahmed Midhat confronted the intricacy of comparing Ottoman and European lifestyles in matters great and small, far more than would be the case today. He had to master the niceties of introductions and calling cards, the gradations in dress required for the congress, and the mores that not only allowed men and women to mingle freely but also required that he know how to play the cavalier. What could be stranger than for a white-bearded professor to kiss the hand of a young woman, rather than the other way round? In Stockholm, where some "oriental" delegates wore Western dress and others did not, Ahmed Midhat discovered that while those in Eastern dress were not expected to know how to behave, Easterners in Western dress would not be forgiven the least mistake. Madame Gülnar's coaching helped him, while reinforcing the point. When he went out in public with the Western-garbed Egyptians, they attracted little notice. But when they went out with the Islamic religious scholars (*ulema*), the sight of the latters' Islamic dress drew thousands of gawkers. At the congress, the European scholars "took fright" of the ulema but showed no reluctance to talk to Egyptians in Western dress.

Europeans also allowed things that Ahmed Midhat found outrageous. The police would intervene if they saw a man in the streets with his trousers unbuttoned but would allow prostitutes to throng the music halls, using foul language and throwing "paper bullets" at men to get their attention. Truly, decorum was one field in which Ottomans most needed a guidebook to Europe. Ahmed Midhat would soon devote a tome to this extensive study. Not all the advantages were on Europe's side, yet if European etiquette was a fit subject for a book, then was all Europe's "moral progress" really decline?

Questions of dress and deportment bring us back to the individual. The most complex issue in East-West comparisons was women's status, another question complicated by the intricacy of nineteenth-century norms. At the reception where Ahmed Midhat first met Madame Gülnar, for example, she told him straight off that she admired everything about Ottoman culture except veiling. Later that evening, the ballet reopened this question, and they both disapproved of the dancers' exposure. In an era when European women were normally almost as covered up as Muslim ones, what justified décolletage and skimpy ballet costumes? Ahmed Midhat had many moments of puzzlement. Upon arrival at Stockholm's Grand Hotel, his request for a bath and a haircut in his room was fulfilled by a woman hairdresser and a woman bath attendant, much to his discomfiture, although he found no fault in the masseuse's respect for the privacy that a Muslim man had to maintain. He commented that women's employment was widespread in Sweden, yet, because both men and women knew how to behave, no impropriety resulted. Thereafter, he encountered many women honorably employed and always commented positively. Did such revelations cause moments of cognitive dissonance for Ottoman readers? If so, they had the larger surprise of Madame Gülnar, the "new woman" who added the honor of accomplishment to that of virtuous behavior.

The greater shock was that of women who did not behave virtuously. Though hardly the kind of anti-Europeanist who depicted all European women as depraved, Ahmed Midhat was shocked by European nightlife, much to Madame Gülnar's amazement. He was horrified by the behavior of prostitutes. No Victorian hypocrisy or prudery, his reaction expresses the "communitarian puritanism" of the Muslim Ottoman reformer whose novels obsessively moralized about the evils of "super-Westernization." Among the many female images presented in his book, it is easy to see where the dancing girls and prostitutes fit into his evaluative scheme of material progress and moral decay. Where, however, did the positive images fit? Contradicting Ottoman norms and contrasting radically with the fallen women, the positively portrayed European women — above all, Madame Gülnar — stand out more than any other human figures in the narrative.

Ahmed Midhat's ideas about family and society provide a larger context for his view of women. Although he met many Europeans who impressed him positively, including entrepreneurs who gave him guided tours of their businesses, he identified European society largely with the pathologies accompanying industrialization. Here, the data correspond best to the picture of material progress and moral decay. He had a sociologist's eye for the atomized family and lonely individual in the modern metropolis. For him, real happiness meant living with one's family in one's own home. He and Madame Gülnar had been amazed to conclude that most dwellers in the fine Parisian buildings did not own their own housing. They agreed — wrongly, in her case, regarding Russia — that 90 percent of families in Istanbul, Moscow, and Petersburg were homeowners. That compensated for the humble aspect of those dwellings and proved that their owners enjoyed "moral prosperity," whereas Parisians had only "outward prosperity."

As for life inside Parisian dwellings, newspaper statistics showed that a third of births were illegitimate. Most families farmed out their children to wet nurses. Family relations, as depicted in "realist" novels, were terrible. Those born illegitimate were denied even the meager comforts of French family life. They grew up without religion. Even nationalism was undermined by partisan political division. Consider the man with no legitimate kin, no property, no faith, adhering politically not to his nation but to one of many political parties, and regarding the others with enmity. Such was the plight of one-third of the 2.5 million Parisians. In contrast, Ahmed Midhat preferred the *vie patriarcale* that his own household embodied.

Madame Gülnar reportedly found these arguments so convincing that though she had once thought Russia not a fit place to live, she began to appreciate its way of life, thanks to Ahmed Midhat. In drawing up his balance sheet of material progress and moral decay, what had consoled him most, he wrote, was that "still-backward peoples like us easterners" preserved a happiness that Europeans had lost. Ottomans must not emulate Europe's moral "progress"; that would deprive them of the spiritual values of their "ancient civilization and Islamic religiosity."[16] The pendant to the Europe of material progress and moral decay was an Ottoman world that was materially poor and backward but morally rich and uncorrupted — an Ottoman world that might, however, be enriched not just by modern machinery but also by some of the ideas and human qualities to be found among Europeans at their best.

AHMED MIDHAT'S JOURNEY was for him a trip from the Europe of his prior imaginings to the "real" Europe. While there, by looking for good in both European Other and Ottoman-Islamic Self, by extending his analysis beyond the topics privileged by Ottoman political thinkers, and by imaginatively introducing exogenous voices — including a female voice — into his narrative, he not only explored the material domain assigned to the Other, he also reflected on the moral or spiritual domain claimed for the Self, a realm essential for the creation of a modern Ottoman culture.

Ahmed Midhat's Occidentalism combined political conformism under an oppressive regime with social, economic, and cultural self-strengthening for Ottoman society. That sufficed to make him a conservative dissident from the political progressives' utopian visions of modernity. Those, however, were visions that could not even be published in Istanbul between about 1880 and the Young Turk revolution of 1908, a period during which the publication and circulation of new ideas nonetheless expanded rapidly. Ahmed Midhat's ideas would later be left behind in the backwash of the emergent, linear, national narrative, yet they are essential for understanding his period, and they have lasting value. The only major Ottoman thinker of the pre-1908 period who sought to achieve a balanced blend of East and West, matter and spirit, he as Occidentalist clearly showed how an Ottoman thinker could creatively engage with Europe and yet resist its cultural power, a power that, if omnipresent, was not omnipotent.

Notes

1. This abridgment introduces readers to the subject, while omitting the theoretical discussion and some of the themes developed in the original essay. Those who wish to use this study for research purposes will find it in their own interest to consult Carter Vaughn Findley, "An Ottoman Occidentalist in Europe: Ahmed Midhat Meets Madame Gülnar," *American Historical Review* 103, 1 (February 1998): 15–49. The theoretical works most basic to this study are Michel Foucault, *Archéologie du savoir* (Paris: Gallimard, 1969); Irvin C. Schick, *The Erotic Margin: Sexuality and Spatiality in Alteritist Discourse* (London: Verso, 1999); and Xiaomei Chen, *Occidentalism: A Theory of Counter-Discourse in Post-Mao China* (New York, 1995).
2. Timothy Mitchell, *Colonising Egypt* (Cambridge, 1988), 32, 149, 172–173; Zeynep Celik, *Displaying the Orient: Architecture of Islam at Nineteenth-Century World's Fairs* (Berkeley, 1992), 181.
3. Ahmed Midhat, *Avrupa'da bir Cevelan* ("Tour in Europe") (Istanbul, 1307/1889–90), 6a: *müsterik* (Orientalist), *müstarib* (here, Occidentalist). He used the term only once, to note the irony of his being sent to the Orientalist Congress; yet the term describes his career rather extensively. Orhan Okay, *Bati Medeniyeti Karsisinda Ahmed*

Midhat (Ahmed Midhat confronts Western civilization) (1975; reprint, Istanbul, 1991).

4. Fatma Muge Gocek, *Rise of the Bourgeoisie, Demise of Empire: Ottoman Westernization and Social Change* (New York, 1996), 3 and chaps. 2–3.

5. M. Sukru Hanioglu, *The Young Turks in Opposition* (New York, 1995), 7–10.

6. Partha Chatterjee, *The Nation and Its Fragments* (Princeton, 1993), 6; Prasenjit Duara, *Rescuing History from the Nation: Questioning Narratives of Modern China* (Chicago, 1995).

7. It was still early to expect a fully developed feminism among Ottoman writers, although the women's press dates as far back as 1868: Serpil Cakir, *Osmanli Kadin Hareketi* (The Ottoman women's movement) (Istanbul, 1994), 22–42; see also Beth Baron, *The Women's Awakening in Egypt: Culture, Society, and the Press* (New Haven, 1994), for similar but slightly later developments in Egypt. Although Ahmed Midhat's position on women had ambiguities, he was not the kind of Westernizer whose "feminism" mimicked European attacks on Islam; see Leila Ahmed, *Women and Gender in Islam: Historical Roots of a Modern Debate* (New Haven, 1992), 152–164, critique of Egypt's Qasim Amin.

8. Ahmed Midhat, *Avrupa'da bir Cevelan*, 131a, 473b, 484b, 508a, 598a, 889a.

9. The Turkish names for the two poles derive from the Italian *alla franca*, "Frankish" or European style, and *alla turca*, Turkish style. For example, in *alaturka* time, the day began at the apparent setting of the sun and the hours were counted in two cycles of twelve, ending with sunset at twelve o'clock the next day.

10. Ahmed Midhat, *Avrupa'da bir Cevelan*, 173a–174b. From the Persian word *gul* (pronounced *gül* in Turkish), meaning "rose" or "flower," *gülnar* means either the wild pomegranate or a deep red double rose. It is one of many women's personal names derived from the word gül, which has important symbolic associations in traditional poetic imagery.

11. Ibid., 443a, 545a, 546a, 687a, 726a–727b, 776a.

12. Ibid., 775a–783b.

13. Ibid.

14. Paul Greenhalgh, *Ephemeral Vistas: The Expositions Universelles, Great Exhibitions and World's Fairs, 1851–1939* (Manchester, 1988), 218–219; Schick, *Erotic Margin*, 115–116, 165–166.

15. Greenhalgh, *Ephemeral Vistas*, 155.

16. Ahmed Midhat, *Avrupa'da bir Cevelan*, 765b, 771b, 1005b.

Siobhan Lambert Hurley

Out of India: The Journeys of the

Begam of Bhopal, 1901–1930

A number of elite Muslim women around the Arab world threw off the burqa and exhibited their "emancipation" in a variety of ways, travel among them, in the twentieth century. Though privileged Muslim women had always had mobility, those who chose to travel received more attention as nationalist movements in places like India, and Egypt highlighted the freedoms "their" women enjoyed. Nawab Sultan Jahan Begam Saheba was a pioneer in this regard, not only because she undertook a variety of trips and tours for the purposes of social reform, but because she wrote extensively about them. Although it seems like a paradox, when the begam undertook such travel for religious, even Islamicist, reasons — initiating all manner of contact with Europeans and fellow Muslims along the way — in fact she demonstrated that Western and non-Western women shared an emergent tradition of transforming the public sphere into a place where ostensibly "private" activities like religious devotion might be seen, appreciated, and accepted. Her association and involvement with British Muslims also demonstrates how crucial traveling women were, and remain, for the creation of transnational communities and the diasporic imagination.

There is a well-known Arab saying that "travel leads to success." The benefits that the civilised countries of the world have enjoyed by means of travel are everywhere manifest at the present day. The principal causes which have determined the progress of civilisation resolve themselves into an exchange of ideas among the various branches of the human race and the increase of knowledge. — Nawab Sultan Jahan Begam of Bhopal, *The Story of a Pilgrimage to Hijaz*

Lhe above quotation was written by Nawab Sultan Jahan Begam Saheba, a social reformer and female Muslim ruler of the small Central Indian state of Bhopal, following her return from the Haj, the Muslim pilgrimage to Mecca, in 1904. Her first journey abroad, as well as her contact with the British in India, had convinced her of the importance of travel as a means to gain knowledge and effect progress. From her ascension to the throne in 1901 until her death in 1930, she remained a strong advocate of this position, touring extensively, not only in her own state and country, but also in many other areas. It was not until the late nineteenth and early twentieth centuries that the women of India and Britain began to participate in the European culture of travel, a construct that had been developed by upper-class British males at a much earlier date. For reasons of work, pilgrimage, study, politics, or simply cultural exchange, an increasingly significant number of women began making the journey between "home" and "abroad." The attitudes and behavior of Sultan Jahan Begam may seem to contrast sharply with the prevailing Western/Orientalist vision of Muslim women as silent and secluded, hidden behind veils and the thick walls of their husband's home. For this reason, it is necessary to begin by placing the begam of Bhopal in the context of the history of her state and other Muslim women of her era.

SULTAN JAHAN BEGAM was the last of four generations of queens who ruled Bhopal throughout the nineteenth and twentieth centuries. Despite numerous threats, the "nawab begams" were able to distinguish themselves as warriors, scholars, builders, and social reformers and assure the independence and prestige of their state under British paramountcy. The dynasty of women rulers officially began in 1819, when the ruling nawab died suddenly, leaving his widow, eighteen-year-old Qudsia Begam, to be invested with the supreme authority of Bhopal State. Appointed regent by the British political agent until her daughter, Sikandar, came of age and married, Qudsia emerged from behind the veil, hired a tutor to teach her the necessary skills of riding and the arts of war, then proceeded to introduce wide-ranging reforms, most notably waterworks. Sikandar Begam followed in this tradition, claiming the throne from her husband, who was renowned for his maladministration and excessive lifestyle. Though he had agreed to allow his wife to remain outside purdah (seclusion), he soon came to blows with her over her continued appearance in public, inflicting a vicious sword wound on her leg shortly before the birth of their only child, Shah Jahan Begam, in 1838. It was after this incident that the three generations of begams removed themselves to a nearby fort, where Sikandar pursued her favorite pastime of devising various methods to terrorize her husband, gracing his presence, not with a loving wife, but with gunfire, arrows, and cavalry charges.[1]

She also proved herself to be a highly competent ruler, distinguishing herself by her loyalty to the British during the Mutiny and also by large-scale administrative reforms.[2] As a result, the British withdrew their proviso that the husband of the begam would become nawab, naming Shah Jahan Begam as sovereign in her own right on the death of Sikandar in 1867. Though she did not display the managerial skills of her mother, she is remembered for her generous support and contributions to Muslim arts and culture, as well as her much criticized marriage to her personal secretary in 1871. This match had disastrous consequences, leading to the alienation of her grandmother and daughter, Sultan Jahan, and the reduction of her status to a figurehead sovereign when her husband persisted in rebellious involvement with anti-British forces.

Despite her long estrangement from her mother, Sultan Jahan succeeded her as ruler in July 1901, beginning a twenty-five-year reign as the last female sovereign of princely Bhopal. Her primary interests and accomplishments lay in the sphere of Muslim female education, which she promoted at every possible opportunity. Though she remained shrouded by a tent-like burqa (veil) until the last years of her life, she campaigned vigorously for schools for girls and women, which would teach basic academic subjects, domestic science, and religious instruction. Within her own state, an area of nearly 7,000 square miles containing around 700,000 people, she made concrete efforts to improve the lives of women by establishing and maintaining various educational institutions, a *zenana* (women's) hospital, a ladies' club, and ladies' prayer rooms in mosques. By 1907, Bhopal city boasted five state-sponsored girls' schools catering to the needs of elite Hindus and Muslims as well as widows, orphans, and other poor girls.[3]

As well as writing extensively on Muslim education, the role of women in Islam, and the history of her state, she was also an active public figure, repeatedly touring India to meet with British officials, give lectures to her coreligionists, and organize conferences and clubs for Muslim ladies. A thorough administrator, she also carried out significant domestic reforms, which included the systematization of land revenue collection, promotion of new farm methods and crafts, and the establishment of a legislative council. Though many of her policies, including her staunch support of the Muhammadan Anglo-Oriental College Aligarh, antagonized the British government, she was able to maintain friendly relations by offering advice on matters of importance to Muslims and loudly proclaiming her loyalty to the Crown. Following her abdication to her son, Hamidullah Khan, in 1926, the begam's activities for women's emancipation became increasingly radical. Before her death in 1930, she made bold pronouncements against child marriage and the male leadership of the women's movement, as well as emerging from behind the purdah.[4]

In the early years of the twentieth century, wives of prominent social and educational reformists began moving into the political sphere, agitating alongside their husbands for female education. While their struggle was initially fought through the print medium, primarily women's magazines, such as *Khatun* and *Tehzib un-Niswan*, women were increasingly seen as having a prominent role to play in emerging forms of organization and protest. Early in the century, when the Ali brothers and their religious preceptor, Maulana Abdul Bari, organized the Khilafat Movement and the Anjuman-e-Khuddam-e-Ka'aba, an organization for the defense of holy cities, "every man, woman, and child" was called into the political arena. As the central female figure in this movement, Bi Amman, mother of the Ali brothers, emerged as the first Muslim woman to play such an active role in national politics. Her example was followed by a troop of female activists who toured the country exhorting large crowds of women to donate their gold ornaments, support their husband's noncooperation efforts, and teach their children religious faith and patriotism.[5] This type of activity was analogous to that of Middle Eastern women who took part in the constitutional agitation in Iran and the revolution of Kemal Ataturk in Turkey.

Other Muslim women of this period, including Sultan Jahan Begam, met together in 1914 to found the All-India Muslim Ladies' Conference. Like concurrent efforts in the Middle East, it was an extremely elitist and rather ineffective organization geared to the furthering of educational reform. While it made a few bold statements on the lessening of purdah restrictions and the abolition of polygamy, its members, unlike their sisters in Egypt and Turkey, generally did not challenge the traditional roles of Muslim women, but rather continued such practices as wearing the veil, as it was a symbol of Muslim culture and their own high status.

Nevertheless, this activity by women is highly significant because it represents the first foray by elite women into the public sphere. By remaining within conventional norms and building on their religious and family duties, "ladies" were able to expand their role in society.[6] Many of these early activists joined with the younger generation and members of other religious groups in 1927 to establish the All-India Women's Conference, a more constructive organization over which the begam of Bhopal presided in 1928.

TRAVEL, AS IT was understood in the early twentieth century, normally referred to an educational process, that is, an activity with the purpose of observation and/or exchange of ideas. This was accepted by the begam of Bhopal, as is evident from the opening quotation, though she did attribute her inspiration to indigenous sources rather than Rousseauian Romanticism, as those in Europe did. The universalizing of this notion of travel has had a distortive effect on history in that it has concealed other forms of movement such as migration, indenture, and slavery, which were common among lower classes of Indians. As Rozina Visram documents in her important study, *Ayahs, Lascars and Princes*, Indians, primarily Muslims, have been in Britain in the capacity of servants, sailors, and laborers since the early eighteenth century.[7] However, it was not until the late nineteenth century that upper-class and high-caste Indians began overcoming religious and cultural taboos about travel and crossing the "black waters."[8] Native princes, in particular, began visiting Europe and Great Britain for both personal and political reasons around the turn of the century in sufficient numbers that their names were regularly noted in London society pages.[9]

For women in India, travel was traditionally undertaken for pilgrimage or to visit relatives; as women were not expected to receive formal education, travel for the purpose of learning was unknown. However, when men, particularly of the Bengali *bhadralok* (middle class), began traveling for secular reasons at the end of the nineteenth century, they were increasingly accompanied by their wives and children. While abroad, some of these women were also provided with educational opportunities.[10] By the turn of the century, Muslim women also began accompanying fathers and husbands on holidays or business trips out of India, providing the companionship expected from ladies in Western and reformed Indian society. Women such as Lady Imam Ali and Begam Shah

Nawaz even participated in political organizations abroad, including the Indian Ladies' Committee and the Muslim League.[11] However, few Muslim women traveled with the express purpose of receiving formal instruction. Reports mention only occasional cases of single girls receiving scholarships to study in England; Begam Shahnawaz, for example, mentions the pioneering case of Mahmooda Begam, a girl from the Central Provinces.[12]

Despite these examples, the numbers of Muslim women who traveled outside of India cannot be considered significant, since their names are well-known, being relatives of prominent politicians, and limited enough to be easily counted. Thus, Sultan Jahan Begam is a somewhat unique figure. Furthermore, though she did not travel alone, being accompanied by her sons, their families, and numerous state officials, she was, if not the only, one of few women of her faith in her time who traveled out of her own conviction. Exceptional Muslim women had, however, ventured out of India before the twentieth century, primarily for religious reasons. Unlike the Hindus, who censured all overseas travel, the Muslim community in India had long accepted voyages for the purpose of Haj and trade, as is evident from the narratives of Ibn Battuta and Alberuni. Such notions of travel enabled Gulbadan, aunt of the Mughal emperor Akbar, to leave India as early as 1575 on a seven-year pilgrimage to Hijaz. Similarly, the second ruling begam of Bhopal, Sikandar, went on Haj in 1863 and was the first Indian ruler, male or female, to successfully complete Haj. She subsequently wrote an account of her journey, entitled *A Pilgrimage to Mecca*.[13] Forty years later, her granddaughter followed in her footsteps, making a five-and-a-half-month journey to the Muslim holy land.

Though the begam's decision to travel to Hijaz was undoubtedly due to a heartfelt desire to complete the Haj, it was a practical choice of destinations for her first excursion out of India, for it could clearly be justified on the grounds of local religious custom; according to the Qur'an, the Haj is one of the principal articles of the Islamic faith, along with the proclamation of the creed, fasting, and charity, and must be completed by every Muslim once in his or her lifetime, if it can be afforded. Due to the prevalence of fatal illnesses, armed bandits, tribal wars, corrupt officials, and transportation mishaps, the expedition to Arabia was extremely perilous during the reign of the begam, and there was a fear that she might not return. However, by flaunting her loyalty and service to the British overlord, she was able to elicit Britain's help in arranging transportation, a medical escort, and a military guard for her traveling party of over three hundred people. She also used her close connections with the imperial power to convince the Turkish government to give her the protection of the sultan and a respectable reception, suggesting that her kind treatment could "cement" friendly relations between the two powers.[14] This careful maneuvering of the influential political forces enabled Sultan Jahan to guarantee that her journey was safe, comfortable, and dignified.

This journey is significant in that it represents her first major contact with what may be seen as a denomination foreign to the Indian subcontinent: orthodox Arabian Islam. Though Sultan Jahan Begam had proved herself to be a steadfast Sunni Muslim before going on Haj from 1903 to 1904, it appears that she was still influenced by the religious ideas that she encountered in Hijaz. Having been raised in the heterogeneous Indian environment, she had regularly encountered members of other Indian(ized) faiths before her initial excursion abroad, shown herself to be open to discussion on religious issues, and even taken part in the festivals of other communities. While she maintained a policy of toleration of non-Muslims after her return from pilgrimage, it seems that the begam increasingly modeled her religious practice on scriptural, rather than customary, Islam and showed only spasmodic interest in other faiths. This growing orthodoxy is reflected in the writings of her contemporaries, who described her in sketches as "extremely pious" and "the most devout of Muslims."[15]

The explicit nature of this change was documented by Louisa Walker, a Quaker missionary who spent many years in Bhopal and had close relations with the ruling family. She wrote to friends in England in 1921 that, initially, the begam of Bhopal was "very friendly" with missionaries, making repeated inquiries about the Gospels and their means of worship, until they felt she was "almost persuaded." After her visit to Mecca, however, she became "a much more ardent follower of the Prophet" and "much more zealous in her own religion."[16] Though the begam continued to permit the institutional work and limited proselytizing activities of the missionaries, she apparently became increasingly suspicious of their religion and defensive about Islam. When the deputation of the Friends' Foreign Mission Association to India came to pay their respects in 1909, they noted that the begam insisted on "[quoting] the Koran as helping her in her life every time any part of the Bible was touched upon.

It seemed as though she looked upon our visit as possibly having an ulterior motive."[17] This attitude was maintained throughout most of her reign. Nevertheless, while discussing prayer with her close friend, Katherine Taylor, in 1928, she betrayed a hint of sympathy for the foreign religion, admitting, "I cannot address Allah as Father as I know you can, it must be very comforting."[18]

Miss Walker also noted in her letters home that the begam's attitudes were again altered by her travels in England and Europe in 1911. This second trip abroad, ostensibly to attend the coronation of the king-emperor and queen-empress, George V and Mary, and to take her son for heart treatment at a health spa, was a more exceptional, though safer journey for a Muslim queen. Joining the various other Indian princes who were "summering" in London, the begam of Bhopal became actively involved in the social life, waiting on the new royals and friends from India, as well as visiting tourist spots, such as the Festival of Empire and Mme. Tussaud's Exhibition.[19] Her attention was also drawn to the neglected mosque at Woking, Surrey, which had been founded in 1889 by the Hungarian orientalist Dr. Leitner to serve the local Muslim population. Built and maintained through the patronage of the begam's mother, Shah Jahan, after whom it was named, it thrived until the death of Dr. Leitner in 1899, at which time it was virtually abandoned. It was as a result of this connection that Sultan Jahan was brought into contact with another form of her religion, that of Ahmadiyya Muslims (a renowned proselytizing sect; heretofore, Ahmadis).

The begam sought to resuscitate the old mosque and its surrounding Muslim community on her return to India by calling on Khwaja Kamaluddin, a member of the Ahmadis, to emigrate to England in 1912 and form a mission at Woking. Her choice of missionary is somewhat surprising, because the Ahmadis were usually shunned by orthodox Muslims for their controversial beliefs; though they claimed to be Muslims, they maintained that Muhammad was not the last Prophet, instead following a Punjabi oracle, Mirza Ghulam Ahmad. Nevertheless, the begam was the primary benefactor of the Woking Muslim Mission until her death. As well as providing financial backing for mission activities, she also wrote extensively, primarily on gender relations in Islam, for Kamaluddin's paper, *Islamic Review*, as both sought a modernist interpretation of the relevant Qur'anic passages and advocated female education.[20] There is almost no mention of the Ahmadi beliefs that would cause dispute.

After the death of her two eldest sons and nearly two and a half decades of rule, the begam of Bhopal again traveled to England, this time to challenge the law of primogeniture, which dictated that her eldest grandson would inherit the throne before her youngest and only surviving son, Hamidullah Khan. Unable to convince the government in Delhi of her claim, she left India for the final time in September 1925 to put her plea before the king-emperor in London. After visiting the begam at her British residence later in autumn, a long-time acquaintance, Lady Glover, commented on her tired condition at this time: "She was suffering much from rheumatism, and was in a very anxious state of mind; she felt no longer able to carry on the very arduous work of governing the State of Bhopal, and was prepared to abdicate."[21] After receiving a positive response from the British government in March 1926, she returned to India in May and placed the rule of her state in the hands of a male for the first time in over a century.

During this trip, the begam's association with the British Ahmadiyya Muslim community at Woking was unequivocally confirmed, even though the Ahmadi *khalifah* (spiritual leader) in India had recently discouraged missionaries from maintaining connections with "ordinary" Muslims. The legitimacy of her succession claim was promoted by Khwaja Kamaluddin and her movements documented in *Islamic Review*. She also made two visits to the mosque at Woking, during which she met Kamaluddin and prominent British converts such as Lord Headley and Khalid Sheldrake. After participating in Friday prayers, she received gifts from the British Muslim Society and congratulated them for their efforts to correct the misrepresentation of Islam in "the West," especially with regard to women's status.[22] She also laid the foundation stone for an extension to the building and donated additional funds for the publication of Kamaluddin's book on the Prophet Muhammad, which was dedicated to her son and successor. Though Sultan Jahan's continued contact and support of the Ahmadis in Britain, a somewhat aberrant group of Muslims, may lead one to question her professed orthodoxy, it seems more appropriate to interpret it as typical of the reaction of "foreigners" in a strange land; as studies of the modern diaspora have disclosed, Indians, as well as other ethnic groups, in the West tend to "club together," regardless of communal or sectarian identities that would divide them at "home."[23]

There were instances, however, when the begam's devotion to foreign powers or principles seemed to overshadow her strict acceptance of Islamic doctrines. The most notable case involved her connection with the sultan of Turkey. On her return journey to India in the autumn of 1911, the begam called on the sultan in Constantinople, renewing ties that had been made during her 1903 visit to Hijaz and ingratiating herself with locals with charitable donations. Nevertheless, when the Ottoman Empire, which included the Muslim holy land, joined the Central Powers in World War I, Sultan Jahan abandoned her religious brethren in favor of the British, donating recruits, artillery, food, and money to the Allied war effort and exhorting Indian Muslims to do their duty to the empire rather than the faltering caliph in Turkey. She justified this stand on the basis of Islam, arguing that Muslims had a duty, according to the Qur'an, to support a government that offered "perfect justice" and never interfered with religion. Furthermore, she stated that the caliph was under the influence of a small group of Turks, who were "in the pay of Germany" and had "never done anything for Islam."[24] Similarly, she defended her support of the Ahmadis on the grounds of "Islamic tolerance."[25] Such pronouncements suggest that, while her attitudes to certain religious questions were affected by travel and contact with non-Indians, her identity as an orthodox Muslim essentially remained unchanged.

BEFORE HER FIRST expedition to England, Sultan Jahan Begam had always shown, not only the greatest respect for the British visitors to her state, but also a distinct admiration for the education, poise, and accomplishments of their female companions. However, after observing these foreign ladies, as well as their lower-class kinswomen, in their own environment, the Muslim queen seemed to experience a change of heart such that she no longer hankered after advancement for Indian women as had been achieved in the West. She was notably impressed by the extent of female education and the training of children, practices that led, in her opinion, to the creation of "polite, free-thinking, patriotic, civilized, high-minded and sympathizing" citizens.[26] But the lack of purdah observance severely challenged her admiration of European culture. It is worth quoting at length her speech to the Ladies' Club upon her return, late in 1911, to illustrate this point:

> In spite of their education I am not in favour of the freedom enjoyed by women of the West where it has passed certain well-defined lines. . . . It is possible that the liberty enjoyed by the women of Europe

is suited to the conditions prevailing there — , or that it is permitted by the teachings of the Christian Faith, but for Indian, and especially Muslim ladies, I think such freedom can, under no circumstances, and at no time, be proper. . . . Musalman women should never hanker after greater freedom than has been granted them by their religion; a freedom, which, while permitting them the fullest enjoyments of their rights, also shields them against all manner of evil.[27]

She encouraged Indian Muslim "ladies" to be selective in their approach to European customs, acting on the Arab saying, "Pick up what is good and leave away what is evil." She begged them not to follow the example of Turkish ladies, who had adopted from their European neighbors not only an interest in education but also the "evil" of unlimited freedom, abandoning Islamic injunctions and "tarnishing" their honor.[28] Similar sentiments are present in the travel writings of other Indian women, such as Parvati Athavale, a Hindu widow, who traveled to the United States in 1918. She claimed that "good points" about the West were "cleanliness, neatness, home teaching [and] dignity," while "bad points" included "love" marriages and employment of women outside of the home.[29] The distinction these women make between "good" and "evil" in European culture echoes the wider discourse on modernity in colonial India, though it is conceptualized in a manner quite different from that of Indian men.

As can be seen, the begam of Bhopal's first trip to Europe caused her to experience another renewal of her faith in Islam, this time relating to the status of women in the religion. Shocked by, as she saw it, the lack of propriety displayed by many English women and the resulting disrespect of their male counterparts, she began to show a new regard in her writings for the chivalrous treatment of women by the Prophet and the protection guaranteed to honorable daughters, wives, and mothers in the Qur'an. Feeling that Islam had been misrepresented in the West, she sought to defend the seemingly repressive practices of her religion to her "Western sisters" by explaining their history and continued importance to women in the contemporary age in a work entitled *Muslim Home. Part I: Present to the Married Couple.* She states this purpose lucidly in the introduction: "Like many other things of Islam the Occident has given a very wrong and, I may say, false notion of the Qur'anic teachings as to the position of woman in Islam. . . . I, however, intend to do something to the enlightenment of my sisters in the West on this subject and write [this] book."[30] Particularly, she sought to justify the institution of purdah, which she rigidly maintained, even while attending the coronation and subsequent banquet in London. This was done in another tract addressed to both European women and Indian reformers, *Al-Hijab or Why Purdah Is Necessary*, which included quotations from the Islamic tradition and Western sources. She chastised supporters of the movement against purdah for aping European manners and customs without thorough consideration of the consequences, arguing that not all customs of the civilized nations were respectable and not all of the so-called savages were barbaric. While she admitted that colonial power was "superior to us [i.e., Indians] in wealth and culture, knowledge and justice and many other noble virtues and good qualities," she stated that the free intercourse of the sexes and nonobservance of purdah was a "blot on the escutcheon of Western civilisation."[31] This was obvious from reading stories in European and American magazines, which told of the degraded moral character of their societies resulting from the increased public role of women. She quoted one writer who succinctly put it, "Take up the newspapers and see the records of divorces, social scandals, and marital woes that fill us with shame and disgust and then tell me that these . . . laws and customs are good things."[32]

The begam of Bhopal was renowned, both at home and abroad, for her bold statements on women's issues, yet her negative reaction to the freedom of the Western women she observed during her 1911 voyage suggests that her Muslim sensibilities overshadowed her efforts for female emancipation. Though her approach to the Qur'an was certainly innovative for her time, her commitment to certain accepted interpretations effectively curtailed her program for Muslim women by limiting it to nominal reform within the boundaries of the Islamic tradition. Women were recognized as equal to men on a religious and moral plane, but required to accept a separate and subservient role in social, political, and economic spheres. By remaining in the home and accepting the authority of her husband, a woman could guarantee that she was not only shielded from assaults to her honor, but also content, because, as Sultan Jahan stated in the conclusion to *Al-Hijab*, a woman gains more pleasure from caring for her family than anything else.[33] She should never hope for liberty like that displayed by the women of Europe, as it only brings misery, frustration, and moral degradation. Such faith in the superiority of one's own culture is far more reminiscent of the attitudes of British women (and men) in India than those of other Muslim social reformers who had traveled to Britain, such as Sayyid Ahmad Khan, who was overcome by the "superiority" of Western civilization during his visit to England in 1869.

DURING HER SECOND sojourn in England, the begam again attended many public functions, including receptions at the India Office and Buckingham Palace, ceremonies at the Cenotaph at Whitehall, and meetings of the Northbrook Society and the National Indian Association.[34] However, she also found time to visit many museums and schools with her daughter-in-law, Maimuna Sultan, and her three granddaughters, such as the Royal School of Art Needlework, which had special relevance to women. She also made practical efforts to help the women of Bhopal by learning skills that she felt would be useful to them, including basket weaving, leather work, and the making of pillow lace. On a personal level, she made a greater effort to become acquainted with Western women and their culture; whereas formal interviews had characterized social interaction during her first visit, friendly gatherings and spontaneous activities were the norm in 1925. Her granddaughter reports that Sultan Jahan Begam regularly socialized with wives of former Indian officials, as well as a motley assortment of other women, holding soirees, often in her bedroom, taking lessons in the harp and violin, and even attending the cinema.

Perhaps most illustrative of her changing attitude to the West, however, was her increasingly liberal attitude to contact between her female dependents and European society. Maimuna Sultan noted in her account of their first journey to Europe that, though she had traveled to Marseille, Paris, London, and other cities, she had seen little more than the inside of hotels. Her powerful mother-in-law would not permit her to sightsee or attend social functions, even in a curtained vehicle or burqa, for fear that she would have her purdah broken by a photographer or absorb "objectionable" foreign ideas. Similarly, she had not permitted Maimuna Sultan, her granddaughters, or other female wards to see Western books, novels, magazines, or films while in Bhopal. Yet, soon after their arrival in London in 1925, Sultan Jahan Begam realized that she could not keep her young charges from the "modern world."[35] English men and women were hired to teach the girls wood carving, pewter work, goldsmithing, leather work, chinese lacquer, music, cookery, and many other skills. The

Bhopali girls became friendly with their teachers and servants, accompanying them around London by bus, Underground, and bicycle to amusement parks, cinemas, theaters, and shops. Their activities, including official outings with the begam, were all photographed freely and reported on in local newspapers, especially the tabloids, which were fascinated by the veiled queen and her lively companions.

Maimuna Sultan's three daughters were also enrolled as Girl Guides and involved in charitable events in London. Particularly, they were required to collect money for war veterans on Poppy Day,[36] an activity that suggests the begam of Bhopal's growing penchant to blend East and West. The girls were sent on to the streets with cans of red flowers but wearing, to their embarrassment, an augmented uniform: Sultan Jahan considered the highland kilts and long socks that were the uniform of the poppy sellers to be "un-Islamic" as they left bare the knees, and, therefore, ordered the girls to also wear *pyjamas* (tight trousers) and a head covering (the girls later adopted a more indigenous uniform, consisting of a khaki-colored *kurta*, pyjamas, and a *dupatta* [shawl] tucked into the belt). The press was delighted with this show of cross-cultural mixing, as is evident from articles in major newspapers. Princess Abida Sultaan, the eldest of the begam's granddaughters, noted, in retrospect, that her grandmother's bid to provide her and her sisters with a combination of Islamic and European education, clothing, and influences was actually an attempt to develop them into living symbols of her ideas of reform: "It was her fervent desire [that] she should provide a girl, a woman, that was an ideal, a mixture between the West and the East, balanced."[37] Ideas such as these, which had developed, or at least matured, during her final journey abroad, also had a definite effect on Sultan Jahan Begam's activities with the women of India upon her return; from 1926 until her death in 1930, her efforts became, not only more numerous, a factor that is not surprising considering her retirement, but also far more progressive.

Though the begam of Bhopal had worked extensively throughout her reign for the emancipation of women, particularly through education, the attention that she had been able to give to this issue had often been restricted by her duties as the autocratic ruler of a large territory. This state of affairs had been exacerbated in the 1920s when personal problems, such as the illnesses and subsequent deaths of her two elder sons, placed even greater pressures on her time. Following her return from Europe and abdication from the throne, she rejoiced in having the opportunity to revitalize her earlier endeavors, many of which had fallen into disarray without her leadership, and to provide personal direction to certain new projects, both in Bhopal and elsewhere in India; as she told members of the Ladies' Club in 1926, "I now intend to freely devote my whole energy to the service of my sex and devotion to God." But, as she stressed to the ladies present, these efforts were also expected to be of a new type: "Bhopal is now entering a new regime, and similarly the scope of your work should enter upon a new phase."[38]

The begam of Bhopal's own reactions to the habits and cultures that she encountered during her trips abroad were subtle and complex, often defying systematized analysis. It is, nevertheless, apparent that travel had an effect on the construction and development of her identity as a Muslim, a woman, and an Indian, as well as altering her perception of the "other." Although her pilgrimage to Mecca confirmed her religious identity as an orthodox Sunni Muslim, making her more suspicious of other creeds, she continued to have confidence in European models of women's emancipation, constructing British women as an ideal. Her first trip to Europe in 1911 led to a renewal of her faith in the morals and social system of Islam, whether propagated by the Muslim establishment or heretical groups like the Ahmadis. Though she remained impressed by the educational system, she reacted negatively to the freedom of women in the West, generally considering their behavior to be indecorous and unrefined. Her final journey abroad in 1925–1926 appears to have led to a mellowing of her views, as she sought to find a happy medium between East and West. She became more personally involved with British women and their society, allowing both herself and her female relatives to be open to new ways and ideas. This development is most clearly exemplified by the remarkable modification of her position on the value of purdah.

Though she was not a wholly unique figure among Muslim women in the early twentieth century, Sultan Jahan Begam of Bhopal can be distinguished from many of her contemporaries in India and the Islamic world by the dauntless spirit that led her to travel at her own volition to Hijaz, Britain, and Europe. The begam's behavior throughout these journeys accents the importance for women of her period of building on socially accepted norms, rather than attacking patriarchy directly. By remaining within the bounds of female respectability and emphasizing her religious devotion, the begam of Bhopal was able to successfully influence Muslim public opinion and incrementally improve the position of women in her state. Unfortunately, she was not so adept at charming British officials: when her succession case was finally resolved in 1926, the secretary of state for India remarked, "I should imagine the old lady is in her seventh heaven. . . . I hope she will spend what remains of it in her own country!"[39]

Notes

1. Princess Abida Sultaan of Bhopal, unpublished manuscript on the history of Bhopal state (1980).

2. Nawab Shah Jahan Begam of Bhopal, *The Taj-ul-Tarikh Bhopal or The History of Bhopal*, trans. H. C. Barstow (Calcutta: Thacker and Spink, 1876), 58–59.

3. For more information, see Nawab Sultan Jahan Begam of Bhopal, *An Account of My Life*, vol. 1, trans. C. H. Payne (London, 1910), vol. 2 (Bombay: The Times Press, 1922), vol. 3 (Bombay; The Times Press, 1927).

4. Nawab Sultan Jahan Begam of Bhopal, speech of Her Highness the Begam-Mother of Bhopal, in *The Second All-India Women's Conference on Educational Reform* (Mangalore: Kanara Printing Works, 1928), 26–27.

5. Gail Minault, "Purdah Politics: The Role of Muslim Women in Indian Nationalism, 1911–1924," in *Separate Worlds*, ed. Gail Minault and Hanna Papanek (Delhi: Chanakya Publications, 1982), 245–259.

6. Shaikh Muhammad, ed., *Ripon ijlas-i Ali India Muslim Ladies' Conference avul Muncaqidah ba-maqam-i 'Aligarh ba-mah-yi March 1914* (Report of the Ise session of the All-India Muslim Ladies Conference held at Aligarh in March 1914) (Aligarh, 1915).

7. Rozina Visram, *Ayahs, Lascars and Princes* (London: Pluto Press, 1986).

8. *Editors' note*: high-caste Hindus were not permitted to cross the sea, which would defile their caste status, with all manner of social and spiritual consequences.

9. "Visiting Indian Chiefs," *The Times*, 7 June 1911, 7a.

10. Inderpal Grewal, *Home and Harem: Nation, Gender, Empire, and the Cultures of Travel* (London: Leceister University Press, 1996), 162–178.

11. India Office Records, 26 July 1924, File L/1/2/6, British Library, London.

12. Jahan Ara Shahnawaz, *Father and Daughter* (Lahore: Nigarishat, 1971).

13. Sikandar Begam of Bhopal, *A Pilgrimage to Mecca* (London: William H. Allen, 1870).

14. Nawab Sultan Jahan Begam of Bhopal, *The Story of a Pilgrimage to Hijaz* (Calcutta: Thacker and Spink, 1909), 241.

15. Lt. Col. John Arthur V. Bolam, *The Life and Times of the 4th Battalion 16th Punjab Regiment* (photocopy of manuscript, 1988), 89.

16. Louisa Walker to H. T. Silcock, 5 February 1921, Records of the Friends' Service Council, File FSC/IN/3, Friends' House, Euston, London.

17. Diary of William Wilson, 10 February 1909, Records of the Friends' Service Council, File FSC/IN/1.

18. Journal letter No. 4 of S. K. Taylor, 11 November 1928, Records of the Friends' Service Council, File FSC/IN/4.

19. "Court Circular" column of *The Times* (London), 8 May to 15 July 1911.

20. Nawab Sultan Jahan Begam of Bhopal, "Relative Position of Men and Women in Islam," *Islamic Review* 4 (1916): 300–305.

21. Lady Glover, *Famous Women Rulers of India and the East* (New Delhi: Deep and Deep Publications, 1989), 97.

22. "Begam . . . of Bhopal at Woking," *Woking News and Mail*, 16 October 1925, 2.

23. Philip Lewis, *Islamic Britain* (London: I. B. Tauris, 1994).

24. Foreign Department, Intl., October 1916, Nos. 13–34, National Archives, New Delhi.

25. Princess Abida Sultaan of Bhopal, personal communication, 29 October 1995.

26. Nawab Sultan Jahan Begam of Bhopal, *A Brief ? Report of the Princess of Wales Ladies' Club, Bhopal* (Calcutta: Thacker and Spink, 1922), 157.

27. Nawab Sultan Jahan Begam of Bhopal, *Al-Hijab or Why Purdah Is Necessary* (Calcutta: Thacker and Spink, 1922), 46.

28. Bhopal, *A Brief ? Report*, 159–160.

29. Grewal, *Home and Harem*, 227–229.

30. Nawab Sultan Jahan Begam of Bhopal, *Muslim Home. Part 1. Present to the Married Couple* (Calcutta: Thacker and Spink, 1916), i.

31. Bhopal, *At-Hijab*, 131.

32. Ibid., 148.

33. Ibid., 180.

34. *Editors' note*: these were two groups where Indians and Britons interested in Indian "social problems" met in London.

35. Princess Abida Sultaan, unpublished manuscript, 201–216.

36. *Editors' note*: a holiday commemorating the English soldiers who died in World War I.

37. Princess Abida Sultaan of Bhopal, personal communication, 20 October 1996.

38. Quoted in Muhammad Amin Zuberi, *Asr-i-Jadid* (The new epoch) (Bombay: The Times of India Press, 1929), 33–34.

39. John Lord, *The Maharajahs* (London: Hutchinson, 1972), 99.

Joseph S. Alter

Celibacy, Sexuality, and
Nationalism in North India

*Bodily reform has been a common concern of anticolonial movements and na-
tionalist ideologues. In many contexts, these discourses have dwelt on the "modernization" of the national body through the application of European regimens
of hygiene, medicine, and science; in South Asia the Hindu concept of* brahmacharya *(celibacy) has occupied a central position in nationalist thought both
during and after the struggle for independence. This essay examines the science
of celibacy in India and the place of these techniques in a gendered discourse of
nationalism that drew on an idealized vision of the masculine restraint articulated in Hindu tradition from the great epics through to the writings of Gandhi
and more recent "self-help manuals" targeted at young men.*

It is well-known that Mahatma Gandhi felt that sexuality and desire
were intimately connected to social life and politics, and that self-
control translated directly into power of various kinds, both public
and private. Gandhi's enigmatic genius and his popular appeal among
India's masses may be attributed, at least in part, to the degree he was able
to embody a powerful ideal of sexual self-control that linked his socio-
political projects to pervasive Hindu notions of renunciation. Affecting
the persona of a world-renouncer, Gandhi was able to mix political, religious, and moral power, thus translating personal self-control into radical social criticism and nationalist goals. Gandhi's mass appeal was partly
effected on a visceral level at which many Hindu men were able to fully
appreciate the logic of celibacy as a means to psychological security, self-
improvement, and national reform. Although my concern in this essay is

not directly with Gandhi's notion of self-control, it is against the larger backdrop of his political legacy that I situate this discussion of sexuality, gender, and nationalism in contemporary India.

My specific purpose is to analyze the Hindu concept of *brahmacharya* (celibacy) as it relates to questions of gender and politics. I will show that a male concern with celibacy is couched in terms of a discourse about truth, and that truth translates directly into the moral politics of nationalism. At the outset, I must point out that the nationalism that emerges out of this discourse is of an oblique and somewhat utopian sort. In other words, it is not formalized or institutionalized in any sense, but takes shape culturally, I would argue, on two primary levels, that of rhetoric on the one hand, and the body on the other. Rhetoric and the body come together in terms of health, for the celibate body is regarded as supremely fit, and as such evokes a divine and heroic mystique of epic proportions. What emerges is a kind of medical poetics in which the male body is sexually analyzed, systematically diagnosed, and, finally, as rhetoric and theory are put into practice, disciplined according to a rigorous regimen. This regimen is thought to produce a citizen who embodies the essence of national integrity and strength.

MANY SCHOLARS HAVE noted that brahmacharya is a concept with social, psychological, medical, and religious significance in Hindu society, and there can be no doubt that semen retention is a theme with powerful resonance in the psyche of many Hindu men who feel that sex is enervating. The basic theory of celibacy has been analyzed and explained in various ways by many authors; my concern is primarily with the technical aspect of the *brahmachari*'s regimen, and with what the logic of those techniques implies. Aside from Gandhi's own writings, there is very little on the mechanics — the science — of being and becoming celibate.

The modern concept of brahmacharya clearly derives from the classical life cycle prescriptions of *dharma*. The fourfold *ashrama* cycle of life stages, of which brahmacharya (initiated studentship) is the first, when understood in conjunction with the "four ends of man" — *dharma, artha, kama,* and *moksha* — clearly articulates an encompassing code of moral, civic, ritual, political, and economic conduct.[1] The status of the initiated student defines one specific phase in the larger structure of society and the "structured" integration of the individual into that society. Specifically, it marks the second birth of Brahman, Kshatriya, and Vaishya boys and sets them on a path of disciplined Vedic learning.[2] In this regard, brahma-charya may be seen as a crucial phase in the articulation of difference within society insofar as the ritual of initiation defines the particular trajectory of the various *Varna* categories and who has what rights and duties within those categories.

Most of the rules of conduct for the brahmachari concern his religious status vis-à-vis his guru and the ritual protocol of his community. It is clearly within the ritualized contexts defined by *The Sacred Laws of the Aryas, Bhagavad Gita,* and the *Ashvalayana Grihya-Sutra* that the bhrahmachari's vow of chastity must be understood. For the initiated twice-born student, chastity in particular and self-control in general were requisite for learning the Vedas, because sex was regarded as both defiling and distracting. In this regard, chastity was a practical pedagogical principle and not a general rule of moral conduct prescribed for all Hindus. Nor was the ritual vow of chastity — as distinct from the modern concept of nationalistic celibacy — medicalized in any sense; the initiated student did not, it seems, practice celibacy as a form of personalized public health. It was simply part of his religious training.

Despite the very narrow, ritualized meaning of celibacy in the classical life cycle scheme of the twice-born, one is able to discern a nascent political agenda in Vedic and post-Vedic discourse on sexuality. In the life cycle of the twice-born male, there was most certainly a time and place for sex. However, the Vedas and other classic texts sought to regulate the nature of who, what, where, and how one might engage in sex (compare with *Kama Sutra*), but not sex itself as a monolithic construct that defined the moral conduct of some equally monolithic Hindu citizen. Social, political, aesthetic, and economic distinctions were all important when reckoning the moral propriety or appropriateness of sex, whereas universal standards were virtually meaningless: what was good for one was by no means good for all, particularly when it came to abstinence. In this regard, the classical authors seemed to see sex as one behavioral facet among many others to be regulated in the interest of maintaining the social hierarchy. The world-renouncer who abstained from sex completely was able to act as a social critic precisely by virtue of his position outside of this hierarchy. Thus, asexuality functioned as a form of sociopolitical power while deriving its authority from the renouncer's mystical, "other-worldly" spirituality. It was this connection between sex, spirituality, and social criticism that Gandhi was able to translate so effectively into his program of militant nonviolence. Although I think the Vedic and post-Vedic perspective on sex is radically different from the modern discourse on sex and nationalism that emerged in the twentieth century — since the classical renouncer, unlike Gandhi and his modern heirs, did not advocate that everyone become like him in order to reform society — it is important to keep in mind that the "laws of dharma" were incipiently political. It is easy, therefore, for modern Hindu advocates of reform to recast the narrow rules of "ancient sex" in terms of social criticism and a more encompassing, nationalistic vision of moral propriety.

Like his classical forebear, the modern brahmachari is, first and foremost, celibate, but to maintain absolute control over his sexual desire his discipline mandates that he must control all of his senses by means of a rigid and carefully regimented program of diet, exercise, and rest. Moreover, control of the senses entails careful management of a wide array of daily activities, including what and how to read, where and how to sleep, and what to wear, among many other things. In other words, brahmacharya is a way of life that is focused on sexuality but includes a much broader spectrum of activities and concerns.

In contemporary North India, a genre of popular/technical literature on brahmacharya is published by large, mainstream establishments as well as by smaller, regional presses. Booklets, pamphlets, and "medical" manuals advocate celibacy, explain its merits, and provide precise instructions on how to control desire and stay healthy. These publications also, and perhaps primarily, offer home remedy treatments to cure specific ailments that threaten to undermine self-control. In virtually all of this literature, the concept of brahmacharya is systematically opposed to Indian modernity. Although it is only logical that this literature should have proliferated in the decades of rapid change and increasing literacy after independence, my argument is that brahmacharya developed as a strategic concept opposed to Westernization. More specifically, it was developed as the moral/physical alternative to various forms of postcolonial desire, both gross and subtle, that were thought to directly afflict the body and undermine its strength and integrity. The forces of postcolonial desire are manifold, and mostly defined by way of contrast to the pristine, natural, and nonerotic environment of "traditional" India. As one critic writes:

> Because the youth of today are destroying their semen they are courting the worst disaster and are daily being condemned to hell. . . .

Mother nature stands, stick in hand, watching their abominable behavior, and for every drop of semen spilled she lashes out and strikes their vital organs. . . .

These days it is common to see the deep wounds of her stick on young people's backs. How many of these unfortunate people lie shaking on their cots like the grievously ill? Some are suffering from the heat. And others, carrying the same deep wounds, pretentiously puff out their chests and walk about piously exchanging garlands while nervously checking their pulse for any sign of illness. There is no trust of God in their hearts, only lust. Now tell me, what future do such people have? . . . They only glow with the light of fireflies, and neither humility nor glory are found in their flickering hypocrisy.[3]

The literature on brahmacharya is directed specifically, but not exclusively, at teenage boys and young men in college, who would be the primary consumers of films, "pornography," and the other effete products of modernity. Books on celibacy are often sold at school bookstores along with classroom texts and other educational literature. Although their precise circulation is unknown, the extent to which young men are familiar with the principles and practice of celibacy indicates that the literature is widely read. Among wrestlers, who constitute a broad class and caste spectrum of society, the practice of brahmacharya is highly developed and provides a clear example of how the discourse on celibacy finds popular, public expression. In many North Indian villages and cities, wrestling is a popular sport that attracts tens of thousands of spectators who are exposed to a dramatic display of how semen retention can enhance the character, strength, and skill of otherwise ordinary men. The wrestling *akhara* (public gymnasium) provides a social environment in which the ideas expressed in the popular literature on celibacy are both confirmed by practice and disseminated among village and neighborhood communities of men. The public gymnasium thus provides a context within which the critique of postcolonial desire finds popular expression. Thereby, a "moral" form of popular culture is pitted against the popular hedonism of modernity.

Numerous scholars have noted that sexual lust and desire are regarded as volatile, dangerous, and chaotic by many in South Asia. Even so, it is not primarily on moral grounds that public sexuality is decried. While one may discern a tone of approbation and indignation in the tracts on brahmacharya, where many authors use words such as "filthy," "dirty," "evil," and "sinful" to describe so-called reprobate sexuality, their concern, ultimately, is with substance and not with the behavioral components of virtue and vice. Celibacy is more of a hydraulic and biochemical problem—an issue of fluid balance and flow that has a powerful moral effect on the individual's overall health—but it is not moral in a puritanical or prudish sense simply by virtue of being intrinsically opposed to sex and sexuality. Thus, a person is good or bad not only because of what he does, but because what he does, sexually speaking, fundamentally changes the biochemical nature of his being. In these terms, moral reform is not so much an issue of "building character" as it is an exercise in building the body in terms of a theory about moral substance. Consequently, there seems to be an inverse correlation between the extent to which brahmacharya is subjected to a microscopic and comprehensive analysis, and the magnitude of those forces that threaten to undermine celibacy. Confronted with the overpowering chaos of transcultural sensuality—Star TV and MTV to name but two of the most recent forces[4]—those who advocate brahmacharya as a strategic form of defensive health do so by way of a scientific discourse designed, at least in part, to combat the nonsense of sexual stimulation with the logical sense of medical knowledge about sex and desire.

RATHER THAN CELEBRATE Independence and the achievements of modern India, those who write about celibacy often point out that postcolonial India is enslaved by its "freedom" to develop and Westernize—enslaved not so much to sex itself, although certainly that, as to the idea that power is a function of potency, and virility the coefficient of modernization. In other words, these authors are adamantly opposed to the institutionalized sex of prostitution and concupiscence, but they are more strongly opposed to a Victorian theory of sexuality that underwrote the vast industry of prostitution and attitude of covert concupiscence in colonial India, a theory whose legacy they regard as a form of neocolonial domination. They would most likely agree with Lawrence Birken's general analysis of modern Western sexuality as a "consuming desire" and with the notion that sexualization and the idiosyncratic nature of desire is a function of radical "neoclassical" individualism.[5]

Those who champion the cause of brahmacharya target for particular criticism the gross manifestations of sex. However, the larger issue they address is the nature of modern sexuality in India and the impact of colonial domination on male identity. As they see it, the basic problem is hydraulic. Modern life, in general, and a discourse preoccupied with intercourse and erotic stimulation both figuratively and literally cause semen to flow and then structure identity in terms of that flow. In the context of postcolonialism, where sex is measured in terms of the gratification it gives, power is defined in relation to the flow and expenditure of semen. You are who you are in terms of the sex you have. For example, one might look, to adapt the rhetoric of the brahmachari, at the way popular film heroes and villains are portrayed; at the accusations leveled against corrupt, licentious policemen; at the proliferation of sex manuals; and, perhaps most alarmingly, at the rate of population growth and all it signifies in the ways men are trying to define themselves and assert their position in society. In other words, everywhere one looks there are more or less horrific signs of men trying to build themselves up by the very means that will ultimately bring them down, quite literally, by drying up their liquid assets.

The celibate, on the other hand, is defined by the sex he does not have and by the semen that he does not allow to flow. However, there is a more fundamental distinction between the brahmachari's conception of sex and that of the postcolonial "libertines" whom he criticizes. For the brahmachari, it is not sex as an act that defines identity, nor is power conceived of in terms of one's sexual prowess — quite the opposite: identity and power are inherent in semen and not in those situations in which semen is made to flow. What this means is that gender gets defined in two radically different ways by the brahmachari and his libertine counterpart. For the postcolonial libertine, masculinity is an ideology of domination, self-gratification, and the control of others, an ideology almost pathologically individualistic in the priority it places on the egocentric self in relation to others. For the brahmachari, on the other hand, gender identity derives from a regimen of self-control, balance, and integration of the self with natural truth. It is, in part, the sheer abomination of contemporary masculinity, the utter waste of vital fluids, that has made celibacy a persuasive form of embodied opposition to the legacy of colonial sexuality.

IN HIS TREATISE on night emission and celibacy, Kaviraj Jagannath Shastri writes:

Today the disease of night emission is widespread. It not only afflicts the young and unmarried, but also those who are married and old. Wherever you look you will see that about 85 percent of the population suffers from this disease. But the greatest sorrow is in the fact that it is these same people who man the rudder of this dear country of ours; who must shoulder the heavy burden of protecting India; who must steer the nation into the future; who provide the standard upon which all else rests; and who are the heart and soul of our society. These students, children, and youth are worn down and left virtually defeated by the battle this evil power wages against them.[6]

Shastri and many others feel that India's vital potential is being wasted on a scale that only those who believe in the phenomenal power of a single drop of semen can truly appreciate. As Shastri concludes, the loss of semen means the total demise of "the nation, the present era, prevailing circumstances, the environment, the natural order of things, and the social order of caste and religion." Although the magnitude of the problem here imagined is noteworthy, it is the nature of the problem that has particular relevance. Shastri and others believe fundamentally that the body is the site of national reform, that nationalism must be embodied to have effect. On the other hand, the nationalism of "pure ideology" is "like the paper tiger, and the loud rhetoric of false prophets." As Shivananda, a leading advocate of bodily reform, writes: "Without reforming the body one will never achieve a state of freedom and satisfaction nor will one ever be successful. There is nothing — no substance or person — who give satisfaction and peace to one whose body is unhealthy. You alone can make yourself free and blissfully happy. In other words, physical reform must be our primary goal, for it is the basis for all of man's other four aims, and essential for our salvation and independence."[7]

As a tangible, corporeal whole, the body is regarded as more fundamental and natural than are ideas and concepts; it is incontrovertible, and therefore moral in a biological rather than an ideological way. As the body is made the site of nationalism, and brahmacharya its agency of reform, the individual is held responsible for embodying such things as freedom, glory, peace, and happiness, as well as more typically physical attributes such as strength and good health. The regimen of celibacy is clearly meant to turn sick men into progressive citizens who could, single-handedly, reform the nation.

Although the nationalism invoked through this kind of rhetoric is embodied on an individual level, where citizenship is constructed as a kind of psychosomatic attribute, there are some important ways the body has an impact on social institutions. As noted above, those who advocate celibacy are critical of postcolonial sexuality in general, but they are adamantly opposed to "legitimate" sexuality as it is practiced within the family. In their view, the family is not a place where one may freely indulge in sex. In fact, it is precisely the notion that one may freely have sex with one's wife as often as one likes — "every hour of every night," as Shivananda sarcastically quips — that makes the family a dangerous and potentially destructive institution, a kind of sanctioned den of iniquity where the veneer of public morality, to say nothing of social status and prestige, hides the truth of a more insidious demise. One's legal rights as a spouse in no way change the biomorality of semen flow.[8] On the other hand, one can certainly be married and remain "celibate" as long as one engages in sex only for procreation. The argument presented for this case is drawn from animals and the natural environment, where relationships are balanced, rather than from the world of modern society, which is corrupt. Men are admonished to draw their genitals up like horses and bulls, thus limiting sex to the act of intercourse while remaining otherwise passively unsexed. Unlike the late-nineteenth-century discourse on "spiritual" nationalism wherein the family was constructed as pure, impervious, and outside the purview of politics, the discourse on brahmacharya not only makes the family a focal site of national reform, but directly criticizes the basic sexual premise on which the family itself is founded.

Although institutionalized sex within the family is generally regarded as itself dangerous precisely because it appears to be "legitimate," brahmacharis reserve their harshest criticism for the practice of child marriage. The logic of this position is not hard to grasp. Youth in general are thought to be easily seduced by the pleasure of sex and particularly apt to take advantage of the sexual license that early marriage provides. To put children in a situation where they can easily satisfy their erotic appetite clearly undermines every principle of self-control and all potential for self-development. Shivananda writes: "In this country we even undermine the potential of our children. Before teaching them how to swim, parents tie the lead weight of a young wife around their sons' necks and then push them out mercilessly into the ocean of life. How can a country in which this kind of thing goes on advance!?"[9]

The nation of which the reformist celibate speaks is both a figment of his utopian imagination, a world where every man is strong, hard working, happy, and free, and a world where the natural order of things—clean air, pure food, cool water, and fresh air—prefigures, and to some extent supersedes the social order. In general, modern social life, which from most perspectives would be the central constituent category of a reformist ideology, is in this case both preempted and subverted. In part, this is because postcolonial modernity is regarded as irredeemably debauched but, in an important sense, Hindu epistemology also makes it difficult to separate out social facts from biological or natural ones. This brings us back to the question of truth and its relationship to the nation and body.

Mahatma Gandhi's autobiography appears in translation as *The Story of My Experiments with Truth* (1927). Although it is an account of his early political and social life, the autobiography is intensely personal and, as Sudhir Kakar has noted, characterized by extreme "candor and honesty."[10] Gandhi was preoccupied with issues of social and political justice and felt that truth was the only means by which justice could be achieved. For Gandhi, however, truth was far from self-evident; one had to experiment in various ways to both realize its nature and subscribe to its tenets. Although he was concerned to some extent with abstract metaphysics, most striking about Gandhi's experiments is their utterly banal character, Gandhi's own virtual obsession with seemingly mundane, utilitarian issues of diet, health, and, above all else, the control of sexual passion. Although Gandhi's own theory of celibacy was derived in more or less equal parts from Christian and Hindu doctrines, the regimens he developed were extreme and highly idiosyncratic. However, it is clear that Gandhi, in keeping with classical Hindu teaching, believed in the power of semen, that there was an intimate connection between the elusive nature of truth and the seductive power of sexuality: to conquer the latter was to realize the former.

Although Gandhi believed in the power of celibacy and was keenly aware of what Kakar refers to as the "metaphysical physiology" of semen, it would seem that for him truth was a somewhat mystical function of the regimen he devised rather than the actual, biomoral substance itself: a problem of overcoming the body in order to realize truth through enlightenment rather than embodying truth as semen itself.[11] At times, Gandhi seems to write as though it is the semen itself that matters, but more often it is what the spillage or waste of semen represents in terms of his personal failure to put mind over matter. For Gandhi, celibacy was a physical and personal means to a sociopolitical, and ultimately spiritual, end.

Unlike Gandhi, whose enigmatic genius was in part the function of his vital suspension between the world of Christian and that of Hindu ethics, contemporary advocates of brahmacharya provide a much more tangible and one-dimensional version of what constitutes truth, and the connection between that truth and national reform. For celibacy is not the means to an end; it is an end in itself, a way to engender nationalism by cultivating the seeds of truth.

Notes

1. *Editors' note*: *dharma*, duty or obligation; *artha*, material gain; *kama*, pleasure; *moksha*, release or salvation from *samsara*, the cycle of birth and rebirth.
2. *Editors' note*: *Brahman*, ritual experts or priests; *Kshatriya*, warriors and rulers; *Vaishya*, merchants. These terms refer to the three highest caste groupings in the classical fourfold varna model of caste. Unlike the fourth varna group (the *Shudra*, agriculturalists), these three groups are all *dvija* (twice-born).
3. Swami Shivananda, *Brahmarharya Hi Jiwan Hai* (Celibacy itself is life) (Allahabad: Adhunik Prakashan Graha, 1984). Unless otherwise noted, all translations are Joseph S. Alter's.
4. Star TV is a relatively new addition to the regular programming on Indian national television. Based in Hong Kong, the Star Network broadcasts foreign films, music videos, and various other forms of popular entertainment throughout India and Southeast Asia. The broadcast of Music Television via this network is particularly noteworthy because it exposes the Indian populace to a form of high-tech, transnational popular culture that is sexually explicit.
5. Lawrence Birken, *Consuming Desire: Sexual Science and the Emergence of a Culture of Abundance, 1871–1914* (Ithaca, N.Y.: Cornell University Press, 1988), 35. See also Louis Dumont, *Essays on Individualism: Modern Ideology in Anthropological Perspective* (Chicago: University of Chicago Press, 1986) for the basis of this kind of individualism.
6. Kaviraj Jagannath Shastri, *Bramacharya Sadhana: Virya Raksha hi Swasthya ka Sar hai* (The means by which to maintain celibacy: Semen protection is the way to health) (Delhi: Dehati Pustak Bhandar, n.d.), 171.
7. Shivananda, *Brahmarharya*, 29.
8. Ibid., 51–52.
9. Ibid., 596.
10. Sudhir Kakar, *Tales of Love, Sex and Danger* (London: Unwin Hyman, 1987), 85.
11. Ibid., 119.

Shoshana Keller

Women's Liberation and Islam in
Soviet Uzbekistan, 1926–1941

The veiled and secluded Muslim woman has functioned as one of the key images used by European empires, missionaries, and reformers to justify colonialism, missionary work, and development projects in the Middle East. In Soviet Central Asia, the Russian state attempted to secure its authority through an aggressive campaign against local Muslim practices, particularly those relating to women (veiling, bride price, and seclusion). In effect, the Soviet campaign for the "liberation of women" became a crucial tool for the secularizing and modernizing drives of the communist state, projects that took on greater importance in Muslim-dominated lands far from the center of Russian imperial power. This essay examines this campaign, the responses from Muslim institutions and leaders in the region, and the invidious position that Uzbeki Muslim women were placed in as they became the key battleground in a struggle for cultural authority between the mullas and the state.

No Soviet initiative caused as much violent upheaval in Uzbek society as the campaign for *raskreposhchenie zhenshchin* (the liberation of women). This was an enormous effort, of which there were two major components. The first began as an administrative assault (*hujum*) on Islamic tradition in 1927–1929 and continued at a less intensive level thereafter, attempting to free women from Muslim social and religious strictures. This encompassed not only unveiling women, but destroying traditional practices of arranged marriage, bride price, the marriage of young girls to adult men, the seclusion of women from public life, polygyny, and other customs. The second component, beginning in

1929–1930, moved large numbers of women into the workforce, primarily on collective farms and in textile and food-processing factories.

The Soviet government used the women's liberation campaign as one of its primary weapons against Islam as a whole, never passing up a chance to declare that Islam must be eliminated because it oppressed women. They also used the campaign as an effective tool to divide the clergy and to pit family members against one another. Although the Soviets achieved significant changes in women's status, particularly among the educated classes, in the end they failed to stamp out any of the traditional practices against which they had campaigned so diligently.

THE ORGANIZATIONS PRIMARILY responsible for carrying out the Soviet women's liberation campaign were the Central Asian Bureau of the Central Committee of the All-Union Communist Party (bolshevik) (Sredazburo TSK VKP[b]) and its Women's Section (Zhenotdel), the Zhenotdel of the TSK VKP(b) itself, the Zhenotdel of the Communist Party of Uzbekistan (KP[b]UZ), the Uzbek Commissariats of Justice and Health, the agitation and propaganda departments of all of the above organs, and the Union of Militant Godless. The Communist Party and state apparatus of Uzbekistan nominally governed the republic but took instructions from Sredazburo, which in turn was subordinate to the Central Committee in Moscow.[1]

Efforts to introduce the new Bolshevik laws on women and the family into Central Asia began early, when a marriage registry office (ZAGS) was set up in Turkestan in November 1919.[2] Party activists organized chapters of the Zhenotdel in the people's republics of Bukhara and Khiva in 1923 and 1924 and founded women's clubs in Ferghana the following year.[3] The Presidium of the Central Executive Committee of the Soviet Union issued a broad statement in February 1925 affirming the "rights of women of the Soviet East" to freedom from all forms of traditional and religious oppression and to full participation in social and political life.[4] At the same time, such propaganda journals as *Bezbozhnik u stanka* (The godless at the workbench) and the *Uzbek Kommunist* began running articles on Muslim women's liberation that emphasized the cruelty of Islamic "fanaticism" and the foolish superstition of mullas.[5] In the face of powerful contradictory forces, however, these early attempts to promote liberation were tentative. The Central Committee of the Communist Party of Turkmenistan discussed outlawing polygyny in 1925, only to decide that they had to work out party policy very carefully in light of "the principle of the necessity of allowing polygyny among national communists, in the first place among responsible workers."[6] In other words, popular support for polygyny was too strong, and the party too weak, for the practice to be eliminated by decree.

Soviet attempts to launch a women's liberation movement were haphazard at best until 1926, when Sredazburo and the all-union Zhenotdel began planning for a campaign to unveil women. On 19 May 1926, Sredazburo's Zhenotdel director, Serafima T. Liubimova, presented a report to the Executive Political Bureau "on party work concerning the liberation of women in Central Asia," in which she outlined the necessity of the task and urged party organizations to begin serious work on educating women and bringing them into the government apparatus and labor force. Liubimova declared that Muslim women's traditional lives were no longer compatible with the world around them: "The way of life [*byt*] which has been preserved until now is women's slavery [*qälim* (bride price), polygyny, seclusion, the giving of underage girls (in marriage)] etc., that is in contradiction to economics and hampers the movement among broad masses of women toward economic independence."[7]

The key to ending such economic and personal misery was to destroy the religious beliefs and customs that kept women in slavery. Liubimova gave several specific examples of how Islam oppressed women and men economically. The practice of sex segregation discriminated against female laborers who wished to work as maids; Islamic law barred women from such work unless they were close relatives of their employers. Marriage in early adolescence and "mutilating birth practices" (*kalechenie rozheni[ts]*)[8] led to such high mortality rates among women that, Liubimova claimed, the Central Asian population ratio stood at an average of 880 women to every 1,000 men. The practices of bride price and polygyny thus placed an undue burden on poor men and perpetuated class-based oppression.[9]

Liubimova's comments reflected the long-standing Bolshevik insistence that women be freed from household duties to find liberation via employment. She considered even domestic service to be superior to leisured seclusion. In 1926, the Soviet government had not yet begun to recruit Central Asian women into the workforce on a large scale, and Liubimova's thinking was based on Western assumptions that did not take into account Uzbek equations of seclusion with wealth, status, and virtuous modesty. This lack of awareness of deep cultural differences was an important factor in the disastrous course the liberation campaign was to take. Liubimova was rather vague on how Islamic practices were to be eliminated, but she did state that it was important for the Uzbek and Turkmen republics to accept the "family-marriage codex and legislation on the illegality of social [*bytovye*] crimes" into their law codes. The law was one of the most important and effective tools used in the campaign, because terms in prison and labor camps could be used to force people to change their behavior. Accordingly, in 1926–1927, Uzbekistan added several articles pertaining to social crimes to its criminal code, penalizing various forms of sexual intercourse with minors, the payment of bride price, male homosexual sex, and forcing women to marry against their will.[10]

The task of implementing and enforcing these laws fell to the Uzbek Commissariat of Justice. The agency began by using the new secular court system to give Muslim women more legal autonomy than they had enjoyed previously under Islamic law. Soviet law gave women the right to demand divorce under easier terms than did Islamic law, and women were much more likely to obtain a divorce in the secular Soviet courts than in the religious Islamic ones. To further guarantee female access to divorce through the secular courts, the commissariat issued a circular in 1926 that forbade religious courts from hearing any divorce cases.[11] In March 1927, the commissariat also issued a general call to form a "united front in the offensive against survivals of the old way of life for the liberation of women," no doubt in connection with the launching of the unveiling campaigns.[12]

However, Zhenotdel workers found that giving Muslim women legal recourse was only part of the battle. Workers who monitored the secular courts to determine whether they were giving women fair hearings reported cases where women who had been assaulted by their husband or male relatives either perjured themselves in court or refused to testify at all against their assailants.[13] For Uzbek women, the act of bringing Uzbek men to Soviet courts additionally opened them to accusations of disloyalty to Islam, to the family, or both. Many women pressed ahead with their charges, but a significant number of them halted prosecution rather than cut themselves off from family and community. Zhenotdel workers also pointed out that the manifest incompetence and indifference of many Soviet courts barred women from trying to prosecute their attackers.[14]

The People's Commissariat of Health played a role in attacking social customs by emphasizing the unhealthiness of veils, early sexual intercourse, and fasting for Ramadan. In April 1929, the Commissariat's Special Commission for the Protection of Mothers and Youth produced a set of guidelines to aid doctors in deciding whether or not a girl was sexually mature. The guidelines stated that the average age for the onset of menses in Uzbek girls was fifteen and a half, and therefore the legal age of marriage should be set minimally at age seventeen, preferably at eighteen and a half. They also listed a series of minimal body measurements (height, weight, etc.) that a girl had to reach in order to be designated "sexually mature." A short while later, the Commissariats of Health and Justice sent a memorandum to Uzbek Komsomol (Communist Youth League) cells on enforcing the guidelines by 15 July 1929. The memorandum shows evidence that a compromise between Russian and Uzbek standards had been reached, because it listed the legal age of marriage as sixteen years. Throughout Uzbekistan, the Soviet government set up hospitals and makeshift clinics to enforce the standards of sexual maturity, and ZAGS was to register for marriage only those young women who had been officially certified mature.[15]

THE PUBLIC FACE of the Soviet women's liberation campaign was not the law codes but the massive propaganda storm launched in Uzbekistan in spring 1927. Sredazburo, the Central Committee of the Communist Party of Uzbekistan, and the Uzbek commissariats all had their own agitation and propaganda sections which devoted much, if not most, of their money and energy on propaganda aimed at women. The Union of Militant Godless strongly emphasized the issue at the all-union and republic levels; the Uzbek Godless journal *Khudasizlär*, published from 1928 to 1931, regularly ran articles on Islamic oppression of women. The head of the all-union godless organizational section, Feodor N. Oleshchuk, urged using women's economic cooperatives in "the East" as a means of taking women away from the influences of their husband and clergy and as good places for conducting intensive antireligious propaganda.[16]

Liubimova and her deputies organized large public demonstrations against the veil, where women tore off and burned their veils in public, read political poetry, viewed plays and movies, and listened to lectures. The hujum, as the assault campaign against the veil was called, officially began on 8 March 1927, International Women's Day. Zhenotdel leaders and other activists addressed the crowds with inspirational speeches and recitations of liberation poetry. They fiercely condemned the old Muslim order and lauded communism as the path to women's freedom. The demonstrations reached their climax when groups of veiled women mounted central stages, dramatically tore off their veils, and threw them into prepared bonfires. According to Massell, these brilliant stagings inspired thousands of women to burn their veils on the spot, then pour through the streets of the old cities yelling revolutionary slogans.[17]

These demonstrations must have been both electrifying and terrifying for all concerned. Many Muslims were offended and angry, their values regarding sexuality and the social order publicly mocked and turned upside-down. The unveiling demonstrations, in conjunction with other aspects of the liberation campaign, touched off a firestorm of violence against women that did not die down for several years and that cost thousands, perhaps tens of thousands, of lives.

No reliable statistical reports summarizing the overall scope of the violence exist. The Soviet secret police (OGPU) produced a report on the rise of "terror in the village" between 1926 and 1928, which stated that the number of political murders had almost doubled during that time but with the important caveat that their agents had not made a systematic catalogue of "terrorist acts," and therefore the data provided were "subject to a certain amount of inexactness and incompleteness." The OGPU's incomplete statistics for eleven months of 1928 recorded 100 cases of "political terror" and 104 cases of assault and murder connected with women's liberation. In the majority of cases, women were victimized by their own or their husband's families.[18]

The Uzbek Supreme Court reported that most homicides of women were due to either jealousy or the liberation campaign. From January 1927 to January 1928, the court investigated seventy-one cases involving sexual or social crimes and convicted 127 people.[19] For 1928 and 1929, the Uzbek Commissariat of Justice estimated that customary crimes made up 7 percent of all crimes in the court system.[20] They did not count the number of victims. The Tashkent Okrug (district) court reported thirty-eight cases connected with women's liberation for 1928, thirteen of them murder.[21] In June 1929 Emelian Iaroslavskii, head of the all-union Union of Militant Godless, estimated that around two hundred women had been murdered for unveiling, some of them hanged by bands of *basmachi* (Central Asian anti-Soviet guerrilla fighters).[22] Ten years later, an article in the journal *Antireligioznik* estimated that 270 Uzbek women had been murdered in 1928 for unveiling.[23]

The deputy chair of the Tashkent Okrug court commented on the indifference of local courts to social crimes: "Concerning social crimes, only one case has come before the [local] court. This demonstrates that, despite the rise of social crime in the okrug and the necessity of resolute struggle against this evil, our regional people's courts have not succeeded in proving themselves in this respect by taking those measures which would ensure that the social crimes which are springing up reach their chambers."[24] Often, when a case was tried in court, the defendant was acquitted or given a lenient sentence. The Khojent Okrug court saw three cases connected to the women's campaign between April and July 1927. The court sentenced one man to two years' imprisonment for forcing a woman into marriage, meted out six years for another man's unspecified crime, and acquitted four of five defendants in the case of a woman's murder (the death sentence of the fifth was immediately appealed).[25] In one unusual case dating from 1932, a Russian chemist employed by the State Planning Commission (Gosplan) was convicted of "buying underage girls for his pleasure." The Uzbek Supreme Court sentenced him to one year and six months in jail, but pardoned him almost immediately because Gosplan could not replace him and lobbied the court on his behalf.[26]

One possible factor behind lenient court judgments was the decision by the USSR Commissariat of Justice not to classify acts against women's liberation as counterrevolutionary crimes. This meant that officials did not refer such crimes to the Uzbek SSR prosecutor's office, but dealt with them locally, granting them lower priority than other cases of anti-Soviet agitation.[27] A more important reason for the courts' leniency was that the judges themselves did not regard these offenses as particularly serious, despite the intensive pro-liberation propaganda going on around them.

On 25 July 1928, perhaps in response to complaints about the courts, the Central Executive Committee of Soviets (TSIK Sovetov) passed a resolution instructing the Commissariat of Justice to create circles of women prosecutors in the okrug-level courts that would systematically apply the 1926 Marriage and Family Code and monitor the Soviet courts to ensure that they were "paying the maximum amount of attention" to exposing social crimes. TSIK Sovetov also instructed the commissariat to work out a more complete program of laws pertaining to the 1926 code.[28]

However, these measures to protect women's interests did little to improve the situation.

At the spring 1929 Uzbek Congress of Soviets, a delegate complained bitterly of the poor performance of the courts regarding customary crimes. He said that not only was bride price flourishing in his area, but that courts were unable to prosecute the crime effectively because no legal guidelines on what penalties to apply existed. Even more seriously, lack of knowledge of legal procedures had resulted in a man going unpunished for beating his wife to death for attending an International Women's Day demonstration.[29] Another delegate at the same congress urged that murderers and bandits should be executed at much higher rates than they had been previously because many death sentences were ultimately commuted to ten years' imprisonment.[30] There was more to this rise in bloodthirst than just the Soviet women's liberation campaign. It was also part of the wrenching upheavals of the First Five-Year Plan and developing Stalinist terror. At the same time, there was a very real problem with trying to stop the wholesale murder of women. Despite many attempts at court reform, the violence had become so acute that it attracted attention from the highest levels of Soviet Central Asian government. Shortly after the Congress of Soviets, Sredazburo head Isaac A. Zelenskii urged that a special law be passed to protect unveiled women, illustrating his argument with grim stories of murder and assault in the Chimkent region that were related to unveiling.[31]

In February 1929, the newspaper *Uzbekistanskaia pravda* lamented: "The murder of women has taken on a mass character. As of February 6, 70 people have been murdered. Social crimes are also taking place: qälim, giving girls in marriage, violence, rape of minors, etc."[32] In its own version of observing Women's Day, the newspaper ran stories illustrating the murderous oppression women suffered under Islam. In late March came "For the Glory of Allah," about a blind young peasant woman named Akhros, who was gang-raped as punishment for not being married to the man with whom she lived. This story was followed a few days later by "The Mulla's Vengeance," about two brothers who murdered Mariam Bikaia Rakhmonkulova, the wife of one of them, when she tried to apply for a divorce through ZAGS. One brother was executed, the other sentenced to ten years in jail. The article expressed horror that local village people had done nothing to either prevent the crime or turn the brothers over for punishment. State officials arrested the brothers more than four months after the fact.[33] While these and similar stories had an obvious propaganda value through the illustration of the misogynistic violence of Muslim men, they were also probably true. By 1929, the violence had reached a point where Communist Party officials felt compelled to call off the "assault" for women's liberation and pursue their goals by more subtle means. This did not change the fact that traditional Uzbek society was under siege and that women who asserted their desires against tradition continued to put themselves at considerable risk.

Not only judges, but other officials ignored or tried to undermine regulations concerning women. Faizulla Abdullaev, a twenty-four-year-old member of the presidium of a Bukhara Okrug political committee, was convicted in 1929 of instructing the local ZAGS to approve illegal marriages (probably of underage girls). In addition, he apparently "publicly insulted" a female cooperative employee by firing a revolver at her.[34] In another case, the deputy chair of the Uzbek TSIK went so far as to praise a group of men for killing an unveiled woman. He was immediately fired, but the attitude he expressed was common.[35] In 1930, the Soviet court convicted a young policeman of marrying a twelve-year-old girl and gave him an unusually heavy sentence of five years' imprisonment on the grounds that his job was to fight against such crimes.[36] The chair of the Katta Kurgan village soviet was convicted in 1933 of helping marry off a girl by providing a false certification of her age and of supplying "alien elements" with other falsified documents.[37]

The myriad difficulties that senior Soviet officials faced in trying to coax or force their subordinates into implementing the liberation campaign were the product of a deep ambivalence, which sometimes spilled over into open resistance, at all levels of the Uzbek party and state bureaucracies. Even dedicated communists had a great deal of trouble adjusting to the revolution in social mores. A transcript of a 1927 party cell discussion of unveiling demonstrated that communists in the Old City of Tashkent were much more comfortable talking about unveiling women in principle than seeing their wives go unveiled. The women themselves refused to walk unveiled in the Old City because of the harassment they experienced.[38] Party members who did not unveil their families or divorce their second wives continued to pose problems even after the liberation campaign was well established. Some commentators found the issue of polygyny particularly troublesome because it revealed Central Asian priorities and the ineffectiveness of Soviet propaganda. All-union Zhenotdel chair A. V. Artiukhina complained: "In the East it often happens that a husband, taking advantage of the still strong influence of the Shari'a, gives his wife a formal divorce via ZAGS and marries another. However, according to the Shari'a he is not divorced from the first wife and continues to live with her. She cannot marry anyone else — no one will take her. Men say [to her]: 'Obtain a divorce according to the Shari'a, and then we will marry you.'"[39] Artiukhina perhaps was not aware that polygyny was not yet illegal in some parts of "the East." Even Central Asian members of the Union of Militant Godless, who had theoretically shed the chains of religious prejudice, could not bring themselves to meet in mixed-gender groups in the first years of the campaign. Instead, the women would gather in one room of a house while the men shouted to them from another room.[40] It was simply not possible for centuries of values and assumptions to be overthrown by decree within the space of a few years.

While eliminating such social crimes as bride price and child marriage was a high priority for the government, published sources rarely referred to the precise details of these crimes. The Amnesty Commission rolls, however, provide a window into this area and include some fascinating details on individual lives not available elsewhere. The amount of bride price varied over time and according to the wealth of the family involved, as did the punishment it incurred. Shady Kurganov, described as a "middle peasant," received a horse, a cow, and a lame bull as bride price for his daughter in 1929.[41] In 1931, a male peasant was paid 50 rubles for bride price.[42] Another received 5,000 rubles in 1934.[43] The same year, a man in Beshkent received one cow for his twelve-year-old daughter.[44] And in an extreme case in 1936, a man sold his adult daughter to five different suitors within two years. Gul-Oi Kushmuratova's starting price was 3,000 rubles, fifteen sheep, one horse, and two cows. Husband number five paid only 900 rubles and 60 *poods* (1 pood = 36 pounds) of grain for her. The account of this case did not state how Kushmuratova left each husband so rapidly, nor the punishment her father, Oi-Saat, received. The case report noted that local party members were aware of what was happening but did nothing.[45]

In these cases, the degree of punishment imposed was determined in large part by the value of the goods exchanged, which in turn was determined by the wealth of the families involved. Prosecutors mainly concerned themselves with those who received bride price rather than those who paid. While dowry also existed in Uzbekistan, the custom was not as widespread as bride price and was not pursued as a crime. The case of Gul-Oi Kushmuratova was atypical, and probably should be regarded as a straightforward financial scam rather than as an example of Muslim intransigence.

The amnesty rolls also reveal something of the state's priorities in prosecuting crime. The most striking aspect is that Soviet authorities showed very little interest in social crimes of any type, preferring instead to go after cases of theft, hooliganism, murder, and bureaucratic corruption. Of the relatively few social crimes that Soviet authorities prosecuted and appealed, the rarest was polygyny. This partly can be explained by the fact that the state did not outlaw polygyny until 1931, but even so, it was mentioned as a factor in only one case out of 5,843 in 1929 — before it had been made a crime in Uzbekistan.[46] Even in the highest reaches of government, officials tolerated, or at least winked at, polygyny, as demonstrated by the early decision of the Turkmenistan Communist Party to allow polygyny among workers, and by the fact that Uzbek President Faizulla Khoiaev had two wives, one Russian and one Uzbek.[47]

The social crime that authorities pursued most vigorously was child marriage. Between 1925 and 1935, twenty out of forty-nine appeals of social crime convictions were for child marriage. The average age of the girls involved was from twelve to fourteen. Child marriage drew a harsher than average penalty of five years' imprisonment, although it was not considered as heinous as murdering unveiled or activist women, which usually drew a sentence of ten years (there were thirteen of these cases in the decade surveyed). In the long run, however, Soviet prosecution failed to eliminate traditional social practices except in the Russianized urban areas, and even there they were not completely successful. In rural Uzbekistan, where the bulk of the population lived, Soviet policy drove old customs underground rather than eliminate them.

This became clear in 1935–1936, when the pressure against religious observance eased somewhat, spurring an immediate resurgence in customary practices. Mullas proclaimed a new era of freedom for Islam, attendance at the mosques and fasting for Ramadan noticeably increased, and women who had gone unveiled donned the *päränjä* once more. Even such activists as the former chair of the Stalin village soviet, Achil-Oi Ruzleva, veiled themselves at least for Ramadan.[48] It was not uncommon to find collective farms where all the women were veiled, including party and Komsomol members.[49] The practice of child marriage either increased or, more likely, had never gone away. The Narodnyi Kommissariat Vnutrennykh Del (NKVD) reported the following statistics to Uzbek Communist Party Chair Akmal Ikramov in spring 1936: "Thus, in 54 districts (out of 61 surveyed) in 1935–36 it was determined that there were 219 instances of giving underage girls into marriage and 172 instances of selling underage girls for bride price, a total of 391 cases of giving away in marriage girls who had not reached the medical age of maturity."[50] Of the 174 people sentenced to jail for these crimes, a little over half (ninety-four) received sentences of two or three years, thirty-one were sentenced to five years, and five received sentences of eight years or more. The courts still did not consider child marriage to be a particularly serious crime.

Aside from the temporary relaxation of the anti-Islamic campaign in the mid-1930s, attacks against women continued because men's attitudes about their honor and power changed very slowly. Many men could not adjust to the idea that they did not wield complete control over the lives of their wives, sisters, and daughters. In the Margelan, Lenin, and Sary-Assiia districts in 1936, men stabbed their wives to death for such acts as removing their veils, going to work, and socializing in public. Nor was this kind of violence limited to rural areas. In Tashkent, a policeman shot at a relative who took off her veil. Even when men allowed their female relatives to labor in factories and cotton fields, women could not work on an equal plane with men. Zhenotdel official Anna Nukhrat complained that men on the collective farms considered cotton picking by hand to be beneath them and that (male) chairmen or brigade leaders assigned women to such backbreaking manual labor while allowing men to drive the few machines available.[51] Women had not been able to escape the vicious bind in which conflicting state and cultural demands put them. If they worked, they risked Uzbek male wrath on the grounds of either personal or cultural betrayal. If they did not work, the government could punish them as shirkers, which would hurt not only women but also their children. In any case, it is doubtful that most Uzbek women viewed the prospect of life in a textile or food-processing plant as truly liberating.

The Uzbek Commissariat of Justice conducted several surveys of local court performance in the late 1930s and early 1940s and found the courts to be sorely lacking in their zeal to prosecute clergy and other religious offenders. The same situation held when it came to pursuing crimes against women. Courts in the Khorezm, Samarkand, and Namangan *oblasts* (provinces) lost crucial case files, bungled prosecutions, or halted investigations entirely for unclear reasons; a prosecutor in Samarkand dropped a case of child marriage because he considered it to be unimportant.[52] The kinds of offenses that came before the courts had not changed very much in ten years. Most of the completed prosecutions were for child marriage; rape and murder received similar (low) priority. What was new was a category of crime known as "preventing women from taking part in society." This category included preventing women from attending school or going to work outside the home. In June 1941, for example, the courts convicted a man under this code for trying to force his wife to wear a päränjä and not talk to other men and beating her when she refused his orders.[53] In other words, fourteen years after the inception of the hujum, women were far from attaining the promised liberation. Real changes were made, to be sure, and in many towns and cities the veil disappeared altogether, but the Soviet campaign had made only a shallow impact on people's beliefs.

AS PART OF the larger anti-Islamic campaign, women's liberation succeeded in splitting the Muslim clergy. The Communist Party openly pursued a policy of creating antagonism between rival clerical factions, for which the changing status of women proved to be an ideal tool.[54] The women's campaign forced the clergy to stretch in previously inconceivable ways to accommodate new conditions and started some of the mullas' most creative and radical responses to the state's anti-Islamic policies.

The majority of Muslim clergy fiercely opposed unveiling and other aspects of the liberation campaign, some directly equating unveiled women with prostitutes.[55] Many clergy were arrested on charges of opposing women's liberation (this included everything from privately criticizing it to murdering Zhenotdel activists), and a few went so far as to commit public suicide to protest unveiling.[56] Conflicts over women's status provoked some of the earliest conservative-reformist battles among official Muslim clerical organizations (called "spiritual administrations"). In summer 1926, an imam named Faziljan Mäksum "raised a storm of protests among the population" against women's meetings in Margelan and "was even forced to leave [the area] . . . for a time." The account of this incident does not identify who forced him to leave, but it does imply a connection between Mäksum's exile and the Ferghana Spiritual Administration, which convened a public hearing in June on his "anti-Shari'a" expressions concerning the "woman question."[57] Public agitation represented a simple type of opposition for the Soviets to quash, however, despite the fact that the government was inefficient in its efforts to find and arrest offenders. The subtler forms of resistance, which included Islamic education and social pressure, proved to be much more difficult to counteract.

For every move the government made, the conservative clergy seemed to have an answer. When Communist Party officials set up zhenotdels in 1924 and 1925, the clergy fought back by organizing their own "zhenotdels," which they dedicated to strengthening women's faith in Islam.[58] While communist propagandists gave impassioned speeches on Islamic misogyny, mullas established private classes in their homes for women, teaching them about the importance of the veil and other religious tenets. In many cases, the mullas' wives became active teaching women, in keeping with Muslim beliefs regarding sex segregation.[59] The message they enforced was that true Muslim women would not be seduced by Soviet blandishments and that to remove their veils was to collaborate with the infidel rulers.

The reformist clergy threatened the communists by co-opting the communist program and using it for their own ends. Although most of the radical reform tactics, such as allowing women into the mosques with men and even designating women clergy, occurred in the Tatar-Bashkir areas, a significant segment of the Uzbek clergy supported an Islamic form of women's liberation. A writer for the all-union agitation/propaganda organ *Kommunisticheskaia revoliutsiia* warned in 1929: "In order to save their position, Muslim clergy are allowing women into the mosque. In religious schools, they are introducing elements of exact science side-by-side with the Qur'an. Nowadays the clergy decides not to approach even the peasants with old, ossified dogmatism. In this sense, reformed religion is more dangerous than unreformed."[60]

Some of the clergy based their arguments directly on the Shari'a, drawing on minority interpretations of the tradition and particularly on Islamic reformist thinking that had begun in the nineteenth century. Their primary motive appears to have been deep personal belief that a less restrictive interpretation of Muslim law was not only possible, but desirable. In response to Faziljan Mäksum's antiliberation protests, Mulla Urunbaev wrote for the Spiritual Administration newspaper *Ferghana*: "According to the Shari'a, according to the testament of Muhammed, women occupy an equal position with men before God. Women may pray five times a day equally with men, they may participate in social life. They also have the right, as men do, to visit [friends], go to the bazaar, study, and receive an education. Women are even allowed to occupy such posts as judge of the Shari'a [*qadi*], *mutawalli*, and other [positions]."[61] Some mullas supported unveiling so strongly that they offered to help the government with its campaign. An official Sredazburo journal, *Za partiiu*, described in italics a remarkable instance of this: "In Kanibad a mulla went to the district committee and told them at great length that there are [strands] in the Koran against the *chächvan* [face veil], that the chächvan is not required according to the law of faith. He even [gave] a written explanation with citations and references and left it with the committee. But in the committee they listened to him, laughed that a mulla would come out in favor of unveiling, and left it at that. No one took up this powerful weapon, no one tried to use this mulla."[62] The author of this article was appalled that the committee had not seen fit to accept the services of the mulla, but in fact the Sredazburo warned against such collaborations for quite some time. Communist officials feared that progressive clergy could gain influence over party organs by working with them and thus ensure their own survival while corrupting communism.[63]

Other reforming clergy supported unveiling for reasons that had more to do with their struggle to retain political power than with personal conviction. Zäkhretdin Aglyäm of Tashkent reportedly chastised his colleagues for not taking the initiative in women's liberation: "We, the clergy, must take the matter of unveiling women into our hands. But now the party has torn the initiative in this matter from our hands. We should have hurried with this business sooner, but now the party has shown the folk that religious people did not do [unveiling], but atheists. We should have acted completely differently; we should have carried this out in the name of religion. Now the masses think that the päränjä was not prescribed by the Shari'a at all, and that the atheists have freed them from it. This is terrible."[64] Aglyäm was not so much concerned that women were unveiling but that the clergy had lost control and was being discredited in the process. His statement also implies that unveiling did enjoy some degree of popular support, at least in Tashkent. The growing Uzbek educated elite showed more inclination to adapt to Russian social legislation than did the rural peasantry, who had little positive incentive to abandon their own customs.

The issue of women's education formed another arena of violent conflict between Central Asian and Soviet social values. While technically nothing in Muslim law barred women from pursuing an education, literate women were exceedingly rare in nineteenth-century Central Asia. When the Russians introduced their Western-style native-language school system in the late nineteenth century, they included a few schools for girls, but most Central Asian parents refused to send children of either sex to them. The new Russian schools and their secular Central Asian (*Jädidist*) counterparts appeared to inspire some response from the Muslim clergy. By 1925, the main Waqf (charitable endowment) Administration of Uzbekistan complained that teenage girls formed the "main contingent" of participants in religious schools and that "In Old Bukhara for every two Soviet schools there are 52 old-method women's schools."[65]

Old Bukhara may have been an anomalous situation at best, even taking into account the strong possibility that the figures mentioned above were intended merely to convey a sense of scale rather than be an accurate census. The Soviet government put a tremendous amount of effort before World War II into improving women's literacy levels, a massive campaign that has yet to be studied, but persuading Uzbeks to send their female children to school was slow, hard work. Clergy protested against girls' education, and secular education in general, as fiercely as they protested unveiling. Many clergy felt, not without reason, that the children were being taken away from them and "made into Russians."[66] Parents, too, were often deeply angered by the new schools. When the Soviet government introduced the law on General Compulsory Primary Education in Turkmenistan in 1930, local peasants were outraged that schools educated girls as well as boys. In 1931, peasants set schools on fire in many districts of Turkmenistan, and the project proved to be largely a failure.[67] The same year in Surkhan-Darya Oblast, Soviets surveyed the number of girls in school. One village soviet chair reported that not a single girl between the ages of eight and fifteen attended school in his village, which was not an unusual situation.[68] Even by the mid-1930s, most girls in Uzbekistan left school beginning at the fifth and sixth levels, often because of betrothal or marriage.[69] According to one study, in 1927–1928, female students made up 26.1 percent (34,735 girls) of the urban school population and 11.5 percent (6,235) of the rural school population. By 1938–1939, these figures increased to 42.7 percent (428,965) of the urban school population and 41.7 percent (337,174) of the rural. On the face of it, this signified a substantial improvement, but the study does not give figures for the general population of school-age children, which was undoubtedly higher than the number of children actually in school, particularly in rural areas.[70] Although the Soviets did succeed in raising Central Asian literacy levels considerably from nineteenth-century statistics, girls still lagged behind boys in overall educational level.

COMMUNIST PARTY ACTIVISTS used the issue of women's oppression as an important tool to draw Uzbeks and other Muslims away from Islam. They argued that the veil and child marriage injured women physically and psychologically, that sex segregation injured them economically, that lack of education and separation from general (male) society injured them intellectually, and that polygyny and other sexual practices were immoral. The government tried to impress its views on the populace through a heavy propaganda campaign, which encompassed public lectures, demonstrations, movies, plays, and newspaper articles. Officials also used the law to summarily enforce the new values, whether Muslims took them to heart or not. The imposition of Russian customs caught Uzbek women in a terrible bind: between remaining loyal to their religion and culture and obeying the state. They risked punishment no matter what choice they made, particularly because the results of their choices were publicly visible and symbolically weighted. In the late 1920s, Uzbek men were losing control over much of their economic lives, their children's education, even the alphabet in which they wrote their language. Many of them clung to controlling the women in their families as a last bastion where they could be assured that they still retained some power. When the Soviets reached into the family as well, many men reacted violently, resulting in the beating, rape, and murder of thousands of women.

The campaign to liberate women both revealed and further exacerbated conflicts among the Muslim clergy. The majority fiercely opposed any change in women's status and encouraged or joined in acts of violence against women who unveiled or acted independently of men. This in turn allowed the government to hold them up for ridicule as fanatics who wanted to keep women in chains of dark ignorance rather than join the "modern" world. Other clergy supported unveiling, either out of personal conviction or political considerations, often feeling that they stood a better chance of retaining power by supporting a movement they could not stop in any case. The clergy who supported women's liberation in turn revealed a split in the government: between those who wanted to use these mullas to further the campaign and those who feared that any collaboration with liberal clergy would taint the atheist credentials of the Communist Party. Ultimately, the anticollaborationist view prevailed, which provided additional motivation to exterminate the liberal clergy.

Religious beliefs, sexual mores, and family structures are intimate, deeply rooted phenomena that evolve slowly over time and are extremely difficult to change by outside fiat, as the Russian colonial experience shows. This was true no less in Central Asia than in China, India, or Africa. The Soviets succeeded in improving women's status in many ways: women were better educated, were able to work and move about publicly, and even attained (low-level) government positions. The veil eventually disappeared in urban and most rural areas. But these changes occurred slowly, not according to the timetable set for the grand assault launched in 1927. Even visible practices such as the veil persisted in rural areas until well after World War II, and polygyny and child marriage faded underground but never disappeared entirely.[71] This was due in large part to the profound ambivalence that even communist Uzbeks felt toward the project, which communicated itself to the unambivalently opposed population. Social change can be achieved when a critical mass of people supports it, but when that support is lacking and the proponents of change are ambivalent, permanent change at a deep level is impossible. For Uzbek women, the changes that were achieved also came with a horribly high price.

Notes

1. The Soviet bureaucracy consisted of two separate but parallel systems, the Communist Party and the state. In Central Asia, a third layer, in the form of the Central Asian Bureau (Sredazburo), was added.

2. Gregory Massell, *The Surrogate Proletariat: Moslem Women and Revolutionary Strategies in Soviet Central Asia, 1919–1929* (Princeton, N.J.: Princeton University Press, 1974), 201.

3. Protocol 9, Management Dept. of Sredazburo, 1 September 1925, fond 62, opis 1, delo 105, list 119, Russian Center for the Preservation and Study of the Documents of Recent History (RTSKhlDNI, formerly TSPA-IML, the Central Party Archive Institute of Marxism-Leninism). References to Russian archival material use the Russian terms *fond* (collection), *opis'* (inventory number), *delo/dela* (file/files), and *list* (page), and are hereafter abbreviated f., op., d./dd., and l./ll., respectively. All translations from Russian are Shoshana Keller's.

4. "V prezidiume TSIK [SSSR]," *Vlast' Sovetov* no. 8 (February 1925): 9.

5. Anna Nukhrat, "Vot, kakie zhestokie nravy na Vostoke," *Bezbozhnik u stanka* no. 10 (1925): 17; "Truzhenitsa Dagestana," *Bezbozhnik u stanka* no. 12 (1925): 6–7; "Prava zheny," and "Neravenstvo za grobom," *Bezbozhnik* (newspaper), no. 42 (1925): 5; M. Razin, "Ozgärtish väqt—khatin-qizlär häräkät" (*Ozbekistan*) *Kommunist* no. 2 (1925): 57–59.

6. Protocol no. 11, Zavotdel Sredazburo, 7 October 1925, f. 62, op. 1, d. 105, l. 204, RTSKhlDNI.

7. Ispolburo Protocol no. 56, f. 62, op. 1, d. 173, l. 94, RTSKhlDNI.

8. Ibid., l. 95.

9. Ispolburo Protocol no. 56, f. 62, op. 1, d. 173, ll. 94–95, RTSKhlDNI.

10. *Sobranie kodeksov UzSSR*, 1st ed. (Samarkand, 1928), 112–113, 121. USSR and Uzbek law codes ignored lesbianism.

11. "O pravovoi zashchite zbenshchin," circular, 25 February 1926, in *Istoriia sovetskogo gosudarstvn i prava Uzbekistana*, 1924–1937 (Tashkent, 1963), 2: 217.

12. "O meropriiatiiakh po raskreposhcheniiu zhenshchin," circular no. 3/1282, 27 March 1927, in *Sbornik tsirkuliarov i rai'iasnii Narodnogo Kommissariata Iustitsii i Verkhoonogo Suda Uzlbekskoi SSR* (Samarkand, 1928), 123–124, quote on 123.

13. Arkhipova, "OTCHET o provedeniem obsledovanik Narsuda 1, 2, 3, i 5 uch. Goroda," Samarkand, 1–5 December 1925, f. 904, op. 1, d. 59, ll. 6–7, TSGA UZ.

14. Ibid.

15. Original Commissariat of Health memorandum, 11 April 1929, f. 837, op. 8, d. 582, ll. 1, 2, TSGA UZ.

16. Oleshchuk (Moscow center) to all Godless organizations, "Razrabota voprosov antireligioznoi raboty v zhenskikh arteliiakh na Vostoke," 20 March 1930, f. 5407, op. 1, d. 17, l.22, State Archive of the Russian Federation (GARF, formerly TSGAOR, Central State Archive of the October Revolution).

17. Massell, *Surrogate Proletariat*, 243–244.

18. Chief of Information for the Plenipotentiary of the OGPU D'iakov and Assistant Chief Ali, "Dokladnaia zapiska—o terrore v kishlake-aule Uzbekistana," January 1929, marked "sovershenno sekretno," f. 62, op. 1, d. 548, ll. 92–94, RTSKhlDNI.

19. Articles 211–215 and 273–278 of the Uzbek Criminal Code.

20. "Otchet NKIu UZSSR o ego deiatel'nosti za 1929 g," f. 904, op. 1, d. 155, l. 27, TSGA UZ.

21. "Otchet. Iz Tashkentskoi Okruzhnoi Ispolkom . . . O deiatel'nosti Tashokrsuda za vremia s 1-go ianvaria po 15-e dekabria 1928 g," f. 904, op. 1, d. 64, l. 69, TSGA UZ.

22. *Stenograficheskii otchet (vtorogo vsesoluznaia s "ezda soiaza voinstvuiushchikh 12 bezbozhnikov)* (Moscow, 1930), 268.

23. F. Popov, "O rabote sredi zhenshchin v Uzbekistane," *Antireligioznik* no. 12 (1938): 14.

24. Dolganov, "Report on the Tashkent Okrug court for the first half of 1928," f. 904, op. 1, d. 64, l. 96, TSGA UZ.

25. F. 904, op. 1, d. 90, l. 162, TSGA UZ.

26. F. 86, op. 1, d. 7956, l. 2, TSGA UZ.

27. "O kvalifikatsii prestuplenii, sovershennoe s tseliu protivodeistviia raskreposhche-niiu zhenshchin," circular no. 3/2366, 16 May 1927, in *Sbornik tsirkuliarov i raz'iasnenii Narodnogo Kommissariata Iustitsii*, 191.

28. F. 904, op. 1, d. 161, l.8, TSGAUZ.

29. *3-ii kurultai sovetov: Stenograficheskii otchet* (Samarkand, 1929), 95.

30. Ibid., 140.

31. Isaac A. Zelenskii, "Raskreposhchenaia uzbekcha trebuet zakona o sniatii parand-zhi," *Vlast'sovetov*, 17 April 1929, 21.

32. "Za podlinnoe raskreposhchenie zhenshchin," *Uzbekistanskaia pravda*, 26 February 1929, 2.

33. "Vo slavu Allakhu," *Uzbekistanskaia pravda*, 20 March 1929, 3; "Mest'Mully," *Uzbekistanskaia pravda*, 25 March 1929, 4.

34. Faizulla Abdullaev was sentenced to four years' imprisonment. F. 86, op. 1, d. 6461, l. 4, TSGA UZ. On earlier cases of official abuse, see Isaac A. Zelenskii, "Bor'ba za raskreposhchenie zhenshchin," *Za pariliiu* no. 4 (1927): 39–44.

35. Massell, *Surrogate Proletariat*, 293.

36. F. 86, op. 1, d. 7951, l. 38, TSGA UZ.

37. F. 86, op. 10, d. 526, l. 73, TSGA UZ.

38. Massell, *Surrogate Proletariat*, 236–238.

39. E. Mostovaia, "Pervoe vsesoiuznoe soveshchanie kommissii po uluchsheniiu truda i byte zhenshchin-vostochnits," *Vlast'sovetov* no. 9 (1928): 8.

40. Stenografislzckii otchet (Moscow, 1930), 335.

41. F. 86, op. 1, d. 5816, l. 33, TSGA UZ.

42. Turab on appeal F. 86, op. 1, d. 7951, l. 7, TSGA UZ.

43. F. 86, op. 10, d. 526, l. 169, TSGA UZ.

44. F. 86, op. 10, d. 1112, l. 232, TSGA UZ.

45. "Report on the marriage of underage girls to adult men," 15 March 1936, f. 58, op. 12, d. 638, l. 96, Party Archive of the Central Soviet-People's Democratic Party of Uzbekistan (PATSS-NDPUZ, formerly the Uzbek Central Party Archive).

46. Takabai Rakhmankulov was sentenced to five years' imprisonment "for polygyny, for bride price, for rape with extreme physical violence, and for the house arrest of his daughter." His request for pardon was refused. F. 86, op. 1, d. 7951, l. 39, TSGA UZ.

47. Marianna Karaeva, interview with author, 6 May 1992. Karaeva was a star with the Uzbek Ballet in the 1930s and 1940s and socialized with many government officials. She also knew the Khojaevs privately, as she regularly went to market with Faizulla's mother, Räihan Säidmurad-qizi/Saidmurodovna. Faizulla's Russian wife was the official one, and she spent years in the Gulag after his arrest in 1937. His unacknowledged Uzbek wife, Mälikä Muhämmäjan-qizi/Mukhammedzhanovna, escaped the camps. Thanks to Roger Kangas for providing me with the names of Faizulla's wives.

48. Deputy Chief NKVD Leonov and Deputy Chief SPO UGB NKVD Zelentso, "NKVD report on religious observances in the villages," 28 December 1935, f. 58, op. 12, d. 638, l. 18, PATSS-NDPUZ.

49. "Report on counterrevolutionary clergy," 10 April 1936, f. 58, op. 12, d. 638, l. 93, PATSS-NDPUZ. E. M. Iaroslavskii, "Ob ocherednykh zadachakh antireligioznoi pro-

pagandy sredi natsionaltnotsei," *Antireligicznik* nos. 8–9 (1938): 23–26 noted the strength of bride price and the veil.

50. "NKVD report to Akmal Ikramov," 19 April 1936, f. 58, op. 12, d. 638, l. 105, PATSS-NDPUZ, emphasis in the original.

51. A. Nukhrat, "Usilim antireligioznuiu propagandu sredi natsionalok," *Antireligioznik* no.1 (1936): 24–25.

52. "Dokladnaia zapiska—O sostoianii rassmotrenniia del v sudakh Samarkandskoi Oblasti, sviazannye s protivodeistviiam raskreposhchenie zhenshchin. s 1 /1–1941 g. po 1 /X-1941 g," f. 904, op. 10, d. 91, l. 60, TSGA UZ.

53. Ibid.

54. Speech by I. G. Khansuvarov at the Thirteenth Sredazburo Plenum, May 1927, f. 62, op. 1, d. 221, l. 151, RTSKhlDNI.

55. Theresa Rakowska-Harmstone, *Russia and Nationalism in Central Asia: The Case of Tadjikistan* (Baltimore, Md.: Johns Hopkins University Press, 1970), 296.

56. F. 62, op. 1, d. 221, l. 212, RTSKhlDNI; f. 86, op. 10, d. 526, l. 16; d. 1114, l. 61; f. 904, op. 1, d. 90, l. 229, TSGA UZ.

57. "Zadachi partii v rabote sredi zhenshchin v sviazi s delatel'nostiu Musul'manskogo dukhovenstva," 18 January 1927, f. 58, op. 3, d. 150, l. 49, PATSSNDPUZ.

58. S. T. Liubimova to Sredazburo, May 1926, f. 62, op. 1, d. 173, l. 96, RTSKhlDNI.

59. K. Shukurova, *Kommunisticheskaia Partiia Uzbekistana* (Tashkent, 1960), 98.

60. A. Arsharuni, "Antireligioznaia propaganda na Sovetskom Vostoke," *Kommunishicheskaia revoliutsiia* no. 1 (January 1929): 73.

61. F. 58, op. 1, d. 150, l. 48, PATSS-NDPUZ.

62. Aleksandr Rogov, "Pod znakom 'Khudjuma,'" *Za pariliiu* no. 1 (1928): 93.

63. Khansuvarov plenum speech, f. 62, op. 1, d. 221, l. 207, RTSKhlDNI.

64. Zäkhretdin Aglyäm, "Material k plenumu—iz doklada o Bukharskom musdukhovenstve," May 1927, f. 62, op. 1, d. 221, l.198, RTSKhlDNI.

65. "Rezoliutsiia po voprosu o zhenskom obrazovanii v Srednei Azlii," f. 62, op. 1, d. 105, l. 148, RTSKhlDNI.

66. P. Sazonova and K. Chernova, "Vnimanie iaslam natsional'nykh raionov," *Revoiloutskka I national'nosti* no. 3 (1934): 54; Shukurova, *Kommunisticheskaia Partiia Uzbekistana*, 54.

67. Sh. A. Ataklychev, "Compulsory Primary Education in Turkmenistan, 1930–1937," *Central Asia Review* 9, no. 3 (1961): 228–233.

68. "Devochek v vozraste ot 8 do 15 let net," *Uzbekistaniskaia pravda*, 4 February 1931, 2.

69. Nukhrat, "Usilim antireligioznuiu propagandu sredi natsionalok," 26; Popov, "O rabote sredi zhenshchin v Uzbekistane," 14.

70. *Uzbekistan za 15 let. Staticheskii sbornik* (Tashkent, 1939), 81.

71. S. Temurova, *Khatin-qizlär aräsdagi dinii säqit vä irim-chirmlärgä qäarshi kuräsh* (Tashkent, 1959).

Mire Koikari

Gender, Power, and U.S. Imperialism:

The Occupation of Japan, 1945–1952

Recent scholarship has highlighted the centrality of imperialism in shaping American culture "at home" and in molding its global military, diplomatic, economic, and cultural objectives. The U.S. occupation of Japan is frequently seen as a benevolent agent that was central in reconstructing and modernizing Japan after its formal surrender in August 1945. A systematic attempt to restructure Japanese gender relations was a crucial aspect of this "civilizing mission," and this essay examines both the role of American women in supporting this program and the ways this project made Japanese women's bodies and female sexuality a battleground in a campaign against "oriental male chauvinism." Here we see the interweaving of race, nation, and gender in debates over sexuality during the occupation and the ways various Japanese groups were forced to reimagine community and tradition under American rule.

About fifty years ago, Sally Butler, president of the National Federation of Business and Professional Women's Clubs, wrote to Douglas MacArthur, then the supreme commander of the Occupation Forces in Japan. Butler congratulated MacArthur on his success in reforming Japan, especially granting suffrage to Japanese women. In response, MacArthur described the enormous changes that he felt the American occupiers were bringing to Japanese women's lives: "Ever since their enfranchisement in the early days of the occupation, it has been my firm purpose to see superimposed here upon a decadent and discredited past a maximum of participation by women. . . . there is coming into Japanese life for the first time the noble influence of womanhood and the home which has done so much to further American stability and progress, and upon which I place most implicit trust that those new and higher ideals toward which the Japanese are now turning their faces will in time be fully understood, cherished and defended."[1]

For many American observers, including Sally Butler, the U.S. occupation of Japan was a noble project. After years of antagonism between the United States and imperial Japan and massive destruction of human lives on both sides, World War II finally ended with Japan's unconditional surrender on 15 August 1945. Immediately, General Douglas MacArthur and his occupation forces invaded bombed-out Japan and occupied it until 1952. MacArthur declared that his intention was to "reorient" and "rehabilitate" Japan into a peaceful and democratic nation. The American occupiers emphatically claimed that, unlike European colonial interventions that had been invasive and exploitative, the U.S. objective in occupying Japan was to civilize, modernize, and, most important, democratize this Asian country that had "gone astray" in the recent war.

Of all the aspects of the U.S. occupation of Japan, liberating women who had hitherto been oppressed under "Oriental male chauvinism" captured the fascination of the American occupiers. Indeed, "saving" Japanese women from patriarchal oppression became a central theme in the American occupiers' discourse. Historical documents indicate that the occupiers felt tremendous zeal and enthusiasm for their project of liberating Japanese women and intervened extensively in Japanese gender relations. For example, on the plane prior to arriving in Japan, MacArthur told his aide that Japanese women should be granted suffrage. Once the occupation began, an American female officer, twenty-two years old and a recent college graduate, successfully wrote the Equal Rights Amendment into the New Japanese Constitution.[2] This reform is particularly remarkable in that at the time, Americans back home were debating, but not at all ready to pass, their own ERA. American women officers were dispatched all over Japan to "enlighten" Japanese women throughout the occupation.

MacArthur's letter to Butler exemplifies Americans' confidence in their ability to accomplish gender reforms in Japan. The same sentiment was shared by MacArthur's staff. The SCAP Records, the official records of the occupation activities, often present the occupation as a "march of progress."[3] In this essay I propose a different, much more critical, interpretation of the U.S. intervention into Japanese gender relations. In analyzing the occupation, I emphasize that it was first and foremost a foreign military intervention. The United States was victor, invader, and occupier; Japan was conquered, invaded, and occupied. Every aspect of the occupation must be analyzed in relation to the enormous power inequities between the two nations. While Japan itself had previously been an imperial force against other Asian countries, the "unconditional surrender" Japan was forced to accept resulted in its dramatic loss of power at the end of the war. At the same time, the Japanese frequently contested the U.S. domination. Despite the seemingly noble and benign intentions of the occupiers, American intervention in Japanese gender relations was never outside of, or unaffected by, the power hierarchy inherent in the occupation. It is crucial to resituate our examination of the U.S. interventions in Japanese gender relations within this complex matrix of power.

My focus on gender in the occupation immediately leads to another crucial observation: gender was always articulated in relation to other categories of power, such as class, race, sexuality, and nationality. Gender did not single-handedly shape the process of the U.S. occupation of Japan. My analysis shows that "a fantastic conflation of the themes of gender, race and class" was distinctly visible in the occupation.[4] The hierarchical relation between the United States and Japan was articulated, but also frequently contested, through gendered language. At the same time, gendered rearticulation was solidly couched in the language of race and sexuality. Similarly, internal differences among Japanese were mediated through more than one discourse. The categories of "respectable Japanese" and "the Other" had temporarily been destabilized as a result of defeat and surrender, but were immediately rearticulated through gendered, racialized, and sexualized discourse. The occupation provides a glimpse of how multiple categories of power were mutually articulated in this large-scale international encounter.

In most discussions of colonial and imperial politics, it is European colonialism that receives the most analytical attention from scholars. Instances of American foreign interventions abound, but less than sufficient attention has been given to these forms of imperialism. The lack of attention to U.S. imperialism is not simply an oversight on the part of the scholars, but evidence that U.S. scholarly communities share a strong compulsion to disassociate the United States from colonialism and to perceive it as inherently anti-imperial since its independence from British rule. Thus, for many U.S. scholars, U.S. imperialism is a contradiction in terms.

Yet, even a cursory glance at the history of U.S. foreign relations shows that the United States had strong ties to European colonialism and has acted as an internal and external colonizing/imperial force in its own right. As Anne McClintock succinctly points out in her discussions of imperial politics, U.S. imperialism "has taken a number of distinct forms (military, political, economic, and cultural), some concealed, some half-concealed." Nonetheless, it could and did exert a coercive power "as great as any colonial gunboat." Thus, one needs to see "continuities in international imbalances in imperial power" between European dominance up to the mid-twentieth century and subsequent "U.S. imperialism without colonies."[5] There are striking similarities in rhetorical and material strategies of domination between European colonialism and U.S. intervention in Japan; I argue that the occupation should be analyzed as one instance of U.S. imperialism.

Framing the occupation as a form of U.S. imperialistic intervention sheds light on power and inequality as fundamental aspects of the U.S.-Japan encounter. I would like to add one cautionary note here. Despite enormous inequalities between the two nations, the way power operated in the occupation process was multidirectional and fluid, not simply top-down. Japan itself had been a colonial power toward other Asian nations, though it had been constantly under the threat from colonial/imperial powers in the West. Its postwar subjugation by the United States was of a relatively short term. Power disparities between the United States and Japan were less dramatic than more prototypical colonial situations. The occupied subjects, especially the existing ruling class, were fairly capable of negotiating with and even occasionally manipulating the American attempt to restructure Japanese domestic order.

Furthermore, the occupation forces did not constitute a unified body of ruling. There were many divisions and conflicts among the occupation authorities, which opened up unexpected political opportunities for the Japanese to exploit. Occupied Japanese did not simply constitute a mass of oppressed subjects under American dominance. Some Japanese collaborated with and even took advantage of the American presence to pursue their own interests in the postwar restructuring of Japan. Thus, observations of the occupation must go beyond binary oppositions of domination versus subordination, oppression versus resistance, and imperial versus anti-imperial and examine the extraordinarily complex operations of power that emerged.

How did the American occupiers perceive the country and people they were supposed to pacify and rehabilitate? One recurrent theme in the occupiers' discourse is that the Japanese were unique and incomprehensible. The "oddity" of the Japanese was traceable to distinctly different historical trajectories of the "West" and the "Orient." One observer articulated this difference in the following terms: "Western culture has evolved through centuries from a humanistic attitude and a seeking to know the truth through observation, theory, experiment and inductive and deductive reasoning. By and large, the Oriental does not have this humanistic philosophy nor the spirit of scientific inquiry."[6] Such an observation about the cultural specificity (or peculiarity) of Japan was often closely tied with another observation about the Japanese "feudal legacy" and "racial character," especially the Japanese "fanatical pride in race."[7] Because of existing feudal legacies, the Japanese were perceived as lacking adherence to abstract principles and willing to subordinate themselves to higher authorities, such as the emperor. Feudal legacies created a very hierarchical and regimented social structure in which individual expression and opinions were suppressed. To Western observers' surprise, blatant denials of individual freedom induced little social dissent among the Japanese, because the Japanese individual was "willing to be regimented . . . [and] happiest when he is told what to do." The Japanese language was another indication of the "inferior" and "incomprehensible character" of the Japanese race; it "belongs to no known family of language" and was perceived as incomprehensible to Western intelligence. Being "wordy and illogical," the Japanese language did "not lend itself to exact and scientific expression." These identified features of the Japanese language were assumed to contribute to the shaping of the fanatical Japanese character. When Japan's feudal legacies and its "fanatical racial character" were combined, Westerners believed the consequences would be devastating: it would produce an "extreme of chauvinism," as was seen in World War II.

Japanese cultural and "racial" character was manifested in Japanese gender relations, which were perceived as peculiar and inferior in comparison to those of the West. Japanese feudal patterns that "have persisted a surprising degree into modern times" placed women in limited and subordinated positions. Japanese woman could occupy only two roles: a familial role as mother and wife, and an extrafamilial role as *geisha*, or prostitute. Mothers and wives were expected to be "obedient, chaste, industrious, and quiet," and they were under the absolute domination of their husband. Prostitutes were "not unhappy as a rule" because "it has been their life since girlhood and in this realm, as in all others in Japan, women are trained not to think or desire beyond their own realm." The portrait of geisha, a sexualized depiction of Japanese womanhood, strikes simultaneously two major themes of the American invasions. On the one hand, legalized prostitution exemplified Japanese women's oppression, and thus their inferior cultural and social condition, which needed to be reformed under the occupation. On the other hand, the geisha constituted a sexualized object of the Western masculine gaze that tried to intrude and possess. Both of these constructions "invited" U.S. intervention in Japan, but in very different and contradictory ways. U.S. intervention in the sphere of sexual politics created one of the most complex and contradictory effects of the occupation.

The American occupiers often believed that their interventions would bring democratization to postwar Japan. Despite the "incomprehensible" and "inferior" nature of Japanese culture and its subjects, the Americans did not take these as permanent or fixed conditions. Like European colonizers before him, MacArthur saw the purpose of the occupation as a liberation of the Japanese from "conditions of slavery," in which freedom of expression, action, and thought had been denied to the Japanese people. Once liberated from their yoke, he argued, "the energy of the Japanese, if properly directed, will enable expansion vertically rather than horizontally."[8]

Like the female colonizers before them, American female occupiers showed great zeal in "civilizing" and "modernizing" Japanese women. For example, Ethel Weed, a female officer in the Civil Information and Education Section who played a central role in the occupation's gender reform, observed that "legally, socially, politically, and economically, the role of the Japanese women up to the time of the occupation was practically a non-existent one," yet "the postwar period in Japan has seen an ever-increasing improvement in the status of women in industry and their emergence from the feudalistic atmosphere in which they have lived and worked for generations." To Weed and other occupiers, it was the American presence and its progressive thoughts and deeds that brought such enormous and positive change to postwar Japan. In the eyes of the occupiers, Japanese culture had been extraordinarily chauvinistic and oppressive toward women, but the civilizing influence of the Americans was transforming this inferior culture: "The remarkable progress of Japanese women as they pull themselves up by their *geta* straps to pioneer in democratic procedures provides an inspiring record of world history. Only by comparison with their previous subjugation under feudalistic tradition little more than one year ago can the full significance of their achievements be realized."[9] Thus, the occupation was a blessing bestowed on Japanese women.

America's imperialist role was enmeshed in rhetoric that constituted its own gender relations as inherently progressive and democratic, in contrast to the image of Japanese gender relations as feudal and repressive. The American family was described as a fundamentally democratic institution where husband, wife, sons, and daughters enjoyed egalitarian relations with each other and where children were socialized to become democratic citizens. It is fairly easy to recognize that the U.S. construction of its own gender relations was narrowly based on the normative standard of white, middle-class experience. The simplistic descriptions of the United States as a democratic society concealed the reality that gender-, race-, and class-based inequalities were pervasive forces that shaped people's experiences there as elsewhere. However, the issue is not about the accuracy of these constructions of American society, but the fact that these constructions allowed the occupiers to claim cultural superiority over Japan. By juxtaposing feudal and repressive Japanese familial and gender relations with modern and democratic American counterparts, the occupiers constructed a culturally and morally superior identity. This is part of a long-standing convention of Western colonial and imperial powers: constructing the West as gender-egalitarian, against which the status of women elsewhere would be unfavorably compared.

With gender, race, and sexuality as central defining features of the difference between the two nations, national differences were never neutral: the United States was the dominant figure over conquered and occupied Japan. Indeed, after the dropping of the atomic bombs, the unconditional surrender, the invasion and disarmament, and the restructuring of Japanese domestic orders, one might expect that U.S. domination over Japan would have been solid and unquestionable. However, the occupied population was neither silent nor compliant. As I show below, the very discursive sites where American superiority and domination were being articulated — gender, race, and sexuality — became battlegrounds where the Japanese asserted their national identity and contested the terms of the occupation imposed by the conqueror. As a result, the occupation encounter was far more disorderly and chaotic than the triumphalist narrative of the occupation would suggest.

While the U.S. occupation of Japan generated tremendous concern about gender democratization, it also brought an enormous number of foreign soldiers to postwar Japan. From the outset, the Japanese expressed anxieties about how to protect "respectable" women, or *ryoke no shijo*,[10] from the hands of foreign soldiers. Fears that the American soldiers would violate Japanese women ran wide and deep among the Japanese. Several prefectural authorities suggested that women should defend their sexual purity even at the expense of their lives, adding that if such determination was not found in women, it should be inculcated through moral and spiritual education. Other precautions that the prefectural and national authorities recommended to Japanese women included staying home and not stepping outside, avoiding places where they would run into foreign soldiers, and staying with Japanese men who could protect them. The authorities also cautioned Japanese women to "behave themselves": women should avoid wearing provocative clothes and makeup and try to look simple and virtuous. The foreign invasion of the nation was understood as a threat to gendered — in this case, female — bodies, which led to closer surveillance of Japanese women and their sexuality.

To protect "respectable" women against "foreign menace," the Japanese authorities took measures: they provided *ianjo*, or brothels, exclusively for American soldiers. Only three days after the surrender, the government-sponsored Recreation and Amusement Center, or RAA, was established under the auspices of the Metropolitan Police Board. Owners of restaurants and sex industries were enlisted for this project, and they were financially compensated by the Japanese government. The RAA put advertisements on the streets and sometimes even in the newspapers that called for "female clerks," age eighteen to twenty-five, who would provide "comfort" for the American soldiers. In return, these women would be provided with places to stay, clothing, and food. There are no historical data that provide exact profiles of the women who worked for the RAA. However, secondary sources indicate that in postwar Japan, where shortage of food, clothes, and shelter constituted pressing problems, women who had no other economic means to support themselves turned to these jobs.[11]

The purpose of the RAA was ultimately defense of the nation, or *Koku-*

tai (national body), against foreign intrusion. This national body was constructed in gender-, race-, and class-specific terms. The central mission of the RAA was to protect the "purity of the Japanese race" and to "contribute to the maintenance of the national body" by protecting respectable women. Sexual and racial purity of respectable (that is, middle-class) women embodied the sanctity of the nation, and the protection of these women from the hands of foreigners was defined as a "postwar emergency measure of national significance." To protect these women who embodied the pure national body, women who were recruited for the RAA — those from precarious economic backgrounds — would be sacrificed as a human *bohatei*, or breakwater. Clearly, class differences that demarcated Japanese women into respectable versus expendable categories were simultaneously articulated through racial, sexual, and nationalistic languages.[12]

This nationalist project, born in the midst of chaos caused by defeat, surrender, and foreign invasion, was very short-lived. Venereal disease started spreading quickly among the American soldiers who visited RAA brothels. Alarmed by the rate of infection, the occupation authorities declared RAA brothels off-limits in March 1946. As a result, the Japanese authorities' "sexual containment policy" failed. The women who worked for the RAA were thrown out onto the streets, and many of them became streetwalkers, or *Pan-Pan*, a derogatory term coined in postwar Japan. Subsequently, fraternization between American soldiers and Japanese women proliferated.

The continuing spread of venereal disease among the soldiers even after the shutdown of the RAA posed an enormous threat to the seemingly successful and orderly occupation. MacArthur's headquarters received many letters from Americans back home inquiring about published reports of "widespread promiscuous relationships between members of the occupation forces and Japanese women of immoral character."[13] The commanders of the military forces urgently communicated to MacArthur that VD was widespread among the soldiers and that, because the Japanese general population held "an extremely large and virulent reservoir of venereal disease," the spread of VD among the soldiers was a "serious and immediate health menace to this command."[14] Importantly, as much as Japanese perceived foreign soldiers as a menace to the purity of respectable women's bodies, the occupation authorities perceived Japanese women's bodies as a threat to "uncontaminated" and thus pure Western bodies.

The proliferation of VD among the U.S. troops brought the lack of unity and cohesion among the occupiers into full relief: the occupation authorities could not come to an agreement regarding the cause of VD. The Public Health and Welfare Section (PHW) argued that the problem originated from East-West differences in medical knowledge and moral and cultural norms: the Japanese lacked social awareness and medical knowledge concerning public health in general, which led to the proliferation of VD. The PHW perceived the problem as compounded by the "moral backwardness of Japanese culture." Unlike the West where prostitution was morally condemned, the PHW argued, the East had customarily accepted prostitution without any moral concern. Thus, Japan was perceived as "a nation whose sexual mores are based on essentially different Oriental traditions," a perspective "supported" by the fact that licensed prostitution was well accepted in Japan.[15]

Because the PHW perceived the problem as originating from Japan's medical and moral backwardness, its policies aimed at amending those aspects of Japanese society. On the one hand, the PHW insisted on treating Japanese women with VD as patients and directed the Japanese government to institute a public health policy regarding VD. On the other hand, in order to address the moral aspects of the problem, the PHW issued an ordinance directing the Japanese government to abolish the existing system of licensed prostitution, stating that "licensed prostitution was in contravention to the ideals of democracy and inconsistent with the development of individual freedom."[16]

The PHW's approach to the problem was a clear contrast to the one adopted by the military commanders. Unlike the PHW, the military commanders defined VD as a criminal matter. A letter, "Venereal Disease Control," dispatched by Headquarters, Eighth Army, to Commanding General 24th Division, stated that infected Japanese women who solicited or had sexual intercourse with American soldiers committed crimes impinging on the security of the American forces. Japanese women, rather than American soldiers, were held accountable for the spread of venereal disease. The crude statement "Any good girl is safe with an American soldier whereas a good soldier is not always safe with any girl" conveys a sentiment widely held by the U.S. military forces.[17]

Without resolving the etiological disagreements between the PHW and the military forces, the occupation authorities and the Japanese government began to arrest Japanese prostitutes and send them for internal medical examination. The attempt to regulate the sexuality of "fallen" and thus "unrespectable" women quickly escalated to regulation of all Japanese women in indiscriminate roundups. The humiliation of arrests and internal medical examinations, which was tantamount to "medical rape," imposed on "innocent" women sparked visible resistance among the Japanese. Middle-class and working-class unionized women bitterly resented the sexual regulation and insisted on their own respectability. Ironically and inadvertently, repressive sexual regulation in occupied Japan provided a rare opportunity for Japanese women to express resistance against the occupation authorities, and against the Japanese government that had implicitly collaborated with the occupiers.

The procedure used to round up Japanese women sparked visible and dramatic protest. One documented case at Ikebukuro Station in Tokyo illustrates the outrageous nature of this particular form of sexual regulation.[18] At around 7 P.M. on 15 November 1946, Japanese women who happened to be around the station were arrested by Military Police (MP) and Japanese railway employees. Among those who were wrongly arrested were female workers on their way home from their union meetings. The women fiercely protested the indiscriminate roundups, but to no avail. They were taken to Itabashi Police Station.

It is not entirely clear from historical documents who was responsible for this indiscriminate roundup. Some women stated that, while the MPs initiated the roundups, it was the Japanese police who actually picked up individual women. Others stated that the roundups were conducted entirely by the MPs, and that the Japanese police were rather apologetic to the Japanese women, saying, for example, "Very sorry, but please follow the MP. We were defeated by the war." Despite the apology, some women felt indignant toward the Japanese police, stating that the Japanese policemen were "too servile."[19]

Once at the police station, these women tried again to prove their innocence by presenting union membership cards or other identification. But the Japanese policemen did not release them. Worse yet, they were humiliated by the Japanese police, who made remarks such as "How often have you been brought here?" and "You must have had intercourse with several men."[20] When women union workers explained that they were late because they were attending labor school, Japanese police responded, "Because you women attend such a labor school, you get into this sort of trouble."[21] Collusion with the occupying forces was not total.

Some Japanese policemen showed sympathy to and tried to release some women who were brought to the police station that day.[22]

After their arrest, the women who had been detained at the police station were loaded into a truck and taken to Yoshiwara Hospital for internal medical examination. During the examinations, the women were subjected to a series of harassing remarks by Japanese doctors and police. MPs were often present in the examination rooms, causing the Japanese women further humiliation. Some of the MPs even tried to pick up particular women and "get friendly" with them. Adding to these insults, the women were required to pay a fee for the medical examination.[23]

Upon release, the female union members took action. First, they contacted their labor union, which sent its representatives to the Itabashi Police Station and the Second Cavalry MP unit stationed at Roppongi, to find out who was responsible for the indiscriminate roundup. The responses the union representatives received were far from satisfactory. The chief of the Itabashi Police Station denied the Japanese police's responsibility, arguing that the roundups were conducted under a directive from the MPs. The MPs' responses to the union representatives were equally dismissive. They stated that the labor representatives had no right to protest against MP actions and that the Japanese police had absolutely no choice but to obey the MPs' orders.

While the union members' meetings with the Japanese and U.S. authorities were futile, their meetings with middle-class women leaders were more productive. The union sent representatives of its women's section to Dietwomen, who by then had heard numerous complaints about indiscriminate roundups. The Dietwomen took a crucial step: they enlisted support from the female occupiers in the Civil Information and Education Section (CI&E). Ethel Weed and other officers immediately responded to these women's appeals and started investigating the matter by contacting the provost marshal, the Public Health and Welfare Section, the Government Section (GS), and the Public Safety Section.[24] The GS identified the indiscriminate roundup as "a serious infringement of the civil rights" of innocent Japanese women and called the involvement of the MPs counterproductive to "all of the beneficial effect of the splendid conduct of the combat troops in the early days of the Occupation."[25]

The controversy surrounding indiscriminate roundups led to a mobilization of Japanese civilians. A major protest rally was held on 15 December 1946.[26] The rally was sponsored by an alliance of numerous political organizations, including the Japan Socialist Party, the Japan Communist Party, the All Japan Congress of Industrial Labor Unions, the Japan Federation of Labor Unions, the Women's Democratic Club, the Women Workers Union, the National Farmers Association, the Japan Women's Christian Temperance Union, and the Youth Communist Federation. These groups represented a wide array of political affiliations, resulting in a coalition ranging from conservative to radical left organizations and individuals.

Importantly, the protestors held the American occupiers as well as the Japanese government accountable for the problems at hand. In their protest speeches, women criticized the existing Japanese government and its economic policies. For example, a woman from the Communist Party argued that poor women out to obtain food were wrongly arrested. Another from the Cooperative Union argued that even though women's equality and freedom were nominally declared, women continued to suffer from economic discrimination. These women condemned the Japanese government and the police system for treating working women as if they were streetwalkers. Each speech was followed by the remark "Down with the Yoshida Cabinet."[27] Japanese protectors also presented a petition addressed to MacArthur. The petition first acknowledged the need for the occupation authorities to combat VD, as it was infecting an increasing number of people "due to the incompetence of the Japanese government to cope with the war and its results." It went on to address the problem of indiscriminate roundups in the following terms: "This matter is of serious concern to society. Please consider and judge for yourself. What would you say if your innocent sisters or loved ones were caught in a net spread for social health and denied explanation, refused the validity of their identification cards, and taken to a certain place? Please consider and judge further. What feelings would you have if you had heard that these innocent girls were compelled to submit to a medical examination at a special hospital built for venereal examination of prostitutes. . . . Haven't the appearance of simple and respectable 'office girls' been more lovely and ladylike than those of prostitutes who are the concubines of the rich?" The petition also discussed the impact of indiscriminate roundups and internal medical examinations on respectable Japanese women. Their resentment of the American occupiers was expressed in terms of a serious violation of the virgin body: "Call it feudalistic and lacking in sex education, but to the pure, young women, they being suspected as being prostitutes is a great shame to them, and furthermore, they practically hold in contempt on their life for being subjected to compulsory medical examination. It will be a hindrance to their marriage."[28]

Clearly, the arguments Japanese protectors directed to the American occupiers were couched in the class-based language of sexual respectability of innocent women. The sexual regulation of unrespectable women was never a concern for the Japanese protectors. The protest occurred because the Americans blatantly transgressed the boundaries between respectable and unrespectable and offended the sanctity of the nation by treating respectable Japanese women as if they were prostitutes and thus unrespectable.

While in this case Japanese protestors carefully chose words to express their resentment toward the occupiers, there were other cases in which the Japanese more explicitly and firmly pointed out contradictions in the occupiers' behavior. One such case was the 1948 petition by S. Yamashita, the chief of the Liaison and Coordination Office in Oita prefecture, located in southern Japan. In this petition, Yamashita pointed out that, despite numerous benefits that the occupation forces had brought to Japan, the MPs' indiscriminate roundups were creating enormous anxieties among the residents in Beppu City in Oita: "Parents and husbands are in an uneasy mind over their daughters and their wives, for their loved ones may at any time be subjected to ignominy and humiliation. Girls are in constant fear while outdoors lest an MP jeep may swoop upon them." Yamashita observed that the MPs' indiscriminate roundups would damage "the cause of democracy" and even "the future friendship between the U.S.A. and this country." He further stated, "The basis of a true democracy to which the Occupation Forces are guiding Japan is regard for individual's rights" but that those very rights were violated by the MPs' conduct. Hence, "it is pathetic to see that people here reverting to the mental attitude in the former days under the militaristic domination think that they must accept them with resignation because such violations are being done by agency beyond their control." He continued: "I am fully aware that the present situation is against the wish of the authorities of the Occupation Forces, for you yourself have on many occasions warned through my office against violations of individual rights on the part of Japanese police. . . . The situation has only been brought about by MPs' overzeal in carrying out their duties and by the lamentable manner on the part of MPs' interpreters. The Japanese Police are not wholly unblamable, for they are not able [*sic*] to advise MPs more strongly."[29] Yamashita's statement was a pointed critique of contradictions in the U.S. occupation of Japan. On the one hand, the Americans endorsed democratic social relations in Japan, but on the other hand, they engaged in antidemocratic practices that would undermine the very purpose of the occupation.

In the process of the U.S. occupation of Japan, women's bodies became a battleground: regulation of gendered — that is, feminine — bodies in the occupied nation became a source of tension and controversy. Gender was clearly a salient factor that shaped the occupation process. A close examination of the gendered aspects of the occupation reveals that the meaning assigned to Japanese women's bodies was fundamentally linked to the sexual, racial, class, and ultimately nationalistic politics developing between the two nations. The struggle to reassert Japanese nationalism encountered an inherent contradiction. The presence of "immoral women," that is, women who consorted with foreign soldiers and were to play a crucial role in maintaining the respectability of the nation, constantly threatened Japan's nationalistic aspiration for a pure and respectable national body from within. The inherently problematic and unstable nature of the Japanese nationalist claim was centrally connected with the sexual and racial politics in occupied Japan.

Japanese women's sexuality posed an enormous threat to Japanese nationalism. While the occupied nation tried to anchor its claim for national respectability in Japanese women's pure sexuality, Japanese women's actual sexual behavior constantly destabilized, even subverted, these claims. For example, an article written by the Japanese Women's Christian Temperance Union (WCTU) shows that the Japanese were deeply concerned with the moral decline of the nation as a result of the behavior of "immoral" women. The article lamented the "unbearably ugly sight" of Japanese prostitutes with foreign soldiers and argued that such behavior by Japanese women contradicted the age-old tradition of morality and virtue. The Japanese WCTU argued that Japanese women misinterpreted the meaning of "freedom" and indiscriminately adopted "Western customs," including immoral sexuality.[30]

At the center of Japanese concern was not prostitution in general, but specifically Japanese women's sexual liaison with non-Japanese men, that is, sexual/racial mixing of indigenous women and foreign men. Several surveys on prostitution conducted by the Japanese government indicate that the Japanese public made a sharp distinction between streetwalking, where the majority of prostitution for foreigners took place, and organized prostitution, which was primarily for Japanese men. While the Japanese surveyed even showed sympathy for women in organized prostitution houses, they strongly condemned and expressed extreme disgust toward the streetwalkers. One response stated that streetwalkers were "gaudy and conspicuous, so they strike the eye," but regarding organized houses, "There had been places like the Yoshiwara since a long time ago, so I don't particularly think they are bad." Another respondent expressed a similar sentiment by stating that "the Pan-Pan are disgusting. Girls in organized houses are to be pitied more than the Pan-Pan." Strong moral disgust toward women engaging in sexual liaisons with foreign soldiers was expressed in broad terms: "They [Pan-Pan] smoke and they wear loud clothes" and "Organized prostitutes don't go out so much, and they don't run loose in the street. They are not as harmful as the Pan-Pan girls."[31] There was an implicit assumption that while those in organized prostitution were in shameful occupations in order to support their poor families, the streetwalkers were pleasure-seekers.

Japanese magazine articles and books often defined immoral women as having distinct lifestyles and "peculiar" physiological and psychological characteristics that set them apart from the rest of the Japanese.[32] For example, Hiroshi Minami, a psychologist, described in detail the lifestyles of "fallen women" and identified physiological and psychological features that he argued were dissimilar to those of respectable Japanese. According to him, the fallen women's outlooks were very different from those of respectable Japanese. Furthermore, they had a strong inferiority complex and aggressive demeanor, which was reflected in their "masculine" style of speech, and an extreme tendency to imitate foreigners (as in using the English language).[33] Minami portrayed these women as distinct from "normal Japanese." Such arguments implied that these women were biologically or psychologically different from the rest of the Japanese, even altogether outside the category of the Japanese race. In other words, these "immoral" women were constructed as racially different from the rest of the normal and virtuous Japanese, and as "Others" would not threaten the Japanese nationalist claim for racial and sexual purity.

Yet such a rhetorical solution for nationalist anxiety fell apart when Japan was confronted with an increasingly visible population of biracial children. Over the course of the occupation, Japanese women began to have children fathered by American soldiers, and many of these biracial children reached the age to enroll at elementary schools. A public debate emerged over whether they should be allowed to go to school with (racially) "pure" Japanese children. Even though the education minister decided to let biracial children enroll at elementary schools, there were continuing public concerns over their entry into schools and their future status in Japan.[34]

These debates produced a variety of opinions regarding biracial children.[35] Some argued that it was fundamentally wrong to stigmatize these children because of their skin color or their mother's immoral behavior and that these children should be treated the same as "pure" Japanese children. Others supported integrating biracial children into schools, but for a more complex reason: if they were isolated and not fully integrated as Japanese, they would become antisocial, even criminals, and create additional social problems in the future. To avoid such problems, they reasoned, it was vital to raise these children as Japanese.

On the other hand, there were those who supported separate education for biracial children, and there were even those who asserted that biracial children should be sent to the United States. A well-known female writer asserted in an open letter to Pearl Buck that biracial children were clearly offspring of American fathers and should therefore be considered American children rather than Japanese children. She argued that it would be best if biracial children were adopted by American families, emphasizing that children fathered by black soldiers in particular should be raised in the United States. According to her, blacks in Japanese society would be completely "foreign elements," but in the United States African Americans had been accepted as respectable citizens and would have no problem raising black children.[36] Such a view clearly originated from Japanese racism toward African Americans as well as the "myth of American democracy" that had been effectively disseminated under the occupation.

Controversies regarding the status of "immoral women" and biracial children were ultimately about where national boundaries should be drawn and who constituted the citizens/subjects in postwar Japan. In the aftermath of its colonial expansion and imperialistic war with the West, Japan faced a sudden reduction of its territories and of the subjects it had previously colonized. Domestically, Japan's imperial subjectivity, centrally based on the emperor and his sovereign power, crumbled during the earliest stage of the occupation, when the Imperial Constitution was nullified. The Japanese faced tremendous anxiety and instability regarding their subjectivity that needed to be resolved. It is notable that with Japan's efforts to reclaim its national identity, women's sexuality became a salient factor. As scholars examining colonial and neocolonial processes have pointed out, the politics of sexuality frequently become a central terrain where colonial power relations are negotiated and crucially shaped by gender, class, and racial dynamics, among others.[37] The continuity of such colonial political processes is clear in the U.S. occupation of Japan. The implications of these particular dynamics throughout the occupation process are disturbing: while "gender democratization" was allegedly pursued under the occupation, middle-class Japanese, including feminist women, implicitly or explicitly deprived the "immoral women" and their biracial children of candidacy for new citizenry/subjectivity.

Occupation narratives have often hailed the occupation as "successful democratization," "the watershed in Japanese women's history," or even as a "feminist revolution." In fact, a far more complex and also politically dynamic process of U.S. intervention into Japanese gender relations occurred. Clearly, the power relations between the two nations were unequal: the United States was the occupier and Japan was the occupied. At the same time, power dynamics between the occupiers and the occupied were far from fixed. The occupied subjects were capable of resisting, negotiating with, and even manipulating the occupiers. Many pursued their respective interests during the political lacuna that briefly existed in postwar Japan. Despite the crumbling of the Japanese imperial nation-state at the end of the war, Japanese nationalist aspiration continued to thrive. Although conquered and subjugated, the nation sought to sustain its claim of national respectability as embodied in middle-class respectable women. Importantly, it was not only Japanese men but also women leaders who participated in this nationalist project. In the process, they implicitly excluded "immoral women" from the category "Japanese." The binary framework that is often used in colonial studies — domination versus subordination, oppression versus resistance, colonial versus anticolonial — is insufficient as an analytical tool in examining cases such as the U.S. occupation of Japan. Reexamining the historical agency of subordinated subjects requires scrutiny of their collaboration with the dominant power.

Clearly, gender mediated the extraordinarily complex power dynamics in the U.S.-Japan encounter. At the same time, gender did not single-handedly shape the occupation process: gender was always articulated in relation to other categories of power, most crucially race, class, and sexuality. One of the most fascinating aspects of the U.S. occupation of Japan is the intersectionality of categories of power. It is critical that historians and others analyze a given category of power through other related and nonstatic categories of power in examining the various historical and political processes at work during this crucial period in U.S.-Japan international relations.

Notes

1. The letter is dated 5 May 1948; Record Group 5, Box 12, Folder "Bus-Buz," the Records of the U.S. Occupation of Japan, MacArthur Archives and Library, Norfolk, Virginia.

2. See Beate Sirota Gordon, *1945 Nen No Kurisumasu: Nihonkoku Kenpo Ni "Danjobyodo" o Kaita Josei No Jiden* (Tokyo: Kashiwa Shobo, 1995).

3. Ibid., 13.

4. "Report of Dr. Florence B. Powdermaker, Visiting Expert, Submitted to the Supreme Commander for the Allied Powers, Tokyo, 15 October 1948"; Record Group 5, Box 112, Folder 3, MacArthur Archives and Library.

5. Quotations in this and the following paragraphs are from *Civil Affairs Handbook, Japan* (Washington, D.C.: Army Service Forces Headquarters, 1944–45); *Army Service Forces Manual*, National Diet Library, Tokyo, 76–81.

6. "Report of Dr. Florence B. Powdermaker, Visiting Expert, Submitted to the Supreme Commander for the Allied Powers, Tokyo, 15 October 1948"; Record Group 5, Box 112, Folder 3, MacArthur Archives and Library.

7. Quotations in this and the following paragraphs are from *Civil Affairs Handbook, Japan* (Washington, D.C.: Army Service Forces Headquarters, 1944–45); *Army Service Forces Manual*, National Diet Library, Tokyo, 76–81.

8. "Message to the American People, 2 September 1945," p. 737, in *Political Reorientation of Japan*, National Diet Library, Tokyo. MacArthur probably meant that, once liberated, the Japanese would focus on their own progress rather than the conquest of neighboring countries.

9. "Progress of Japanese Women, Prepared by the Women's Affairs Branch of the CI&E for General Federation of Women's Clubs in Washington, D.C., 7 January 1947," Box 5247, File: Weed, Ethel, Feature Stories, SCAP Records.

10. The literal translation is "women from good families."

11. Masayo Duus, *Haisha No Okurimono* (Tokyo: Kodansha Bunko, 1995); Daijiro Kobayashi and Akira Murase, *Minnawa Shiranai Kokka Baishun Meirei* (Tokyo: Yuhikaku Shuppan, 1992); Akiko Rugiyama, "Haisen To R.A.A.," *Josei Gaku Nenpo 9* (1988); Toshio Sumimoto, *Senryo Hiroku* (Tokyo: Mainichi Shinbunsha, 1952).

12. *Fujin Mondai Shiryo Shusei*, vol. 1, *Jinken* (Domesu Shuppan, 1978), 535–536.

13. "Press Release," 2 April 1946, Record Group 25, Box 1, Folder 21, MacArthur Archives and Library.

14. "Venereal Disease Control in Army Air Force Personnel, From Pacific Air Command, U.S. Army to Supreme Commander for the Allied Powers," 21 November 1946, AG 726.1 Sur-1. 2191, File: Solicitation of the Troops for the Purpose of Prostitution, SCAP Records. There were several memos of similar content in this file.

15. "Check Sheet from Legal Section to Government Section, Regarding Bill for the Punishment of Prostitution and Related Activities," 15 June 1948, 2191, File: Solicitation of the Troops for the Purpose of Prostitution, SCAP Records.

16. "Memorandum for Imperial Japanese Government," Enclosure 3, 9321, File: Summary Report: VD Control, October 1945–December 1949, SCAP Records.

17. "Venereal Disease Indoctrination Course, General Headquarters, Far East Command," December 1947, 9370, File: VD Control, 1947–1948, SCAP Records.

18. 2191, File: Solicitation of the Troops for the Purpose of Prostitution, and 5250, File: Prostitution, SCAP Records. Also see Hussey Papers, Reel 9, 82B, National Diet Library, Tokyo.

19. "Information Report from Miss Renko Takokawa," CI&E, 5 December 1946, 5250, File: Prostitution, SCAP Records.

20. "Round up of Prostitutes," 5250, File: Prostitution, SCAP Records, and "Report on Conference on Connection with the Round-up of Japanese Women for VD Examination, Check Sheet from CI&E to GS," 5 December 1946, Hussey Papers, Reel 9, 82B.

21. "Report of Actual Circumstances: Japanese Movie and Stage Workers Union," Hussey Papers, Reel 9, 82B.

22. "Round-up of Prostitutes, Interview with Miss Sakakibara et al.," 29 November 1946, 5250, File: Prostitution, SCAP Records.

23. "Round-up of Prostitutes," 5250, File: Prostitution, SCAP Records.

24. "Report in Conference in Connection with the Round-up of Japanese Women for VD Examinations, Check Sheet from CI&E to GS."

25. "Memorandum for the Record, Alleged Maladministration of V.D. Control by Japanese Police and Unwarranted Interference by Military Police," GS, 6 February 1947, 2191, File: Solicitation of the Troops for the Purpose of Prostitution, SCAP Records; "Memorandum for the Chief, GS, Petition of Various Japanese Organizations with Respect to Handling of Women," Hussey Papers, Reel 9, 82B.

26. "Rally to Protest Round-ups," 5250, File: Prostitution, SCAP Records.

27. "Rally to Protect Women," 5250, File: Prostitution, SCAP Records.

28. "Petition to General MacArthur," Hussey Papers, Reel 9, 82B.

29. "Petition Concerning the Control of Prostitution, From Chief, Oita Liaison and Coordination Office, To the Commanding Officer, Oita Military Government Team," 4 December 1948, 9936, File: VD Control, Staff Visits, SCAP Records.

30. Japanese Women's Christian Temperance Organization, "Fuuki Ni Taisuru Ikensho," *Fujin Shinpo* 563 (1946).

31. "Survey Series: The Japanese People Look At Prostitution," 30 June 1949, 9321, File: Summary Report: VD Control, October 1945–December 1949, SCAP Records.

32. Examples include the following: Yoji Watanabe, *Gaisho No Shakaigakuteki Kenkyu* (Tokyo: Rankosha, 1950); Hiroshi Minami, "Pan Pan No Sekai," *Kaizo* 30 (1949); Etsuji Sumitani, "Gaisho No Jittai," *Josei Kaizo* 29 (1950); Kiyoshi Kanzaki, "Kanpan

Ni Agatta Pan Pan," *Kaizo* 34 (1953); Ikutaro Shimizu, "Kanashimubeki Henken Ni Tsuite," *Fujin Koron* 39 (1953); Kiyoshi Kanzaki, "Motto Hokorio: Kichi To Teiso No Kiki Ni Tsuite," *Fujin Koron* 39 (1953).

33. Hiroshi Minami, "Sengo Nihon Ni Okeru Baishofu No Tokushitsu," *Fujin No Seiki* 8 (1949).

34. Kiyoshi Kanzaki, "Shiro To Kuro," *Fujin Koron* (1953); Kennichi Maki, "Konket-suji No Mondai," *Shakai Jigyo* 36 (1953).

35. "Konketsuji O Dosuruka," *Fujin Koron* (1953), cites various opinions on the issue collected through survey.

36. Yaeko Nogami, "Konktesuji O Kofukuna Michi E," *Fujin Koron* 37 (1952).

37. McClintock, *Imperial Leather*; Aihwa Ong, *Spirits of Resistance and Capitalist Discipline* (Albany: State University of New York Press, 1987); Stoler, *Carnal Knowledge and Imperial Rule* (Berkeley: University of California Press, 2002) and "Rethinking Colonial Categories: European Communities and the Boundaries of Rule," *Comparative Studies in Society and History* 31, 1 (January 1989): 134–161.

Hyun Sook Kim

History and Memory:

The "Comfort Women" Controversy

While postwar Japanese society was recast by the U.S. occupation, Japan itself has struggled to come to grips with the legacies of the imperial system it created in Asia and the Pacific. A central feature of the Japanese empire was coercion and exploitation of colonized women, many of whom were forced to serve in "comfort stations" as sexual slaves for the Japanese military. This essay explores the ways both colonizing (Japan) and colonized (Korea) nations have dealt with this traumatic history of coercion, violence, and exploitation by juxtaposing accounts of the Japanese empire from Japanese and Korean history textbooks. The second half of the essay contrasts the strategies of evasion, silencing, and the erasure of colonialism found in these texts, with the accounts of the empire produced by "comfort women" themselves. These powerful narratives, memoirs, and poems not only hold nation-states to account for the wrongs of the past, but also puncture received "truths" about the place of gender and sexuality in the construction of empires and nations, underscoring the ways memory can unsettle the authoritative historical accounts sponsored by nation-states.

The year 1995 provided a particularly active site for the contestation of history and memory. The fiftieth anniversary of the atomic bombing of Hiroshima and Nagasaki at the end of the Pacific War and the beginning of decolonization from Japanese imperialism in formerly occupied areas such as Korea has brought up new and old politics of remembering and forgetting past events. The stories of the so-called comfort women—the estimated one hundred thousand to two hundred thousand young girls who were kidnapped and coerced into sexual slavery for the Japanese military during World War II — initiate a new set of debates.[1] These debates focus on the organized, strategic "forgetting" of the comfort women issue in history writing.

Since December 1991, over one hundred women in South Korea have registered with the Korean government as former comfort women. By identifying themselves publicly, these women ruptured the long-imposed official silence regarding the systemized rape of colonized women during the Pacific War. In their narratives, we find that the women, who are now called *halmôni* (grandmothers) by Koreans because of their advanced age, consider their stories to be collective and political, not just personal. The women testify about their experiences of exploitation and violence in terms of the larger socioeconomic, cultural, and political issues — the difficult circumstances that they and their families faced under colonialism. They reveal the ways the women sacrificed their lives and youth for their families and the nation. The comfort women were and continue to be colonized Korean women who have faced material poverty, gender and ethnic discrimination, and physical hardship under Japanese colonial domination. The most remarkable and historically unprecedented aspect of the comfort women "movement" is that the women survivors speak out by asserting their multivocal identities: they state that they are elders, women, poor, and subjects who were subordinated by both imperial/colonial and national governments because of their gender and ethnicity. The women's self-identification as former comfort women is by itself a political act that is symbolic (and may be cathartic) on both personal and national/collective levels.

While reflecting on the fluid relationship between history writing and memory construction, this essay looks at school textbooks as a site of the 1990s political struggle between the state and the comfort women. What is the state view on the comfort women issue, and how is it represented in school textbooks in Korea and Japan? What political and cultural space do the comfort women occupy in the state discourse about the nation's wartime/colonial past? Reading the textbooks as representations of the state discourse, this essay explores the nature of the contestation between officially constituted public memory and personal memories by women who survived military sexual enslavement during the Pacific War.

The conflicts around the historical representation of a wartime past reveal that war and war making concern not simply immediate matters of physical force, organized violence, and state coercion but questions of national and collective identities as well. While the state memory and official history of war and war making may be recorded as "business as usual," the women survivors and some Japanese students are challenging their governments to recognize that war making is preeminently about bodies in pain and violence against selected subjects. In this context, the countermemories of the surviving comfort women make visible the psychological, emotional, and physiological impact of an unofficial war weapon — namely, organized rape — that was used to capture, subordinate, and silence the colonized female subjects.

SINCE 1991, THE comfort women debate has invited challenges to the state's practice of history writing from new voices within Japan. The state-approved textbooks used in Japanese schools in the 1990s are not silent but continue to be selective about the representation of wartime history. The state discourse on wartime history is represented in a two-volume set of Japanese school textbooks published in 1993 and 1994 by the International Society for Educational Information (ISEI), an affiliate of the Japanese Ministry of Foreign Affairs founded in 1957.[2] Precisely because they are published by the state itself, these two volumes can be treated as an important source of information about state views on national history and history education in Japan. They reveal the strategies used by the state, including the construction of Japanese as victims, to erase the differences between the Japanese colonial power and the victimized colonies in Asia.

This series on Japanese school textbooks, titled *Japan in Modern History*, one volume for primary schools and another for junior high schools, has been published to inform the international community of the content of social studies taught to Japanese students. In particular, ISEI published the series to counter statements such as the following: "Young people in Japan might not be taught enough about their country's modern history, particularly in regard to Japan's role in the world during the past century."[3] As stated in the preface to *Japan in Modern History*, through the publication of such volumes, ISEI seeks to accomplish several objectives: first, to deepen international understanding in line with the trend toward "internationalization" in the 1990s; second, to deepen understanding of "different cultures" via the study of the history of exchanges with other nations and other peoples; third, to give Japanese children an "understanding of social life" and to encourage an "understanding of, and love for, the Japanese land and the nation's history"; and finally, to foster in Japanese children the foundations of the "public spirit" necessary to form a "democratic, peaceful nation and society living in international society."[4]

The first volume, titled *Japan in Modern History (Primary School)*, contains three of the eight social studies textbooks used by sixth-grade students, all of which have been sanctioned by the Ministry of Education as adequately satisfying *gakushus shido ōyōryo* (national curriculum standards, officially translated as "course of study" in government publications).[5]

Atarashii, written and compiled by Uzawa Hirofumi, Terasaki Masao, and thirty others and published by Tokyo Shoseki in February 1993, is the most widely used textbook. "Atarashii" literally means "new." It could be translated as "revisionist," too, depending on the context, especially concerning the recent movement to rewrite Japanese history (focusing on school textbook narratives). A group of nationalist intellectuals in Japan began their move to appeal to the public for the need to "re-write" their national history by presenting a popular history book as well as a school textbook that highlights heroic figures and celebratory events only while silencing or redressing the aggressive warfare and atrocity that Japan had engaged in (especially in the modern era). The group—which appealed much to the general public by writing what they liked to hear when the economy plummeted after the bubble burst over the last fifteen years—is called a committee for making a new (atarashii) history textbook. It presents the Pacific War through visual representations. The impact of the Pacific War on various nationalities is generalized; this textbook also emphasizes that because the war "dragged on" and "became fiercer," Koreans and Chinese were "brought forcibly to Japan." On the page focused on the theme "The Peoples of Asia during the War," the textbook displays three photographs and the narrative asks the question: How were the peoples of the occupied areas treated by the Japanese army? One photograph shows a caravan of Imperial Japanese Army troops in trucks and on bicycles entering a city plaza. The caption below the photo reads: "Japanese forces occupying a town in Southeast Asia." The description of the photograph states, "Japanese forces parading through the newly occupied capital of Vietnam."[6] Another photograph, titled "Soldiers of the Chinese Army Training," is presented; the caption below this photo states: "Members of the People's Army training for the fight against Japan." The third photo shows "a family [Japanese] saying goodbye to a soldier [Japanese] going to the front." The grouping and juxtaposition of these three photographs together create the impression that the war inevitably affected greater Asia by forcing Japanese soldiers to separate from their families in Japan and go to faraway places such as Vietnam, and also by mobilizing Chinese soldiers to fight against Japan. The photos represent Vietnam, China, and Japan simply as the geographical markers and landscape of the war; Japan's colonial occupation of Asia and its domination of colonial subjects are not revealed in the photos. At the same time, the photos create an impression that Japanese soldiers were also the victims because they were sent off to Vietnam and were forced to fight the Chinese. The visual representation of the war in this manner effectively erases Japan's position as imperial power and colonial oppressor by eliding Japan with its former colonial subjects. In contrast to the visual representation of the war, the narrative that accompanies the three photographs is clearer about the impact of Japan's colonial and imperialist war policies as applied to colonial subjects. The narrative reads as follows: "The Japanese forces forced the peoples of the area they occupied to work for the war and made off with the resources of those areas also. Such things heightened ill feelings toward Japan in the areas concerned, and many of their peoples began to resist the Japanese forces. As the war dragged on and became fiercer, Japan began to suffer a shortage of labor, and large numbers of Koreans, and even Chinese, were brought forcibly to Japan, where they were put to work under terrible conditions in factories and mines. The Koreans in particular were subjected to intolerable treatment; they were forced, for example, to change their names to Japanese-sounding ones."[7]

It may surprise many critics to find that these Japanese primary school textbooks actually present an extensive discussion of the war. At the same time, however, there is a perfunctory treatment not only of the events of the 1941–1945 period of the Pacific War, but also of the tangled story of the Japanese advance into the occupied areas of Manchuria, China, and Southeast Asia. In contrast to the discussions of the bombings of Hiroshima and Nagasaki and of the general suffering that Japanese civilians endured during the war, the history of Japan's treatment of people from Asian colonies is merely glossed over. Instead, the focus is on Japan itself and how the Japanese people and the nation suffered. The short chronology of "Main Events" of the 1938–1944 period, which is presented in the textbook on the same page as the three photographs mentioned above, further conveys this point. From 1938 to 1944, the chronology tells how the Japanese nation, including middle school students, were mobilized for the war effort. It also mentions the recruitment of Chinese and Korean laborers who endured harsh conditions in mines and factories. Not surprisingly, the books do not mention the stories of women who are euphemistically called *ianfu*, or comfort women. Rather, the key lesson seems to be that Japanese adults and children and the people from neighboring Asian countries all suffered from the war and that the collective suffering of Asians together could not be avoided.

Within this collective victimology trope, the stories of the comfort women are expunged, an act that invalidates these women's memories and personal histories. Moreover, by depicting the war from a pacifist stance, the texts only reinforce the lesson, through photo images, that "all Asians are victims of war" and "war is destructive." All people, the colonizer and the colonized subjects alike, are assumed to occupy the same victim position. What is troubling about this pacifist approach toward wartime history is not the antiwar position, but its leveling effect: the actual imbalance of power that exist(ed) between the colonizer (Japan) and the colonized subjects (other Asians) is leveled as if they stand as equals. The pacifist stance creates a moral judgment about the destructive nature of war, but by doing so, it reduces the complex ways in which Japanese colonialism, Western imperialism, and militarism together produced cultural, material, psychological, and physical violence for the colonized subjects. The selective remembrance and representation of the war in the primary textbooks create an impression that the Japanese and other Asians shared harmonious interdependence and unity.

By comparison, how do junior high school books treat the comfort women issue? The second volume of the collected textbooks by ISEI, entitled *Japan in Modern History (Junior High School)*, presents selected materials from three textbooks. They are *Atarashii shakai: Rekishi* (New social studies: History), most widely used in Japanese schools since 1993; *Chugaku shakai: Rekishiteki bunya* (Social studies for junior high schools: History); and *Shimpan chugaku shakai: Rekishi* (Social studies for junior high schools: History, new edition). As in the first volume, selections from these three textbooks are presented in the Japanese original on one page and in English translation on the facing page.

Shimpan chugaku shakai: Rekishi presents a full-page discussion on the theme "War and the Lives of the People." The one photograph included on this page shows a young Asian woman who is hunched over, working in a munitions factory. Her ethnicity and nationality are not specified; she can be Japanese, Korean, Chinese, or whatever, and she signifies simply a young woman who contributed her labor to the war effort. The caption accompanying the photo states, "Girl students at work in an arms factory." The lengthy commentary on the war begins with a view that with the growing intensity of the war, the daily lives of ordinary people became increasingly difficult. This commentary suggests that faced with the adversity of war, especially with a shortage of wartime labor, the Japanese government and military conscripted Japanese adults and children to work in the factories and mines. The next two paragraphs (in two or three sentences each) describe the lives of non-Japanese people under colonial occupation. The book states that "the approximately seven-hundred thousand Koreans and forty thousand Chinese who were brought forcibly to Japan were set to doing heavy manual labor in the mines and elsewhere. In addition, many Taiwanese and Korean men were sent to the front as soldiers under the conscription system. Furthermore, large numbers of Korean and other women were sent to the battlefield under the name *teishintai* (volunteer corps, or comfort women)."[8] This term, which was used euphemistically during the war, is merely repeated in the textbook rather than problematized. It may come as a surprise to some readers that the text does, in fact, discuss the conscription of men and women from Korea and Taiwan, as well as the harsh conditions under which they labored. However, at the same time, the book states that the "women sent to the battlefield" were the "necessary spoils" of a racial war against Western imperialism.

In *Atarashii shakai: Rekishi*, two pages are dedicated to a discussion of the Japanese colonization of Korea, the anti-Japanese resistance movements led by Koreans, and the forced recruitment of Koreans for the Japanese war effort. One photograph, titled "Korean Soldiers in the Japanese Army," shows young Korean men wearing their Japanese names sewn to their Imperial Japanese Army uniforms, listening with stern faces to a speaker (possibly a Japanese army officer) who is not shown in the photograph. The caption below the photograph contains the following information: "As the progress of the war worsened, people from the colonies of Korea and Taiwan were drafted into the army. The photograph shows Korean volunteer soldiers."[9]

In *Chugaku shakai: Rekishiteki bunya*, another popular textbook, additional photographs exhibit images of the imperial Japanese government and military and the military treatment of Korean male laborers. One photograph presents an image of a dozen Korean men in peasant work clothes who are pushing carts heavily loaded with stones on a narrow, steep road. The caption reads as follows: "Korean people mobilized to work on the construction of a hydroelectric power plant. This was to provide a source of electric power for military factories in Korea and Manchuria."[10]

Next to this photograph, three other pictures are juxtaposed; together, these photos, again, create a leveling effect between Imperial Japan and its colonies. One photo shows young men lined up in a single file. The caption states, "Young Taiwanese mobilized into the Japanese army." Another photo shows Japanese families waving the flag of Imperial Japan and the caption below the photo states, "Sending off the troops." The last photo displays two Chinese children standing alone on a dirt mound. The caption states, "Children who lost their parents after their home was burned down in the war (China)." Here, Korea, Taiwan, China, and Japan are equalized. No narrative is provided about *who* mobilized Koreans and Taiwanese into the Japanese army, nor about *how* and *why*. The orphaned and homeless Chinese children are simply depicted as victims of "the war." Yet, ironically, the photo of Japanese people waving the flag of the Rising Sun is shown to depict their loyalty and patriotism to Imperial Japan.

On the following page, however, the accompanying narrative, titled "The Time of the Forcible Recruitments," states: "One after another they took away anyone on the street or working in the fields who looked like they might be useful. They just put them in trucks and then onto ships and brought them to Japan. It wasn't conscription; it was kidnapping."[11] Again, it may surprise some Koreans that the Japanese textbook clearly indicates that Koreans were "kidnapped," not "conscripted," from the street or fields. But who actually did the "kidnapping"? Were only the men kidnapped, and no women or children? What meaning(s) does the "kidnapping of Koreans" suggest to young Japanese schoolchildren? What do this "record" and these photos, together, convey to the readers about the relationship between Koreans and Japanese during the war?

Again, the colonial ruler and the colonized subject are presented as occupying the same position. This depiction of the sameness or commonness neutralizes the dominant-subordinate power relationship between Japan and Korea. The leveling method produces the following images and effects of the colonizer-colonized relationship: (1) the Japanese, like other Asians, become subjects similarly victimized by Western imperialists; (2) as victims of a war against the West, all Asians suffer the same; (3) regardless of ethnicity, all Asians are mobilized together to defend Asian territory; and (4) Japan's defense of Asia is not an act of aggression or invasion but a necessary measure to secure the "Greater East Asia Co-Prosperity Sphere." This presentation of the war not only obliterates actual historical power relations between Japan and the Asian countries it colonized, but it also mythologizes the Pacific War and diminishes the impact of Japanese imperialism on the colonies. The myth recreated in the textbooks is that the Co-Prosperity Sphere was the unfortunate consequence of wartime exigencies, in which all Asians were forced to unite and mobilize together to defend Asia from Western imperialists. While the Pacific War was also referred to as the "Greater East Asian War" to convey "a new Asia throwing off the West,"[12] the Asian colonies were not liberated from Japanese colonialism nor did they enjoy "coprosperity." By creating a myth of harmony among Asians, this presentation effectively erases past and present conflicts between the Western imperialists, the Japanese colonizers, and the other Asian nations subjugated under both Japanese and Western domination.

The trope of Asian unity/harmony enables Japan to ignore its own role as colonizer by seeing only the West as the aggressor. In this one-sided, defensive posture, the colonized people are not shown as the colonized subjects they were, but as "lesser" Asians who supported and needed Japan's protection. The victim trope, in turn, implies that Japan has never been a perpetrator of ethnic and sexual violence against "lesser" Asians. By employing terms such as *teishintai* (voluntary corps) and ianfu (comfort women), the state trope of victimization and pacifism literally equates military sexual slaves with "volunteer corps" who "comforted" soldiers with their bodies.

Intentional or not, the downplaying of imperial Japan's power position as an aggressor conceals its imperialist policy and its ideology of the master race, or *Yamato minzoku* (Yamato race). In fact, the notion of "proper place"—a notion that created a hierarchy among and within races, ethnic groups, nations, cultures, gender, and family—was integral to the division of labor within the Greater East Asia Co-Prosperity Sphere.[13] Boldly elucidated by military leader Lt. Colonel Ishiwara Kanji, the Co-Prosperity Sphere was systematically formulated. The Japanese would provide the political and cultural leadership and develop large industry; the Chinese would provide labor and small industry; the Koreans would produce rice; the Manchus would engage in animal husbandry; and the southern regions would provide raw materials and other resources.[14] Furthermore, to ensure its leadership over Asia in the 1940s, the Japanese government made its myth of racial superiority integral to the Japanese imperial power structure: "We, the Yamato race, are presently spilling our 'blood' to realize our mission in world history of establishing a Greater East Asia Co-Prosperity Sphere. In order to liberate the billion people of Asia, and also to maintain our position of leadership over the Greater East Asia Co-Prosperity Sphere forever, we must plant the 'blood' of the Yamato race in this 'soil.'"[15]

Embedded in the comfort women issue is Japan's postwar and postimperial ambivalence toward its failure to realize the myth of racial superiority reflected in the above passage. Japan's official silence and its selective omission of images of its wartime aggression, especially those dealing with violence against colonized subjects in the form of military sexual slavery, appear premised on Japan's ambivalence toward the question of its racial superiority as a nation.

THE SOUTH KOREAN government, like its Japanese counterpart, has upheld a masculine-nationalist posture toward women exploited as military sexual slaves. For example, the postwar authoritarian governments have admonished the women who tried to expose the comfort women issue. Considering the issue a nuisance, government officials continued to ignore and discourage women activists who tried to expose wartime rape as a gender/sexual-based war crime. The Korean Council for the Women Drafted for Military Sexual Slavery by Japan, a coalition group composed of labor, human rights, Christian, Buddhist, and women's groups, among others, in 1991 proposed the construction of a memorial monument dedicated to comfort women at the Independence Memorial Museum. But the Korean government rejected the proposal, stating that there was "insufficient land" available for a new monument and that "the landscape around the memorial building" would make construction difficult.[16]

The history textbooks used in junior high and high schools throughout South Korea usually make no mention of comfort women, or at best, portray them as marginal historical figures. *Kuksa* (National history), the textbook that is currently used in all South Korean junior high and high schools, underscores the moral and ethical lesson that patriotic Koreans must preserve their national culture and identity.

The 1992 version of *Kuksa* for high schools devotes one chapter to the National Independence Movement. The first subsection focuses on *minjokui sunan* (national suffering) and presents an official nationalist narrative on "The Colonial Rule of Obliteration of the [Korean] Nation." The hypernationalist ideology evident in this high school textbook is replicated in the same vein in the 1994 version of *Kuksa* for junior high schools. This textbook reiterates the same trope of victimization — that of Korea as a colonized national-ethnic subject — in a moralistic tone and language. For example, one chapter, titled "The Campaign to Preserve National Culture," examines the theme of "imperial Japan's policy to destroy the Korean nation." This chapter highlights Japan's invasion of Korea through the masculinized national narrative. We find this theme illustrated in the following excerpt:

> The Korean peninsula became a strategic military zone for imperial Japan's invasion of Asia. Reduced to an instrument of Japan's imperialist invasion, our nation and culture faced the danger of complete destruction. In the name of the Unification of Korea and Japan, Koreans, as imperial subjects, were banned from using the Korean language and teaching Korean history in schools. Moreover, publication of newspapers in the Korean language was made illegal. Because of an incident involving the Korean Language Society, Korean language scholars were arrested, with the result that their scholarship was interrupted, and research on Korean language and history was forbidden. The Korean nation was forced to worship at Japanese shrines, which were erected throughout Korea. Furthermore, the family names and given names of Koreans were forcefully changed to Japanese names. During the Pacific War, when Japanese faced a short supply of raw materials and labor, our youths were conscripted to work in mines and factories where their labor was exploited. Even students in their teens were taken to various fronts in the name of the Student Volunteer Corps. In addition, even the women became the object of sacrifice for the war under the name *chonsidae* [comfort women]. In such a way, not only our raw materials but our labor, too, was forcibly mobilized for the Japanese war of invasion.[17]

The sentence from the above passage that states "even the women became the object of sacrifice for the war under the name of comfort women" is the only new information added to the textbook since 1992.

The official view of the colonial past is presented here in terms of the collective grief, sorrow, suffering, and humiliation of Koreans as a nation. The collective memory of the colonized Korean nation is shaped through the remembering of the Japanese obliteration of Korean national and ethnic cultures and the ways Korean men and women, young and old, were forced to sacrifice their lives for the colonialist/imperialist war effort. In the textbook, the cruelty and crimes of Japanese colonists clearly dominate the landscape of collective memory; these lines from the textbook suggest that the colonial oppression should not be forgotten. Thus, the language of loss, grief, and suffering, which recognizes the "sacrifice" of Korean women as chongsindae, nurtures and instills nationalist and patriotic sentiments among the young Korean students. The subliminal message here is a moral one: it is a view that condemns Japanese imperialism and colonialism for bringing humiliation and emasculation of the Korean nation by forcing Korea to "sacrifice" the women of the nation.

The mention of comfort women in the textbook thus serves only to arouse anti-Japanese, Korean nationalist sentiments in students; the superficial one-liner is not meant to provoke a discussion about the fate of the women under patriarchy or to create an understanding of how and why women were made subjects of sexual and racial exploitation under colonialism and war. If the state recognized the comfort women issue as being worthy of inclusion in national history writing, the textbook would discuss the women's experiences in the Japanese military camps and the nature of women's "sacrifice." The sexual violence and subjugation of women that accompanied the colonial patriarchal project might discuss the capture and conscription of Korean girls into the Women's Patriotic Labor Corps or the Women's Voluntary Labor Corps, by both Koreans and Japanese, the systematically organized and militarized nature of wartime rape, the establishment of comfort stations throughout Asia, and the deaths, suicides, poverty, and ostracism that women faced upon returning home to Korea after the war.

The marginal treatment of this issue in the textbooks, however, is neither accidental nor due to a lack of information. Rather, the marginality reflects a method of official silencing and a patriarchal bias embedded in the official state ideology toward women. The masculinized nationalist state rhetoric presented in the Korean textbooks necessarily suppresses the comfort women discussion because the rape of Korean women by soldiers of the colonial ruler evokes the decentering of the Korean national, ethnic, and patriarchal identities. Attached to the comfort women issue are core issues of Korean ethnic identity and masculinized nationalism, which are essentialized in terms of morality. Once "chaste" and "pure," feminine virtues that are praised in the Confucian patriarchal ideology, Korean women who were raped and sexually exploited by Japanese soldiers represent damaged, disgraceful, and unchaste female bodies that lack the "feminine essence." In the reconstitution of the Confucian, patriarchal, and paternalistic political order of postcolonial South Korea, the comfort women were effectively subordinated and silenced within the nation. The government and the national elites have treated the comfort women issue as an embarrassment. Viewed as a "woman's problem," private and individual, the plight of comfort women was not considered a matter worthy of public or national attention until 1991. The recuperation of the Korean national identity by the postwar state in South Korea has relied on strategies of excommunicating the raped women from mainstream Korean society and marginalizing their place in national history.

Reading the history textbooks, one quickly confronts the lesson that Koreans, as a unified plural self, have the responsibility to preserve Korean ethnic and national culture. This lesson finds constant reinforcement in the moralistic and hypernationalist ideology of the South Korean state. As was evident in the Japanese school textbooks, the national history presented in Korean textbooks also dramatizes its own victimology. For example, the memory of the Japanese ruling Other evokes a vulnerable image of Self vis-à-vis the Korean. One aspect of this vulnerability is seen in the weak position of the Korean nation as an emasculated, colonized subject. Koreans did not and could not overthrow the colonizer from within. In spite of the militant strikes, demonstrations, revolts, and independence struggles that Koreans organized continuously until the end of the war, the Japanese military and police were too strong, too repressive, and too dominant to be overthrown by the Koreans themselves. Faced with the colonialist strategy of relying on terror, aggression, and repression, the Korean nation did not possess the necessary military power to challenge the colonizer during the thirty-five to forty years that Korea was occupied and ruled by Japan. The weak military and political position of South Korea vis-à-vis Japan during most of the twentieth century made actual confrontation with the conqueror-colonist an impossibility. Its weakness as a patriarchal power and a nation-state is one of the reasons that could explain why the postwar authoritarian governments in South

Korea have more or less silenced the comfort women issue from collective memory. Furthermore, it is through the deployment of a binary construction or imagining of the Korean nation as the victim and the Japanese colonizer as the oppressor/perpetrator that the postwar South Korean state has delineated its national identity. The reliance on the victimology trope enables the postwar South Korean state to instill hypermasculine nationalist sentiments among Koreans while, at the same time, it disavows its self-image as the colonized nation and patriarchy that failed to protect the victimized Korean men and women. It must be emphasized that although the weak military and political position of South Korea during most of the twentieth century indeed made actual confrontation with the conqueror-colonist an impossibility, the postwar authoritarian governments have disavowed the image of South Korea as a weak nation and patriarchy.

Therefore, fear of emasculation is in part responsible for the state's silencing of the memory of comfort women in South Korea. The women are living symbols that remind the nation of its patriarchal weakness and paternal failure, namely, the inability of Korean men to protect the lives and bodies of their own wives, daughters, and sisters. Questioning why the military sexual slavery and rape of females during colonialism and war continue to be issues of which the Korean state cannot speak openly leads us to ponder the following question: What is the collective memory that the comfort women evoke for the state and the nation? More damaging to the collective psyche of postwar Korea than the bodies of the women survivors themselves is, therefore, what those bodies continue to represent: the symbolic emasculation of the Korean national, state, and patriarchal elites.

AS ILLUSTRATED IN the analyses of textbooks, the Japanese and Korean governments have selectively ignored, suppressed, and sanitized the wartime experience of the comfort women. In contrast to the official history constituted by the state, the countermemories of women survivors are transmitted and shaped through personal testimonials. Nearly fifty years of official silence on the comfort women issue, both in Japan and South Korea, have brought major protests and demonstrations since 1992. Speaking out against the governments' denial of their existence, former comfort women have mobilized as new political actors no longer hidden from the public view. They have put the comfort women issue on the national and international political agenda, with the assistance of various activist groups and individual supporters, both inside and outside Korea. Since early 1992, women survivors, with the aid of researchers, have also produced powerful personal testimonies about their memories of wartime sexual violence and exploitation. Curiously, however, the testimonies have quickly become reified as "information" and "data," and they are treated as hard facts and the truth about the past — "facts" that must be verified. This approach to reading testimonies as mere evidence or data, however, misses the crucial meaning and power inherent in the women's testimonials. Consequential matters concerning the meanings embedded in the process of the remembering itself and the memory of rape, which contradicts the official reconstruction of wartime events, need to be more carefully examined.

Indeed, the women's testimonials are a means by which the personal and the political converge. From ethnogendered perspectives, the stories of comfort women transmit a collective voice that speaks for plural identities — of poor, female, colonized subjects who are Korean and of other Asian ethnic cultures. Maria Rosa Henson, a woman from the Philippines who has written her own biography about the experience of sexual slavery for Japanese soldiers, recounts her memory of having been the poor, illegitimate daughter of a big landowner and a supporter of a resistance army, who was physically and sexually assaulted by Japanese soldiers because of her identity as a Filipina.[18]

The testimony-narratives of women survivors, such as the autobiography of Maria Rosa Henson, typically begin with the speakers' female socialization as girls and young women in rural villages, stories of poverty and hardship faced by their families under Japanese colonial rule, and descriptions of their roles as daughters, mothers, and wives who repeatedly survived against difficult odds. The women also express their anger, humiliation, and moral outrage in the testimonials. Although the events occurred fifty years ago, by sharing their memories in public for the first time, the women release the angst and pain of their past trauma as if the events had occurred only yesterday. By telling their stories of forced recruitment, hunger, confinement, torture, beatings, disease, rape, death, and humiliation, the women reconstitute both private and public memories of the past.

Hwang Kum-ju is among the first women to testify in public. She kept her experience buried and hid her past for most of her seventy years. As a young girl, Hwang, along with other girls from her village in South Korea, was recruited with the promise of work in a factory. Hwang says, "I was put on several trains and [we] were told we would be given manufacturing jobs like thousands of men drafted into forced labor." She recalls that after several days, they were taken to the Japanese army barracks, where they were "kept like animals." She suffered from daily rapes, sexual diseases, and brutal treatment: "There were so many soldiers. Sometimes, we had to do it with twenty to thirty soldiers a day. I think ours was the only comfort station in that area, and soldiers and officers came whenever they had some spare moments. Higher-ups came freely, and at night we usually slept with officers. Women who contracted venereal diseases were simply left to die or shot. Anyone resisting the advances of the men was beaten."[19]

Hwang states that she always lived with a feeling of having been "wronged" and wanted to tell her story to the government, but it was impossible to do so. But in 1992 she testified and, once her story was televised, other women, such as Kang Tok-kyong, also voiced their memories of rape, pain, fear, and terror: "The military policeman wore a red rank-patch with three stars. I learned that he was Kobayashi Tateo, a corporal. . . . He took me to a low hill. It was pitch dark, and he raped me. I was so scared and didn't know anything about men that I didn't even resist. I should have killed myself by biting my tongue, but at that time, I was only seized with terror. . . . After three days, Kobayashi came and raped me again. Then other soldiers began to come."[20]

Kim Tok-chin's anger is aimed at the Korean government. More than the actual experience of military sexual slavery itself, she tells us about the deeper psychological wound she suffered from being stigmatized, excluded, and rejected by Korean society and the Korean government. Kim states:

> Until now I have lived with all my resentment and anger buried deep in my heart. I went to one of my nephews, a high school teacher, whom I had helped to educate. I told him about my past and asked if I should register at the Council. . . . He pleaded with me not to register. I discussed the matter with another nephew living in Taejon. He wept as he listened to my story and advised me not to register. He said, "It will break your son's heart. What will your stepson in the United States say when he hears all this?" But I felt uneasy and couldn't sleep

at all. So one day I went to a broadcasting station and told my story. I came home and slept soundly. I told my son about the whole thing, and he wept uncontrollably, saying, "Mother, you have lived so courageously even with such a rough past. I am proud of you." My heart moves more and more towards the meetings of the Council. Of course Japan is to blame, but I resent the Koreans who were their instruments even more than the Japanese they worked for. I have so much to say to my own government.[21]

As reflected in these testimonies, the women survivors speak in detail about the pain, abuse, and violence they endured. The women remember the names of those who abused them, testify about the ways they were recruited, and reveal how they were confined to comfort stations run by the Japanese military. In particular, the women demand that their "lost youth" (i.e., their health, respectability, chastity, dignity, etc.) be returned to them. But the women also challenge us to recognize their complete identity as Koreans and women and to restore their social standing by not judging them as disgraced and disgraceful women. The sorrow and pain that the women survivors face, as well as their desire that others recognize the violence they suffered for so long, are expressed in *Katusa* (struggle or fight), a song sung by Yi Yang-su:

> I can't live with this bitterness
> Give me back my youth
> Apologize and make reparation,
> Japan, apologize and make reparation for
> Taking us and trampling on us
> Mother, father, can you hear
> Your daughter crying
> Now my Korean brothers and sisters help me along.[22]

These poignant lines express women's courage to speak and call for recognition. Women no longer remain quiet, obedient, and invisible. Rather, with the help of a women's movement that is growing in Asia, and by telling their stories and protesting in public, the women are now struggling to liberate themselves from fifty years of silence. They also display their moral outrage against both the Japanese and South Korean governments by challenging those states for reparation and redress, for recognition of their rights, and for revision of the textbooks. The demand for reparation, as expressed here by Yi, should be read, not with indifference, embarrassment, and nuisance—the reaction of the South Korean and Japanese governments—but as a call for recognition and commitment to provide the basic survival needs of former comfort women and their families.

Finally, we must not confuse the fact that it was not the men nor the governments but the women survivors themselves, in their advanced age as septuagenarians, who have ruptured the silence around this issue. Although these women were subjects who experienced victimization by and subjection to men—rape, abuse, lack of control of their own bodies, and society's silencing—they have emerged as new political actors who are demanding recognition, rights, and reparation. The testimonials clearly depict that the women have been and are conscious of their oppression, which stems from military, colonial, and Confucian-patriarchal domination.[23] By urging us to listen to their public testimonies, the women survivors, though poor, aged, and suffering from illnesses, are asserting the "subjectivity" that the Korean state and society have denied them for so long.

At the same time, the structures of symbolic representation that the women survivors use to construct their narrative of the self enable us to move beyond the level of simple reflection of their emotions. An examination of women's views of their bodies and selves, as reflected in their testimonies, helps us to recuperate the suppressed identities and submerged voices of the raped and colonized women. These views call on us, researchers and activists alike, to intervene in making sense of the women's testimonies and in obtaining a public validation of their personal memories as collective memories. Rather than merely collecting and disseminating their stories as facts, we are called on to investigate in depth and interpret the complex nature of their experiences in wartime military sexual slavery. By examining the meanings embedded in the testimonies and the language used by the women survivors to reconstruct their memories, we can incorporate their racial/ethnic, gender, and sexuality location as fundamental sites for reconstructing both collective and personal histories.

AGAINST THE BACKDROP of the politics of memory and history writing, the testimonials of women survivors and their demand that the wartime rape issue be included in the textbooks symbolize more than a simple cry for the recognition of injustice. Reading the women's testimonies merely as protests for including them in and correcting history weakens the power of the testimonials. Rather, the women are challenging us to question the received "truths" about imperialism, colonialism, nationalism, and gender oppression and patriarchy and to revise the narratives of national history through which we have come to understand our collective present. Their testimonials provide an alternative source from which we can direct our thinking about how the female subjectivity of formerly colonized women is constructed, about whose story will be reconstituted into the narrative of national history, and about how the national narrative will come to represent the past for the present and future. What is immediately at stake in the comfort women issue is who gets to speak and whether or not the public discussion about female sexuality and rape, as well as the voices of surviving comfort women, will gain legitimacy. The larger issue is what happens now that the discourse about comfort women has become a public debate. The comfort women controversy is the ground on which collective memory, identity, and tales of the nations' pasts and presents are being contested and reconstructed, both in postimperial Japan and postcolonial South Korea. The testimonials and textbooks reveal a power conflict as to whether or not the women survivors will be recognized as conscious subjects with agency. At the same time, these materials question the style in which the postcolonial Japanese and South Korean states are imagining their past, present, and future identities as collective nations.

Notes

1. The comfort women were/are commonly referred to as *jugun ianfu* or *teishintai* (volunteer corps) in Japanese, and *wianbu* or *chôngsindae* in Korean. The vulgar Chinese term *p'i* (vagina) is also used to describe the women.

"Comfort women" is a direct translation from "wianbu" in Korean (and "ianfu" in Japanese). "Chongsindae" is a different term, originally, referring to the more generic "labor force" that was specially mobilized for Japan's war effort before and during the Asian-Pacific War. Thus, chongsindae includes the old and young, men and women, Japanese and non-Japanese, and so forth. However, in Korea in the last few years before the end of the war when Japan made its "total war" effort in the colony, the term was increasingly used specifically for women who were conscripted for labor and who had to make up for the demands of the empire when most men were in the battlefield. And many of them were deceived and coerced to become sex slaves for the Japanese imperial troops until the end of the war. So, in Korea, chongsindae became a general term for those sex slaves for Imperial Japan. But, accurately speaking, chongsindae and wianbu are two different categories.

2. International Society for Educational Information (ISEI), *Japan in Modern History*, 2 vols. (Tokyo: ISEI, 1993–94).

3. Ibid., 1: 9.

4. *Shogakjo gakushu yoryo*, pt. 2, chap. 2: Social Studies (1989), 28, cited in ISEI, *Japan in Modern History*, 1:13.

5. The three textbooks are *Atarashii shakai* 6 (New social studies 6), *Shimpan shakai* 6 (New social studies 6), and *Watashitachi no shogaku shakai* 6 (Our primary school social studies 6). Since April 1992, these three books have been the most popular texts used in Japan.

6. ISEI, *Japan in Modern History*, 94–95.

7. Ibid., 95.

8. ISEI, *Japan in Modern History Junior High School*, 507.

9. Ibid., 144–145.

10. Ibid., 144.

11. Ibid., 334–337.

12. See Saburo Ienaga, *The Pacific War, 1931–1945* (New York: Pantheon, 1978), 154.

13. John Dower, *War without Mercy: Race and Power in the Pacific War* (New York: Pantheon, 1986), 277.

14. William Theodore de Bary, ed., *Sources of Japanese Tradition* (New York: Columbia University Press), 2: 801–805.

15. Quoted in Dower, *War without Mercy*, 277.

16. Yi Sun-in, "Iljepihae (chongsindae) ch'öngwonsimsa chilmun," in *Chongsindae munje charyojip* (Seoul: Korea Council, 1992), 2: 27–32.

17. Kuksa P'yonch'an Wiwonhoe (National History Compilation Committee), *Kuksa* (Seoul: Ministry of Education, 1992), 133; my translation.

18. See Maria Rosa Henson, *Comfort Woman: Slave of Destiny* (Manila: Philippine Center for Investigative Journalism, 1996), 41–47.

19. Korean Council, *Chongsindae munje Charyojip* (Seoul: Korean Council, 1992), 7–9; Korean Council, *Kangjero kkulryogan Chosonin Kunvoianbudul* (Seoul: Hanwul, 1993), 93–106; Korean Council, *Witness of the Victims of Military Sexual Slavery by Japan* (Seoul: Korean Council, n.d.), 87–100.

20. Korean Council, *Witness of the Victims*, 5.

21. Korean Council, *Kangjero kkulryogan*, 57.

22. See Korean Council, *Witness of the Victims*, 86.

23. On the relationship between the patriarchal culture/ideology and the politics of comfort women, see Chungmoo Choi, "Korean Women in a Culture of Inequality," in *Korea Briefing*, ed. Donald N. Clark (Boulder, Colo.: Westview Press, 1992).

Melani McAlister

"One Black Allah": The Middle East in
the Cultural Politics of African American
Liberation, 1955–1970

When the African American boxer Cassius Clay declared he was a Muslim and adopted the name Muhammad Ali in 1964, the links between blacks in the United States and Muslim communities more generally were made clear to all the world. And yet the history of the deeper, more systematic ties between African Americans, the Nation of Islam, and transnational Islamic movements in the twentieth century has not been evident until recently. This essay contextualizes the stories of Ali and LeRoi Jones (later, Amiri Baraka) by tracking the involvement of African Americans — civil rights leaders, artists, and ordinary folks — not simply in international affairs but in the geopolitics of the 1960s and 1970s, specifically with respect to the Middle East. If the fighting body of Ali was one entrée into debates about the Israeli state and Palestinian self-determination, it was just one of many avenues (cultural and political) that African Americans had for articulating their relationship to a wider world (including through a critique of their "internal colonization" in the United States). Castro of Cuba, Nkrumah of Ghana, and Nasser of Egypt were also iconic, and the connections they allowed between anticolonial resistance and black power, underappreciated perhaps today, remind us that although Ali remains celebrated for his global consciousness, in fact he represents the cosmopolitan and highly politicized consciousness of much of black America in the late twentieth century.

Two events, separated by just over a year, in two very different spheres of cultural activity, marked the extraordinary influence of Islam in the African American community in the 1960s. Two prominent African American men, one an athlete, the other a poet and a playwright, took highly visible and conscious steps away from their old identities and affiliations and began instead to articulate a black consciousness and politics based on the teachings of Islam. These two public transformations — rituals of self-identification and self-naming — point to an often neglected genealogy of black political and cultural affiliation: an African American imagined community in which the Arab Middle East is central.

On 25 February 1964, the twenty-three-year-old fighter Cassius Clay defeated Sonny Liston and took the world heavyweight boxing title, the most lucrative prize in professional sports. On the day after his triumph, Clay, who had already become one of the most well-known and controversial figures in the boxing world, announced at a press conference that he was a Muslim.[1] Until that day, Clay had been known as a playful, rather apolitical youngster with a fondness for pink Cadillacs, extravagant bragging, and comic poetry. But in the months before the fight, rumors of his association with the Nation of Islam (NOI) had circulated widely; he had been seen frequently in the company of Malcolm X, whom he had invited to his training camp in Miami. A few weeks after the victory, Elijah Muhammad, the leader of the Nation of Islam, bestowed on Clay his Muslim name, Muhammad Ali. Ali's victory and subsequent announcement were widely reported; his association with the NOI was often viewed with skepticism or anger. In the spring of 1964, when Malcolm X left the Nation, Ali stayed, and quickly became the most famous Black Muslim in the country and one of the Nation of Islam's most prominent spokespersons. Just a few months later, Ali embarked on a tour of Africa and the Middle East. When he returned, he announced to the press: "I'm not an American; I'm a black man."[2]

In 1966, Ali's status as a political figure took a new direction when he refused his induction into the U.S. Army, saying, "I'm a member of the Black Muslims, and we don't go to no wars unless they're declared by Allah himself. I don't have no personal quarrel with those Viet Congs."[3] That refusal — that risky stand on behalf of the politics of his religious belief — transformed Ali's image: he soon became one of the most visible and influential antiwar figures in the country. He was, in the words of poet Sonia Sanchez, "a cultural resource for everyone in that time," a man whose refusal to fight in Vietnam became an emblem of the far-reaching influence of the black nationalist critique of American nationalism and U.S. foreign policy.[4]

In 1965, a little over a year after Muhammad Ali's highly public conversion, the poet and playwright LeRoi Jones left his literary circles in Greenwich Village to move uptown to Harlem, where he founded the Black Arts Repertory Theatre / School (BARTS). In Harlem, Jones turned his back on his earlier ties with Beat poetry and even his more recent success with plays on race relations (*The Dutchman* had won an Obie award in 1964). He focused instead on the task of building a community theater and on developing the themes and writing styles that would launch the Black Arts Movement. During his time at BARTS, Jones wrote *A Black Mass*, a one-act play that presented in dramatic form the Nation of Islam's central myth: the story of Yacub, the evil scientist who "invented" white people. Then, in 1968, Jones changed his name to Ameer (later to Amiri) Baraka. He studied Sunni Islam under the tutelage of Hajj Heesham Jaaber, who had been affiliated with Malcolm X near the end of his life. By then, Baraka, whom his contemporaries considered to be "the most promising black writer" in the nation, was also the best-known representative of the Black Arts Movement, a champion of black cultural nationalism, a significant theorist of the reemergence of committed art, and an articulate critic of U.S. imperialism. Baraka would turn away from Islam and toward Maoism in the 1970s. But from at least 1965 until 1973, he and others saw Islam as a primary nationalist cultural resource, an authentically black religion that would be central to the requisite development of an alternative black culture and a liberated spirituality.

This essay analyzes the significance of the Middle East in African American cultural politics in the late 1950s and 1960s. In particular, it explores the impact of Islam as a religious practice and as a cultural poetics, including its more diffuse impact even on those who were not converts. By 1965 or 1966, one need not have ever entered a Muslim temple nor read a Nation of Islam newspaper to know that, in the African American community, Islam had moved far beyond the sectarian curiosity it had been just ten years earlier. In a cultural field that ranged from poetry and plays to highly charged sports matches, from local community theaters to the boxing ring, Islam was a significant presence. In various manifestations, Islam, and the Nation of Islam in particular, played a central role in reconfigurations of black radicalism, challenging both the hegemony of black Christianity's religious values and the politics of integration associated with it. At the same time, the centrality of the Middle East to Islamic histories and to many Muslim rituals encouraged the increasing visibility of Arab cultures and Arab politics in African American communities. In particular, we begin to see the ways in which African American investments in, and interpretations of, the Arab-Israeli conflict developed, at least in part, out of the religious and cultural alternatives to black Christianity that became influential in the 1960s.

THE NATION OF Islam emerged as a significant social and political force in the black community in the late 1950s, after a period of disarray and declining membership in the 1940s. When Malcolm X was released from Norfolk Prison in 1952, he quickly came to play a major role in the organization's expansion, establishing temples in cities all over the country. By December 1959, the Nation had fifty temples in twenty-two states; the number of members in the organization is difficult to estimate, but by 1962 was probably in the range of 50,000 to 100,000, with many more supporters. In 1962, *Muhammed Speaks*, the major NOI newspaper, founded by Malcolm X, had the largest circulation of any black paper in the country.[5]

Although the Nation of Islam was an avowedly "black nationalist" organization, its vision of black nationalism cannot be fully understood separately from either its explicitly religious content or its insistently transnational dimensions. In fact, the religious and the transnational aspects were intimately related: while the Nation of Islam was *unorthodox* Islam, Elijah Muhammad had, since the 1930s, consistently affirmed the significance of its connection to other Muslim communities around the globe, particularly those in the Middle East. The Nation challenged the assumption that African Americans were simply or primarily a subset of all Americans; its political imaginary never posited black nationalism as a self-contained subnationalism, even when Elijah Muhammad or Malcolm X made claims for the right to control specific tracts of land within the United States. Instead, the NOI built on the fact that Islam was a major world religion with a strong transnational orientation; Muslim governments and Muslim communities often forged ties across borders, political and cultural, as well as religious. Drawing on this global vision, the NOI developed a model of community that linked African Americans both to Africa and to "Asia" (by Asia, Elijah Muhammad seemed to mean primarily what is usually called the Middle East). By the time it began to reach a larger audience in the 1950s, the Nation of Islam's vision drew on several decades of black anticolonialist activity, led by intellectuals and activists from W. E. B. Du Bois to Paul Robeson to Walter White, which had envisioned African Americans as part of a pan-African diaspora. At the same time, the Nation's theological politics departed from that earlier activism's primary focus on Africa, opting for a more expansive transnationalism that included much of the nonwhite world (Latin America is something of an exception). Like the pan-Africanist intellectual and cultural movements of the 1930s and 1940s, however, Elijah Muhammad described the connections between African Americans and colonized peoples through a language of naturalized race. Muhammad simply claimed both Africa and the Middle East as black heritage, insisting that the Arabian peninsula and the Nile Valley were the historic home of what he called the "Afro-Asiatic black man" now living in America.

The significance of this religious and racial geography was profound. In the NOI temples being rapidly established in urban areas in the late 1950s and early 1960s, ministers brought a message of worldwide black Islam to thousands of African American converts. The Nation taught that Islam was the "natural religion of the black man," which had been stripped from the Africans who were sold into slavery and taught their masters' Christianity. Lectures in the temples often harshly indicted the traditional Christianity of the African American church and argued that African Americans should recognize their true heritage as the descendants of the Muslim prophet Muhammed. Arabic, the Nation taught, was the original language of black people, not only because many of the Africans who were taken into slavery and carried to the new world spoke Arabic, but also because "the so-called Negroes" in America were descendants of the original Arabic-speaking peoples to whom Islam was revealed. As the religious service began, the minister greeted his parishioners with the Arabic greeting *Assalaam-alaikum* (peace be with you) and the members responded, *wa-Alaikum as-salaam* (and also with you). At the Islamic schools set up by the Nation, Arabic lessons were an integral part of the curriculum: Arabic language instruction was said to begin at the age of three.[6]

The Nation's theology included an alternative genealogy for black Americans, who were understood to be descendants of the original inhabitants of Asia in general and Mecca in particular. As Elijah Muhammad wrote in his 1965 treatise, *Message to the Blackman in America*: "It is Allah's (God's) will and purpose that we shall know ourselves. . . . He has declared that we are descendants of the Asian black nation and the tribe of Shabazz . . . the first to discover the best part of our planet to live on . . .

the rich Nile Valley of Egypt and the present seat of the Holy City, Mecca, Arabia."[7]

The Nation of Islam's assertion that all black people were by nature Muslims was part of its critique of black Christianity, a critique that was at once theological, political, and historical. NOI meetings often had a display, drawn on a blackboard, featuring two flags: on one side of the board was a U.S. flag with a cross beside it and underneath it the caption "Slavery, Suffering, and Death." On the other side was drawn a flag bearing the Crescent and underneath it the words "Islam: Freedom, Justice, and Equality." Beneath both was a question: "Which one will survive the War of Armageddon?"[8] Elijah Muhammad's message to African Americans focused on pride and transformation. The Christianity of their slave masters had functioned to continue their spiritual enslavement, he argued, but Islam, which built upon the teachings of the Bible but succeeded them with additional revelations, would provide the key for understanding old teachings in the way they were intended, rather than through the perversions of white Christianity. In this way, NOI teaching revised, without discarding, important aspects of Christian symbolism that were salient in the black community. At the same time, this teaching also carried with it a racial, political, and moral geography: it pitted (black) Islam against (white) Christianity in a worldwide and historic struggle.

This religious mapping of the world, a practice certainly not unique to Islam or the Nation, was directly opposed to contemporary black Christian constructions of the Middle East as a "Holy Land" in which Israel (both ancient and modern) was a strong source of religious and political identification. Black Christianity had traditionally presented African American history as a not-yet-completed retelling of the Hebrew story, a potential site for the reentry of God into history on the side of a people. By the late 1950s, the Christian-dominated civil rights movement was making highly effective use of the Exodus as a figure for African American liberation. The alliance between African Americans and Jews in the early civil rights movement, though grounded in the active Jewish participation in the movement, was almost certainly strengthened by a strong metaphorical affiliation between the narrative of ancient Hebrew liberation from bondage and the purposeful imagining of African American liberation from discrimination in the United States. The Exodus trope was a link, one articulated in churches and meetings, in songs and in sermons, as well as in the writings of African American intellectuals and activists, from Martin Luther King Jr. to James Baldwin to Joseph Lowrey.

The connection that Black Christians felt with the Hebrew story extended into contemporary international politics. The establishment of modern Israel in 1948 was a source of enthusiasm and even inspiration for many African Americans. In 1947, Walter White, the executive director of the NAACP, had played a crucial role in lobbying African nations to vote for the UN resolution partitioning Palestine into Jewish and Arab areas. Ralph Bunche, the UN secretary for peacekeeping, was active in negotiating the end to the Arab-Israeli War in 1948 on terms generally considered favorable to Israel. And in 1948, the NAACP passed a resolution stating that "the valiant struggle of the people of Israel for independence serves as an inspiration to all persecuted people throughout the world."[9]

The Nation of Islam's vision of a worldwide Islamic alliance confronting white Christianity challenged the black Christian sanctification of ancient Israel and offered an alternative sacred geography, with Mecca as its center. Significantly, Elijah Muhammad taught that the stories told in the Christian Bible were prophesies rather than histories, and that, as prophesy, they spoke of the contemporary experiences of African Americans rather than the historical experiences of the ancient Hebrews: "Before the coming of Allah (God), we being blind, deaf, and dumb, had mistaken the true meanings of these parables as referring to the Jews. Now, thanks to Almighty God, Allah . . . who has opened my blinded eyes, and unstopped my ears, loosened the knot in my tongue, and has made us to understand these Bible parables are referring to us, the so-called Negroes and our slave masters."[10]

Within the NOI paradigm, Jews were not those whose ancient history was the prototype for contemporary liberation, as was the case for King and other civil rights leaders, but those whose putative status as "the chosen people" had usurped the position of the black people in relation to God. This scriptural interpretation did complex cultural work for the Nation. Surely, this metaphorical removal of Jews from the stories of the Old Testament had particular salience in terms of the domestic tensions that were already rife in urban areas between African Americans and Jews. Obviously, it carried the kernels of the NOI's anti-Semitism, which became more and more pronounced over the decade. But the specifically religious content also worked affirmatively as well, by mobilizing, appropriating, and refashioning an honored tradition to claim for African American Islam, as earlier Christianity had done with Judaism and as the Romans did with Greek mythology.

This mixture of denigration and affirmative appropriation was also apparent in the Nation's attitude toward modern Israel. Like earlier black nationalist movements, the NOI saw in the success of Zionism an example and motivation for black nationalism. Malcolm X often referred to Israel respectfully in his speeches and interviews, even as he insisted on the rightness of the Palestinian cause, as in this remarkably ambiguous passage from his *Autobiography*: "If Hitler *had* conquered the world, as he meant to — that is a shuddery thought for every Jew alive today. The Jew will never forget that lesson. . . . the British acquiesced and helped them to wrest Palestine away from the Arabs, the rightful owners, and then the Jews set up Israel, their own country — the one thing that every race of man in the world respects, and understands."[11]

This grudging respect did not translate into emotional identification with Zionism's success, as it did within much black Christian discourse, but it did further establish the complex meanings the Middle East held for the Nation of Islam and its members. If, as nationalists, they respected and even hoped to emulate Jewish nationalism, they nonetheless saw the Arab struggle with Israel as a parallel to the Nation of Islam's struggle for national self-determination in the United States, where the Nation claimed the right to "separate" from the rest of the United States by taking control of three or four states in the South for black people. Both the Arab (largely Muslim) population in Israel/Palestine and the black ("originally Muslim") population in the United States were in a struggle over land: control over that land was essential to nationalism and political rights.

Of the many connections the Nation established, those with Egypt were particularly important. The focus on Egypt developed for several reasons. First, like most black nationalists, NOI leaders believed emphatically that Egypt was a black nation and that the greatness of ancient Egyptian civilization was proof of the historical greatness of black culture. Second, Egypt was (and is) largely a Muslim nation; therefore, it embodied the link between ancient black greatness and contemporary Islam. Finally, there was Egypt's leader, Gamal Abdel Nasser, who had come to power in a bloodless coup against the British-backed king in 1952. In the mid-1950s, Nasser had emerged as the most important nationalist leader of the Arab world and as one of the major figures of the anticolonial nonaligned movement. Along with figures like Castro in Cuba and Kwame Nkrumah in Ghana, Nasser represented an emotionally explosive convergence of anticolonial defiance and postcolonial global consciousness.[12] But Nasser, as the leader of Egypt, also represented a particular connection between black and Arab anticolonialism: just as Egypt was geographically positioned at the intersection of the Middle East and Africa, in the years after Bandung, Nasser positioned himself as a leader in connecting African and Asian anticolonial movements.

In 1956, Nasser became an anti-imperialist icon when he nationalized the Suez Canal Company after President Eisenhower had refused to support U.S. loans for the construction of the Aswan High Dam. In response to the nationalization of the canal, Britain (the former colonial power), France, and Israel invaded Egypt; both the United States and the Soviet Union (for different reasons) demanded the immediate withdrawal of the invading forces.[13] The U.S. opposition to the invasion was widely viewed as a refusal to back the imposition of old-style colonialism in the Middle East; not coincidentally, it was also an assertion of American dominance in the region.

But Nasser emerged from Suez the real winner. His successful weathering of an invasion by the colonial powers made him a hero in the decolonizing nations, as well as among many African Americans. Nasser, an avowed Arab nationalist, also came to represent black and African defiance. Not surprisingly, the Nation of Islam endorsed the Egyptian seizure of the Suez Canal and opposed the invasion in its various publications. And though the Suez crisis did not receive as extensive coverage as Bandung had in the rest of the black press (which was focused on the Montgomery bus boycott and other developments in the emergent civil rights movement), many black intellectuals also responded critically. Right after Suez, W. E. B. Du Bois, a long-time supporter of Israel, hailed Nasser (and criticized Israel's role in the invasion) in a poem published in *Masses and Mainstream*: "Beware, white world, that great black hand / Which Nasser's power waves / Grasps hard the concentrated hate / Of myriad million slaves."[14] Observers would later look back on Suez as something of a turning point in African American perceptions of the Middle East: the moment in which Arab anticolonialism came home to black Americans.

The Nation of Islam identified with colonized nations politically, from the standpoint of a "colored" nation oppressed by whites, but it also drew very specifically on cultural and religious identifications with Arab nations, which were understood to be also racial and historical. A year after Suez, in December 1957, Malcolm X organized a meeting on colonial and neocolonial issues that included representatives from the governments of Egypt, the Sudan, Ghana, Iraq, and Morocco. That meeting, hosted by the Nation, sent a cable from Elijah Muhammad to Nasser, who was hosting the Afro-Asian People's Solidarity Conference in Cairo. In it, Elijah Muhammad, describing himself as the "Spiritual Head of the Nation of Islam in the West," addressed Nasser and the other national leaders as brothers, as coreligionists, and as peers:

> As-Salaam-Alikum. Your long lost Muslim brothers here in America pray that Allah's divine presence will be felt at this historic African-Asian Conference, and give unity to our efforts for peace and brotherhood.
>
> Freedom, justice, and equality for all Africans and Asians is of far-reaching importance, not only to you of the East, but also to over 17,000,000 of your long-lost brothers of African-Asian descent here in the West. . . . May our sincere desire for universal peace which is being manifested at this great conference by all Africans and Asians, bring about the unity and brotherhood among all our people which we all so eagerly desire.[15]

The cable, and Nasser's friendly reply, circulated widely within the Nation; these contacts later facilitated Malcolm X's trip to Egypt in 1959, where he laid the groundwork for Elijah Muhammad's visit to Mecca in 1960.

The Nation of Islam made explicit the link between a shared heritage and a shared origin: a myth of commonality remapped the dominant imaginative geography that separated the Middle East from Africa, instead uniting Africa and North West Asia (the Middle East) into one geographical space deemed "black Asiatic-African." The vision of one black culture meant that blackness was no longer simply a synonym for Africans and people of recent African descent, but a *literal* linking together of large groups of non-Europeans — the "Asians and Africans" connected, in Malcolm X's words, by history and "by blood."

As cultural source and resource, then, the Nation of Islam functioned through diverse sites. As a religious and political organization, it took culture and media representation quite seriously, but it also had an impact in many spaces/locations that Elijah Muhammad did not directly control, and thus wielded significant influence well beyond its membership. One site for this more general diffusion of Islamic sensibility was the remarkable infusion of NOI mythology into the cultural products of the emerging Black Arts Movement, which would in turn influence the direction of black liberation politics as the decade drew to a close. The signs of the Nation were frequently incorporated into the productions of a new generation of young writers, who took the symbols and myths of this African American Islamic sect as part of the raw material for the production of a new, black, postnational culture.

LEROI JONES LEFT Greenwich Village to found Harlem's Black Arts Repertory Theatre/School in 1965. Malcolm X had just been killed, and young African American intellectuals and activists found themselves and their communities in upheaval, in shock, torn by heated debates over the split between Malcolm X and Elijah Muhammad and by questions of who was responsible for the assassination. Then *The Autobiography of Malcolm X* was released; it became an immediate best-seller, creating a sensation in the circles of young, increasingly radicalized men and women who had listened to Malcolm X's speeches and were now riveted by the story of his life. It was in this context, coming to terms with the death of the country's most important spokesperson for black radicalism, that Jones/Baraka set out to form a community-based popular theater and to invent a form and language that would reach a broad African American audience with a message of black (post)nationalism. As Baraka later wrote, he and his colleagues wanted "an art that would reach the people, that would take them higher, ready them for war and victory, as popular as the Impressions or the Miracles or Marvin Gaye. That was our vision and its image keep us stepping, heads high and backs straight."[16]

Though BARTS was short-lived (it collapsed within a year), its founding was an inspiration to a new generation of poets and playwrights. Black theater and poetry burst onto the national scene, a flowering of African American cultural production unlike anything since the Harlem Renaissance. Within a year, small community theater groups were being formed around the country (in San Francisco, Detroit, Chicago, Washington, D.C., Los Angeles). The new community theaters produced plays and held poetry readings, not only in theaters, but also in schools, at local meetings, and in the street. Baraka himself was also a model; his transformation from highly literary poet into a radical artist committed to straightforward poetic language and generally short, accessible plays inspired the young writers who were publishing and performing in his wake (and quite consciously in his debt): Ed Bullins, Sonia Sanchez, Marvin X, Ben Caldwell, and Nikki Giovanni, among others.

The Black Arts Movement defined political struggle as cultural struggle; this cultural transformation, in turn, required a new spirituality. In literary circles, Islamic symbolism and mythology were incorporated into the self-conscious construction of a new black aesthetic and a revolutionary black culture. The aim was to establish a basis for political nationalism through the production of a set of cultural and spiritual values "in tune with black people." Those seeking black power were called on to understand the significance of culture. As Baraka argued, "The socio-political must be a righteous extension of the cultural. . . . A cultural base, a black base, is the completeness the black power movement must have. We must understand that we are replacing a dying [white] culture, and we must be prepared to do this, and be absolutely conscious of what we are replacing it with."[17] The attempt to construct a new black culture was deeply intertwined with the search for religious alternatives to mainstream Christianity, a search that included not only Islam, but also a renewed interest in the signs and symbols of pre-Islamic and traditional African religions (such as the Yoruban religion) and the study of ancient Egypt. These influences were often mixed together, in Baraka's thought as elsewhere, in an eclectic, sometimes deliberately mystical, mix.

Baraka's *A Black Mass* exemplifies the cross-fertilization and appropriation that linked Islam and the Black Arts Movement in the self-conscious production of a black mythology. The play was based on the story of Yacub, the evil scientist who created white people, as told by Elijah Muhammad and recounted repeatedly in publications and speeches. "Yacub's History" was "the central myth" of the Nation; it told the story of black origins and explained the current plight of black people, while reversing the traditional associations of Eurocentric Christianity, making "whiteness" the category associated with evil and thus in need of explanation. (The story also provided the background and justification for the Nation's provocative practice of referring to whites as "devils.") *A Black Mass* was written in 1965 while Baraka was at BARTS; it was first performed in Newark in May 1966 (after BARTS folded and Baraka moved to Newark to form Spirit House) and a month later was published in the little magazine *The Liberator*. In 1969, it was included in Baraka's collection, *Four Black Revolutionary Plays*.[18]

When Baraka wrote *A Black Mass*, he was not a member of the Nation of Islam, not even identified as a Muslim, though he would affiliate with orthodox Sunni Islam a few years later. Baraka would always mix Islam with his support of Kawaida, Ron Karenga's syncretic doctrine based on traditional African religions, but his fascination with the story of Yacub and his general interest in the myths of the Nation of Islam was not idiosyncratic. Thus, though *A Black Mass* was not produced as often as some of Baraka's more explicit social commentary, Black Arts critics admired it. The editor and essayist Larry Neal, who was also Baraka's friend and colleague, described it as Baraka's "most important play," because "it is informed by a mythology that is wholly the creation of the Afro-American sensibility."[19] The play was an early, explicit statement of the ways that, even after the death of Malcolm X and even with suspicions about Elijah Muhammad's role in his murder, the beliefs of the Nation of Islam were often presented as black culture, influencing and infusing a new black sensibility even for those who were not NOI adherents. In this sense, *A Black Mass* was both symptomatic and anticipatory of what would happen in the sphere of black cultural production in the next few years.

The play was a revision and a condensation of "Yacub's History," which explained the creation of white people from Earth's original black inhabitants as the product of generations of genetic breeding. In *A Black Mass*, Yacub, now called Jacoub, is introduced as one of three "Black Magicians" who together symbolize the black origin of all religions: according to the stage directions, they wear a skullcap, a fez, and an African fila. The play's title alludes to the necessity of black revisions of religious ritual, and the play itself is designed to revise and rewrite implicitly white-centered origin myths (and, not incidentally, to explain and define the theological problem of evil as represented in white people).

Castigated by the other magicians for his arrogance, Jacoub nonetheless proceeds with his experiment; as he does so, the natural world is disturbed by raging seas and thundering skies that have a Lear-like portentousness. Three women run in from outside, upset and frightened; they wail and moan, serving as a chorus and as representatives of "the people" who will be destroyed by Jacoub's creation. Undeterred, Jacoub pours his solutions together: there is an explosion, out of which leaps a cold white creature in a lizard-devil mask. The creature vomits and screams, "slobberlaughing" its way through the audience (30). The women and the other magicians are horrified by the creature, but Jacoub insists that he can teach the beast to talk. But the creature has only two words, incessantly repeated: "Me!" and "White."

The beast immediately tries to attack the women, and it soon bites one of them, Tilia, who is quickly transformed into another monster, white-blotched and slobbering. With this "bite-caress," Baraka adds Dracula to his stock of popular culture referents, and in so doing brings sexuality to the forefront: the depraved and dangerous — and decidedly unsexy — red-caped beast infects the women first, using its lust to spread its "white madness." If the play allegorically represents the rape of black women by white men, it also constructs "Woman" as the first and most susceptible possible site of the spread of "whiteness," thus reproducing the tendency of many nationalist ideologies to make women's bodies the sites of both nationalist reproduction and potential cultural impurity. As Philip Brian Harper[20] has pointed out, Black Arts Movement rhetoric consistently associated proper blackness with proper masculinity, a move that not only marginalized women but also meant that racial identification was figured in terms of a potent heterosexuality. Gender and sexuality infused the cultural/political rhetoric of Black Arts authenticity.

At the end of the play, Tilia and the beast become hideous Adam and Eve substitutes: the two of them then attack and kill the other women and the rest of the magicians, including Jacoub. With his dying breath, Jacoub condemns the two "white beasts" to the caves of the north. These two creatures will reproduce and eventually will create the white race that comes to dominate and enslave the rest of the world. Thus, if *A Black Mass* describes white people as the spawn of monsters, a crime against the natural order, distorted reproduction is the unspoken but crucial undercurrent.[21]

At the end of *A Black Mass*, a final narrator voice-over issues a call to racial struggle, now framed in mythical and theological terms: "And so Brothers and Sisters, these beasts are still loose in the world. Still they spit their hideous cries. There are beasts in our world, Brothers and Sisters. . . . Let us find them and slay them. . . . Let us declare Holy War. The Jihad. Or we cannot deserve to live. lzm-el-Azam. Ism-el-Azam. lzm-el-Azam. lzm-el-Azam" (39). The call for *Jihad* (Arabic for "righteous struggle" or Holy War) becomes a religious and moral response to the problem of evil, the answer of the present to the history presented in the play. The language of Islamic militancy is mobilized for black militancy; religious struggle and racial struggle are made one.

THE CULTURAL AND religious influence of Islam would play an important role in African American responses to the 1967 Arab-Israeli War, a war that marked the first major armed conflict in eleven years between Israel and Arab states, and which for the first time made Palestinians (the "refugees" from the founding of Israel in 1948) into a highly visible component of the conflict. In May 1967, the ongoing tensions between Israel, Egypt, and Syria escalated dramatically. Egyptian president Nasser, involved in a war of words with conservative Arab regimes over the direction of Arab politics, had recently been criticized by Jordan and Syria for hypocrisy and cowardice in continuing to allow UN troops to be stationed on the Egyptian side of the border with Israel. The UN troops had been positioned in the Sinai in 1957 to guard the peace after the Suez crisis, but Israel had refused to allow UN peacekeepers on its side of the border. Nasser, stung by the accusations and attempting to regain his prestige as the region's preeminent nationalist leader, moved his own troops into the Sinai in May 1967 and asked the United Nations to withdraw. Several days later, Nasser provocatively closed the Strait of Tiran to Israeli shipping. As American and European diplomats scrambled to cobble together a multilateral diplomatic and/or military response (the United States was particularly concerned to act carefully in light of the increasing controversies over the war in Vietnam), Israel insisted on the right of navigation through the international waters of the Strait and declared the closure an act of war. On 5 June, with tensions escalating on all sides, Israel launched an air attack that virtually destroyed both the Egyptian and Syrian air forces on the ground. Immediately, Jordan also entered the battle, attacking Israel with artillery and air power. In just six days, the war was over, with Israel the clear victor. As a result of the conflict, the Israelis conquered several territories that had been previously controlled by Arab countries: the Gaza strip (Egypt), East Jerusalem and the West Bank (Jordan), and the Golan Heights (Syria).

The mainstream African American reaction to the war was generally muted, though decidedly on the side of Israel. But the younger black liberation movement, now moving in an increasingly radical direction, had a very different response. Already, young black activists, building on the cultural politics articulated by leaders like Malcolm X and Baraka and influenced by the writings of anticolonialist and Marxist Frantz Fanon, had begun to describe the situation of African Americans as one of internal colonization. Increasingly, they drew parallels to the struggles for decolonization: from Muhammad Ali's jubilant affirmation that he was "not an American" but "a black man," to the young activists carrying around worn copies of *Wretched of the Earth*. These are "the Last Days of the American Empire," Jones/Baraka wrote in 1964, and for African Americans to love America would be to become "equally culpable for the evil done to the rest of the world."[22]

This was nowhere more true than in the Student Nonviolent Coordinating Committee (SNCC), which, though it had been originally allied with the Southern Christian Leadership Council (SCLC) and the Christian-based civil rights organizations, had become increasingly identified with the internal colonization model for understanding African American oppression. In May 1967, the organization made its internationalist approach apparent by declaring itself a human rights organization, establishing an International Affairs Commission, applying for nongovernmental organization (NGO) status at the United Nations, and announcing that it would "encourage and support the liberation struggles against colonialism, racism, and economic exploitation" around the world.[23] This internationalist approach was not an innovation, or a radical departure; it built on both the anticolonial activism of earlier generations of black Americans and the more recent cultural and political influence of Islam and African-based religions. But SNCC's stance was seen — as it was intended to be seen — as a clear indication that the organization was making a decisive break with the mainstream civil rights organizations and their model of liberation in one country.

It was in this context that the SNCC newsletter, in the summer of 1967, printed an article about the Arab-Israeli War. In June, just after the six-day war erupted, the Central Committee had requested that SNCC's research and communications staff investigate the background to the conflict. A few weeks later, the organization newsletter carried an article that described the war and the postwar Israeli occupation of the West Bank and Gaza in a decidedly pro-Arab fashion. The list of facts about "the Palestine problem" was highly critical of Israel (and not just the recent war): "Did you know that the Zionists conquered Arab homes through terror, force, and massacres? Did you know . . . that the U.S. government has worked along with Zionist groups to support Israel so that America may have a toehold in that strategic Middle East location, thereby helping white America to control and exploit the rich Arab nations?"[24] The article was accompanied by two cartoons and two photographs that many people considered anti-Semitic: one of the cartoons depicted Nasser and Muhammad Ali, each with a noose around his neck; holding the rope was a hand with a Star of David and dollar signs. An arm labeled "Third World Liberation Movements" was poised to cut the rope. One of the photos showed Israeli soldiers pointing guns at Arabs who were lined up against a wall, and the caption read: "This is Gaza, West Bank, not Dachau, Germany."[25]

The newsletter, and the statements supporting it, were widely denounced in the mainstream press and the Jewish community; the executive director of the American Jewish Congress called it "shocking and vicious anti-Semitism."[26] SNCC historian Clayborne Carson has argued that the article was "unauthorized" and based on the opinions of one individual, a staff writer who had been influenced by the Nation of Islam and had Palestinian friends in college. But as Carson also points out, SNCC's Central Committee had surely expected a pro-Palestinian orientation to the investigation they had requested, and they generally supported the conclusions it drew.

Carson believes that SNCC's decision to take up the Arab-Israeli War was part of a general trend toward making "gratuitous statements on foreign policy issues"; by 1967, he concludes, support for Third World liberation struggles was the only ideological glue that could hold the fracturing organization together. Others mark the SNCC leaflet as an indicative moment, the coming out of a whole generation of young blacks who were "using Israel as the benchmark for their repudiation of their civil rights past."[27] Certainly it was the case that the 1967 Arab-Israeli War galvanized Jewish identity in the United States; thus, criticism of Israel became a highly charged issue for Jews precisely at the moment that SNCC was making its public statements.

In general, these assessments have built on the assumption that, up to 1967, all available narratives of black liberation had placed African Americans in a de facto and unproblematic alliance with Israel, an alliance that would have continued had it not been for some individual or collective failure to sustain the domestic relationship forged between African Americans and American Jews in the civil rights movement. The fact that mainstream civil rights leaders quickly condemned the SNCC article and made statements in support of Israel seems at first to confirm this argument: the leaders of the old civil rights coalition, influenced by the black Christian narratives of Exodus and the model of Zionism for black liberation, and perhaps appreciative of the role that Jews had played in the movement, felt an emotional commitment to Israel.

But this division over the Arab-Israeli conflict also points to another story, the story of how the religious and cultural influence of Islam in the black community intersected with the increasing importance of decolonization movements worldwide. Placing SNCC's response to the 1967 Arab-Israeli War in the context of black Islam and its role in the radicalization of African American culture and politics helps us reframe the questions we ask about that moment and about the history of black-Jewish and black-Arab relations overall.

This alternative analysis avoids the common conflation of black-Jewish relations in the United States, and the concomitant issues of racism and anti-Semitism, with the meanings and significance of the Middle East for African Americans. While it is clear that the two issues, domestic relationships on the one hand, and representations of Israel and the Arab Middle East, on the other, are related, too often the assumption has been that African American views of the Middle East must reflect black-Jewish relations in the United States, and must be, to the degree that these views are critical of Israel or express affiliation with Arabs, an expression of black anti-Semitism.

This is not to say that anti-Semitism was not present in the black community and the Black Arts Movement. It was, and sometimes virulently. And though it is useful to point out the ways in which economic tensions in urban areas framed anti-Jewish feeling, it is not sufficient to say, as James Baldwin once did, that blacks were anti-Semitic because they were antiwhite.[28] In the case of Baraka, and in many of the pronouncements of the NOI, there is a profound difference, both qualitative and quantitative, in the ways that white ethnicities were targeted. For example, in one well-known poem, "Black Arts," Baraka made offhand remarks about several groups, commenting in the violent rhetoric that was often typical of him, that ideal poems would "knockoff . . . dope selling wops" and suggesting that cops should be killed and have their "tongues pulled out and sent to Ireland." But as Baraka himself later admitted, he held a specific animosity for Jews, as was apparent in the different intensity and viciousness of his call in the same poem for "dagger poems" to stab the "slimy bellies of the owner-Jews" and for poems that crack "steel knuckles in a jewlady's mouth."[29]

Certainly, anti-Jewish feeling did have a bearing on the ways some people (black and white) formed their understandings of the Arab-Israeli conflict: there were instances at the time of the 1967 war — and there have been since — of people who began by talking about the Arab-Israeli issue and who ended by criticizing Jewish store owners or political leaders in the United States for matters unrelated to foreign policy. (Of course, the tendency to conflate criticism of Israeli actions with criticism of Jews is not limited to African Americans.) But these anti-Semitic expressions simply don't explain the pro-Arab feelings of many African Americans in this period: it is quite possible to be both anti-Jewish and anti-Arab, as the example of some Christian fundamentalist groups illustrates.

I suggest that African American investments in the Arab-Israeli conflict have a significant history aside from the tensions of black-Jewish relations, a history that developed *within* the black community as part of a search for religious and cultural alternatives to Christianity. This search was simultaneously part of an ongoing process of redefining "blackness" in the United States. The struggle to define a black culture was never separable from the process of constructing transnational definitions of blackness — definitions that connected African Americans to people of color and anticolonialism all over the world, including, quite centrally, the Middle East.

MUCH OF THE discourse of civil fights viewed blackness as a subnational identity and saw the African American struggle as a striving for rights that would, if successful, transform the nation itself. At the same time, black nationalist writers tended to see blackness as a separate national identity, which would necessarily in time develop its own foreign policy, based on alliance with other peoples in a similar structural position as colonized people. But flowing through both of these visions has been another: that of blackness as a transnational identity and African Americans as players in a truly global drama.

Thus, African American cultural production in the era of black liberation challenged the very notion of a national identity by undermining the categories — of land, of culture, of politics — that underlay it. That is one reason it matters. Not because transnational identities are magically unproblematic; the cultural radicalism of the 1960s often framed black identity in terms that were ahistorical, masculinist, and anti-Semitic. This is its irony, its limit, and its loss. But the intervention was significant: a remapping of the world, an alternative moral geography, and a new imagined community that did not begin and end with Africa. This alternative was far more than a policy critique, it was a redefinition and a remapping. It was the search for an identity that would be, as both Baraka and Neal put it, "post-American": something outside of, and in opposition to, the expanding role of the United States on the world stage. Often centered in constructions of spirituality and religious belief, this African American narrative of countercitizenship mobilized the Middle East as both a crucial signifier and a utopian gesture in the process of constructing black identities within and across national borders.

Notes

1. On the day after the fight, Clay announced that he "believed in Allah"; at a second press conference the following day, he clarified his membership in the Nation of Islam. See Thomas Hauser, *Muhammad Ali: His Life and Times* (New York, 1991), 81–84.
2. Robert Lipsyte, "Cassius Clay, Cassius X, Muhammad Ali," *New York Times Magazine*, 25 Oct. 1964, 29.
3. Bill Jaus, "Cassius: I'm Still Unfit," *New York Post*, 21 Feb. 1966. See Henry Hampton and Steve Fayer, *Voices of Freedom* (New York, 1990), 321–334; Hauser, *Muhammad Ali*, 142–201.
4. Sanchez is quoted in Hampton and Fayer, *Voices of Freedom*, 328.
5. Mathias Gardell, *In the Name of Elijah Muhammad* (Durham, N.C., 1996), 65.
6. According to C. Eric Lincoln, *Black Muslims in America* (Boston, 1973), 120.
7. Elijah Muhammad, *Message to the Blackman* (Chicago, 1965), 31.
8. Described by Malcolm X, *The Autobiography of Malcolm X* (with Alex Haley) (New York, 1964, 1992), 224–225.
9. Robert Weisbord and Richard Kazarian Jr., *Israel in the Black American Perspective* (Westport, Conn., 1985), 20–22.
10. Muhammad, *Message to the Blackman*, 95–96.
11. *The Autobiography of Malcolm X*, 320.
12. See Brenda Gayle Plummer, *Rising Wind: Black Americans and U.S. Foreign Policy, 1935–1960* (Chapel Hill, N.C., 1996), 257–272.
13. See Donald Neff, *Warriors at Suez: Eisenhower Takes America into the Middle East* (New York, 1981).
14. W. E. B. Du Bois, "Suez," originally published in *Masses and Mainstream*, Dec. 1956, reprinted in *Creative Writings of W. E. B. Du Bois*, ed. Herbert Aptheker (White Plains, N.Y., 1985), 45–46.

15. Quoted by Lincoln, *Black Muslims in America*, 225.

16. Amiri Baraka, *The Autobiography of LeRoi Jones/Amiri Baraka* (New York, 1984), 204.

17. Amiri Baraka, "The Need for a Cultural Base to Civil Rites and BPower Movements," originally published in *The Black Power Revolt*, reprinted in *Raise, Race, Rays, Raze: Essays since 1965* (New York, 1971), 43–46.

18. Publication history from Jeff Decker, ed., *The Black Arts Movement: Dictionary of Literary Biography Documentary Series* v. 8 (Detroit, 1990), 120–121; Amiri Baraka, *Four Black Revolutionary Plays* (New York, 1969).

19. Larry Neal, "The Black Arts Movement," in *Visions of a Liberated Future: Black Arts Movement Writings*, ed. by Michael Schwartz (New York, 1989), 73.

20. Philip Brian Harper, *Are We Not Men? Masculine Anxiety and the Problem of African-American Identity* (New York, 1996).

21. Ibid., 76.

22. LeRoi Jones, "The Last Days of the American Empire (Including Some Instructions for Black People)," reprinted in *Home: Social Essays* (1966; Hopewell, N.J., 1998).

23. Clayborne Carson, *In Struggle: SNCC and the Black Awakening of the 1960s* (Cambridge, Mass., 1981), 192–198, 266.

24. Quoted in Weisbord and Kazarian, *Israel in the Black Perspective*, 33.

25. "Third World Round Up: The Palestine Problem: Test Your Knowledge," SNCC *Newsletter*, June–July 1967. The cartoons and photos are described in Weisbord and Kazarian, *Israel in the Black Perspective*, 35–36.

26. "Third World Round Up: The Palestine Problem: Test Your Knowledge."

27. Murray Friedman, *What Went Wrong: The Creation and Collapse of the Black-Jewish Alliance* (New York, 1995), 227–233.

28. James Baldwin, "Negros Are anti-Semitic because They Are anti-White," in *The Price of the Ticket: Collected Non-Fiction, 1948–1985* (1967; New York, 1985).

29. "Black Art," originally published in *The Liberator* (Jan. 1966) and collected in *Black Magic* (1969), reprinted in *Selected Poetry*. See Amiri Baraka, "I Was an AntiSemite," *Village Voice*, 20 Dec. 1980, 1.

Tony Ballantyne and Antoinette Burton

Postscript: Bodies, Genders, Empires:

Reimagining World Histories

When the Italian traveler Girolamo Benzoni arrived in Venezuela in 1541, among his very first encounters was with an Indian woman "such . . . as I have never before nor since seen the like of." He went on: "My eyes could not be satisfied with looking at her for wonder. . . . She was quite naked, except where modisty [*sic*] forbids, such being the custom throughout all this country; she was old, and painted black, with long hair down to her waist, and her ear-rings had so weighed her ears down, as to make them reach her shoulders, a thing wonderful to see. . . . her teeth were black, her mouth large, and she had a ring in her nostrils . . . so that she appeared like a monster to us, rather than a human being."[1]

Anyone familiar with exploration and travel writing from the New World knows how common such observations are. Benzoni's anatomical catalogue, which materializes the woman in Benzoni's sights *as body*, registers a preoccupation with the physical embodiment of indigenous populations that was a constitutive feature of such accounts. Benzoni and those who followed after him established the female body in particular as a recurrent emblem of native savagery and monstrosity, to be wondered at as one of the many astonishing "resources" of the world beyond Europe. Here as elsewhere, the body becomes an occasion for a taxonomical reflection as well as for translations of "the native woman" to European audiences. In the context of uneven power relations, bodies in contact provided a unique opportunity for the production of knowledge around gender and sexual difference, knowledge that, in turn, offered apparent proof of the comparative humanity of European civilization. *Bodies in Contact* suggests that the knowledges generated by such highly gendered contact had, and continue to have, ramifications far beyond the history of empires and colonialism per se. Although, as Adele Perry has remarked, colonialism is "very prosaically an exercise in gender" insofar as it produces gender itself as a terrain of contested power, its centrality to the making of global regimes and their histories is not necessarily self-evident.[2] Offering students of world history the chance to understand the extent to which such powerfully embodied colonial encounters structured the workings of transnational communities and global circuits of power has been the chief purpose of this volume.

Zones of Engagement: The Body as Method

Ever since Mary Louise Pratt coined the term "contact zones" in her 1992 book *Imperial Eyes*, students of empires and colonialisms have attempted to harness it to their analyses of cultural encounter.[3] For Pratt, contact zones are both real and imagined spaces in which cultures and their agents come together in circumstances of asymmetrical power. They are also uncharted terrains from which new, hybridized, cultural forms often emerge. The body has, arguably, been crucial to the experience of such encounters, though its capacity as an archive for the pleasures of human experience and the violences of history, colonial or otherwise, has only begun to be tapped by scholars.[4] Thanks to the work of Michel Foucault, the social body can no longer be taken for granted merely as a metaphor. His notion of "biopower" allows us to see with particular vividness the variety of somatic territories that modern states have identified as the grounds for defining and policing the normal, the deviant, the pathological, and, of course, the primitive. Following Foucault, much recent work on the body has acknowledged its power as both a discursive and a material resource.[5] Judith Butler's argument about "bodies that matter" is exemplary in this regard, even if her attention to historical specificity is wanting.[6] And although Foucault himself was notoriously myopic about the domain of the colonial in his analyses of both the history of sexuality and of state-sponsored surveillance, historians of empire have scrutinized both the successes and the failures of colonial regimes that focused on the regulation of bodies as a means to promote their civilizing missions.[7] Indeed, the body is in many ways the most intimate colony, as well as the most unruly, to be subject to colonial disciplines, a fact that officials, missionaries, and travelers were always quick to realize, even though they might not have articulated it in quite those terms.

To return to Pratt, the body itself has been and remains a zone of management, containment, regulation, conformity, and resistance as well as of contact tout court. Under a variety of social, economic, and political constraints it has exhibited a remarkable flexibility and resilience as both a category and as the matériel of history, even while it has also been the site of suffering, the subject of humanitarian intervention and military invasion, and the object of violence and trauma. Far from serving as passive slates on which the past has written, bodies have consistently been agents in their encounters with history — agents that command our attention as much as war, migration, religion, dynastic succession, the environment, law, capitalism, modernity, or any of the other major rubrics through which we understand world history.

The body is such a provocative investigative modality that Kathleen Canning has recently called on historians to develop a theoretical framework for "the body as method."[8] This is a tremendously challenging disciplinary task, in part because the body's oxymoronic status as a *discursive object* means that its ideological work as sign or symbol tends to exclude from view the very real stories about labor, leisure, mobility, political economy, the household, the family, and the state (among other things) that it has to tell. *Bodies in Contact* responds to this challenge by suggesting that the body-as-contact-zone is a powerful analytical term *and* a useful pedagogical tool for understanding the nature and dynamics of imperial, colonial, and world histories — precisely because it allows us to navigate the dynamic relationship between representation and "reality" and to see the work of mediation that embodied subjects perform between the domestic and the foreign, the quotidian and the cyclical, the dynamic and the static. So, for example, the discourses about Nahua sexuality that the Franciscan Bernadino de Sahagún attempted to consolidate in Book 10 of his *Florentine Codex* tell us much about how justifications for ecclesiastical colonialism developed on the ground in sixteenth-century New Spain. But those discourses also constitute an archive in which we can read in great detail about how the Church attempted to regulate the dress, behavior, and sexual cosmology of indigenous women — as well as how that particular civilizing project failed. Alternatively, something as physical as the game of football among Irish Catholics sponsored a series of discourses about manliness, political viability, and cultural revivalism which, in turn, shaped the very nature and direction of political nationalism in modern Ireland. Indeed, something as em-bodied as the tattoo, something as intimate as body markings, can help us read the impact of colonial practices in southern Mozambique — a claim provocative of debates about the body as method which are joined rather than resolved here, and which can and should animate undergraduate classrooms and lecture halls. *Bodies in Contact* abounds with similar examples across time and space, giving readers the chance to see bodies in action, to assess their role in national, regional, and transnational contexts, and to ask what kinds of evidence they offer for the writing of new kinds of history.

It should be emphasized that the essays in this collection do not necessarily share an agenda, methodologically or otherwise, about the body as a tool of historical investigation. Some authors privilege the physical body quite explicitly, as in Joseph Alter's piece on celibacy and Jennifer Morgan's on African and Amerindian female bodies in early modern European travel accounts. Some see the body as a mediator, both literal and figurative, between cultures, as Julia C. Wells's and Adele Perry's essays on conjugality demonstrate. Still others use it as a metaphor for a national body politic that is diseased (Quinlan), emergent (McDevitt), segregated (Sinha), or in crisis (Camiscioli). For others, like Lambert Hurley and Findley, it is travel and the particular forms of mobility and contact that individual bodies take up that is of interest, especially when those bodies (an Indian Muslim woman and an Ottoman man, respectively) are not typically thought to be in motion. Or, in the case of Lucy Eldersveld Murphy's work on creole women in the American Midwest, it is understanding how people live in community that quietly dramatizes how mixed-raced bodies both create and transgress local, regional, national, and colonial borders. Still others, like Melani McAlister's essay that begins with Muhammad Ali, show how famous bodies can be used as a jumping-off point for seeing connections between local communities (African Americans during the cold war) and transnational events with global significance (the Arab-Israeli War and the international Islamicist movement). As we suggest in our introduction, whether interpreted broadly or narrowly, the category "bodies in contact" can enable us to appreciate histories we might not otherwise have seen and to make visible connections between the colonial and the global that scholars are, in some instances, just beginning to make into "history."

Embodied Subjects: Opening World History to Women, Gender, and Sexuality

In marked contrast to the attention paid by feminists in recent years to gender and the problem of transnationalism and globalization, historians of women and gender have not viewed world history per se as their stage.[9] The early exceptions to this are, of course, the variety of textbooks, written mostly in the 1980s, that attempted to tell the stories of Western civilization (and, to a lesser degree, world civilization) from a gendered perspective.[10] Other notable exceptions are the series spearheaded by Cheryl Johnson-Odim and Margaret Strobel, "Restoring Women to History," which focused on the non-West and eventuated in single volumes on Asia, Africa, and Latin America, and Bonnie Smith's forthcoming three-volume *Women's and Gender History in Global Perspective*.[11] Taken together, these syntheses and collections are invaluable reference points for those of us who wish to reimagine college and university survey courses as places where the histories of women, gender, and sexuality can be situated squarely at the center of the aptly called "master narratives" of imperialism and globalization across the longue durée. This has proven difficult at more than a generic level because overall, scholars interested in the body as a site of gendered agency have not taken world history as their purview either, despite a genuine and often highly nuanced appreciation for the cross-cultural influences and geopolitical resonances of embodied experience.[12]

On the other hand, even though the reinvention of world history as an important area of concentration in North American graduate schools and, more generally, as a significant subfield within professional academic history in the late 1980s and early 1990s coincided with the growing authority of women's history and the emergence of gender as a key analytical category within humanities scholarship in general, world historians have shown limited interest in either women's or gender history. The *Journal of World History*, the official journal of the World History Association, was launched as a "new forum for global history" in 1990 and has been at the forefront of discussions of both world history research and pedagogy. Women have been barely visible in the fourteen volumes published to date; aside from Nikki Keddie's essay on women in the Muslim world in the first issue, just two essays, by Judith P. Zinsser and Helen Wheatley, have focused on women.[13] Following on from this, Michelle Maskiell's recent essay on shawls and empires is the only essay published in the *Journal of World History* that has deployed gender as an analytical category in any sustained or sophisticated manner.[14] Equally revealing is the almost total absence of gender as an important theme for research and teaching in the field of world history in the programmatic statements published by George E. Brooks, Philip D. Curtin, T. E. Vadney, Andre Gunder Frank, and David Christian in early issues of the journal.[15] To be sure, there are other venues for world history beyond the *Journal of World History*, most particularly, the *World History Bulletin*, H-World (the heavily subscribed e-list), and, most recently, the e-journal *World History Connected* (www.worldhistoryconnected.org). Readers may find more attention to gender in these forums because of the pedagogical questions such venues deliberately address — a gendered division that is as instructive as it is unfortunate.[16] In light of this imbalance, the *Journal of World History* may well be functioning as a redoubt to which historians resistant to both women's and gender history have retreated, even as, over the same decade, the *Journal of Women's History* and *Gender and History* have been "globalizing," both by design and as a result of the increasingly self-conscious transnational agenda of women's and gender history.

Clearly, the challenge of what Judith P. Zinsser has called "women's world history" is to resist "essentializing women on a global scale." And, we would add, to understand how narratives of women's experiences can be matched with gendered analyses so that more historically nuanced accounts of the "transcultural ideal of all women's subordination to men" (also Zinsser's phrase) can reach students of world history.[17] In this respect, the challenge that *Bodies in Contact* poses to traditions of world history is considerable. For despite repeated calls for engagement with women's history and feminist scholarship more generally, gender has not featured prominently as a problematic or analytical tool in world history as a subfield of the discipline as a whole either. Gerda Lerner's landmark *The Creation of Patriarchy*, which documented the construction of a gendered division of labor and political power that ensured male dominance and female subordination in ancient Mesopotamia, indicated the importance of studying women and gender relations for world history. But this work ultimately had a greater impact on women's history than on the practice of world history, even as feminists have labored to challenge some of the universalisms Lerner herself produced.[18] Other scholars have examined the role of gender in shaping the development of the societies that have traditionally been at the core of world history: China, India, Mesopotamia, Greece, and Rome. Unfortunately, this scholarship has had a civilizational focus, effacing the cross-cultural exchanges and networks that stand at the center of world history's distinct approach to the past. In part, this erasure of women, or at least their consignment to being integral to local, national, or civilizational stories rather than cross-cultural or global narratives, reflects the thematic foci that have dominated writing on world history: exploration, long-distance trade, missionary activity, empire building, and the rise of nationalism. These endeavors, which have frequently been directed by hierarchical institutions, intellectual elites, or powerful commercial interests, have been seen as integral to accounts of cultural contact, increased interregional interdependence, and the rise of Europe. Effectively, the large-scale perspective of world history has tended to render women invisible; or, alternatively, where women were prominent they are imagined as either oddities or exemplars because of their gender.

Though, again (as indicated in the introduction), we recognize that the body is not necessarily coterminous with women, gender, and sexuality, a lack of attention to embodied practices and regimes has followed from these overlooked categories of analysis. World history's effacement of women and gender not only arises out of its neglect of the histories of the family, sexuality, domestic work, and faith that have been the staple of women's history since World War II, but also reflects the kinds of sources used in reconstructing cross-cultural contact and patterns of interregional integration. Travel narratives, the archives of commercial companies and industrial concerns, the records of large religious institutions, and the mass of documentation produced by empires have traditionally been produced by men and have reflected their concerns.[19] In many imperial contexts, colonized women are rendered doubly marginal because both their gender and their position as colonized and female voices in many, if not all, colonial archives are fleeting and fragmentary. Thus, women are much less prominent in types of sources that have traditionally been used in world history, and the quest to recover female agency and subjectivities, the project of women's history as a transformative, revisionary undertaking is often frustrated by the very nature of these archives.

Most important, however, world historians have been slow to recognize that gender is a relational category: even beyond the textbook digests, "gender" has typically been identified as a synonym for "woman" among practitioners of the genre. They have struggled to imagine in gendered terms those activities in the past that were seen as the domain of men largely because this historical approach has generally been resistant to the linguistic turn and cultural history. World history has been deeply grounded in a materialistic vision of the past and has been energized by interdisciplinary affiliations with economics, environmental studies, and sociology rather than with literary studies, anthropology, and gender studies, which were three of the key vectors that transformed the writing of European, North American, and South Asian history in the late 1970s and early 1980s. Even though "discourse," "representation," and "identity" have slowly begun to enter the vocabulary of world historians over the past decade, there is considerable resistance to these concepts, and questions of economics, environmental change, and technology remain at the core of the subdiscipline.

Perhaps not surprisingly, race has received much more attention from world historians than gender. This again reflects the kind of questions and problems that world historians have been exploring, and, in particular, it points to the centrality of slavery and imperialism in modern world history scholarship. Slavery has long been one of the central concerns and most fiercely contested issues in world history. While many historians have explored slavery's long and varied history in Europe, the Mediterranean, the Islamic world, and Asia, the bulk of research on the history of slavery has focused on the transplantation of slaves from Africa to the Caribbean and the Americas during the early modern period. This emphasis on the African slave trade and the place of slavery in the evolution of the plantation system reflects the sheer enormity of this trade—with probably 11 million Africans transported across the Atlantic from 1500 to 1850—and the importance of this population transfer in reshaping the demographic structure of the "Atlantic World." More broadly, the labor of Africans on the plantations of the New World has been identified as a key passage in the transition to modernity, where new systems of labor, production, and consumption emerged and capitalism became a truly global phenomenon. Even though the central historiographical disputes about slavery— the exact size of the trade, the profitability of the trade and of plantation agriculture, and reasons that slave-based agricultural production was abolished, abandoned or supplanted — have hinged on demographic and economic issues, questions of race and racial difference have always remained prominent in this scholarship. In a similar vein, many of the debates on the role of imperialism in world history conducted from the 1950s to the 1990s — the relationship between the periphery and the metropole, the relationship between colonialism and capitalism, and the place of empires in both "modernization" and "underdevelopment" — hinged on economic and political questions. Yet, even before the work of Edward Said, numerous historians explored the place of racial thought in justifying or even driving European empire building, and race was a staple concern in the national historiographies of the United States and the British settler colonies (Canada, but especially South Africa, Australia, and New Zealand). Certainly, within world history scholarship race has rarely been given primacy as either a motor of history or even as an analytical tool, but its importance has been consistently recognized in ways that gender has not: although race and gender are frequently invoked together, these problematics occupy very different positions in the subdiscipline of world history.

As Jennifer Morgan remarks in her essay on images of African women in early modern travel writing, we are less interested in championing the primacy of gender over race than we are in providing students the opportunity to see how a variety of systems — ideological and material, symbolic and real — operate, and are entangled, in the most mundane and the most monumental of historical circumstances. We believe that it reshapes our understandings of the localized politics of slave regimes as both Atlantic and Eurasian institutions when we examine, for example, the ability of concubines in neo-Mamluk Egypt to accumulate substantial capital and construct patronage networks of their own — and see that their sexual and marital choices were heavily constrained in the process. Extending the geographical reach of the body-as-contact-zone to sites like Egypt reflects as well our commitment to engaging larger disciplinary questions in the process of reimagining women, gender, and the body in world history.

Work on women, gender, and sexuality — again, targeting the micro and macro levels and historicizing in material and discursive registers — clearly contributes to the larger project of remapping historical narratives and challenging the chronologies of "the West" and "the rest" that tend to undergird if not world history per se, then at the very least its practical pedagogical face: the undergraduate classroom. Does it not deexceptionalize the West to know that travel writers in the Qing period mobilized consistently gendered and sexualized discourses about Taiwanese, Vietnamese, and even southern Chinese women, in a tone that both resembles and is distinct from a Western "colonial" perspective? Does it not remind us that, to borrow from Richard Eaton, Islamic history *is* global history when we read about the far-ranging travels of the begam of Bhopal and learn that her travel writing did as much transnational political work as that of her English male contemporaries?[20] Or that the profoundly gendered observations of the Ottoman litterateur and traveler Ahmed Midhat returned to Europe a highly skeptical gaze, designed to encompass, evaluate, criticize, and even sometimes admire the so-called progress of Western civilization? Does it not reorient conventional understandings of the gender dynamics of non-Western societies to learn that Indian women were some of the keenest critics of the clubland culture in British India, even while their male elite counterparts sought to replicate it? Does not a detailed reading of the symbolic and spiritual power accorded to semen and other bodily properties in discussions of national character in twentieth-century India challenge commonplace understandings of the sources and scope of anticolonial thought?

The complementary as well as the oppositional character of gendered historical experience which these few examples illustrate gets us out of a binary model by emphasizing the relational character of gendered societies in colonial and global contexts.[21] It also tells us much about the limits of teleological narratives of Western civilization models, not to mention about the operation of "native" agency through a variety of embodied strategies — strategies of negotiation, compromise, conformity, capitulation, resistance, and refusal. In many cases, the ability to put a name to a phenomenon or track a particular embodied experience can add weight and dimension to extant historiographical generalizations, something a textbook can do but that requires space so that the detail can be presented and absorbed. Here again, the idea of bodies-as-contact-zone is instructive for materializing all manner of local and global dimensions and, perhaps, for derailing conventional presuppositions about how people acted in concert with or reacted against systemic change or structural forces. Admittedly, many of the essays herein deal with relatively elite subjects and their narratives, reflecting the limits of the conventional archive, at least, even for the project of transforming world history. Yet arguably, even elite stories have the capacity to provide what

Julie Codell calls "imperial co-histories" by reminding us of the complexities of power, status, and identity in the context of imperial world systems.[22] A number of essays demonstrate the ability of subaltern communities to contest and resist imperial projects and, in the case of Hyun Sook Kim's essay, dramatize the ways exploited groups such as "comfort women" could puncture received and authoritative visions of national and imperial pasts. Whether by correcting, complicating, or reinforcing dominant narratives, the bodies that these essays cast into bold relief contribute to a more complex set of realities, thereby producing new knowledges about world history in a variety of temporal and spatial contexts.

New Imperial Histories in Global Perspective

Many of the visions articulated in this volume have grown, it must be said, out of the "new imperial history," an initially Anglocentric project entailed (in the broadest sense) by the collision of histories of empire with the historical fact of decolonization. The range of approaches that are gathered under this umbrella term display some marked continuities with the recent directions in world history and, in some cases, are explicitly increasingly engaged with the perspective of world history. Although many identify Edward Said's *Orientalism* as initiating a profound transformation of the study of empire because of its analysis of literary texts, focus on discourse and representation as analytical categories, and its exploration of Foucault's power/knowledge nexus, the intellectual projects of the new imperial history emerged as much out of the translation of social history to the realm of European empires.[23] During the 1980s, models of both British and French imperial history that focused on politics and the worlds of both colonial and indigenous elites were challenged by the work of the Subaltern Studies collective in South Asia and a wider group of social historians in Asia, the Middle East, Africa, and Latin America. These scholars drew on local archives, indigenous language sources, and oral histories to explore the history of women, families, and local communities.[24] Their works examined the experience of women, the role of race, and the operation of class (and their interrelationships) in ways that marked them off clearly from the earlier, elite-focused works produced by both nationalist and imperial historians as well as early traditions of Marxist social history.

From the late 1980s these revisionist approaches to the history of imperialism were increasingly brought into dialogue with and challenged by scholars energized by the "cultural turn" in humanities scholarship. The impact of poststructuralist thought (especially Foucault), the growing authority of Said's work on empire and representation, and the work of feminist historians committed to the study of gender as a relational category rather than women's history opened up a new range of approaches to the history of empires. Commonly, this shift is identified as a turn to the study of colonial discourse, but an equally important result of the cultural turn in the study of empire was the identification of new sites of inquiry for the historians of colonialism and empires. If, as we have seen, Foucault's notion of biopower transformed understandings of the relationship between individual bodies and the state, the influence of Foucault's work on power/knowledge encouraged historians to imagine the hospital, asylum, police station, museum, and even the colonial archive itself as institutions that were fundamental to the construction of colonial authority and as productive analytical sites.[25] As a result, the disciplinary power of the colonial state became an increasingly important theme in the historiography of empires, as did questions of intimacy and conjugality.[26]

One of the chief results of the new imperial history has been to reshape spatial understandings of empire and its geographies of power. Fundamental to this project has been the reimagining of the relationships between the metropole and its colonies. Imperial histories generally emerged out of a metropolitan-focused tradition that saw power, modernity, and even "civilization" as emanating in the imperial center and being projected out to the colonies. In this view, the colonies themselves were transformed by empire, absorbed into a capitalist system, civilized, modernized, or, for some, impoverished by empire while metropolitan societies simply enjoyed the economic benefits or carried the cost of empire.[27] It is perhaps no coincidence that historians of women and gender have been at the forefront of these reconceptualizations: their determination to read the false divisions between public and private, between home and the world accounts at least in part for their agility in and commitment to bridging the gap between "domestic" and imperial histories.[28] Scholarship on imperial masculinities and feminisms, on non-Europeans who visited or lived in Europe, and on the place of empire in both popular and elite European culture has destabilized this polarized image of empire by reconstructing the colonial encounters that occurred at the very "heart of the empire" and demonstrating the ways metropolitan cultures were not only transformed by but actually constituted out of imperialism.[29] Remaking the cultural geographies of empire has also involved mapping the larger networks, institutions, and exchanges that integrated the empire. Rather than seeing imperial systems as containing a metropole and a series of distinct colonies, recent work has instead invoked an integrated if uneven "imperial social formation" or the "webs of empire" to refocus attention on the cultural traffic that wove colonies together into imperial systems as well as linking colonies to the imperial center.[30] These works, which coalesce in significant ways around James Blaut's critiques of Eurocentrism and the "colonizer's model of the world," are not only arguing against visions of imperialism that imagine an unproblematized Europe at the core of modern world history, but also reflect a growing engagement with anthropological and sociological studies of contemporary transnational exchanges and an awareness that the history of modern empires are profoundly implicated in our current global moment.[31]

Here as well the stories that *Bodies in Contact* have to tell put pressure on the imperial narratives that are often at the heart of global histories. We emphatically do not wish to suggest that world history can be equivalent, or should be reduced, to imperial history, let alone to the history of empires per se. Given the national chauvinisms at the heart of modern imperial historiography, together with the aspirations of a revived politically conservative British imperial history, such an equation has the potential merely to reinscribe canonical views of Europe and "the rest" as well as to re-embed triumphant nationalist narratives at the heart of research and pedagogy.[32] Nor do we wish to imply that empires acted as juggernauts, razing everything in their wake or exercising anything like total power in situ. Indeed, one of the greatest challenges of reimagining colonial histories in a global context is precisely to balance the fact of imperial power with its fragility and precariousness in the face of local history, "native" practice, and indigenous forms of authority and culture.[33] But by the same token, teachers and students of world history need a more nuanced understanding of how imperial mentalities, policies, and regimes have contributed to discourses of globalization. They need be able to see — in more refined and more detailed ways than we now have available — how and why this was so, as well as when it was *not*, in order to have more than a crude understanding of imperial power in the past and into the present. The ways gendered images of racial health and national reproduction circulated and contributed to discourse and policy about a eugenic interwar France remind us, for example, of how implicated histories other than Britain's are in modern world imperialism—and of how crucial the policing of all manner of "foreign" bodies was to that project. Anxieties over gender and racial boundaries at the edge of empires, from British Columbia to Australia's Northern Territory, underscore colonial modernity's persistent equation of the bodily integrity of colonists and the integrity of the colonial body politic in the face of contact with both colonized indigenous populations and mobile non-European peoples. The fact that African Americans in the 1960s were intimately acquainted with debates about war in the Middle East and Vietnam because of some communities' involvement with the Nation of Islam (and one of its most famous spokesmen, Muhammad Ali, one of America's most celebrated "black bodies") should give us pause as well. In a similar vein, the prominence of purdah and the practice of veiling in Soviet attempts to "modernize" the Muslims of Uzbekistan reminds us that gender has not only been central in British, French, and, more recently, American incursions into the Muslim world, but also was crucial in the secularizing imperialist project of communism. And archival work on American Indian communities that uses the term "colonial" to describe the contexts of displacement and removal, surveillance and discipline of creole bodies is equally apposite, bringing what Amy Kaplan and Donald Pease have called "cultures of U.S. imperialism" squarely into line with those of other would-be world powers in the recent past.[34]

The collective weight of these essays, therefore, not only calls into question many of the narratives produced, nurtured, and cherished by nations and empires, it also presents a range of critical visions of the making of the modern world. In their consistent foregrounding of the negotiation of community identities and boundaries, materializing histories of both repression and resistance, and their sensitivity to the complex interconnections among the local, national, imperial, and global, the works collected here reveal the power struggles that have shaped histories big and small. Most important, they insist that colonialism and empires are fundamental to histories of cross-cultural relations, interregional integration, and the emergence of global institutions and cultural forms. They undercut naïvely utopian visions of an integrated global order based on liberal capitalism that supposedly marks the "end of history" by in fact suggesting that critical histories are crucial to making sense of our current global moment and the ways its pasts are entangled with the long history of imperialism.[35]

Conclusion: World Histories in the New Millennium

As the preceding essays demonstrate, bodies, though policed, do not necessarily respect boundaries, and tracking the historical trajectories of bodies that either transgress or reconsolidate boundaries helps us de-naturalize the geographies we have inherited in women's and gender and world histories. The contribution of this volume lies in its determination to decenter Europe in the narratives of colonial and global history; its emphasis on both the agency of indigenous people and the structural conditions of imperial and colonial power; its recovery of local histories of encounter and resistance; its genuinely transnational reach; its commitment to placing "personal stories" as well as collective community experiences at the heart of global stories; and, above all, its presumption that gender and sexuality are central to, if not constitutive of, both old and new world orders. Research shows that even before September 11, 2001, North American undergraduates, at any rate, were resistant to the critiques of imperial modernity and historicity that a gendered global history has the power to offer, though they remain intrigued by imperialism as a world system and a source of cultural hegemony.[36] Given the events of the first three years of the new millennium, when quite familiar forms of Anglo-American imperialism have reemerged on the world stage in the twin contexts of discourses about globalization and very real violences against and in the name of women and children, students of world history around the globe have never been in greater need of original and innovative scholarship that takes bodies seriously as agents of global power and transnational identities.[37] The question of how to rewrite grand narratives so that they are inclusive of, and transformed by, the stories on offer here remains among the most vital challenges for world history as an intellectual, political, and pedagogical project. Among other things, such a project raises questions about the tenability of linear-driven narratives as against the fragment, the episode, or the fugitive subaltern subject; it raises questions, in other words, about the viability of those very distinctions and in turn throws open the problem of history writing to the kind of critique that has (with the notable exception of Subaltern Studies) only begun to be written in the past decade or so.[38] How to translate these revised narratives to classrooms beyond the college and university setting (i.e., to secondary school audiences) is equally daunting, though it is arguably of paramount importance for a truly educated citizenry in the twenty-first century.[39] *Bodies in Contact* points out some pathways in this direction. It is intended to enable students to juxtapose diverse imperial regimes, to bring together work on celibacy, intermarriage, and sports with scholarship on migration, citizenship, and the law, and to see a range of contrasts across time and space, thus marking a beginning, rather than an end, to the project of making visible the material consequences of colonial regimes for embodied subjectivities, their communities, their economic systems, and their political cultures across the globe.

Notes

1. Girolamo Benzoni, *History of the New World* (1572), trans. W. H. Smyth (London, 1857), 3–4; cited in Jennifer Morgan, this volume.

2. Adele Perry, private e-mail communication, fall 2003.

3. Mary Louise Pratt, *Imperial Eyes: Travel Writing and Transculturation* (Routledge, 1992).

4. For two very different but equally illuminating approaches, see Alan Sekula, "The Body and the Archive," *October* 39, 3 (1986): 3–64, and Zine Magubane, "Which Bodies Matter? Feminism, Poststructuralism, Race and the Curious Theoretical Odyssey of the 'Hottentot Venus,'" *Gender and Society* 15, 6 (2001): 816–834.

5. For a thorough review of this literature, see Kathleen Canning, "The Body as Method? Reflections on the Place of the Body in Gender History," *Gender and History* 11, 3 (November 1999): 499–513.

6. Judith Butler, *Bodies That Matter* (Routledge, 1992).

7. See Ann Laura Stoler, *Race and the Education of Desire* (Duke University Press, 1995) and *Carnal Knowledge and Imperial Power* (University of California Press, 2002).

8. Canning, "The Body as Method?"

9. See, for example, Caren Kaplan et al., *Between Woman and Nation: Nationalism, Transnational Feminisms and the State* (Duke University Press, 1999); Sonita Sarker and Esha Niyogi Day, eds., *Trans-Status Subjects: Gender in the Globalization of South and Southeast Asia* (Duke University Press, 2002); and the special issue of *Signs* 26, 4 (summer 2001), "Gender and Globalization."

10. Bonnie S. Anderson and Judith P. Zinsser, *A History of Their Own: Women in Europe from Prehistory to the Present*, rev. ed. (Oxford University Press, 2000); Bonnie Smith, *Changing Lives : Women in European History since 1700* (D.C. Heath, 1989); Marilyn J. Boxer and Jean H. Quataert, eds., *Connecting Spheres: Women in a Globalizing World, 1500 to the Present*, 2nd ed. (Oxford University Press, 2000).

11. Bonnie Smith, *Women's and Gender History in Global Perspective* (University of Illinois Press, forthcoming); Marysa Navarro, Kecia Ali, and Virginia Sanchez Korrol, *Women in Latin America and the Caribbean* (Indiana University Press, 1999); Guity Nashat and Judith E. Tucker, *Women in the Middle East and North Africa* (Indiana University Press, 1999); Barbara N. Ramusack and Sharon Sievers, *Women in Asia* (Indiana University Press, 1999); Iris Berger, E. Frances White, and Cathy Skidmore-Hess, *Women in Sub-Saharan Africa* (Indiana University Press, 1999). Bonnie Smith's NEH seminar at the Institute for Research on Women at Rutgers University (July 5–6, 2000, "Women's History and Gender History in a Global Perspective") was a landmark event in the history of rethinking world history; see Margaret Strobel and Marjorie Bingham, "The Theory and Practice of Women's History and Gender History in Global Perspective" (unpublished manuscript, forthcoming, provided courtesy of Margaret Strobel).

12. See, for example, Jennifer Terry and Jacqueline Urla, eds., *Deviant Bodies: Critical Perspectives on Science and Popular Culture* (Indiana University Press, 1995).

13. Nikki R. Keddie, "The Past and Present of Women in the Muslim World," *Journal of World History* 1, 1 (1990). 77–108, Helen Wheatley, "From Traveller to Notable: Lady Duff Gordon in Upper Egypt, 1862–1869," *Journal of World History* 3, 1 (1992): 81–104; Judith P. Zinsser, "From Mexico to Copenhagen to Nairobi: The United Nations Decade for Women, 1975–1985," *Journal of World History* 13, 1 (2002): 139–168. See also Carol Devens, " 'If We Get the Girls, We Get the Race': Missionary Education and Native Girls," *Journal of World History* 3 (1992): 219–238.

14. Michelle Maskiell, "Consuming Kashmir: Shawls and Empires, 1500–2000," *Journal of World History* 13, 1 (2002): 27–65.

15. George E. Brooks, "An Undergraduate World History Curriculum for the Twenty First Century," *Journal of World History* 2, 1 (1991): 65–79; David Christian, "The Case for 'Big History,' " *Journal of World History* 2, 2 (1991): 223–238; Philip D. Curtin, "Graduate Teaching in World History," *Journal of World History* 2, 1 (1991): 81–89; Andre Gunder Frank, "A Plea for World System History," *Journal of World History* 2, 1 (1991): 1–28; T. E. Vadney, "World History as an Advanced Academic Field," *Journal of World History* 1, 2 (1990): 209–223.

16. We are grateful to Ian Fletcher and Yael Simpson Fletcher for encouraging us to consider this point.

17. Judith P. Zinsser, "Women's History, World History and the Construction of New Narratives," *Journal of Women's History* 12, 3 (2000): 198, 205.

18. Gerda Lerner, *The Creation of Patriarchy* (Oxford University Press, 1986) and *The Majority Finds Its Past: Placing Women in History* (Oxford University Press, 1981).

19. A pivotal discussion of these questions can be found in Gayatri Chakravorty Spivak, "The Rani of Sirmur: An Essay in Reading the Archives," *History and Theory* 24, 3 (1985): 247–273.

20. Richard Eaton, *Islamic History as Global History* (American Historical Association, 1990). For a list of pamphlets on global history produced by the American Historical Association, go to http://www.theaha.org/pubs/titles.htm.

21. Thanks to Durba Ghosh for underscoring this point for us.

22. Julie F. Codell, ed., *Imperial Co-Histories: National Identities and the British and Colonial Press* (Fairleigh Dickinson University Press, 2003).

23. Edward W. Said, *Orientalism* (Routledge and Kegan Paul, 1978).

24. Ranajit Guha, ed., *Subaltern Studies: Writings on South Asian History and Society I* (Oxford University Press, 1982); David Prochaska, *Making Algeria French: Colonialism in Bône, 1870–1920* (Cambridge University Press, 1990); Charles van Onselen, *Studies in the Social and Economic History of the Witwatersrand 1886–1914*, 2 vols. (Longman, 1982).

25. See Tony Ballantyne, "Rereading the Archive, Opening up the Nation State in South Asia (and Beyond)," in *After the Imperial Turn*, ed. Antoinette Burton (Duke University Press, 2003); David Arnold, *Colonizing the Body: State Medicine and Epidemic Disease in Nineteenth-century India* (University of California Press, 1993); James H. Mills, *Madness, Cannabis and Colonialism: The 'Native-only' Lunatic Asylums of British India, 1857–1900* (Macmillan, 2000); Timothy Mitchell, *Colonising Egypt* (Cambridge University Press, 1988).

26. Antoinette Burton, ed., *Gender, Sexuality and Colonial Modernities* (Routledge, 1999); Stoler, *Carnal Knowledge and Imperial Power*; Stoler, *Race and the Education of Desire*; Frederick Cooper and Ann Laura Stoler, eds., *Tensions of Empire: Colonial Cultures in a Bourgeois World* (University of California Press, 1997).

27. See, for example, P. J. Cain and A. G. Hopkins, *British Imperialism: 1688–2000*, 2nd ed. (Longman, 2002); David Hancock, *Citizens of the World: London Merchants and the Integration of the British Atlantic Community, 1735–1785* (Cambridge University Press, 1995); and the essays in Akita Shigeru, ed., *Gentlemanly Capitalism, Imperialism and Global History* (Palgrave-Macmillan, 2002).

28. See Nupur Chaudhuri and Margaret Strobel, eds., *Western Women and Imperialism: Complicity and Resistance* (Indiana University Press, 1992) and Catherine Hall, *Civilising Subjects* (University of Chicago Press, 2002).

29. Entry points into this scholarship include Antoinette Burton, *At the Heart of the Empire: Indians and the Colonial Encounter in Late-Victorian Britain* (University of California Press, 1997); Antoinette Burton, *Burdens of History: British Feminists, Indian Women, and Imperial Culture, 1865–1915* (University of North Carolina Press, 1994); Alice L. Conklin, *A Mission to Civilize: The Republican Idea of Empire in France and West Africa, 1895–1930* (Stanford University Press, 1997); Alice L. Conklin and Ian Christopher Fletcher, eds., *European Imperialism, 1830–1930: Climax and Contradiction* (Houghton Mifflin, 1999); Catherine Hall, Keith McClelland, and Jane Rendall, *Defining the Victorian Nation: Class, Race, Gender and the British Reform Act of 1867* (Cambridge University Press, 2000); Catherine Hall, ed., *Cultures of Empire: Colonizers in Britain and the Empire in the Nineteenth and Twentieth Centuries* (Routledge, 2000); John M. MacKenzie, ed., *Imperialism and Popular Culture* (Manchester University Press, 1986); John MacKenzie, *Orientalism: History, Theory and the Arts* (Manchester University Press, 1995).

30. Mrinalini Sinha, *Colonial Masculinity : The "Manly Englishman" and the "Effeminate Bengali" in the Late Nineteenth Century* (Manchester University Press, 1995); Tony Ballantyne, *Orientalism and Race: Aryanism in the British Empire* (Palgrave-Macmillan,

2001); Alan Lester, *Imperial Networks: Creating Identities in Nineteenth-century South Africa and Britain* (Routledge, 2001).

31. See J. M. Blaut, "Colonialism and the Rise of Capitalism," *Science and Society* 53 (1989): 260–296, and *The Colonizer's Model of the World: Geographical Diffusionism and Eurocentric History* (Guilford, 1993). We would like to thank Mrinalini Sinha for reminding us of this point.

32. See, for example, Peter Stansky et al., NACBS *Report on the State and Future of British Studies in North America* (November 1999), and Antoinette Burton, "When Was Britain? Nostalgia for the Nation at the End of the 'American Century,'" *Journal of Modern History* 75 (June 2003): 359–374.

33. Thanks to Adele Perry for urging us to specify this tension.

34. Amy Kaplan and Donald Pease, eds., *Cultures of U.S. Imperialism* (Duke University Press, 1995).

35. Francis Fukuyama, *The End of History and the Last Man* (Penguin, 1992).

36. See Heather Streets, "Empire and 'the Nation': Institutional Practice, Pedagogy, and Nation in the Classroom," in Burton, *After the Imperial Turn*, 57–69.

37. For one example of the rush to capitalize on these events, see Niall Ferguson, *Empire: How Britain Made the Modern World* (Allen Lane, 2003).

38. See, for example, Robert F. Berkhofer, *Beyond the Great Story: History as Text and Discourse* (Harvard University Press, 1995).

39. The American Historical Association has several teaching tools to help in this endeavor; see their Web site, http://www.theaha.org/teaching/. According to Margaret Strobel, "On the AP front . . . Marjorie Bingham and Susan Gross, of the now-closed Upper Midwest Women's History Center for Teachers in the Twin Cities got an NEH grant to revise their Women in World Area Studies books to put them and other stuff on George Mason's History Matters website as a resource for people teaching AP world history." E-mail correspondence, June 26, 2003.

CONTRIBUTORS

JOSEPH S. ALTER teaches in the Anthropology Department at the University of Pittsburgh. His research is in the field of medical anthropology and he has published on a range of topics, including sports, sexuality, physical fitness, nationalism, health, and medicine in South Asia. He is currently completing a book manuscript entitled *Yoga in Modern India: The Body between Philosophy and Science* (Princeton University Press, forthcoming). Previous publications include *The Wrestler's Body: Identity and Ideology in North India* (University of California Press, 1992), *Knowing Dil Das: Stories of a Himalayan Hunter* (University of Pennsylvania Press, 2000), and *Gandhi's Body: Sex, Diet and the Politics of Nationalism* (University of Pennsylvania Press, 2000).

TONY BALLANTYNE is Senior Lecturer in History at the University of Otago in New Zealand. His research focuses on knowledge production in the British empire and the networks that connected the Pacific to South Asia in the eighteenth and nineteenth centuries. His publications include *Orientalism and Race: Aryanism in the British Empire* (Palgrave, 2001) and the edited collection *Science, Empire and the European Exploration of the Pacific* (Ashgate, 2004).

ANTOINETTE BURTON teaches British, imperial, colonial, women's, and world history at the University of Illinois at Urbana-Champaign. She is most recently the author of *Dwelling in the Archive: Women Writing House, Home and History in Late-Colonial India* (Oxford University Press, 2003) and the editor of *After the Imperial Turn: Thinking with and Through the Nation* (Duke University Press, 2003).

ELISA CAMISCIOLI is Assistant Professor of History at Binghamton University, State University of New York, where she teaches gender history and colonial culture. She is completing a book entitled *Embodying the French Race: Immigration, Reproduction, and National Identity in France, 1900–1939*. By exploring the realms of pronatalism, prostitution, the marriage contract, racial mixing, and the rationalization of labor and the body, her work reframes the early-twentieth-century debate on immigration and citizenship to highlight the salience of racial hierarchies and reproductive practices. She has also begun a new project on the French experience in Pondicherry, South India.

MARY ANN FAY received her Ph.D. in Middle East history from Georgetown University. The focus of her work has been elite women in early modern Egypt and the relationship between property ownership and women's status. Her work has appeared in the *Journal of Women's History*, the *International Journal of Middle East Studies*, and several collections. A monograph on elite Egyptian women is in progress. She has taught at the American University of Sharjah in the UAE and is now scholar-in-residence and academic advisor to the Arab Studies Program at American University, Washington, D.C.

CARTER VAUGHN FINDLEY, Professor of History at Ohio State University, is now writing a study of "Turkey, Nationalism and Modernity." His other writings include *The Turks in World History* (Oxford University Press, forthcoming), *Twentieth-Century World* (with John Rothney, 5th edition, Houghton Mifflin, 2002), *Ottoman Civil Officialdom: A Social History* (Princeton University Press, 1989), and *Bureaucratic Reform in the Ottoman Empire: The Sublime Porte, 1789–1922* (Princeton University Press, 1980). Former president of the World History Association (2000–2002), he has received the Ohio State University Distinguished Scholar Award (2000) and J. S. Guggenheim, NEH, and other fellowships.

HEIDI GENGENBACH is a historian whose research and teaching focus on women's and gender history, oral history, and colonial history in southern Africa, particularly Mozambique. Her work has been published in the *International Journal of African Historical Studies*, the *Journal of Southern African Studies*, and the *Journal of Women's History*. She is currently living in Boston, where she is finishing the manuscript for an electronic book entitled *Where Women Make History: Gendered Accounts of Community and Change in Magude, Mozambique.*

SHOSHANA KELLER is an Associate Professor of History at Hamilton College. She is the author of *To Moscow, Not Mecca: The Soviet Campaign against Islam in Central Asia, 1917–1941* (Praeger, 2001). She is currently working on an anthology of resources on modern Eurasia, 1800–2000.

HYUN SOOK KIM is Associate Professor at Wheaton College in Massachusetts. She received her M.A. and Ph.D. in sociology from New School for Social Research. Her research focuses on gender, state, nationalism, and ethnic conflicts in the contexts of postcolonial Korea and Vietnam. She has published articles on the topics of gender and nationalism; gendered memorialization of war and conflict; military prostitution and wartime rape; and history, memorialization, and national reconciliation. Her current work in progress is titled *Massacres and Memories: The Politics of Gender, Violence and Modernity in Postcolonial Korea.*

MIRE KOIKARI is an Associate Professor in the Women's Studies Program at the University of Hawai'i at Manoa. She is currently completing a book on the cold war culture and feminist mobilization during the U.S. occupation of Japan from 1945 to 1952, forthcoming from Duke University Press. Her research and teaching interests include American and Japanese feminism, nationalism, and imperialism and their consequences in the Asia-Pacific region in the nineteenth and twentieth centuries.

SIOBHAN LAMBERT HURLEY is Senior Lecturer in Modern History at Nottingham Trent University in the United Kingdom. Currently, she is coediting a volume with Avril Powell entitled *Rhetoric and Reality: Gender and the Colonial Experience in South Asia* and revising her book manuscript on the begam of Bhopal and the emergence of a Muslim women's movement in India. Her most recent publications are "Introduction: A Princess Revealed" in Abida Sultaan's *Memoirs of a Rebel Princess* (Oxford

University Press, 2003) and "Fostering Sisterhood: Muslim Women and the All-India Ladies' Association," *Journal of Women's History* 16, 2 (summer 2004).

MELANI MCALISTER is Associate Professor of American Studies at George Washington University. She is the author of *Epic Encounters: Culture, Media, and U.S. Interests in the Middle East, 1945–2000* (University of California Press, 2001). She is also a contributor to "September 11 and History," a special issue of the *Journal of American History*. Professor McAlister writes and teaches about foreign policy, popular culture, religion, and globalization. She has published analysis and commentary about U.S. perceptions of the Middle East in the *New York Times*, the *Washington Post*, the *Chronicle of Higher Education*, and *The Nation*.

PATRICK MCDEVITT is an Assistant Professor of History at the University at Buffalo, State University of New York. He is the author of *May the Best Man Win: Sport, Masculinity and Nationalism in Great Britain and the Empire, 1880–1935* (Palgrave-Macmillan, 2004).

JENNIFER L. MORGAN is an Assistant Professor of History and Women's and Gender Studies at Rutgers University. Her research examines the intersections of gender and race in colonial America. She is the author of *Laboring Women: Gender and Reproduction in the Making of New World Slavery* (University of Pennsylvania Press, 2003).

LUCY ELDERSVELD MURPHY is Associate Professor of History at Ohio State University, Newark, and author of *A Gathering of Rivers: Indians, Métis and Mining in the Western Great Lakes, 1737–1832* (University of Nebraska Press, 2000). She was coeditor with Wendy Hamand Venet of *Midwestern Women: Work, Community, and Leadership at the Crossroads* (Indiana University Press, 1997). Currently, she is working on a study of the experiences of the old fur trade families in Wisconsin and Michigan during the demographic transitions of the mid-nineteenth century. With Rebecca Kugel, she is also working on an edited collection on theory and methodology for Native American women's history.

ROSALIND O'HANLON is a Fellow of Clare College at the University of Cambridge. Her work focuses on South Asian historiography as well as the history of gender and caste in western India. Her publications include *Caste, Conflict and Ideology: Mahatma Jotirao Phule and Low Caste Protest in Nineteenth-century Western India* (Cambridge University Press, 1985) and *A Comparison between Women and Men: Tarabai Shinde and the Critique of Gender Relations in Colonial India* (Oxford University Press, 1994).

REBECCA OVERMYER-VELÁZQUEZ is an Assistant Professor of Sociology at Whittier College. She recently completed her dissertation at the University of California, Santa Barbara, on the Consejo Guerrerense 500 Años de Resistencia Indígena, an indigenous peoples movement in Guerrero, Mexico. The dissertation explores the relationship between indigenous peoples and the Mexican state in the 1990s within the longer historical context of the development of state Indian policy and an international discourse of indigenous rights.

FIONA PAISLEY is deputy director of the Centre for Public Culture and Ideas and lectures in Australian history at Griffith University, Brisbane, Australia. She has published widely on settler colonial history in transnational context and is the author of *Loving Protection? Australian Feminism and Aboriginal Women's Rights, 1919–1939* (Melbourne University Press, 2000). Currently she is completing a book-length study of women's internationalism in the Pacific region, focusing on cultural internationalism and its critics in the regional women's movement of the 1920s to 1950s.

ADELE PERRY teaches history at the University of Manitoba, where she is Canada Research Chair in Western Canadian Social History. She is the author of *On the Edge of Empire: Gender, Race, and the Making of British Columbia* (University of Toronto Press, 2001) and is currently working on the relationship between immigration and aboriginal policies in turn-of-the-century Canada and the history of transcolonial connections in eighteenth- and nineteenth-century western North America.

SEAN QUINLAN is an Assistant Professor of History at the University of Idaho. He was a Mellon postdoctoral fellow at UCLA and has been the recipient of a Fulbright IIE fellowship in Paris. His scholarly work has appeared in *Social History*, *Eighteenth-Century Studies*, *History of European Ideas*, *History Workshop*, and *French History*. He is currently completing a book manuscript entitled *The Morbid Social Body: Reforming Self, Sexuality, and Society in French Medicine, ca. 1750–1850.*

MRINALINI SINHA is Associate Professor of History and Women's Studies at Pennsylvania State University. She is the author of *Colonial Masculinity: The "Manly Englishman" and the "Effeminate Bengali" in the Late Nineteenth Century* (Manchester, 1995). She has edited *Selections from Katherine Mayo's Mother India* (1999) and coedited *Feminisms and Internationalism* (University of Michigan Press, 1999). She is currently working on a book on the changes in imperial politics in India in the interwar period.

EMMA JINHUA TENG is an Associate Professor of Chinese Studies at the Massachusetts Institute of Technology and the Class of 1956 Career Development Chair. Her publications include "The Construction of the 'Traditional Chinese Woman' in the Western Academy: A Critical Review," *Signs* (Fall 1996) and "Artifacts of a Lost City: Arnold Genthe's *Photographs of Old Chinatown* and Its Intertexts," in *Re/collecting Asian America: Readings in Cultural History*, ed. Y. Matsukawa, I. Lim, and J. Lee (Temple University Press, 2002). Her book, *Taiwan's Imagined Geography: Chinese Travel Writing and Pictures, 1683–1895*, is forthcoming from Harvard University Asia Center. She is currently working on a book on representations of the Eurasian.

JULIA C. WELLS is an Associate Professor in the History Department of Rhodes University; she teaches gender in South Africa history, public history, and colonial thought in Africa. She is the author of *We Have Done with Pleading: The Women's 1913 Anti-pass Campaign* (Ravan Press, 1991) and *We Now Demand! The History of Women's Resistance to Pass Laws in South Africa* (Witwatersrand University Press, 1993). Her latest publications have been on the eccentric missionary James Read, though now she is mostly doing work on community involvement in taking ownership over its own history and turning it into usable commodities. She is also an elected municipal councilor in the Makana Municipality, chairing the Portfolio Commitee, which deals with heritage.

INDEX

Journal of Women's History 10, 1 (1998): 20–44 are reprinted with the permission of Indiana University Press.

Selections from Mire Koikari, "Rethinking Gender and Power in the U.S. Occupation of Japan, 1945–1952," *Gender and History* 11, 2 (1999) are reprinted with permission from Blackwell Publishers.

Selections from Hyun Sook Kim, "History and Memory: The 'Comfort Women' Controversy," *positions* 5, 1 (1997): 73–105 are reprinted with permission from Duke University Press.

Selections from Melani McAlister, " 'One Black Allah': The Middle East in the Cultural Politics of African American Liberation, 1955–1970," *American Quarterly* 51, 3 (September 1999): 622–656 © The American Studies Association. Reprinted with permission of The Johns Hopkins University Press.

Tony Ballantyne is a Senior Lecturer in History at the
University of Otago. Antoinette Burton is Professor of
History at the University of Illinois, Urbana-Champaign.

Library of Congress Cataloging-in-Publication Data
Bodies in contact : rethinking colonial encounters in
world history / Tony Ballantyne and Antoinette Burton, eds.
p. cm.   Includes bibliographical references and index.
ISBN 0-8223-3455-0 (cloth : alk. paper)
ISBN 0-8223-3467-4 (pbk. : alk. paper)
1. Body, Human — Social aspects — Cross-cultural studies.
2. Body, Human — Symbolic aspects — Cross-cultural studies.
3. Sex role — Cross-cultural studies. 4. Colonization.
5. Imperialism. 6. Globalization.
I. Ballantyne, Tony II. Burton, Antoinette M.
GT495.B62 2005   908'.2 — dc22
2004018697